SKILLS For SUCCESS

with Microsoft® Word 2010

COMPREHENSIVE

TOWNSEND | HOVEY | FERRETT

Prentice Hall

Boston   Columbus   Indianapolis   New York   San Francisco   Upper Saddle River
Amsterdam   Cape Town   Dubai   London   Madrid   Milan   Munich   Paris   Montréal   Toronto
Delhi   Mexico City   São Paulo   Sydney   Hong Kong   Seoul   Singapore   Taipei   Tokyo

Library of Congress Cataloging-in-Publication Data
Townsend, Kris.
  Skills for success with Word 2010 comprehensive / by Kris Townsend.
      p. cm.
  Includes bibliographical references and indexes.
  ISBN 978-0-13-508830-2 (alk. paper)
  1. Microsoft Word.   2. Word Processing.   I. Title.
Z52.5.M52T69 2011
005.52—dc22   2010019633

Editor in Chief: *Michael Payne*
AVP/Executive Acquisitions Editor: *Stephanie Wall*
Product Development Manager: *Eileen Bien Calabro*
Editorial Project Manager: *Virginia Guariglia*
Development Editor: *Vonda Keator*
Editorial Assistant: *Nicole Sam*
AVP/Director of Online Programs, Media: *Richard Keaveny*
AVP/Director of Product Development, Media: *Lisa Strite*
Editor—Digital Learning & Assessment: *Paul Gentile*
Product Development Manager, Media: *Cathi Profitko*
Media Project Manager, Editorial: *Alana Coles*
Media Project Manager, Production: *John Cassar*
Director of Marketing: *Kate Valentine*
Senior Marketing Manager: *Tori Olsen Alves*
Marketing Coordinator: *Susan Osterlitz*

Marketing Assistant: *Darshika Vyas*
Senior Managing Editor: *Cynthia Zonneveld*
Associate Managing Editor: *Camille Trentacoste*
Production Project Manager: *Camille Trentacoste*
Senior Operations Supervisor: *Natacha Moore*
Senior Art Director: *Jonathan Boylan*
Art Director: *Anthony Gemmellaro*
Text and Cover Designer: *Anthony Gemmellaro*
Manager, Rights and Permissions: *Hessa Albader*
Supplements Development Editor: *Tina Minchella*
Full-Service Project Management: *MPS Content Services, a Macmillan Company*
Composition: *MPS Content Services, a Macmillan Company*
Printer/Binder: *WorldColor/Kendallville*
Cover Printer: *Lehigh/Phoenix*
Typeface: *Minion 10.5/12.5*

Credits and acknowledgments borrowed from other sources and reproduced, with permission, in this textbook appear on appropriate page within text.

Prentice Hall
is an imprint of

www.pearsonhighered.com

10 9 8 7 6 5 4 3 2 1
ISBN-10:   0-13-508830-5
ISBN-13: 978-0-13-508830-2

Contents in Brief

Table of Contents

Contents in Brief

About the Authors

Kris Townsend is an Information Systems instructor at Spokane Falls Community College in Spokane, Washington. Kris earned a bachelor's degree in both Education and Business, and a master's degree in Education. He has also worked as a public school teacher and as a systems analyst. Kris enjoys working with wood, snowboarding, and camping. He commutes to work by bike and enjoys long road rides in the Palouse country south of Spokane.

This book is dedicated to the students at Spokane Falls Community College. Their adventures, joys, and frustrations guide my way.
—KRIS TOWNSEND

Christie Jahn Hovey is a Professor of Business & Technologies at Lincoln Land Community College in Springfield, Illinois. Christie has a bachelor's degree in Education from Illinois State University, a master's degree in Education/Human Resource Development from the University of Illinois at Urbana-Champaign, and is A.B.D. in Community College Leadership, at the University of Illinois at Urbana-Champaign. She has taught high school and was a corporate training consultant for Fortune 500 companies, as well as for state government and numerous small businesses.

This book is dedicated to anyone who has the desire to learn . . . especially my students, my husband Robyn, and my son Will.
—CHRISTIE JAHN HOVEY

Robert L. Ferrett recently retired as the Director of the Center for Instructional Computing at Eastern Michigan University, where he provided computer training and support to faculty. He has authored or co-authored more than 70 books on Access, PowerPoint, Excel, Publisher, WordPerfect, Windows, and Word. He has been designing, developing, and delivering computer workshops for more than two decades.

I'd like to dedicate this book to my wife Mary Jane, whose constant support has been so important all these years.
—ROBERT L. FERRETT

Contributors

We'd like to thank the following people for their work on Skills for Success:

Instructor Resource Authors

Afi Chamlou	*Northern Virginia Community College*	Robert Porche	*Bucks County Community College*
Andrea Leibach	*Harrisburg Area Community College*	Karen Smith	*Technical College of the Lowcountry*
Burton Neumeier	*Hillsborough Community College*	Steve St. John	*Tulsa Community College*

Technical Editors

Hilda Wirth Federico	*Jacksonville University*	Steve Rubin	*California State University—Monterey Bay*
Elizabeth Lockley		Eric Sabbah	
Linda Pogue	*Northwest Arkansas Community College*	Jan Snyder	

Reviewers

Darrell Abbey	*Cascadia Community College*	Tara Cipriano	*Gateway Technical College*
Bridget I. Archer	*Oakton Community College*	Paulette Comet	*Community College of Baltimore County—Catonsville*
Laura Aagard	*Sierra College*		
John Alcorcha	*MTI College*	Gail W. Cope	*Sinclair Community College*
Barry Andrews	*Miami Dade College*	Susana Contreras de Finch	*College of Southern Nevada*
Natalie Andrews	*Miami Dade College*	Chris Corbin	*Miami Dade College*
Wilma Andrews	*Virginia Commonwealth University School of Business*	Janis Cox	*Tri-County Technical College*
		Tomi Crawford	*Miami Dade College*
Bridget Archer	*Oakton Community College*	Martin Cronlund	*Anne Arundel Community College*
Tahir Aziz	*J. Sargeant Reynolds*	Jennifer Day	*Sinclair Community College*
Greg Balinger	*Miami Dade College*	Ralph DeArazoza	*Miami Dade College*
Terry Bass	*University of Massachusetts, Lowell*	Carol Decker	*Montgomery College*
Lisa Beach	*Santa Rosa Junior College*	Loorna DeDuluc	*Miami Dade College*
Rocky Belcher	*Sinclair Community College*	Caroline Delcourt	*Black Hawk College*
Nannette Biby	*Miami Dade College*	Michael Discello	*Pittsburgh Technical Institute*
David Billings	*Guilford Technical Community College*	Kevin Duggan	*Midlands Technical Community College*
Brenda K. Britt	*Fayetteville Technical Community College*	Barbara Edington	*St. Francis College*
Alisa Brown	*Pulaski Technical College*	Donna Ehrhart	*Genesee Community College*
Eric Cameron	*Passaic Community College*	Hilda Wirth Federico	*Jacksonville University*
Gene Carbonaro	*Long Beach City College*	Tushnelda Fernandez	*Miami Dade College*
Trey Cherry	*Edgecombe Community College*	Arlene Flerchinger	*Chattanooga State Tech Community College*
Kim Childs	*Bethany University*	Hedy Fossenkemper	*Paradise Valley Community College*
Pualine Chohonis	*Miami Dade College*	Kent Foster	*Withrop University*
Lennie Coper	*Miami Dade College*	Penny Foster-Shiver	*Anne Arundel Community College*

Arlene Franklin	*Bucks County Community College*
George Gabb	*Miami Dade College*
Barbara Garrell	*Delaware County Community College*
Deb Geoghan	*Bucks County Community College*
Jessica Gilmore	*Highline Community College*
Victor Giol	*Miami Dade College*
Melinda Glander	*Northmetro Technical College*
Linda Glassburn	*Cuyahoga Community College, West*
Deb Gross	*Ohio State University*
Rachelle Hall	*Glendale Community College*
Marie Hartlein	*Montgomery County Community College*
Diane Hartman	*Utah Valley State College*
Betsy Headrick	*Chattanooga State*
Patrick Healy	*Northern Virginia Community College—Woodbridge*
Lindsay Henning	*Yavapai College*
Kermelle Hensley	*Columbus Technical College*
Diana Hill	*Chesapeake College*
Rachel Hinton	*Broome Community College*
Mary Carole Hollingsworth	*GA Perimeter*
Stacey Gee Hollins	*St. Louis Community College—Meramec*
Bill Holmes	*Chandler-Gilbert Community College*
Steve Holtz	*University of Minnesota Duluth*
Margaret M. Hvatum	*St. Louis Community College*
Joan Ivey	*Lanier Technical College*
Dr. Dianna D. Johnson	*North Metro Technical College*
Kay Johnston	*Columbia Basin College*
Warren T. Jones, Sr.	*University of Alabama at Birmingham*
Sally Kaskocsak	*Sinclair Community College*
Renuka Kumar	*Community College of Baltimore County*
Kathy McKee	*North Metro Technical College*
Hazel Kates	*Miami Dade College*
Gerald Kearns	*Forsyth Technical Community College*
Charles Kellermann	*Northern Virginia Community College—Woodbridge*
John Kidd	*Tarrant County Community College*
Chris Kinnard	*Miami Dade College*
Kelli Kleindorfer	*American Institute of Business*
Kurt Kominek	*NE State Tech Community College*
Dianne Kotokoff	*Lanier Technical College*
Cynthia Krebs	*Utah Valley University*
Jean Lacoste	*Virginia Tech*
Gene Laughrey	*Northern Oklahoma College*
David LeBron	*Miami Dade College*
Kaiyang Liang	*Miami Dade College*
Linda Lindaman	*Black Hawk College*
Felix Lopez	*Miami Dade College*
Nicki Maines	*Mesa Community College*
Cindy Manning	*Big Sandy Community and Technical College*
Patri Mays	*Paradise Valley Community College*
Norma McKenzie	*El Paso Community College*
Lee McKinley	*GA Perimeter*
Sandy McCormack	*Monroe Community College*
Eric Meyer	*Miami Dade College*
Kathryn Miller	*Big Sandy Community and Technical College, Pike Ville Campus*
Gloria A. Morgan	*Monroe Community College*
Kathy Morris	*University of Alabama, Tuscaloosa*
Linda Moulton	*Montgomery County Community College*
Ryan Murphy	*Sinclair Community College*
Stephanie Murre Wolf	*Moraine Park Technical College*
Jackie Myers	*Sinclair Community College*
Dell Najera	*El Paso Community College, Valle Verde Campus*
Scott Nason	*Rowan Cabarrus Community College*
Paula Neal	*Sinclair Community College*
Bethanne Newman	*Paradise Valley Community College*
Eloise Newsome	*Northern Virginia Community College—Woodbridge*
Karen Nunan	*Northeast State Technical Community College*
Ellen Orr	*Seminole Community College*
Carol Ottaway	*Chemeketa Community College*
Denise Passero	*Fulton-Montgomery Community College*
Americus Pavese	*Community College of Baltimore County*
James Gordon Patterson	*Paradise Valley Community College*
Cindra Phillips	*Clark State CC*
Janet Pickard	*Chattanooga State Tech Community College*
Floyd Pittman	*Miami Dade College*
Melissa Prinzing	*Sierra College*
Pat Rahmlow	*Montgomery County Community College*
Mary Rasley	*Lehigh Carbon Community College*
Scott Rosen	*Santa Rosa Junior College*
Ann Rowlette	*Liberty University*
Kamaljeet Sanghera	*George Mason University*
June Scott	*County College of Morris*
Janet Sebesy	*Cuyahoga Community College*

Contributors continued

Jennifer Sedelmeyer	*Broome Community College*	Margaret Taylor	*College of Southern Nevada*
Kelly SellAnne	*Arundel Community College*	Martha Taylor	*Sinclair Community College*
Teresa Sept	*College of Southern Idaho*	Michael M. Taylor	*Seattle Central Community College*
Pat Serrano	*Scottsdale Community College*	Roseann Thomas	*Fayetteville Tech Community College*
Amanda Shelton	*J. Sargeant Reynolds*	Ingrid Thompson-Sellers	*GA Perimeter*
Gary Sibbits	*St. Louis Community College—Meramec*	Daniel Thomson	*Keiser University*
Janet Siert	*Ellsworth Community College*	Astrid Hoy Todd	*Guilford Technical Community College*
Robert Sindt	*Johnson County Community College*	Barb Tollinger	*Sinclair Community College*
Karen Smith	*Technical College of the Lowcountry*	Cathy Urbanski	*Chandler Gilbert Community College*
Robert Smolenski	*Delaware County Community College*	Sue Van Boven	*Paradise Valley Community College*
Robert Sindt	*Johnson County Community College*	Philip Vavalides	*Guildford Technical Community College*
Gary R. Smith	*Paradise Valley Community College*	Pete Vetere	*Montgomery County Community College—West Campus*
Patricia Snyder	*Midlands Technical College*		
Pamela Sorensen	*Santa Rosa Junior College*	Asteria Villegas	*Monroe College*
Eric Stadnik	*Santa Rosa Junior College*	Michael Walton	*Miami Dade College*
Mark Stanchfield	*Rochester Community and Technical College*	Teri Weston	*Harford Community College*
Diane Stark	*Phoenix College*	Julie Wheeler	*Sinclair Community College*
Neil Stenlund	*Northern Virginia Community College*	Debbie Wood	*Western Piedmont Community College*
Linda Stoudemayer	*Lamar Institute of Technology*	Thomas Yip	*Passaic Community College*
Pamela Stovall	*Forsyth Technical Community College*	Lindy Young	*Sierra Community College*
Linda Switzer	*Highline Community College*	Matt Zullo	*Wake Technical Community College*

A Microsoft® Office textbook that recognizes how students learn today-

Skills for Success

with Microsoft® Word 2010 *Comprehensive*

- **10 x 8.5 Format –** Easy for students to read and type at the same time by simply propping the book up on the desk in front of their monitor

- **Clearly Outlined Skills –** Each skill is presented in a single two-page spread so that students can easily follow along

- **Numbered Steps and Bulleted Text –** Students don't read long paragraphs or text, but they will read information presented concisely

- **Easy-to-Find Student Data Files –** Visual key shows students how to locate and interact with their data files

Start Here – Students know exactly where to start and what their starting file will look like

Outcome – Shows students up front what their completed project will look like

Skills List – A visual snapshot of what skills they will complete in the chapter

Sequential Pagination – Saves you and your students time in locating topics and assignments

Skills for Success

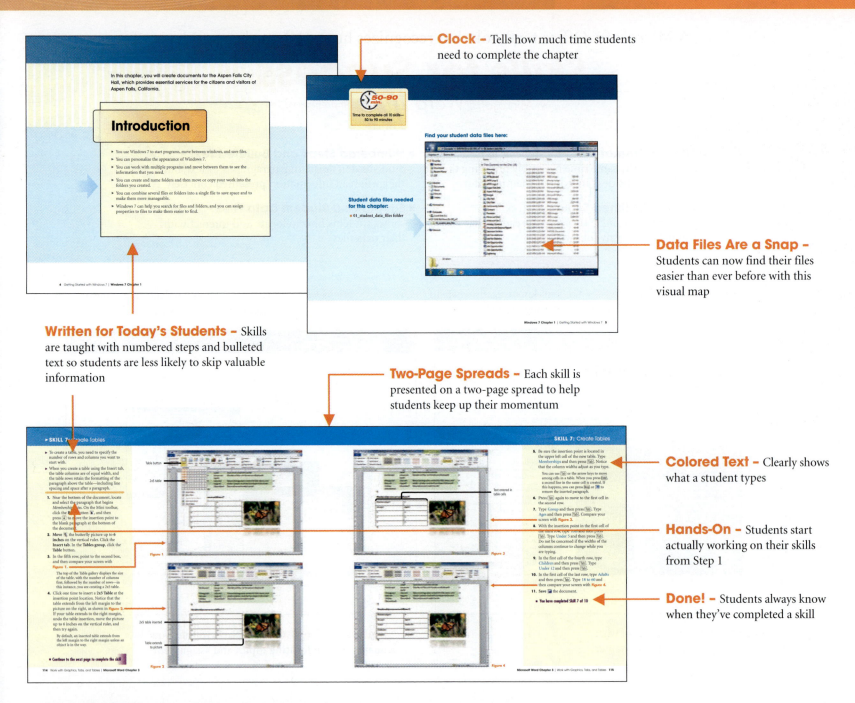

Clock – Tells how much time students need to complete the chapter

Data Files Are a Snap – Students can now find their files easier than ever before with this visual map

Written for Today's Students – Skills are taught with numbered steps and bulleted text so students are less likely to skip valuable information

Two-Page Spreads – Each skill is presented on a two-page spread to help students keep up their momentum

Colored Text – Clearly shows what a student types

Hands-On – Students start actually working on their skills from Step 1

Done! – Students always know when they've completed a skill

Skills for Success

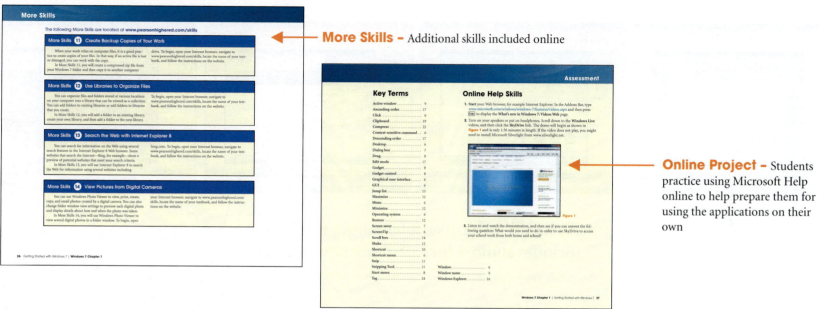

More Skills – Additional skills included online

Online Project – Students practice using Microsoft Help online to help prepare them for using the applications on their own

End-of-Chapter Material – Several levels of assessment so you can assign the material that best fits your students' needs

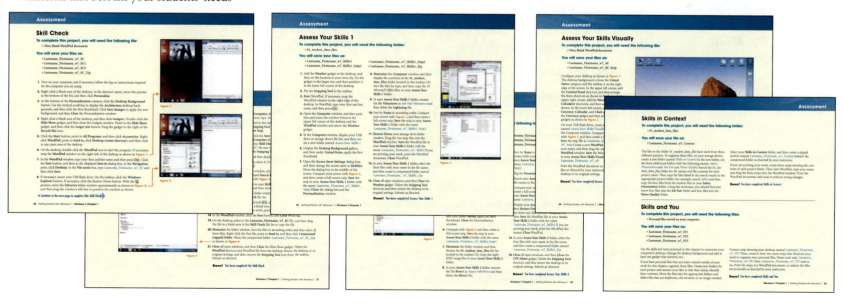

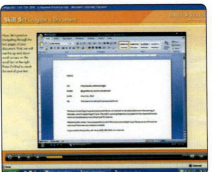
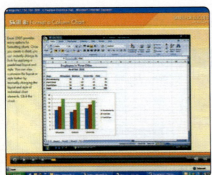
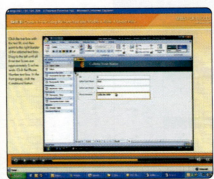
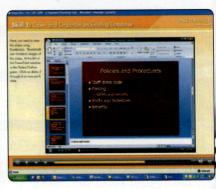

Videos! – Each skill within a chapter comes with a video that includes audio, which demonstrates the skill

NOTE: These videos are only available with *Skills for Success with Office 2010 Volume 1*

Instructor Materials

All Instructor materials available on the IRCD

Instructor's Manual – Teaching tips and additional resources for each chapter

Assignment Sheets – Lists all the assignments for the chapter, you just add in the course information, due dates and points. Providing these to students ensures they will know what is due and when

Scripted Lectures – Classroom lectures prepared for you

Annotated Solution Files – Coupled with the scoring rubrics, these create a grading and scoring system that makes grading so much easier for you

Power Point Lectures – PowerPoint presentations for each chapter

Prepared Exams – Exams for each chapter

Scoring Rubrics – Can be used either by students to check their work or by you as a quick check-off for the items that need to be corrected

Syllabus Templates – for 8-week, 12-week, and 16-week courses

Test Bank – Includes a variety of test questions for each chapter

Companion Website – Online content such as the More Skills Projects, Online Study Guide, Glossary, and Student Data Files are all at www.pearsonhighered.com/skills

SKILLS For SUCCESS

with Microsoft®
Word 2010

COMPREHENSIVE

Common Features of Office 2010

▶ The programs in Microsoft Office 2010—Word, Excel, PowerPoint, and Access—share common tools that you use in a consistent, easy-to-learn manner.

▶ Common tasks include opening and saving files, entering and formatting text, and printing your work.

Your starting screen will look like this:

SKILLS

Skills 1-10 Training

At the end of this chapter, you will be able to:

Skill 1 Start Word and Navigate the Word Window

Skill 2 Start Excel and PowerPoint and Work with Multiple Windows

Skill 3 Save Files in New Folders

Skill 4 Print and Save Documents

Skill 5 Open Student Data Files and Save Copies Using Save As

Skill 6 Type and Edit Text

Skill 7 Cut, Copy, and Paste Text

Skill 8 Format Text and Paragraphs

Skill 9 Use the Ribbon

Skill 10 Use Shortcut Menus and Dialog Boxes

MORE SKILLS

More Skills 11 Capture Screens with the Snipping Tool

More Skills 12 Use Microsoft Office Help

More Skills 13 Organize Files

More Skills 14 Save Documents to Windows Live

Outcome

Using the skills listed to the left will enable you to create documents similar to this:

Visit Aspen Falls!

Aspen Falls overlooks the Pacific Ocean and is surrounded by many vineyards and wineries. Ocean recreation is accessed primarily at Durango County Park. The Aspen Lake Recreation Area provides year round fresh water recreation and is the city's largest park.

Local Attractions

- Wine Country
  - Wine Tasting Tours
  - Wineries
- Wordsworth Fellowship Museum of Art
- Durango County Museum of History
- Convention Center
- Art Galleries
- Glider Tours

Aspen Falls Annual Events

- Annual Starving Artists Sidewalk Sale
- Annual Wine Festival
- Cinco de Mayo
- Vintage Car Show
- Heritage Day Parade
- Harvest Days
- Amateur Bike Races
- Farmer's Market
- Aspen Lake Nature Cruises
- Aspen Falls Triathlon
- Taste of Aspen Falls
- Winter Blues Festival

Contact Your Name for more information.

You will save your files as:

Lastname_Firstname_cf01_Visit1
Lastname_Firstname_cf01_Visit2
Lastname_Firstname_cf01_Visit3

In this chapter, you will create documents for the Aspen Falls City Hall, which provides essential services for the citizens and visitors of Aspen Falls, California.

Common Features of Office 2010

▶ Microsoft Office is the most common software used to create and share personal and business documents.

▶ Microsoft Office is a suite of several programs—Word, PowerPoint, Excel, Access, and others—that each have a special purpose.

▶ Because of the consistent design and layout of Microsoft Office, when you learn to use one Microsoft Office program, you can use most of those skills when working with the other Microsoft Office programs.

▶ The files you create with Microsoft Office need to be named and saved in locations where they can be easily found when you need them.

Time to complete all
10 skills – 50 to 90 minutes

Find your student data files here:

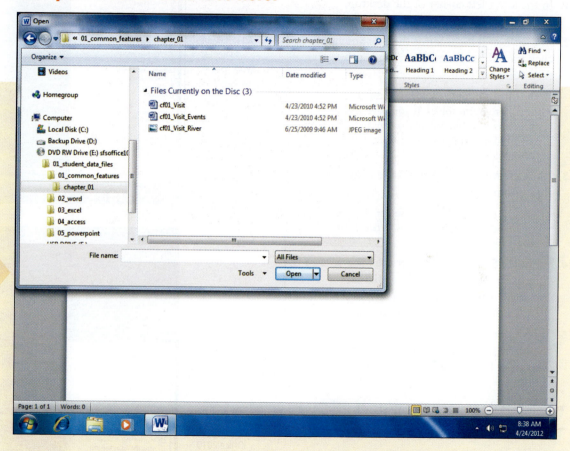

**Student data files needed
for this chapter:**

- cf01_Visit
- cf01_Visit_Events
- cf01_Visit_River

▶ The Word 2010 program can be launched by clicking the Start button, and then locating and clicking the *Microsoft Word 2010* command.

▶ When you start Word, a new blank document displays in which you can type text.

1. In the lower left corner of the desktop, click the **Start** button 🔵 .

2. In the lower left corner of the **Start** menu, click the **All Programs** command, and then compare your screen with **Figure 1**.

    The Microsoft Office folder is located in the All Programs folder. If you have several programs installed on your computer, you may need to scroll to see the Microsoft Office folder.

3. Click the **Microsoft Office** folder, and then compare your screen with **Figure 2**.

    Below the Microsoft Office folder, commands that open various Office 2010 programs display.

4. From the **Start** menu, under the **Microsoft Office** folder, click **Microsoft Word 2010**, and then wait a few moments for the Microsoft Word window to display.

5. If necessary, in the upper right corner of the Microsoft Word window, click the Maximize button 🔳 .

■ **Continue to the next page to complete the skill** ➤

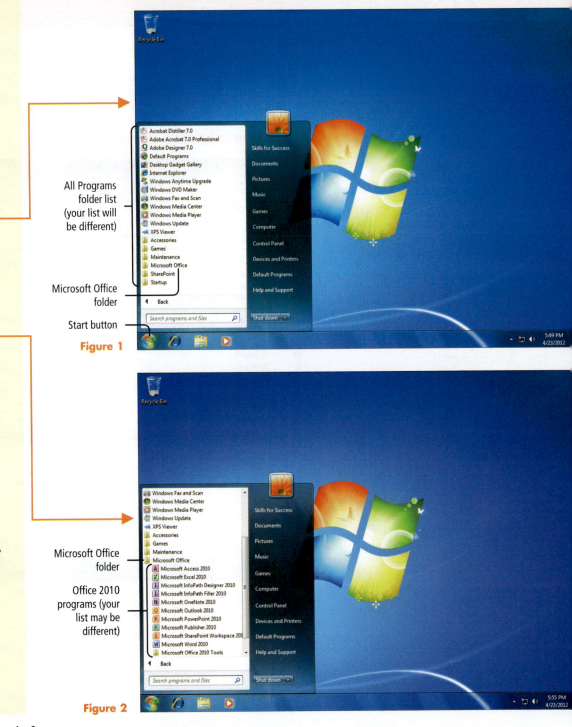

All Programs folder list (your list will be different)

Microsoft Office folder

Start button

Figure 1

Microsoft Office folder

Office 2010 programs (your list may be different)

Figure 2

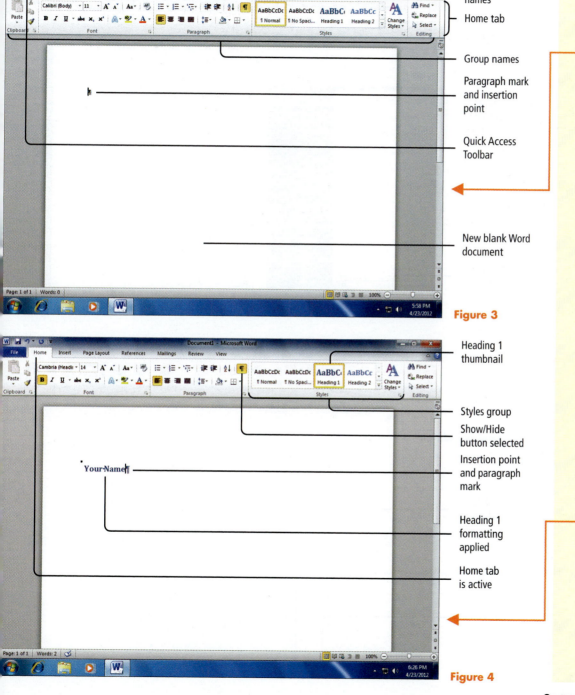

Ribbon tab
names

Home tab

Group names

Paragraph mark
and insertion
point

Quick Access
Toolbar

New blank Word
document

Figure 3

Heading 1
thumbnail

Styles group

Show/Hide
button selected

Insertion point
and paragraph
mark

Heading 1
formatting
applied

Home tab
is active

Figure 4

6. On the Ribbon's **Home tab**, in the **Paragraph group**, click the **Show/Hide** button ¶ until it displays in gold indicating that it is active. Compare your screen with **Figure 3**.

   Above the blank Word document, the Quick Access Toolbar and Ribbon display. At the top of the Ribbon, a row of tab names display. Each Ribbon tab has buttons that you click to perform actions. The buttons are organized into groups that display their names along the bottom of the Ribbon.

   In the document, the *insertion point*— a vertical line that indicates where text will be inserted when you start typing—flashes near the top left corner.

   The Show/Hide button is a *toggle button*— a button used to turn a feature both on and off. The paragraph mark (¶) indicates the end of a paragraph and will not print.

7. In the document, type your first and last names. As you type, notice that the insertion point and paragraph mark move to the right.

8. On the **Home tab**, in the **Styles group**, point to—but do not click—the **Heading 1** thumbnail to show the *Live Preview*—a feature that displays the result of a formatting change if you select it.

9. Click the **Heading 1** thumbnail to apply the formatting change as shown in **Figure 4**. If the Word Navigation Pane displays on the left side of the Word window, click its Close ☒ button.

■ **You have completed Skill 1 of 10**

▶ When you open more than one Office program, each program displays in its own window.

▶ When you want to work with a program in a different window, you need to make it the active window.

1. Click the **Start** button ⊙ , and then compare your screen with **Figure 1**.

Your computer may be configured in such a way that you can open Office programs without opening the All Programs folder. The Office 2010 program commands may display as shortcuts in the Start menu's pinned programs area or the recently used programs area. Your computer's taskbar or desktop may also display icons that start each program.

2. From the **Start** menu, locate and then click **Microsoft Excel 2010**. Depending on your computer, you may need to double-click—not single click—to launch Excel. Compare your screen with **Figure 2**. If necessary, click the Maximize button ⊡ .

A new blank worksheet displays in a new window. The first *cell*—the box formed by the intersection of a row and column—is active as indicated by the thick, black border surrounding the cell. When you type in Excel, the text is entered into the active cell.

The Quick Access Toolbar displays above the spreadsheet. The Excel Ribbon has its own tabs and groups that you use to work with an Excel spreadsheet. Many of these tabs, groups, and buttons are similar to those found in Word.

On the taskbar, two buttons display—one for Word and one for Excel.

■ **Continue to the next page to complete the skill**

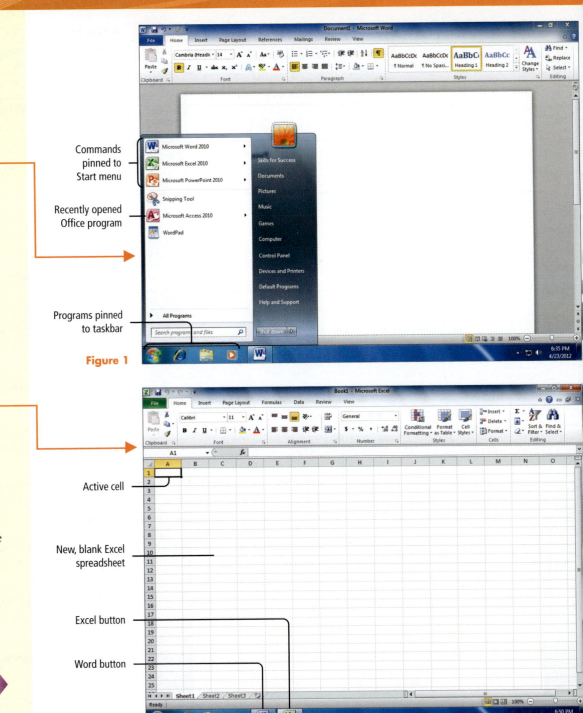

Commands pinned to Start menu

Recently opened Office program

Programs pinned to taskbar

Figure 1

Active cell

New, blank Excel spreadsheet

Excel button

Word button

Figure 2

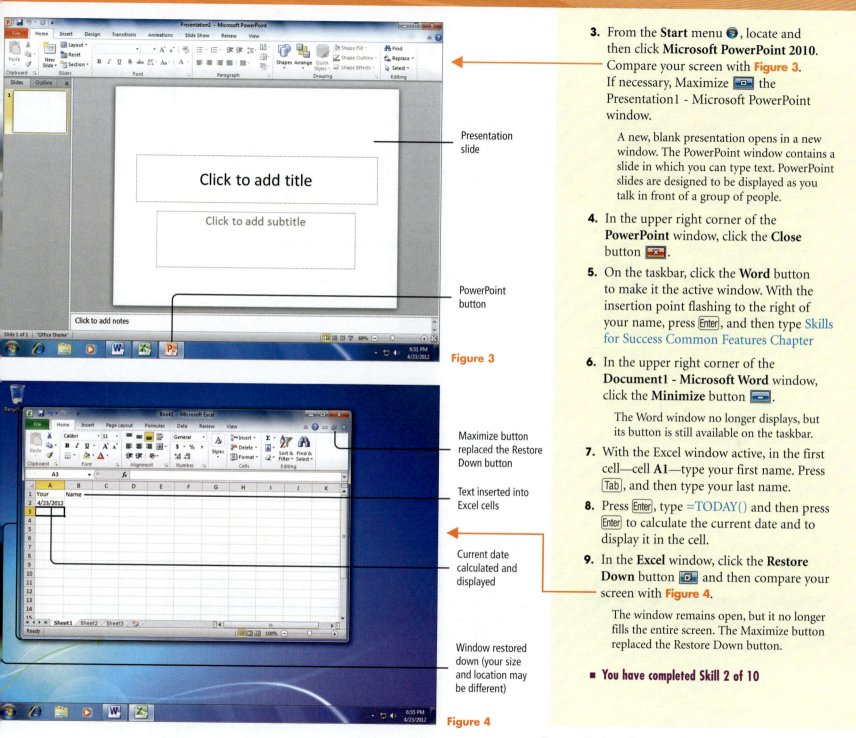

Presentation slide

PowerPoint button

Figure 3

Maximize button replaced the Restore Down button

Text inserted into Excel cells

Current date calculated and displayed

Window restored down (your size and location may be different)

Figure 4

3. From the **Start** menu, locate and then click **Microsoft PowerPoint 2010**. Compare your screen with **Figure 3**. If necessary, Maximize the Presentation1 - Microsoft PowerPoint window.

   A new, blank presentation opens in a new window. The PowerPoint window contains a slide in which you can type text. PowerPoint slides are designed to be displayed as you talk in front of a group of people.

4. In the upper right corner of the **PowerPoint** window, click the **Close** button.

5. On the taskbar, click the **Word** button to make it the active window. With the insertion point flashing to the right of your name, press Enter, and then type Skills for Success Common Features Chapter

6. In the upper right corner of the **Document1 - Microsoft Word** window, click the **Minimize** button.

   The Word window no longer displays, but its button is still available on the taskbar.

7. With the Excel window active, in the first cell—cell **A1**—type your first name. Press Tab, and then type your last name.

8. Press Enter, type =TODAY() and then press Enter to calculate the current date and to display it in the cell.

9. In the **Excel** window, click the **Restore Down** button and then compare your screen with **Figure 4**.

   The window remains open, but it no longer fills the entire screen. The Maximize button replaced the Restore Down button.

■ **You have completed Skill 2 of 10**

▶ A new document or spreadsheet is stored in the computer's temporary memory (*RAM*) until you save it to your hard drive or USB flash drive.

1. If you are saving your work on a USB flash drive, insert the USB flash drive into the computer now. If the Windows Explorer button 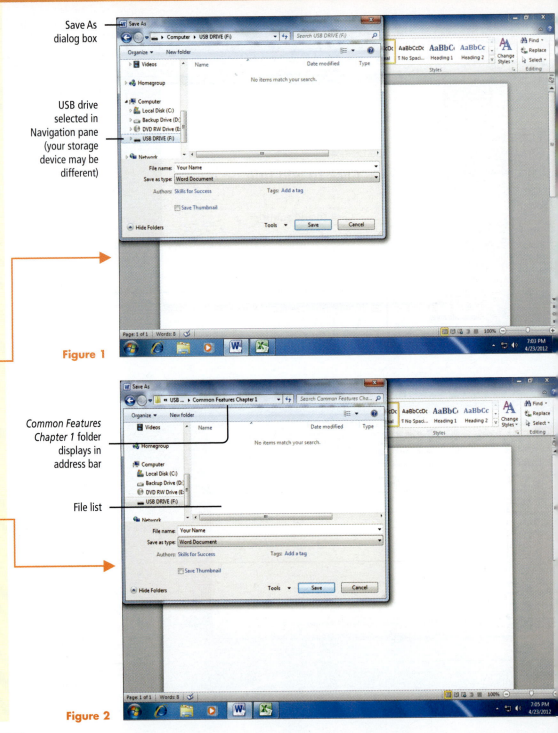 flashes on the taskbar, right-click the button, and then on the Jump List, click Close window.

2. On the taskbar, click the **Word** button to make it the active window. On the **Quick Access Toolbar**, click the **Save** button.

> For new documents, the first time you click the Save button, the Save As dialog box opens so that you can name the file.

3. If you are to save your work on a USB drive, in the Navigation pane scroll down to display the list of drives, and then click your USB flash drive as shown in **Figure 1**. If you are saving your work to another location, in the Navigation pane, locate and then click that folder or drive.

4. On the **Save As** dialog box toolbar, click the **New folder** button, and then immediately type Common Features Chapter 1

5. Press Enter to accept the folder name, and then press Enter again to open the new folder as shown in **Figure 2**.

> The new folder is created and then opened in the Save As dialog box file list.

■ **Continue to the next page to complete the skill**

Save As dialog box

USB drive selected in Navigation pane (your storage device may be different)

Figure 1

Common Features Chapter 1 folder displays in address bar

File list

Figure 2

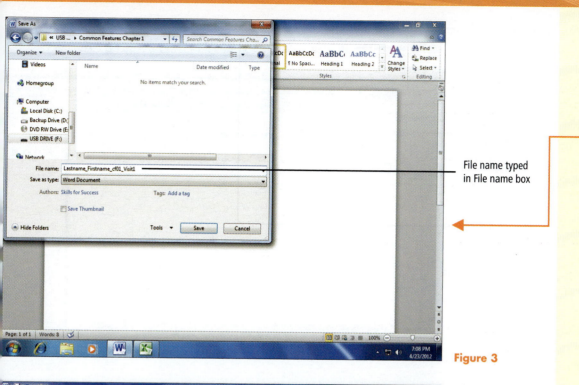

File name typed
in File name box

Figure 3

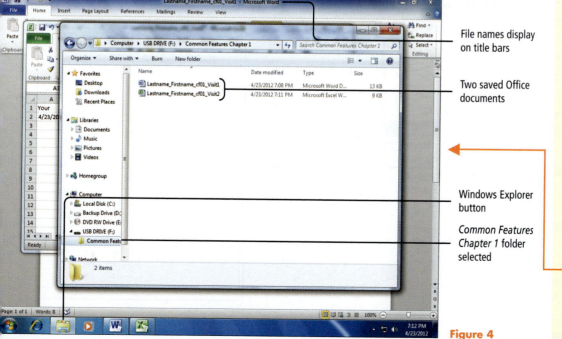

File names display
on title bars

Two saved Office
documents

Windows Explorer
button

*Common Features
Chapter 1* folder
selected

Figure 4

6. In the **Save As** dialog box, click in the **File name** box one time to highlight all of the existing text.

7. With the text in the **File name** box still highlighted, type Lastname_Firstname_cf01_Visit1

8. Compare your screen with **Figure 3**, and then click **Save**.

   After the document is saved, the name of the file displays on the title bar at the top of the window.

9. On the taskbar, click the **Windows Explorer** button . In the folder window **Navigation** pane, open the drive on which you are saving your work, and then click the **Common Features Chapter 1** folder. Verify that *Lastname_Firstname_cf01_Visit1* displays in file list.

10. On the taskbar, click the **Excel** button to make it the active window. On the Excel **Quick Access Toolbar**, click the **Save** button .

11. In the **Save As** dialog box **Navigation** pane, open the drive where you are saving your work, and then click the **Common Features Chapter 1** folder to display its file list.

    The Word file may not display because the Save As box typically displays only files created by the program you are using. Here, only Excel files will typically display.

12. Click in the **File name** box, replace the existing value with Lastname_Firstname_cf01_Visit2 and then click the **Save** button.

13. On the taskbar, click the **Windows Explorer** button, and then compare your screen with **Figure 4**.

■ **You have completed Skill 3 of 10**

► Before printing, it is a good idea to work in *Page Layout view*—a view where you prepare your document or spreadsheet for printing.

1. On the taskbar, click the **Excel** button, and then click the **Maximize** button.

2. On the Ribbon, click the **View tab**, and then in the **Workbook Views group**, click the **Page Layout** button. Compare your screen with **Figure 1**.

   The worksheet displays the cells, the margins, and the edges of the paper as they will be positioned when you print. The *cell references*—the numbers on the left side and the letters across the top of a spreadsheet that address each cell—will not print.

3. On the Ribbon, click the **Page Layout tab**. In the **Page Setup group**, click the **Margins** button, and then in the **Margins** gallery, click **Wide**.

4. Click the **File tab**, and then on the left side of the Backstage, click **Print**. Compare your screen with **Figure 2**.

   The Print tab has commands that affect your print job and a preview of the printed page. Here, the cell references and *grid lines*—lines between the cells in a table or spreadsheet—do not display because they will not be printed.

5. In the **Print Settings**, under **Printer**, notice the name of the printer. You will need to retrieve your printout from this printer. If your instructor has directed you to print to a different printer, click the Printer arrow, and choose the assigned printer.

■ **Continue to the next page to complete the skill**

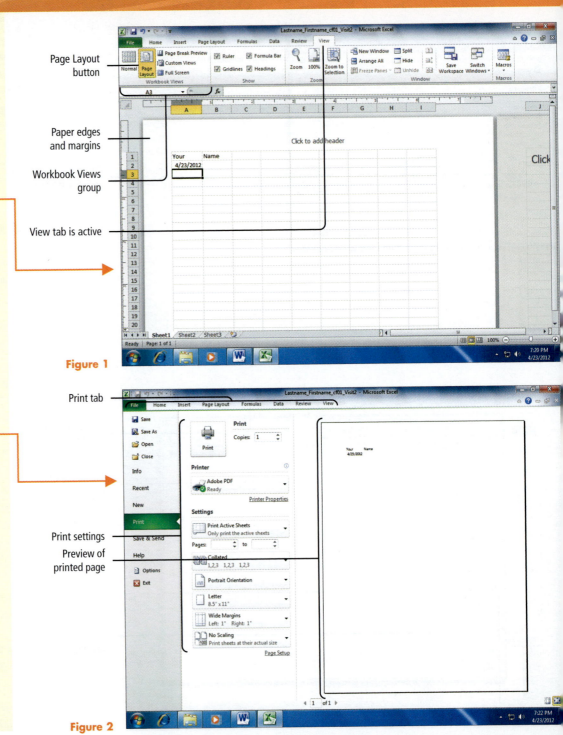

Page Layout button

Paper edges and margins

Workbook Views group

View tab is active

Figure 1

Print tab

Print settings

Preview of printed page

Figure 2

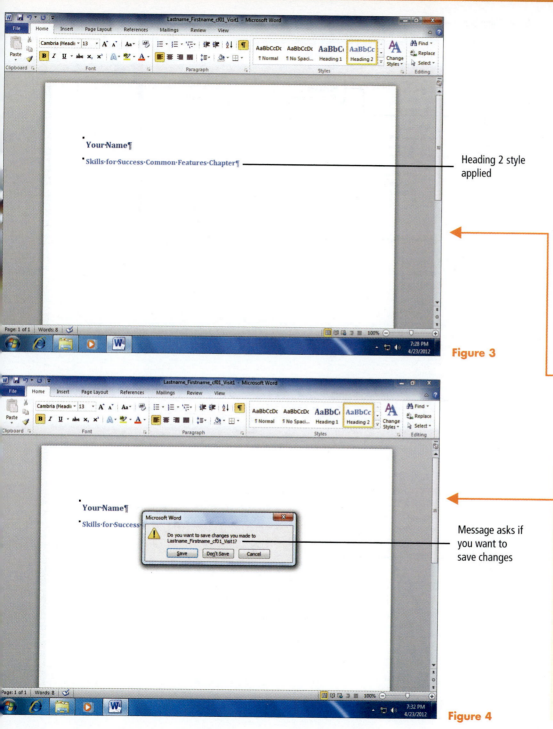

Heading 2 style
applied

Figure 3

Message asks if
you want to
save changes

Figure 4

6. Check with your *Course Assignment Sheet* or *Course Syllabus,* or consult with your instructor to determine whether you are to print your work for this chapter. If you are to print your work, at the top left corner of the Print Settings section, click the Print button. If you printed the spreadsheet, retrieve the printout from the printer.

7. On the **File tab**, click **Save**.

   Because you have already named the file, the Save As dialog box does not display.

8. On the **File tab**, click **Exit** to close the spreadsheet and exit Excel.

9. In the Word document, verify that the insertion point is in the second line of text. If not, on the taskbar, click the Word button to make it the active window.

10. On the **Home tab**, in the **Styles group**, click the **Heading 2** thumbnail. Compare your screen with **Figure 3**.

11. On the **File tab**, click **Print** to display the Print tab. If you are printing your work for this chapter, click the Print button, and then retrieve your printout from the printer.

12. On the **File tab**, click **Exit**, and then compare your screen with **Figure 4**.

    When you close a window with changes that have not yet been saved, a message will remind you to save your work.

13. Read the displayed message, and then click **Save**.

   ■ **You have completed Skill 4 of 10**

▶ This book often instructs you to open a student data file so that you do not need to start the project with a blank document.

▶ The student data files are located on the student CD that came with this book. Your instructor may have provided an alternate location.

▶ You use Save As to create a copy of the student data file onto your own storage device.

1. If necessary, insert the student CD that came with this text. If the AutoPlay dialog box displays, click Close ▣.

2. Using the skills practiced earlier, start **Microsoft Word 2010**.

3. In the **Document1 - Microsoft Word** window, click the **File tab**, and then click **Open**.

4. In the **Open** dialog box **Navigation** pane, scroll down and then, if necessary, open ▷ Computer. In the list of drives, click the CD/DVD drive to display the contents of the student CD. If your instructor has provided a different location, navigate to that location instead of using the student CD.

5. In the file list, double-click the **01_ student_data_files** folder, double-click the **01_common_features** folder, and then double-click the **chapter_01** folder. Compare your screen with **Figure 1**.

6. In the file list, click **cf01_Visit**, and then click the **Open** button. Compare your screen with **Figure 2**.

   If you opened the file from the student CD, the title bar indicates that the document is in ***read-only mode***—a mode where you cannot save your changes.

■ **Continue to the next page to complete the skill** ▶

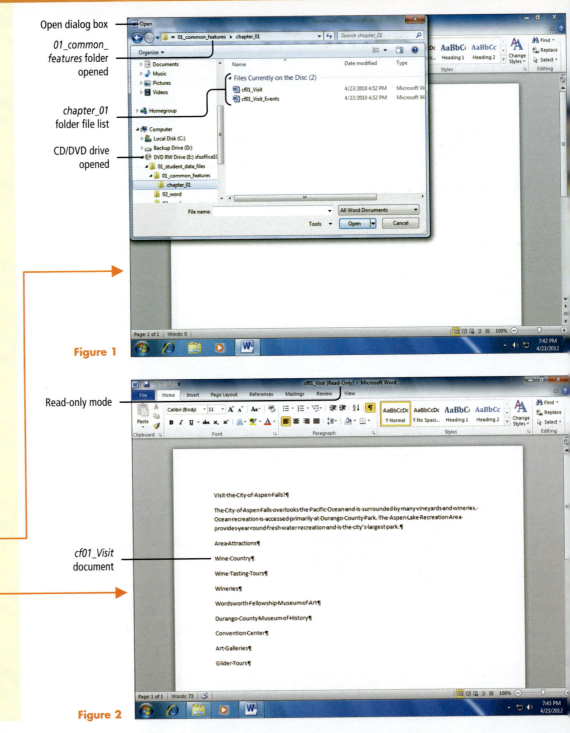

Open dialog box

01_common_ features folder opened

chapter_01 folder file list

CD/DVD drive opened

Figure 1

Read-only mode

cf01_Visit document

Figure 2

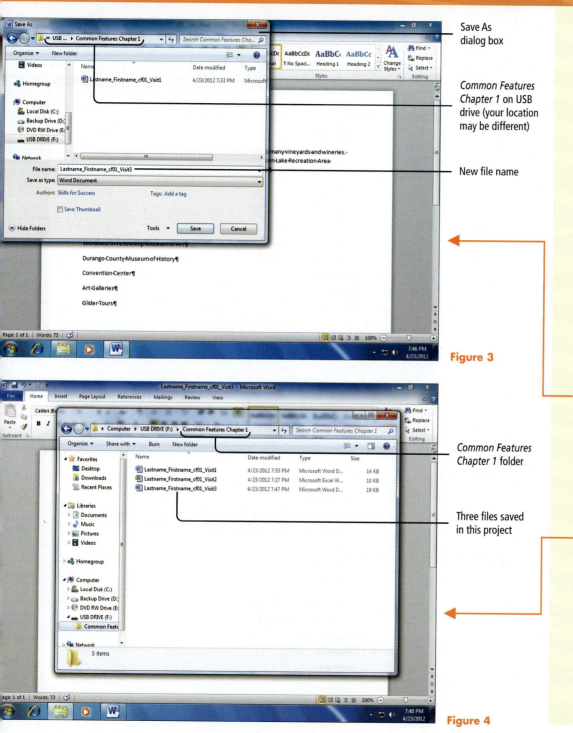

Save As dialog box

Common Features Chapter 1 on USB drive (your location may be different)

New file name

Figure 3

Common Features Chapter 1 folder

Three files saved in this project

Figure 4

7. If the document opens in Protected View, click the Enable Editing button.

Protected View is a view applied to documents downloaded from the Internet that allows you to decide if the content is safe before working with the document.

8. Click the **File tab**, and then click **Save As**.

Because this file has already been saved with a name in a specific location, you need to use Save As to create a copy with a new name and location.

9. In the **Save As** dialog box **Navigation** pane, navigate to the **Common Features Chapter 1** folder that you created previously—open ▷ the drive on which you are saving your work, and then click the **Common Features Chapter 1** folder.

10. In the **File name** box, replace the existing value with Lastname_Firstname_cf01_Visit3 Be sure to use your own first and last names.

11. Compare your screen with **Figure 3**, and then click the **Save** button.

12. On the title bar, notice the new file name displays and *[Read-Only]* no longer displays.

13. On the taskbar, click the **Windows Explorer** button. Verify that the three files you have saved in this chapter display as shown in **Figure 4**.

14. In the Windows Explorer window, navigate to the **student CD**, and then display the **chapter_01** file list.

15. Notice that the original student data file—*cf01_Visit*—is still located in the **chapter_01** folder, and then **Close** the Windows Explorer window.

■ **You have completed Skill 5 of 10**

► To *edit* is to insert text, delete text, or replace text in an Office document, spreadsheet, or presentation.

► To edit text, you need to position the insertion point at the desired location or select the text you want to replace.

1. With the **Word** document as the active window, in the first line, click to the left of the word *Aspen*. Press [Bksp] 12 times to delete the words *the City of*. Be sure there is one space between each word as shown in **Figure 1**.

   The Backspace key deletes one letter at a time moving from right to left.

2. In the second line of the document, click to the left of the words *The City of Aspen Falls*. Press [Delete] 12 times to delete the phrase *The City of*.

   The Delete key deletes one letter at a time moving from left to right.

3. In the line *Area Attractions*, double-click the word *Area* to select it. Type Local and then compare your screen with **Figure 2**.

   When a word is selected, it is replaced by whatever you type next.

■ **Continue to the next page to complete the skill**

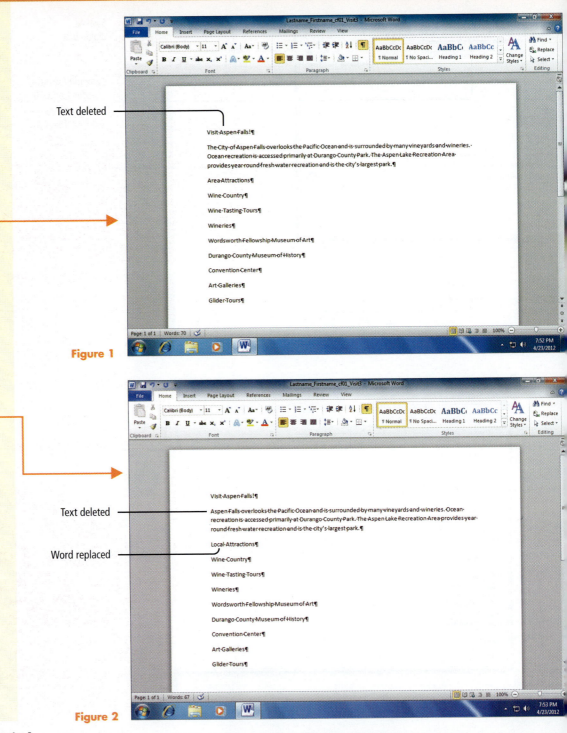

Figure 1

Figure 2

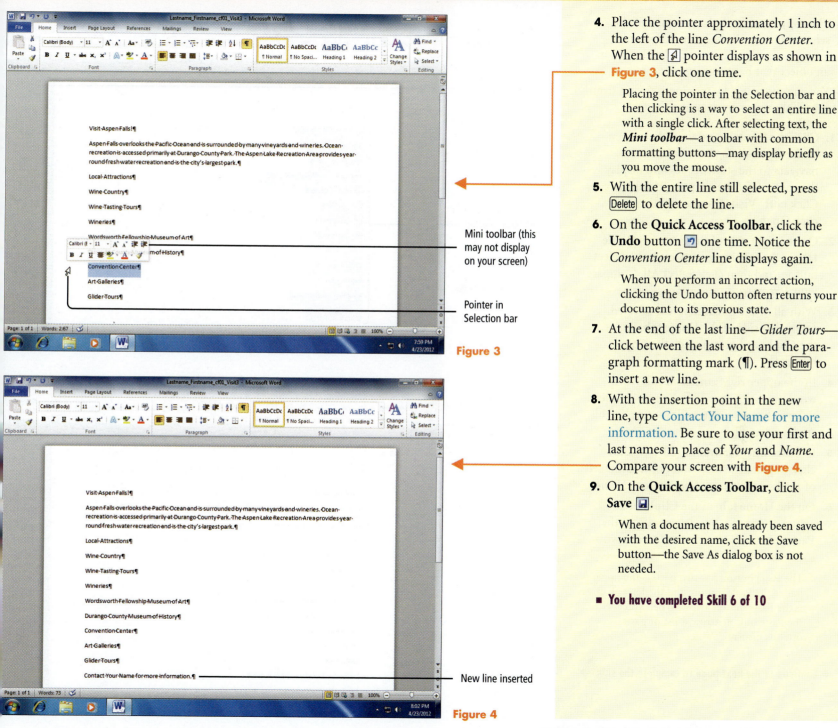

Mini toolbar (this may not display on your screen)

Pointer in Selection bar

Figure 3

New line inserted

Figure 4

4. Place the pointer approximately 1 inch to the left of the line *Convention Center*. When the pointer displays as shown in **Figure 3**, click one time.

   Placing the pointer in the Selection bar and then clicking is a way to select an entire line with a single click. After selecting text, the *Mini toolbar*—a toolbar with common formatting buttons—may display briefly as you move the mouse.

5. With the entire line still selected, press Delete to delete the line.

6. On the **Quick Access Toolbar**, click the **Undo** button one time. Notice the *Convention Center* line displays again.

   When you perform an incorrect action, clicking the Undo button often returns your document to its previous state.

7. At the end of the last line—*Glider Tours*—click between the last word and the paragraph formatting mark (¶). Press Enter to insert a new line.

8. With the insertion point in the new line, type Contact Your Name for more information. Be sure to use your first and last names in place of *Your* and *Name*. Compare your screen with **Figure 4**.

9. On the **Quick Access Toolbar**, click **Save**.

   When a document has already been saved with the desired name, click the Save button—the Save As dialog box is not needed.

■ **You have completed Skill 6 of 10**

► The *copy* command places a copy of the selected text or object in the *Clipboard*— a temporary storage area that holds text or an object that has been cut or copied.

► You can move text by moving it to and from the Clipboard or by dragging the text.

1. Click the **File tab**, and then click **Open**. In the **Open** dialog box, if necessary, navigate to the student files and display the contents of the chapter_01 folder. Click **cf01_Visit_Events**, and then click **Open**.

2. On the right side of the Ribbon's **Home tab**, in the **Editing group**, click the **Select** button, and then click **Select All**. Compare your screen with **Figure 1**.

3. With all of the document text selected, on the left side of the **Home tab**, in the **Clipboard group**, click the **Copy** button.

4. In the upper right corner of the Word window, click **Close**. You do not need to save changes—you will not turn in this student data file.

5. In **Lastname_Firstname_cf01_Visit3**, click to place the insertion point to the left of the line that starts *Contact Your Name*.

6. On the **Home tab**, in the **Clipboard group**, point to—but do not click—the **Paste** button. Compare your screen with **Figure 2**.

The Paste button has two parts—the upper half is the Paste button, and the lower half is the Paste button arrow. When you click the Paste button arrow, a list of paste options display.

■ **Continue to the next page to complete the skill**

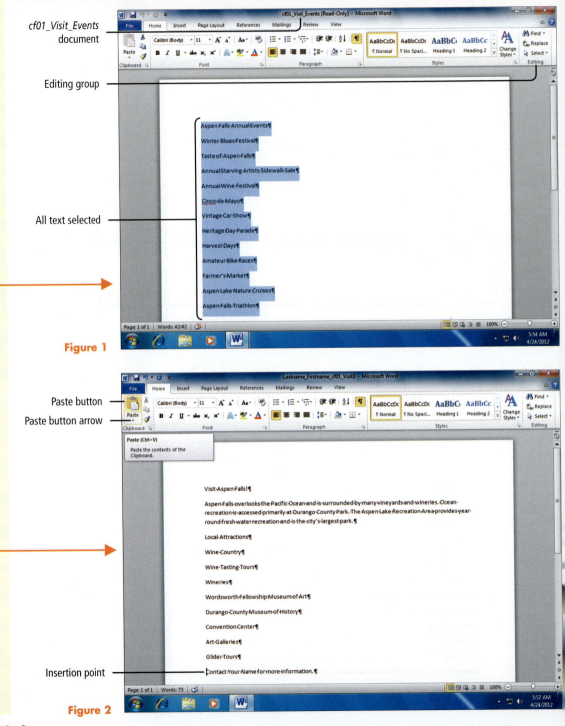

cf01_Visit_Events document

Editing group

All text selected

Figure 1

Paste button

Paste button arrow

Insertion point

Figure 2

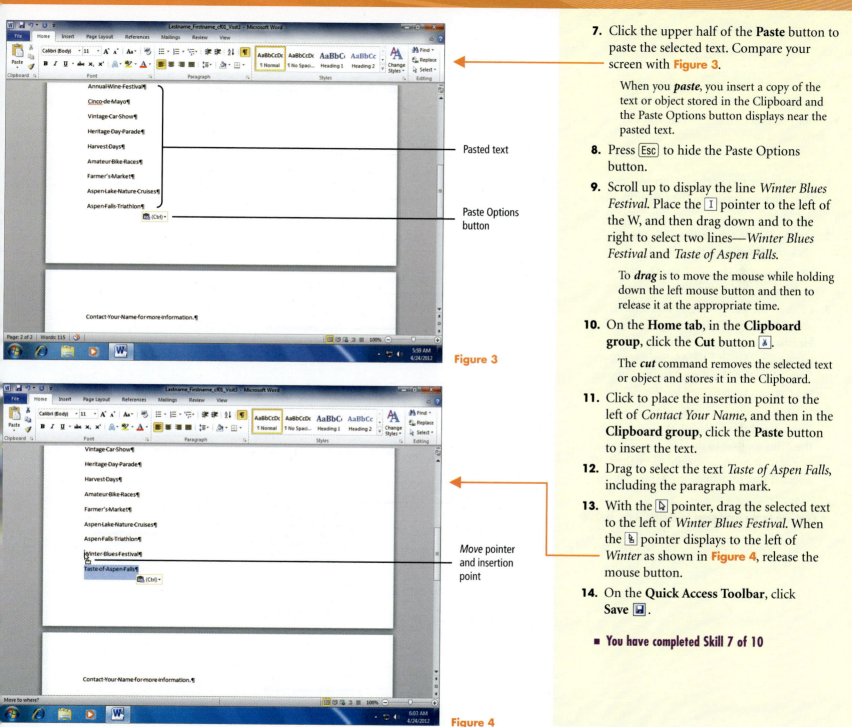

Pasted text

Paste Options button

Figure 3

Move pointer and insertion point

Figure 4

7. Click the upper half of the **Paste** button to paste the selected text. Compare your screen with **Figure 3**.

   When you *paste*, you insert a copy of the text or object stored in the Clipboard and the Paste Options button displays near the pasted text.

8. Press (Esc) to hide the Paste Options button.

9. Scroll up to display the line *Winter Blues Festival*. Place the (I) pointer to the left of the W, and then drag down and to the right to select two lines—*Winter Blues Festival* and *Taste of Aspen Falls*.

   To *drag* is to move the mouse while holding down the left mouse button and then to release it at the appropriate time.

10. On the **Home tab**, in the **Clipboard group**, click the **Cut** button .

   The *cut* command removes the selected text or object and stores it in the Clipboard.

11. Click to place the insertion point to the left of *Contact Your Name*, and then in the **Clipboard group**, click the **Paste** button to insert the text.

12. Drag to select the text *Taste of Aspen Falls*, including the paragraph mark.

13. With the pointer, drag the selected text to the left of *Winter Blues Festival*. When the pointer displays to the left of *Winter* as shown in **Figure 4**, release the mouse button.

14. On the **Quick Access Toolbar**, click **Save** .

   ■ **You have completed Skill 7 of 10**

► To *format* is to change the appearance of the text—for example, changing the text color to red.

► Before formatting text, you first need to select the text that will be formatted.

► Once text is selected, you can apply formatting using the Ribbon or the Mini toolbar.

1. Scroll to the top of the document, and then click anywhere in the first line, *Visit Aspen Falls.*

2. On the **Home tab**, in the **Styles group**, click the **Heading 1** thumbnail.

When no text is selected, the Heading 1 style is applied to the entire paragraph.

3. Click in the paragraph, *Local Attractions,* and then in the **Styles group**, click the **Heading 2** thumbnail. Click in the paragraph, *Aspen Falls Annual Events,* and then apply the **Heading 2** style. Compare your screen with **Figure 1**.

4. Drag to select the text *Visit Aspen Falls!* Immediately point to—but do not click—the Mini toolbar to display it as shown in **Figure 2**. If necessary, right-click the selected text to display the Mini toolbar.

■ **Continue to the next page to complete the skill**

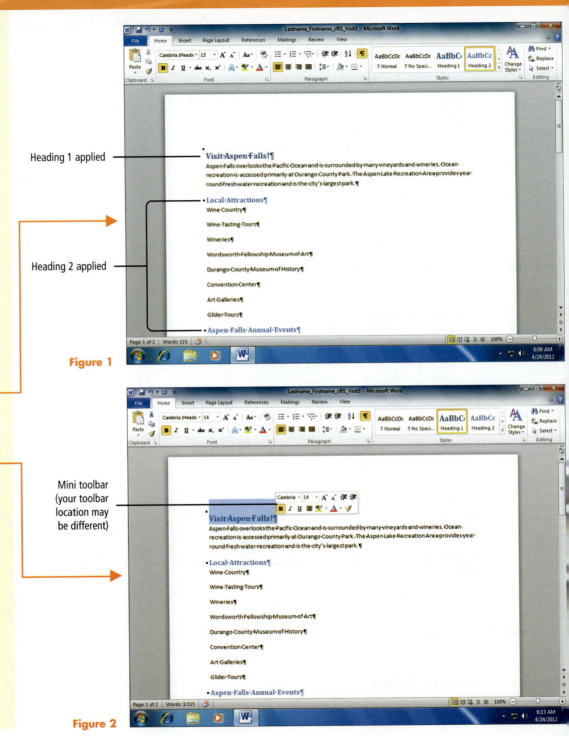

Heading 1 applied

Heading 2 applied

Figure 1

Mini toolbar (your toolbar location may be different)

Figure 2

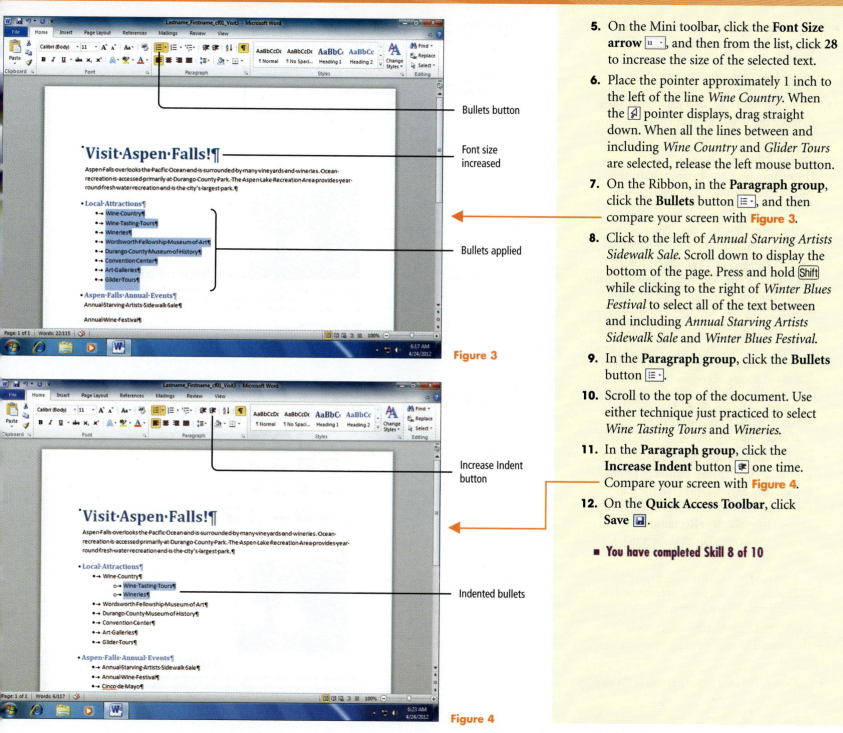

Figure 3

Figure 4

5. On the Mini toolbar, click the **Font Size arrow** ⊞⊡, and then from the list, click **28** to increase the size of the selected text.

6. Place the pointer approximately 1 inch to the left of the line *Wine Country*. When the ⊠ pointer displays, drag straight down. When all the lines between and including *Wine Country* and *Glider Tours* are selected, release the left mouse button.

7. On the Ribbon, in the **Paragraph group**, click the **Bullets** button ⊞⊡, and then compare your screen with **Figure 3**.

8. Click to the left of *Annual Starving Artists Sidewalk Sale*. Scroll down to display the bottom of the page. Press and hold ⓈⓗⒾⒻⓉ while clicking to the right of *Winter Blues Festival* to select all of the text between and including *Annual Starving Artists Sidewalk Sale* and *Winter Blues Festival*.

9. In the **Paragraph group**, click the **Bullets** button ⊞⊡.

10. Scroll to the top of the document. Use either technique just practiced to select *Wine Tasting Tours* and *Wineries*.

11. In the **Paragraph group**, click the **Increase Indent** button ⊞ one time. Compare your screen with **Figure 4**.

12. On the **Quick Access Toolbar**, click **Save** ⊟.

■ **You have completed Skill 8 of 10**

Bullets button

Font size increased

Bullets applied

Increase Indent button

Indented bullets

► Each Ribbon tab contains commands organized into groups. Some tabs display only when a certain type of object is selected—a graphic, for example.

1. Press and hold `Ctrl`, and then press `Home` to place the insertion point at the beginning of the document.

2. On the **Ribbon,** to the right of the **Home tab**, click the **Insert tab.** In the **Illustrations group**, click the **Picture** button.

3. In the **Insert Picture** dialog box, navigate as needed to display the contents of the student files in the **chapter_01** folder. Click **cf01_Visit_River,** and then click the **Insert** button. Compare your screen with **Figure 1**.

   When a picture is selected, the Format tab displays below Picture Tools. On the Format tab, in the Picture Styles group, a *gallery*—a visual display of choices from which you can choose—displays thumbnails. The entire gallery can be seen by clicking the More button to the right and below the first row of thumbnails.

4. On the **Format tab**, in the **Picture Styles group**, click the **More** button to display the **Picture Styles** gallery. In the gallery, point to the fourth thumbnail in the first row—**Drop Shadow Rectangle**—to display the ScreenTip as shown in **Figure 2**.

   A *ScreenTip* is informational text that displays when you point to commands or thumbnails on the Ribbon.

5. Click the **Drop Shadow Rectangle** thumbnail to apply the picture style.

■ **Continue to the next page to complete the skill**

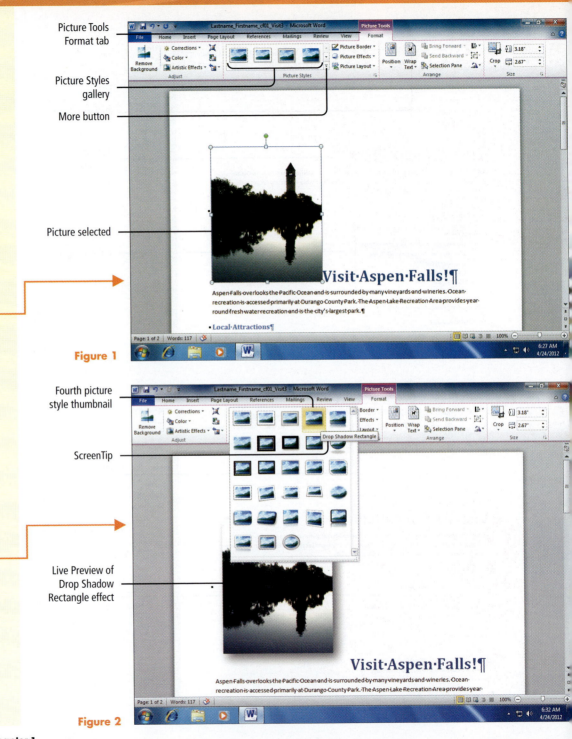

Picture Tools Format tab

Picture Styles gallery

More button

Picture selected

Figure 1

Fourth picture style thumbnail

ScreenTip

Live Preview of Drop Shadow Rectangle effect

Figure 2

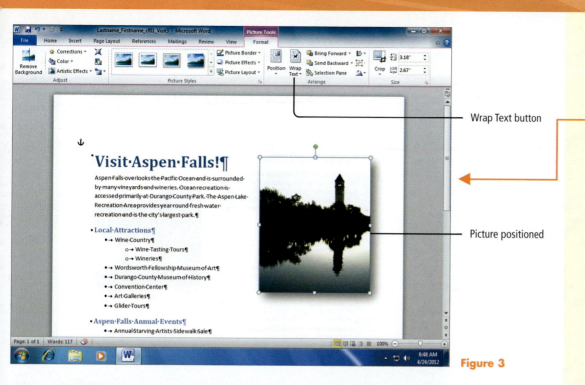

Wrap Text button

Picture positioned

Figure 3

6. On the **Format tab**, in the **Arrange group**, click the **Wrap Text** button, and then from the list of choices, click **Square.**

7. Point to the picture, and then with the pointer, drag the picture to the right side of the page as shown in **Figure 3.**

8. Click a blank area of the page, and then notice the Picture Tools Format tab no longer displays.

9. On the **Page Layout tab**, in the **Themes group**, click the **Themes** button.

10. In the **Themes** gallery, point to—but do not click—each of the thumbnails to display the Live Preview of each theme. When you are done, click the **Civic** thumbnail.

11. On the **View tab**, in the **Zoom group**, click the **One Page** button to display the entire page on the screen. If necessary, adjust the position of the picture.

12. On the **View tab**, in the **Zoom group**, click the **100%** button.

13. Select the text *Visit Aspen Falls!* without selecting the paragraph mark. Press [Alt] to display *KeyTips*—keys that you can press to access each Ribbon tab and most commands on each tab. Release [Alt], and then press [H] one time to display the Home tab. Compare your screen with **Figure 4.**

    With KeyTips displayed on the Home tab, pressing [2] is the same as clicking the Italic button [I]. In this manner, you select Ribbon commands without using the mouse.

14. Press [2] to apply the Italic format to the selected text.

15. **Save** the document.

■ **You have completed Skill 9 of 10**

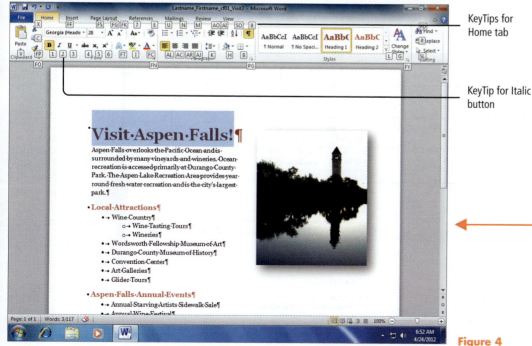

KeyTips for Home tab

KeyTip for Italic button

Figure 4

▶ Commands can be accessed in *dialog boxes*—boxes where you can select multiple settings.

▶ You can also access commands by right-clicking objects in a document.

1. In the paragraph that starts *Aspen Falls overlooks the Pacific Ocean*, **triple-click**—click three times fairly quickly without moving the mouse—to highlight the entire paragraph.

2. On the **Home tab**, in the lower right corner of the **Font group**, point to the **Font Dialog Box Launcher** as shown in **Figure 1**.

The buttons at the lower right corner of most groups open a dialog box with choices that may not be available on the Ribbon.

3. Click the **Font Dialog Box Launcher** to open the Font dialog box.

4. In the **Font** dialog box, click the **Advanced tab**. Click the **Spacing arrow**, and then click **Expanded**.

5. To the right of the **Spacing** box, click the **By spin box up arrow** three times to display *1.3 pt*. Compare your screen with **Figure 2**, and then click **OK** to close the dialog box and apply the changes.

■ **Continue to the next page to complete the skill** ▶

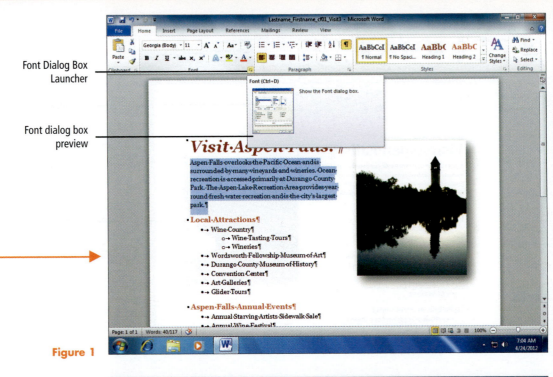

Font Dialog Box Launcher

Font dialog box preview

Figure 1

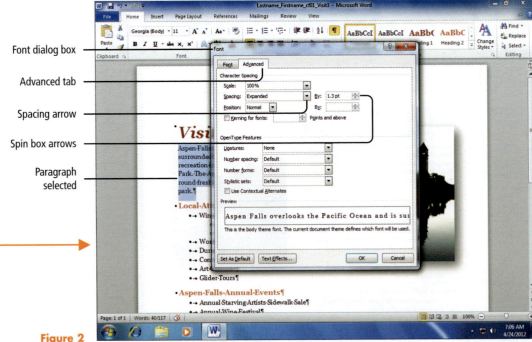

Font dialog box

Advanced tab

Spacing arrow

Spin box arrows

Paragraph selected

Figure 2

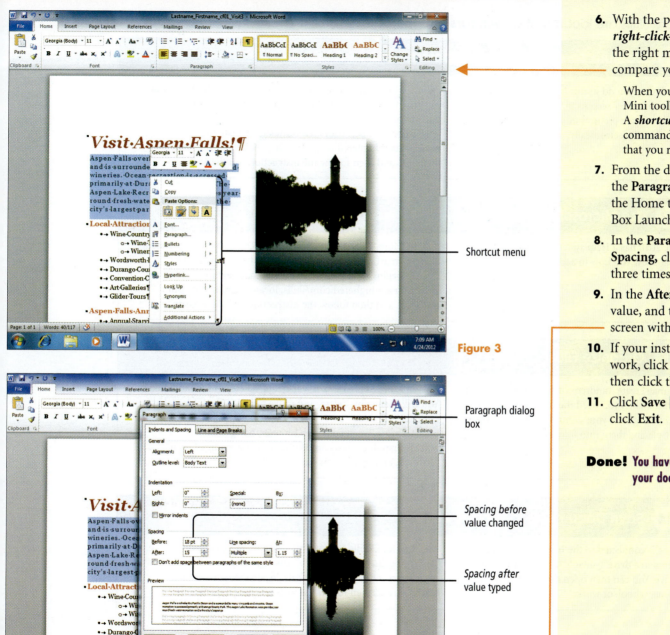

Shortcut menu

Figure 3

Paragraph dialog box

Spacing before value changed

Spacing after value typed

Figure 4

6. With the paragraph still selected, *right-click*—click the paragraph with the right mouse button—and then compare your screen with **Figure 3**.

   When you right-click selected text, the Mini toolbar and a shortcut menu display. A *shortcut menu* displays a list of commands related to the type of object that you right-click.

7. From the displayed shortcut menu, click the **Paragraph** command. Alternately, on the Home tab, click the Paragraph Dialog Box Launcher.

8. In the **Paragraph** dialog box, under **Spacing**, click the **Before spin up arrow** three times to display *18 pt.*

9. In the **After** box, highlight the existing value, and then type 15 Compare your screen with **Figure 4**, and then click **OK**.

10. If your instructor asks you to print your work, click the File tab, click Print, and then click the Print button.

11. Click **Save**, click the **File tab**, and then click **Exit**.

Done! You have completed Skill 10 of 10, and your document is complete!

More Skills

The following More Skills are located at **www.pearsonhighered.com/skills**

More Skills Capture Screens with the Snipping Tool

Some of the work that you do in this book cannot be graded without showing your computer screens to the grader. You can use the Snipping Tool to create pictures of your screens. Snip files can be printed or submitted electronically.

In More Skills 11, you will use the Snipping Tool to create a picture of your screen and then copy the picture into a Word document.

To begin, open your web browser, navigate to www.pearsonhighered.com/skills, locate the name of your textbook, and then follow the instructions on the website.

More Skills Use Microsoft Office Help

Microsoft Office 2010 has a Help system in which you can search for articles that show you how to accomplish tasks.

In More Skills 12, you will use the Office 2010 Help system to view an article on how to customize the Help window.

To begin, open your web browser, navigate to www.pearson highered.com/skills, locate the name of your textbook, and then follow the instructions on the website.

More Skills Organize Files

Over time, you may create hundreds of files using Microsoft Office. To find your files when you need them, they need to be well-organized. You can organize your computer files by carefully naming them and by placing them into folders.

In More Skills 13, you will create, delete, and rename folders. You will then copy, delete, and move files into the folders that you created.

To begin, open your web browser, navigate to www.pearsonhighered.com/skills, locate the name of your textbook, and then follow the instructions on the website.

More Skills Save Documents to Windows Live

If your computer is connected to the Internet, you can save your Office documents to a drive available to you free of charge through Windows Live. You can then open the files from other locations such as home, school, or work.

In More Skills 14, you will save a memo to Windows Live.

To begin, open your web browser, navigate to www.pearsonhighered.com/skills, locate the name of your textbook, and then follow the instructions on the website.

Key Terms

Online Help Skills

1. **Start** Word. In the upper right corner of the Word window, click the **Help** button . In the **Help** window, click the **Maximize** button.

2. Click in the search box, type Create a document and then click the **Search** button. In the search results, click **Create a document**.

3. Read the article's introduction, and then below **What do you want to do**, click **Start a document from a template**. Compare your screen with **Figure 1**.

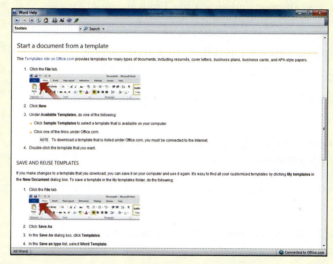

Figure 1

4. Read the Start a document from a template section to see if you can answer the following: What types of documents are available as templates? On the New tab, under Available Templates, what are the two general locations that you can find templates?

Matching

Match each term in the second column with its correct definition in the first column by writing the letter of the term on the blank line in front of the correct definition.

____ **1.** A feature that displays the result of a formatting change if you select it.

____ **2.** A line between the cells in a table or spreadsheet.

____ **3.** A mode where you can open and view a file, but you cannot save your changes.

____ **4.** A view where you prepare your document or spreadsheet for printing.

____ **5.** Quickly click the left mouse button two times without moving the mouse.

____ **6.** To insert text, delete text, or replace text in an Office document, spreadsheet, or presentation.

____ **7.** A command that moves a copy of the selected text or object to the Clipboard.

____ **8.** A command that removes the selected text or object and stores it in the Clipboard.

____ **9.** To change the appearance of the text.

____ **10.** A menu that displays a list of commands related to the type of object that you right-clicked on.

A Copy

B Cut

C Double-click

D Edit

E Format

F Grid line

G Live Preview

H Page Layout

I Read-only

J Shortcut

Multiple Choice

Choose the correct answer.

1. The flashing vertical line that indicates where text will be inserted when you start typing.
   A. Cell reference
   B. Insertion point
   C. KeyTip

2. A button used to turn a feature both on and off.
   A. Contextual button
   B. On/Off button
   C. Toggle button

3. The box formed by the intersection of a row and column.
   A. Cell
   B. Cell reference
   C. Insertion point

4. Until you save a document, it is stored only here.
   A. Clipboard
   B. Live Preview
   C. RAM

5. The combination of a number on the left side and a letter on the top of a spreadsheet that addresses a cell.
   A. Coordinates
   B. Cell reference
   C. Insertion point

6. A temporary storage area that holds text or an object that has been cut or copied.
   A. Clipboard
   B. Dialog box
   C. Live Preview

7. A toolbar with common formatting buttons that displays after you select text.
   A. Gallery toolbar
   B. Mini toolbar
   C. Taskbar toolbar

8. Informational text that displays when you point to commands or thumbnails on the Ribbon.
   A. Live Preview
   B. ScreenTip
   C. Shortcut menu

9. A visual display of choices from which you can choose.
   A. Gallery
   B. Options menu
   C. Shortcut menu

10. An icon that displays on the Ribbon to indicate the key that you can press to access Ribbon commands.
    A. KeyTip
    B. ScreenTip
    C. ToolTip

Topics for Discussion

1. You have briefly worked with three Microsoft Office programs: Word, Excel, and PowerPoint. Based on your experience, describe the overall purpose of each of these programs.

2. Many believe that computers enable offices to go paperless—that is, to share files electronically instead of printing and then distributing them. What are the advantages of sharing files electronically, and in what situations would it be best to print documents?

Create Documents with Word 2010

▸ Microsoft Office Word is one of the most common programs that individuals use on a computer.

▸ Use Word to create simple documents such as memos, reports, or letters and to create sophisticated documents that include tables and graphics.

Your starting screen will look similar to this:

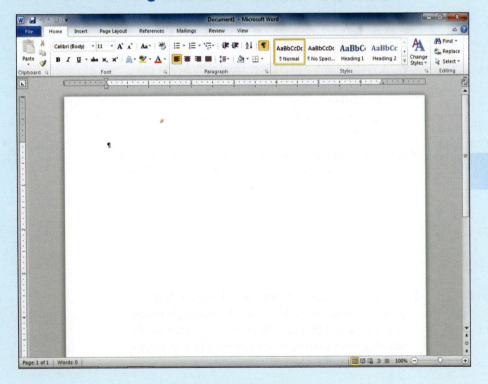

SKILLS

Skills 1-10 Training

At the end of this chapter, you will be able to:

Skill 1 Create New Documents and Enter Text
Skill 2 Edit Text and Use Keyboard Shortcuts
Skill 3 Select Text
Skill 4 Insert Text from Other Documents
Skill 5 Change Fonts, Font Sizes, and Font Styles
Skill 6 Insert and Work with Graphics
Skill 7 Check Spelling and Grammar
Skill 8 Use the Thesaurus and Set Proofing Options
Skill 9 Create Document Footers
Skill 10 Work with the Print Page and Save Documents in Other Formats

MORE SKILLS

More Skills 11 Split and Arrange Windows
More Skills 12 Insert Symbols
More Skills 13 Use Collect and Paste to Create Documents
More Skills 14 Insert Screen Shots into Documents

Outcome

Using the skills listed to the left will enable you to create documents like these:

ASPEN FALLS PUBLIC LIBRARY
255 Elm Street
Aspen Falls, CA 93463

May 5, 2012

Dr. Janis Imlay
Aspen Falls Community College
1 College Drive
Aspen Falls, CA 93464

Dear Dr. Imlay:

Subject: New Logo for Library

Thank you so much for your letter offering the services of your graphic design students for library-related projects. We currently have a project in mind that might benefit both the library and your students.

We want to update our logo to more accurately reflect the wide variety of services offered in a modern library. A logo contest would be a great idea. Call me at (805) 555-1011 to discuss this further.

I have attached a list of library activities to give the students an idea of some of the things we do.

Sincerely,

Douglas Hopkins, Director

Lastname_Firstname_w01_Library

Book Discussion Groups

There are several different book discussion groups, all led by volunteer moderators from the community. Some discussion groups focus on different types of books, such as biographies, history, fiction, classics, science and technology, and Spanish language literature.

Computer Training

Computer training is offered in the computer lab of the main branch only. The following classes are offered once a month and others are offered intermittently:

- Introduction to Computers
- Microsoft Word
- Microsoft Excel
- Adobe Photoshop
- Windows XP and Vista
- Using the Internet

Speakers and Entertainers

The library brings in noted authors once a month for an ongoing lecture series. Folk singers, small jazz ensembles, and other musical groups perform in the Hawken Community Room as they can be booked.

Bookmobile

A second bookmobile has been added, and routes are displayed on the library website. Bookmobiles visit each school in the district at least once a week.

Story Time

Story times are available in the Hawken Community Room on Saturday morning for toddlers, Saturday afternoon for early elementary students, and Sunday afternoon for kids interested in chapter books.

Game Night

Games are played in the Hawken Community Room on Friday evenings after the library closes at 6 p.m. Among the more popular games are chess, bridge, and backgammon. Experts are available to help patrons learn the games or improve their skills.

Electronic Book Downloads

More than 1,000 eBooks are available for download to an MP3 player. Library patrons can check these books out for three weeks, and can renew them one time. The books range from today's popular fiction to the classics.

Lastname_Firstname_w01_Library

You will save these documents as:

Lastname_Firstname_w01_Library
Lastname_Firstname_w01_Library_2003

In this chapter, you will create documents for the Aspen Falls City Hall, which provides essential services for the citizens and visitors of Aspen Falls, California.

Introduction

▶ Entering text, formatting text, and navigating within a Word document are the first basic skills you need to work efficiently with Word.

▶ You can change the font and font size, and add emphasis to text, but use caution not to apply too many different formats to your text. This can be distracting to the reader.

▶ It is easy to insert a picture into a Word document, and doing so increases the visual appeal and the reader's interest. Pictures should be clearly associated with the surrounding text and should not be inserted just to have a picture in the document.

▶ It is never acceptable to have errors in spelling, grammar, or word usage in your documents; you can use Word to prevent this from happening.

Time to complete all
10 skills – 50 minutes

Find your student data files here:

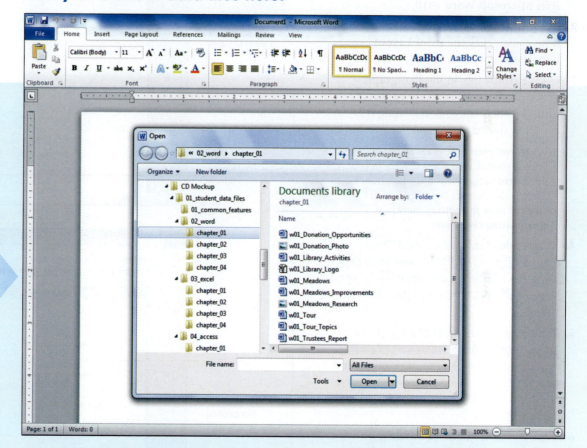

Student data files needed for this chapter:

- New blank Word document
- w01_Library_Activities

► When you start Microsoft Office Word 2010, a blank document displays.

► The first time you save the document, give it a name and choose a storage location. Then, save your changes frequently.

1. On the taskbar, click the **Start** button 🔵. From the **Start** menu, locate and then start **Microsoft Word 2010**.

2. In the lower right corner of your screen, if necessary, click the **Print Layout** button 🔲.

3. On the **Home tab**, in the **Paragraph group**, click the **Show/Hide** button ¶ until it displays in gold indicating it is active, as shown in **Figure 1**.

   When you press Enter, Spacebar, or Tab on your keyboard, characters display in your document to represent these keystrokes. These characters do not print and are referred to as *formatting marks* or *nonprinting characters*.

4. In all uppercase letters, type ASPEN FALLS PUBLIC LIBRARY and press Enter. Type 255 Elm Street and press Enter. Type Aspen Falls, CA 93463 and press Enter two times.

5. Type May 5, 2012 and press Enter three times; type Dr. Janis Imlay and press Enter; type Aspen Falls Community College and press Enter; type 1 College Drive and press Enter; and type Aspen Falls, CA 93464 and press Enter.

6. Type Dear Dr. Imlay: and press Enter. Type Subject: New Logo for Library and press Enter. Compare your screen with **Figure 2**.

■ **Continue to the next page to complete the skill**

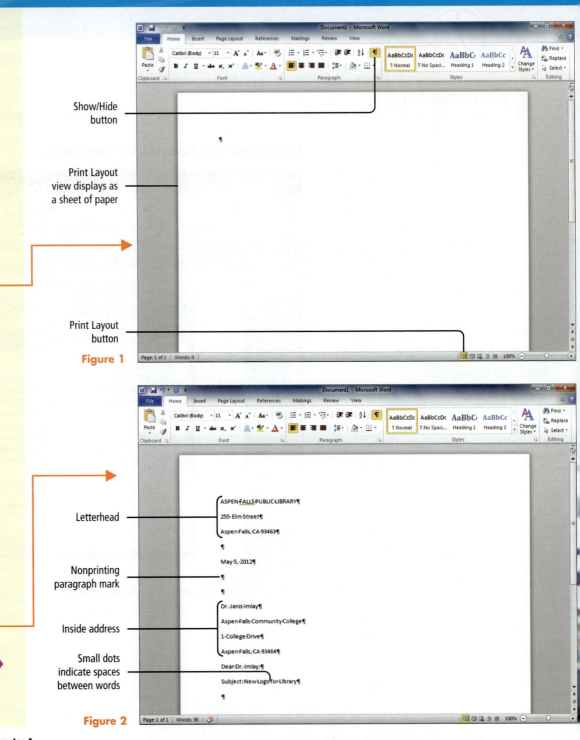

Show/Hide button

Print Layout view displays as a sheet of paper

Print Layout button

Figure 1

Letterhead

Nonprinting paragraph mark

Inside address

Small dots indicate spaces between words

Figure 2

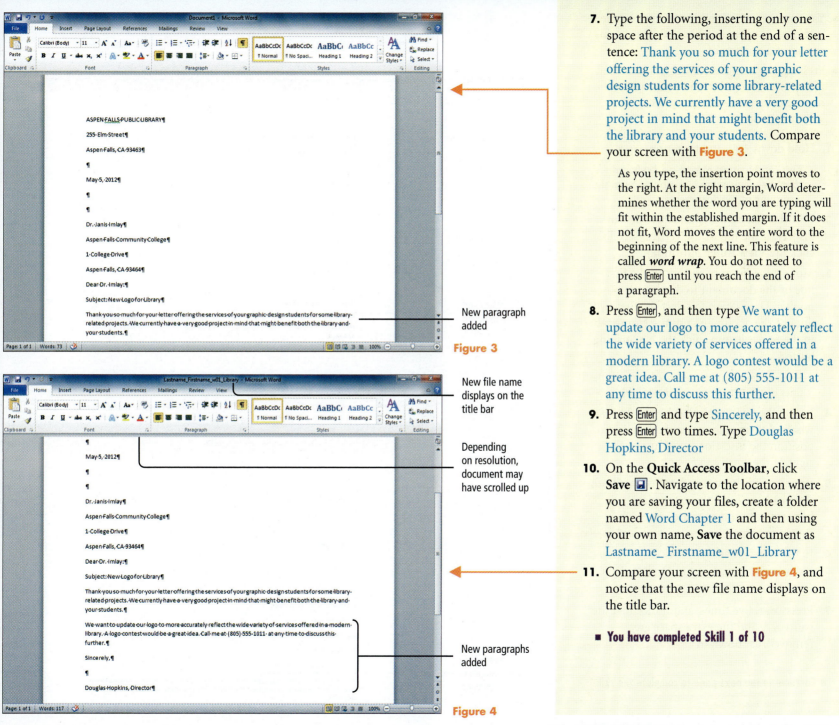

Figure 3

Figure 4

New paragraph added

New file name displays on the title bar

Depending on resolution, document may have scrolled up

New paragraphs added

7. Type the following, inserting only one space after the period at the end of a sentence: Thank you so much for your letter offering the services of your graphic design students for some library-related projects. We currently have a very good project in mind that might benefit both the library and your students. Compare your screen with **Figure 3**.

As you type, the insertion point moves to the right. At the right margin, Word determines whether the word you are typing will fit within the established margin. If it does not fit, Word moves the entire word to the beginning of the next line. This feature is called *word wrap*. You do not need to press Enter until you reach the end of a paragraph.

8. Press Enter, and then type We want to update our logo to more accurately reflect the wide variety of services offered in a modern library. A logo contest would be a great idea. Call me at (805) 555-1011 at any time to discuss this further.

9. Press Enter and type Sincerely, and then press Enter two times. Type Douglas Hopkins, Director

10. On the **Quick Access Toolbar**, click **Save** 🖫. Navigate to the location where you are saving your files, create a folder named Word Chapter 1 and then using your own name, **Save** the document as Lastname_ Firstname_w01_Library

11. Compare your screen with **Figure 4**, and notice that the new file name displays on the title bar.

■ **You have completed Skill 1 of 10**

► You can use a combination of keys on the keyboard to move quickly to the beginning or end of a document.

► Pressing ⌐Bksp⌐ removes characters to the left of the insertion point, and pressing ⌐Delete⌐ removes characters to the right of the insertion point.

1. Hold down ⌐Ctrl⌐, and then press ⌐Home⌐.

    This combination of keys—a **keyboard shortcut**—moves the insertion point to the beginning of the document.

2. If horizontal and vertical rulers do not display, at the top of the vertical scrollbar, click the **View Ruler** button ▣.

3. Move the pointer to the left of the first line of the document to display the ▨ pointer. Drag down to select the first two lines of the document. On the **Home tab**, in the **Styles group**, click the **No Spacing** button.

    Extra space should be removed between the lines of the letterhead and inside address.

4. Locate the paragraph that begins *Thank you*, and then in the second line, click to position the insertion point just to the right of the word *good*.

5. Press ⌐Bksp⌐ five times, and notice that both the word *good* and the extra space between *very* and *good* are removed, as shown in **Figure 1**.

6. In the same paragraph, click to position the insertion point just to the left of the word *very*.

7. Press ⌐Delete⌐ five times, and notice that the word *very* and the extra space are removed, as shown in **Figure 2**.

■ **Continue to the next page to complete the skill**

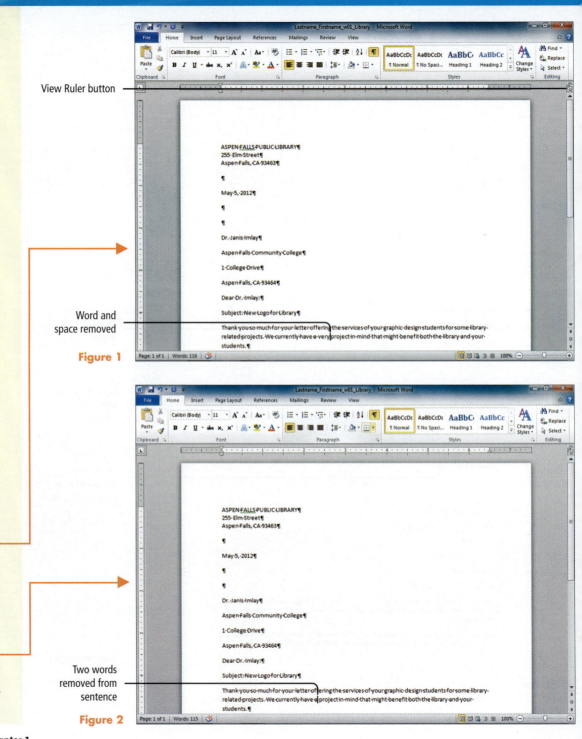

View Ruler button

Word and space removed

Figure 1

Two words removed from sentence

Figure 2

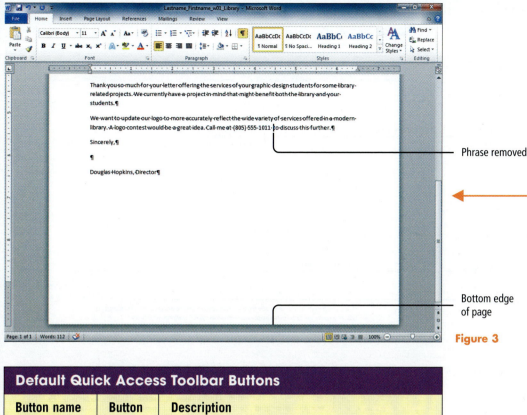

Phrase removed

Bottom edge
of page

Figure 3

Default Quick Access Toolbar Buttons

Button name	Button	Description
Save	💾	Saves the current document. If the document has not been saved, the button displays the Save As dialog box.
Undo	↩	Reverses the last action or series of actions.
Repeat	↻	Repeats the last action; shares the same button location as the Redo button.
Redo	↪	Displays instead of the Repeat button if the Undo command has been used; reverses the action of the Undo button.

Figure 4

8. Press Ctrl + End to move to the end of the document.

> The insertion point is positioned at the end of the last paragraph, and the bottom edge of the page displays at the bottom of the screen.

9. In the last paragraph of the letter body, which begins *We want to update*, locate the phrase *at any time*. Use either Bksp or Delete to remove the phrase and the extra space, and then compare your screen with **Figure 3**.

10. On the **Quick Access Toolbar**, click the **Save** button 💾. Alternately, hold down Ctrl, and then press S.

> This new saved version of your file over-writes the previous version.

11. Take a moment to examine the default buttons on the Quick Access Toolbar—your toolbar may display additional buttons—summarized in the table in **Figure 4**.

12. Press Ctrl + Home to move the insertion point to the beginning of the document and display the top edge of the page.

■ **You have completed Skill 2 of 10**

▶ To format text, first select the text, and then make formatting changes. You can also select text and then delete it.

▶ You can insert text at the insertion point by typing new text. You can also insert text by selecting existing text and then typing new text.

1. In the first line of the document, point just to the left of *ASPEN*. Hold down the left mouse button, and then drag to the right to select the entire line, including the paragraph mark. Notice that selected text is highlighted.

2. From the Mini toolbar, click the **Center** button ▤ to center the first line of text.

3. Repeat this procedure to center the second and third lines of the library address.

4. In the paragraph that begins *Thank you,* in the first line, point to the word *some,* and then double-click. Notice that double-clicking in this manner selects a single word and the Mini toolbar displays, as shown in **Figure 1**.

5. With the word *some* selected, press ⌈Delete⌋.

   When you double-click to select and delete a word, the selected word is deleted, along with its following space.

6. In the paragraph *Dr. Janis Imlay*, point to any word and triple-click. Notice that the entire paragraph is selected. On the **Home tab**, in the **Styles group**, click the **No Spacing** button.

7. Repeat this procedure to remove the extra spacing from the two paragraphs below *Dr. Janis Imlay.* Compare your screen with **Figure 2**.

■ **Continue to the next page to complete the skill**

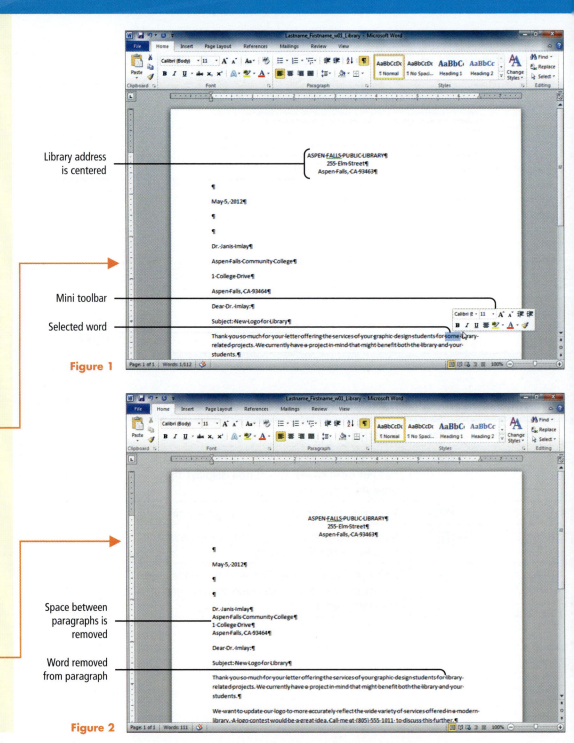

Library address is centered

Mini toolbar

Selected word

Figure 1

Space between paragraphs is removed

Word removed from paragraph

Figure 2

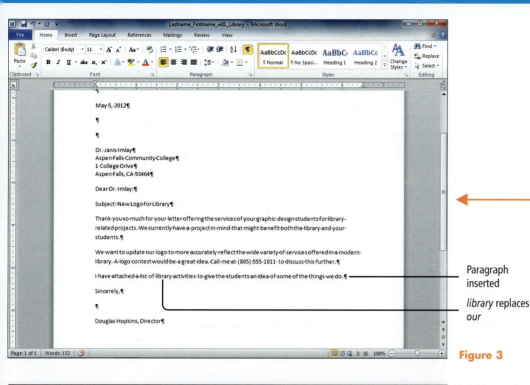

Figure 3

Paragraph inserted

library replaces *our*

8. In the paragraph that begins *We want to,* click to position the insertion point at the end of the paragraph—following the period after *further.*

9. Press Enter one time, and then type I have attached a list of our activities to give the students an idea of some of the things we do.

10. In the same paragraph, double-click the word *our* to select it, type library and then compare your screen with **Figure 3**.

   Recall that when you select a word, phrase, sentence, or paragraph, anything you type will replace all of the selected text.

11. In the paragraph that begins *Thank you,* move the pointer into the left margin area next to the first line of the paragraph. When the 🔏 pointer displays, double-click. Notice that the entire paragraph is selected.

12. Click anywhere in the document to deselect the text. Hold down Ctrl, and then press A. Notice that all of the text in the document is selected. Alternately, display the 🔏 pointer in the left margin and triple-click to select the entire document.

13. Press Ctrl + Home.

   Using a keyboard shortcut to move the insertion point also deselects any selected text.

14. **Save** 💾 the changes, and then take a moment to examine some ways to select text, described in the table in **Figure 4**.

   ■ **You have completed Skill 3 of 10**

Selecting Text in a Document

To select	Do this
A portion of text	Hold down the left mouse button and drag from the beginning to the end of the text you want to select.
A word	Double-click the word.
A sentence	Hold down Ctrl, and then click anywhere in the sentence.
A paragraph	Triple-click anywhere in the paragraph.
A line	Move the pointer to the left of the line. When the 🔏 pointer displays, click one time.
The entire document	Hold down Ctrl and press A. Alternately, display the 🔏 pointer in the left margin and triple-click.

Figure 4

► Objects, such as a text file or a graphic, can be inserted into a document.

► Inserted text displays at the insertion point location.

1. Press Ctrl + End to move the insertion point to the end of the document.

2. Press Ctrl + Enter to create a page break, as shown in **Figure 1**.

   A ***manual page break***—forcing a page to end at a location you specify—is added at the end of Page 1, and a new blank page is created. A manual page break indicator also displays below the text at the bottom of Page 1.

3. Press Ctrl + Home to move to the top of the document, and then notice that the active page and the number of pages in the document display on the status bar. Press Ctrl + End to move to the end of the document.

   The insertion point moves to the blank paragraph at the top of Page 2, and the top portion of Page 2 displays near the top of the Word document window.

4. On the Ribbon, click the **Insert tab**.

5. In the **Text group**, click the **Object button arrow**, and then compare your screen with **Figure 2**.

   The Object button is used to insert ***objects***—items such as graphics, charts, or spreadsheets created by Word or other programs—or text from another Word file.

▪ **Continue to the next page to complete the skill**

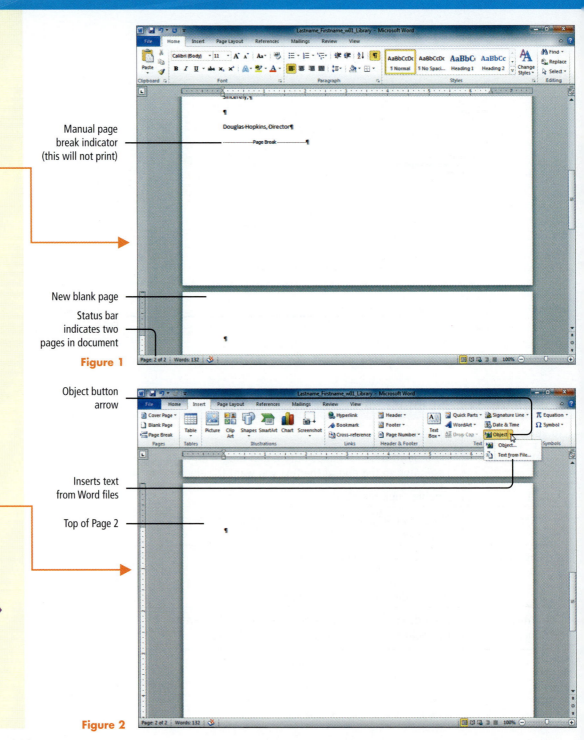

Manual page break indicator (this will not print)

New blank page

Status bar indicates two pages in document

Figure 1

Object button arrow

Inserts text from Word files

Top of Page 2

Figure 2

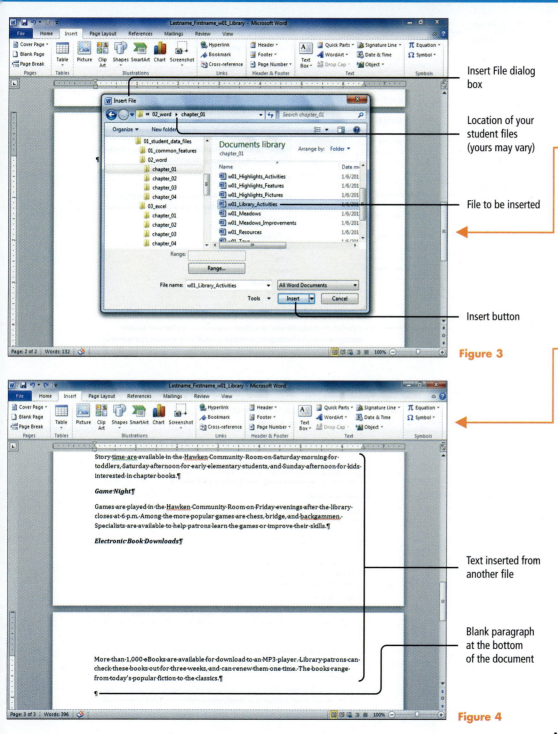

Insert File dialog box

Location of your student files (yours may vary)

File to be inserted

Insert button

Figure 3

Text inserted from another file

Blank paragraph at the bottom of the document

Figure 4

6. From the displayed list, click **Text from File** to display the **Insert File** dialog box.

   The Insert File dialog box is similar to the Open dialog box.

7. Navigate to the location of your student files, and then click the **w01_Library_ Activities** file. Compare your screen with **Figure 3**.

8. In the lower right corner of the **Insert File** dialog box, click the **Insert** button.

   All of the text from the w01_Library_ Activities file is copied into the current document at the insertion point location. The original file remains unchanged. The spelling and grammar errors in the inserted document will be corrected in Skill 7.

9. If necessary, press Ctrl + End to move to the end of the document, and notice that an extra blank paragraph displays, as shown in **Figure 4**.

10. Press Bksp one time to remove the blank paragraph from the end of the document.

11. Press Ctrl + Home to move the insertion point to the beginning of the document, and then **Save** 🖫 the changes.

   ■ **You have completed Skill 4 of 10**

► A *font* is a set of characters with the same design and shape.

► One way to format text is to change the font or font size.

► You can also add bold, italic, or underline emphasis to make text stand out from surrounding text. Bold, italic, and underline are referred to as *font styles*.

1. Click the **Home tab**. In the **Font group**, notice that Word's default font is **Calibri (Body)**, and the default font size is **11**.

   Fonts are measured in *points*, with one point equal to 1/72 of an inch.

2. Scroll so that you can view Page 2, click anywhere in the text, and then notice that the font is **Cambria (Headings)** and the font size is **12**.

3. Press Ctrl + A to select all of the text in the document. In the **Font group**, click the **Font arrow** [Calibri (Body)], and then from the displayed list, point to—but do not click—**Arial Black**. Notice that Live Preview displays what the text would look like if you select the Arial Black font, as shown in **Figure 1**.

4. From the displayed **Font** list, click **Calibri (Body)** to change all of the text in the document to Calibri.

5. With the text still selected, in the **Font** group, click the **Font Size arrow** [11], and then click **11**.

6. On Page 2, click anywhere in the text to cancel the selection. Notice the change to the font and font size, as shown in **Figure 2**.

■ **Continue to the next page to complete the skill**

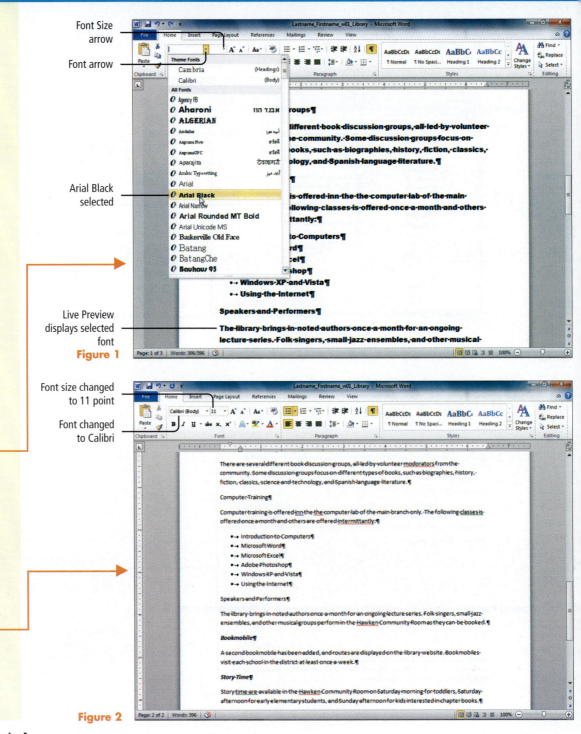

Font Size arrow

Font arrow

Arial Black selected

Live Preview displays selected font

Figure 1

Font size changed to 11 point

Font changed to Calibri

Figure 2

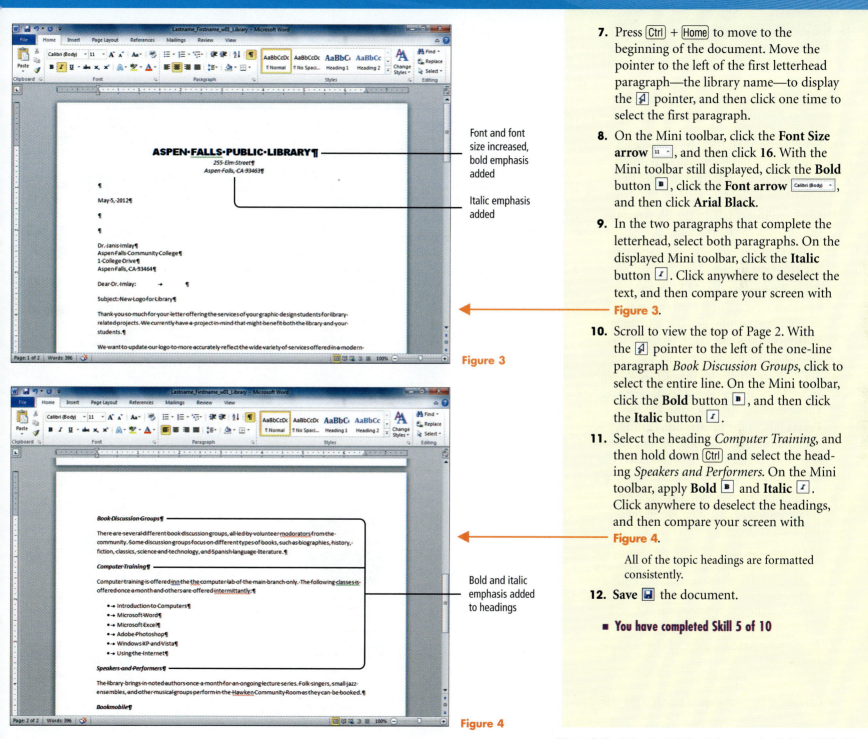

Font and font
size increased,
bold emphasis
added

Italic emphasis
added

Figure 3

Bold and italic
emphasis added
to headings

Figure 4

7. Press Ctrl + Home to move to the beginning of the document. Move the pointer to the left of the first letterhead paragraph—the library name—to display the 🔏 pointer, and then click one time to select the first paragraph.

8. On the Mini toolbar, click the **Font Size arrow** 11, and then click **16**. With the Mini toolbar still displayed, click the **Bold** button B, click the **Font arrow** Calibri (Body), and then click **Arial Black**.

9. In the two paragraphs that complete the letterhead, select both paragraphs. On the displayed Mini toolbar, click the **Italic** button I. Click anywhere to deselect the text, and then compare your screen with **Figure 3**.

10. Scroll to view the top of Page 2. With the 🔏 pointer to the left of the one-line paragraph *Book Discussion Groups*, click to select the entire line. On the Mini toolbar, click the **Bold** button B, and then click the **Italic** button I.

11. Select the heading *Computer Training*, and then hold down Ctrl and select the heading *Speakers and Performers*. On the Mini toolbar, apply **Bold** B and **Italic** I. Click anywhere to deselect the headings, and then compare your screen with **Figure 4**.

    All of the topic headings are formatted consistently.

12. **Save** 💾 the document.

- **You have completed Skill 5 of 10**

► You can insert *clip art*—graphics and images included with Microsoft Office or obtained from other sources—anywhere in a document.

► You can also insert pictures that have been saved as files on your computer.

1. Scroll to position the top of Page 2 on your screen, and then click to position the insertion point to the left of the *B* in *Book Discussion Groups.*

2. Click the **Insert tab**. In the **Illustrations group**, click the **Clip Art** button.

3. In the **Clip Art** task pane, in the **Search for** box, type library

4. Click the **Results should be arrow**, and then clear all of the check boxes except **Illustrations**. Select the **Include Office.com content** check box, and then click the **Go** button.

5. Scroll down to display the picture shown in **Figure 1**. If you do not see this image, **Close** the Clip Art task pane. On the **Insert tab**, in the **Illustrations group**, click **Picture**, and navigate to your student files for this chapter. Select and insert the **w01_Library_Logo** file, and skip to **Step 8**.

6. In the **Clip Art** pane, click the library image indicated in Figure 1, and then compare your screen with **Figure 2**.

   The image is inserted at the insertion point location. By default, the image is inserted in the text in exactly the same manner that a character is inserted from the keyboard. Some of the text at the bottom of Page 2 moves to a new Page 3.

7. In the **Clip Art** task pane, click the **Close** button ☒.

■ **Continue to the next page to complete the skill** ➤

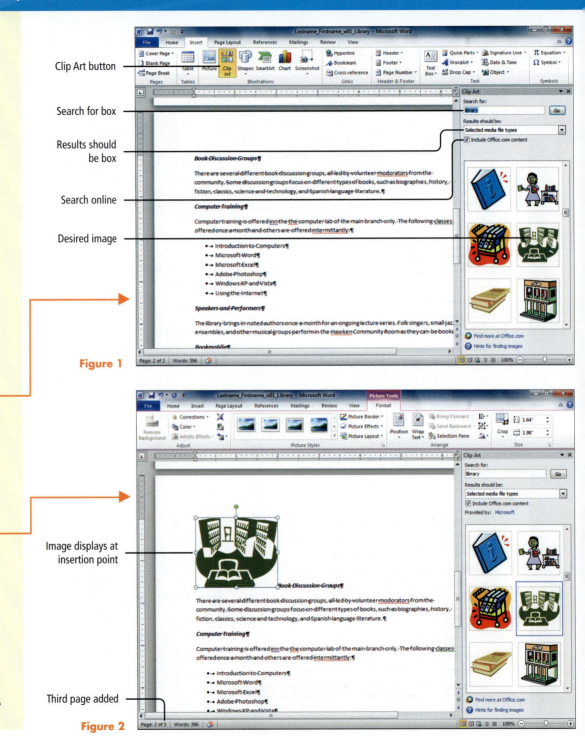

Clip Art button

Search for box

Results should be box

Search online

Desired image

Figure 1

Image displays at insertion point

Third page added

Figure 2

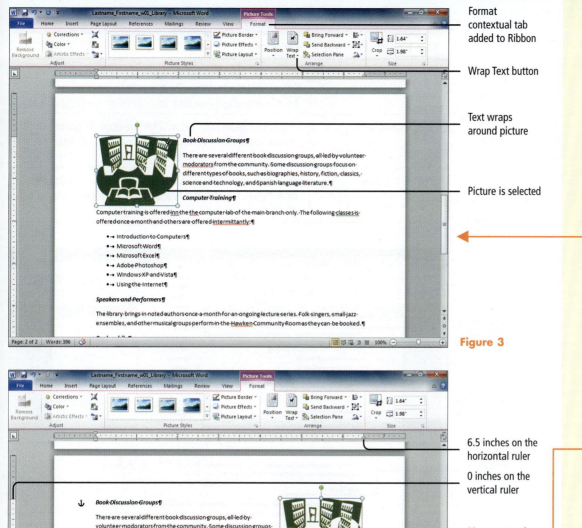

Format contextual tab added to Ribbon

Wrap Text button

Text wraps around picture

Picture is selected

Figure 3

6.5 inches on the horizontal ruler

0 inches on the vertical ruler

Picture moved

Document is two pages long

Figure 4

8. If necessary, click the picture to select it, and then notice that small circles and squares display at the corners and edges of the borders, indicating that the picture is selected. Notice also that a new tab—the **Format** contextual tab—is added to the Ribbon.

9. On the **Format tab**, in the **Arrange group**, click the **Wrap Text** button, and then take a moment to examine the various options for *text wrapping*—the manner in which text displays around an object.

10. From the displayed list, click **Square**, and then compare your screen with **Figure 3**.

11. Be sure the rulers display at the top and left of your document window; if necessary, click the **View tab**, and then in the **Show group**, select the **Ruler** check box.

12. Point to the selected picture until the 🔧 pointer displays.

13. By using the rulers as a visual guide, drag the picture to the right, positioning the upper right corner of the picture at **6.5 inches** on the horizontal ruler and at **0 inches** on the vertical ruler. Compare your screen with **Figure 4**. Notice that by wrapping the text around the picture, the number of pages in the document returns to two pages.

14. Adjust the position of the picture as necessary to match the figure, and then **Save** 💾 the changes.

■ **You have completed Skill 6 of 10**

► You can respond to potential spelling and grammar errors one at a time, or you can check the entire document.

► The number of potential grammar errors displayed by Word depends on your settings.

1. In the paragraphs near the picture, notice the wavy red, green, and blue lines, which indicate potential errors in spelling, grammar, and word use as outlined in the table in **Figure 1**.

   One or more of the wavy line colors may be missing, depending on your program settings.

2. Scroll through Page 2 and notice that the name *Hawken* has a wavy red underline in three locations.

   The wavy red underline means the word is not in the Office 2010 main dictionary. Many proper names are not in the main dictionary and are flagged as misspellings.

3. In the middle of Page 2, in the paragraph that begins *The library*, point to *Hawken* and right-click. Compare your screen with **Figure 2**.

   Possible corrected spellings display, although this proper name is spelled correctly.

4. From the list, click **Ignore All** to remove the underline from all instances of the word *Hawken* in the document.

5. Scroll to the top of Page 2. Right-click the word *inn* that is flagged with a wavy blue line, which indicates the potentially incorrect use of a word. If your word is not flagged, select the word *inn*, correct the spelling to **in**, and go to **Step 7**.

6. From the shortcut menu, click *in*, to correct the word usage.

■ **Continue to the next page to complete the skill**

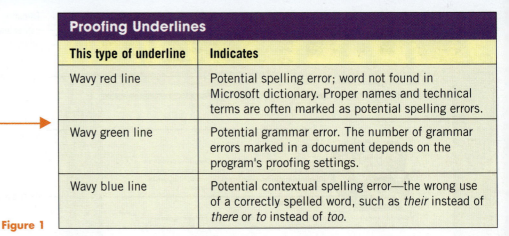

Proofing Underlines	
This type of underline	**Indicates**
Wavy red line	Potential spelling error; word not found in Microsoft dictionary. Proper names and technical terms are often marked as potential spelling errors.
Wavy green line	Potential grammar error. The number of grammar errors marked in a document depends on the program's proofing settings.
Wavy blue line	Potential contextual spelling error—the wrong use of a correctly spelled word, such as *their* instead of *there* or *to* instead of *too*.

Figure 1

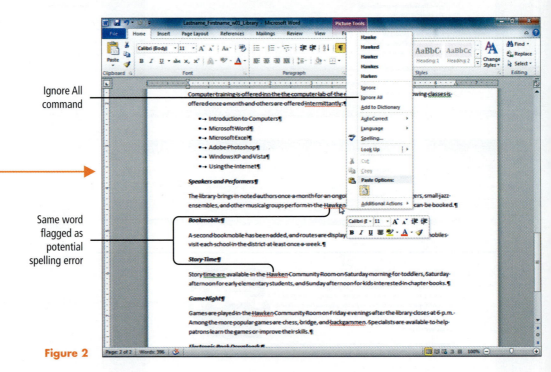

Ignore All command

Same word flagged as potential spelling error

Figure 2

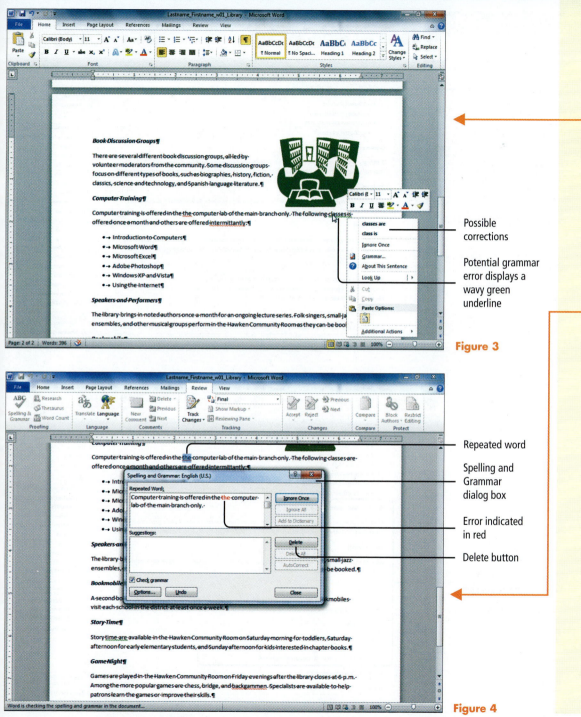

Possible corrections

Potential grammar error displays a wavy green underline

Figure 3

Repeated word

Spelling and Grammar dialog box

Error indicated in red

Delete button

Figure 4

7. Right-click *modorators*, which displays a wavy red line. Click the correct spelling **moderators**.

8. Right-click the text *classes is*, which displays a wavy green line indicating a potential grammar error. Compare your screen with **Figure 3**.

9. From the displayed list, click **classes are** to correct the grammatical error.

10. Scroll down and notice that there are additional spelling and grammar errors in the document. Press Ctrl + Home to move to the beginning of the document. Click the **Review tab**, and then in the **Proofing group**, click the **Spelling & Grammar** button. If a *Verb Confusion* error displays for *ASPEN FALLS*, click **Ignore Once**, and then compare your screen with **Figure 4**.

The Spelling and Grammar dialog box displays a potential error—a repeated word.

11. In the **Spelling and Grammar** dialog box, click the **Delete** button to delete the repeated word. For the next selected error, notice under **Suggestions** that the correct spelling—*intermittently*—is highlighted. Click the **Change** button to correct the spelling.

12. For the grammatical error *time are*, click **times are**, and then click **Change**.

13. Correct the misspelled word *backgammen* by clicking **Change**.

14. Ignore any other errors, and then when a message indicates that the spelling and grammar check is complete, click **OK**. Save your document.

- **You have completed Skill 7 of 10**

► Proofing tools include Spelling & Grammar checking, a Thesaurus, and Research tools.

► You can set proofing options to provide readability statistics for your document.

1. Scroll to the middle of Page 2 and locate the heading *Speakers and Performers*.

2. Double-click anywhere in *Performers* to select the word. On the **Review tab**, in the **Proofing group**, click the **Thesaurus** button. Notice that a **Research** task pane displays lists of similar words, as shown in **Figure 1**.

   A *thesaurus* lists words that have the same or similar meaning to the word you are looking up.

3. In the **Research** task pane, locate and point to *Entertainers*. To the right of the word, click the displayed arrow, and then click **Insert**. Notice that *Entertainers* replaces *Performers*. If an extra space displays to the left of *Entertainers*, remove the space.

4. In the second line of the paragraph that begins *Games are played*, locate and click anywhere in the word *Specialists*. In the **Proofing group**, click the **Thesaurus** button, and use the technique you just practiced to replace *Specialists* with **Experts**. Compare your screen with **Figure 2**.

5. In the **Research** task pane, click the **Close** button ⊠.

6. On the **Review tab**, in the **Proofing group**, click the **Word Count** button. Notice that the document statistics display, and include the number of pages, words, paragraphs, lines, and characters.

■ **Continue to the next page to complete the skill**

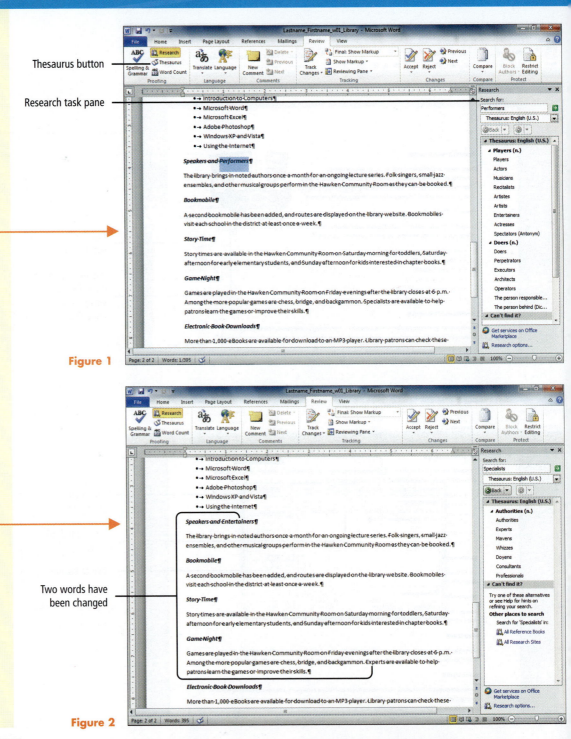

Thesaurus button

Research task pane

Figure 1

Two words have been changed

Figure 2

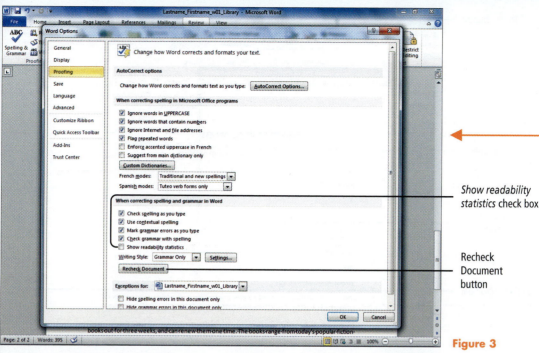

Show readability statistics check box

Recheck Document button

Figure 3

Readability statistics

Figure 4

7. In the **Word Count** dialog box, click the **Close** button.

8. Click the **File tab**. On the left side of the **Backstage**, click **Help**, and then on the **Help page**, click **Options**. On the left side of the **Word Options** dialog box, click **Proofing**, and then compare your screen with **Figure 3**.

   The Proofing options give you control over which potential spelling and grammar errors will be flagged, and lets you choose which items or rules to ignore.

9. In the **Word Options** dialog box, under **When correcting spelling and grammar in Word**, select the **Show readability statistics** check box, and then near the bottom of the dialog box, click **Recheck Document**.

10. Read the message, and then click **Yes** to recheck the spelling and grammar. Click **OK** to close the Word Options dialog box.

11. In the **Proofing** group, click the **Spelling & Grammar** button, and then ignore any errors that display. Notice that when the check is complete, a **Readability Statistics** dialog box displays, as shown in **Figure 4**.

    The Readability Statistics dialog box includes some of the information found in the Word Count dialog box, but it also includes information on the length of paragraphs, the number of words in sentences, and the reading level—shown at the bottom of the dialog box.

12. **Close** ▣ the **Readability Statistics** dialog box. Repeat **Steps 8** and **9**, clear the **Show readability statistics** check box, and then close the dialog box. **Save** ▣ the document.

■ **You have completed Skill 8 of 10**

► A *header* and *footer* are reserved areas for text, graphics, and fields that display at the top (header) or bottom (footer) of each page in a document.

► Throughout this book, you will insert the document file name in the footer of each document.

1. Press Ctrl + Home to move to the beginning of the document.

2. Click the **Insert tab**, and then in the **Header & Footer group**, click the **Footer** button. Compare your screen with **Figure 1**.

   Word provides several built-in footers. When you want to enter your own text, the Edit Footer command at the bottom of the gallery is used.

3. In the **Footer** gallery, use the vertical scroll bar to examine the footer formats that are available.

4. Below the **Footer** gallery, click **Edit Footer**. Notice that at the bottom of Page 1, below **Footer**, the insertion point is blinking in the footer, and the **Design** contextual tab displays on the Ribbon, as shown in **Figure 2**.

■ **Continue to the next page to complete the skill**

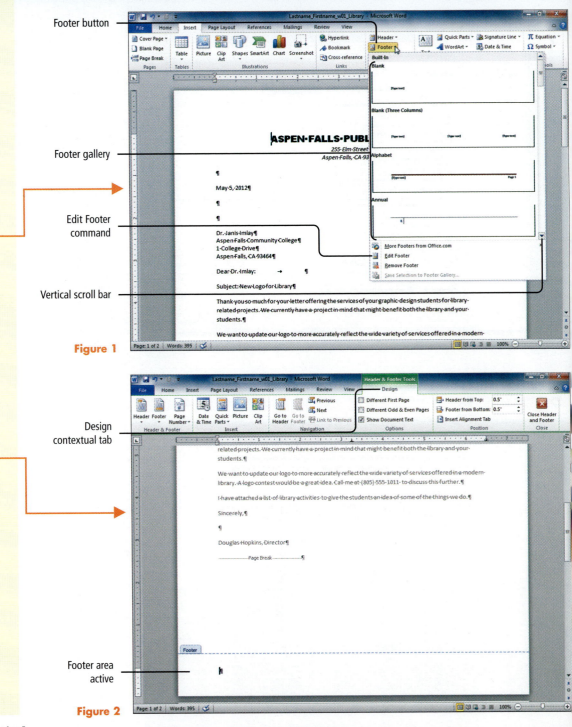

Footer button

Footer gallery

Edit Footer command

Vertical scroll bar

Figure 1

Design contextual tab

Footer area active

Figure 2

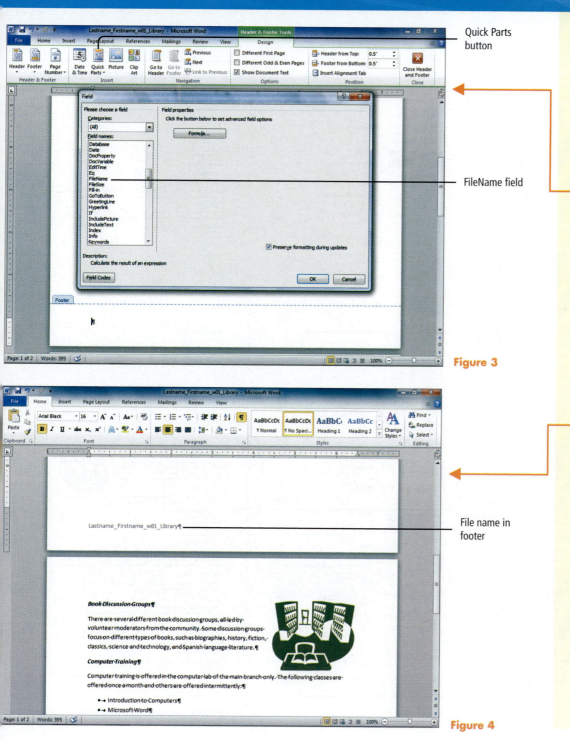

Quick Parts
button

FileName field

Figure 3

File name in
footer

Figure 4

5. On the **Design tab**, in the **Insert group**, click the **Quick Parts** button.

6. From the displayed list, click **Field**.

A *field* is a category of data—such as a file name, a page number, or the current date—that can be inserted into a document.

7. Under **Field names**, use the vertical scroll bar to see what types of fields are available, and then locate the **FileName** field. Compare your screen with **Figure 3**.

When a field name consists of two or more words, the spaces between the words are removed.

8. Under **Field names**, click **FileName**. Under **Format**, be sure (**none**) is selected, and then at the bottom of the **Field** dialog box, click **OK**.

The file name is added to the footer.

9. On the **Design tab**, in the **Close group**, click the **Close Header and Footer** button.

10. Scroll to display the bottom of Page 1 and the top of Page 2, and then compare your screen with **Figure 4**.

The text in the footer area displays in gray because the footer is inactive; while the document text is active, the footer text cannot be edited. When the footer area is active, the footer text is black, the document text is gray, and the footer text can be edited.

11. Save 🖫 the document.

■ **You have completed Skill 9 of 10**

▶ Before you print a document, it is good practice to preview it on your screen so that you can see any final changes that are necessary.

▶ Using the Backstage Print page, you can choose which printer to use, which pages to print, and how many copies of the document to print.

▶ You can save documents in different formats so that people who do not have Word can read them.

1. Press [Ctrl] + [Home] to move to the beginning of the document.

2. Click the **File tab**. On the left side of the **Backstage**, click **Print**, and then compare your screen with **Figure 1**.

   Recall that print settings display on the left side of the Print page, and a preview of the current page of the printed document displays on the right. The Zoom percent displays at the bottom of the preview; yours may vary depending on your screen resolution.

3. Below the document preview, click the **Zoom In** 🔍 button as necessary to change the zoom level of the preview to **100%**.

4. Click the **Zoom percent** to display the **Zoom** dialog box. Under **Zoom to**, select the **Whole Page** option button, and then click **OK**.

5. On the right side of the **Print** page, at the bottom of the vertical scroll bar, click the **arrow** ▼ to display Page 2, as shown in **Figure 2**. Notice that the footer text is no longer gray in the preview.

6. At the top of the vertical scroll bar, click ▲ to display Page 1.

   ■ **Continue to the next page to complete the skill**

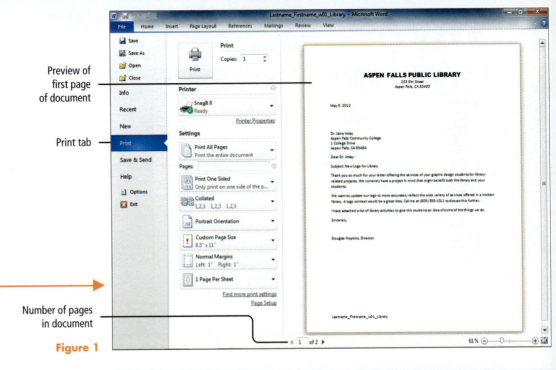

Preview of first page of document

Print tab

Number of pages in document

Figure 1

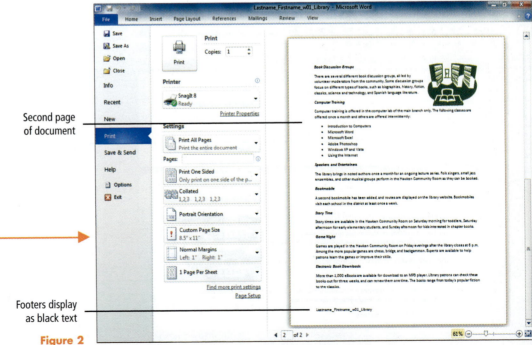

Second page of document

Footers display as black text

Figure 2

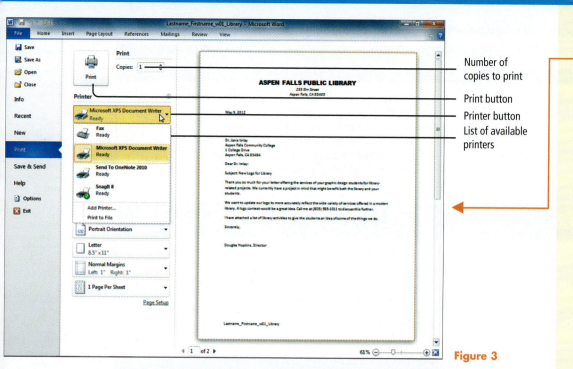

Number of copies to print

Print button

Printer button

List of available printers

Figure 3

7. Under **Printer**, click the **Printer** button, and then compare your screen with **Figure 3**.

   A list of printers that are available to your computer displays, as do other document destinations.

8. From the **Printer** list, select the printer you would like to use.

   You can use the Print page to select a printer, select the number of copies to print, and specify which document pages to print.

9. Be sure that the **Copies** is set to **1**. If you are printing your work for this project, at the top of the **Print** page, click the **Print** button—otherwise, do not click the **Print** button.

10. On the left side of the **Backstage**, click **Save As**. In the **Save As** dialog box, click the **Save as type** box, and then take a moment to examine the most common file formats for Word documents, which are summarized in the table in **Figure 4**.

11. From the list, click **Word 97-2003 Document**. Navigate to the **Word Chapter 1** folder, rename the file Lastname_Firstname_w01_Library_2003 and then click **Save**.

    Saving a document in an older format enables people with older software to open the document.

12. Display the footer area, right-click the file name, and then click **Update Field**. Close the footer area.

13. Click the **File tab**, and then under **Help**, click **Exit**.

14. Submit your printout or files as directed by your instructor.

Word Save As File Formats

Format	Descriptions
Word Document	Saves the document using the Word 2010 file format.
Word Template	Saves the document so that it can be used over and over, without altering the original document.
Word 97-2003 Document	Saves the file in earlier Word formats so that individuals using earlier versions of the program can open the document.
PDF	Saves the document in the popular Portable Document Format (PDF) display format, which can be opened on most computers.
XPS Document	Saves the document in the Microsoft XPS display format.
Other Formats	Lets you save a document as plain text with no formatting, in a universal file format such as Rich Text Format, or as a web page.

Figure 4

Done! You have completed Skill 10 of 10 and your document is complete!

More Skills

The following More Skills are located at **www.pearsonhighered.com/skills**

More Skills Split and Arrange Windows

You can split the Word screen, which lets you look at different parts of the same document at the same time. In a multiple-page document, this is convenient for viewing both the first page and the last page at the same time. You can also view two different documents side by side and make comparisons between the two.

In More Skills 11, you will open a multiple-page document, and split the screen. Then, you will open a second document and view both documents at the same time.

To begin, open your web browser, navigate to www.pearsonhighered.com/skills, locate the name of your textbook, and then follow the instructions on the website.

More Skills Insert Symbols

There are many symbols that are used occasionally, but not often enough to put on a standard computer keyboard. Some examples of commonly inserted symbols include copyright and trademark symbols, mathematical operators, and special dashes that are longer than hyphens. These symbols can be found and inserted from the Symbols group on the Insert tab.

In More Skills 12, you will open a document and insert several symbols from the Special Characters list in the Symbol dialog box.

To begin, open your web browser, navigate to www.pearsonhighered.com/skills, locate the name of your textbook, and then follow the instructions on the website.

More Skills Use Collect and Paste to Create Documents

To create a document by using text and objects from a variety of different sources, first collect all of the documents and images into the Office Clipboard, and then paste them into a new document.

In More Skills 13, you will open a document, collect two text files and two images on the Office Clipboard, and then construct a document from the collected items.

To begin, open your web browser, navigate to www.pearsonhighered.com/skills, locate the name of your textbook, and then follow the instructions on the website.

More Skills Insert Screen Shots into Documents

When you are working on a document, you may want to include a screen shot from your computer—such as a screen from another program or a website—as a graphic in the document.

In More Skills 14, you will use a browser to go to a government website, and then create a copy of the screen and store it in the Clipboard. You will then paste the screen into a document.

To begin, open your web browser, navigate to www.pearsonhighered.com/skills, locate the name of your textbook, and then follow the instructions on the website.

Key Terms

Online Help Skills

1. **Start** 🌐 Word. In the upper right corner of the Word window, click the **Help** button 📷. In the **Help** window, click the **Maximize** 🔲 button.

2. Click in the search box, type page numbers and then click the **Search** button 🔍. In the search results, click **Add or remove headers, footers, and page numbers**.

3. Read the article's introduction, and then below **What do you want to do?**, click **Add a page number without any other information**. Compare your screen with **Figure 1**.

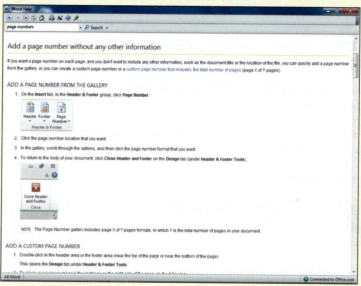

Figure 1

4. Read the section to see if you can answer the following: What is a quick way to open a header or footer? How can you show page numbers in the *Page X of Y* format—for example, *Page 3 of 12*?

Matching

Match each term in the second column with its correct definition in the first column by writing the letter of the term on the blank line in front of the correct definition.

____ **1.** A character that indicates a paragraph, tab, or space on your screen, but that does not print when you print a Word document.

____ **2.** The color of the wavy line that indicates a potential spelling error.

____ **3.** The color of the wavy line that indicates a potential grammar error.

____ **4.** Forces a page to end, and places subsequent text at the top of the next page.

____ **5.** Graphics and images included with Microsoft Office or obtained from other sources.

____ **6.** A technology that shows the result of applying a formatting change as you point to it.

____ **7.** A unit of measurement for font sizes.

____ **8.** Automatically moves text from the right edge of a paragraph to the beginning of the next line as necessary to fit within the margins.

____ **9.** A reserved area for text, graphics, and fields that displays at the top of each page in a document.

____ **10.** A category of data—such as a file name, the page number, or the current date—that can be inserted into a document.

A Clip art

B Field

C Formatting mark

D Green

E Header

F Live Preview

G Manual page break

H Point

I Red

J Word wrap

Multiple Choice

Choose the correct answer.

1. Formatting marks such as paragraph symbols and dots for spaces are also called:
   A. Nonprinting characters
   B. Symbols
   C. Objects

2. When you are typing text and a word will not fit within the established right margin, this Word feature moves the entire word to the next line in the paragraph.
   A. AutoComplete
   B. Word wrap
   C. Alignment

3. To delete the character to the left of the insertion point, press:
   A. Bksp
   B. Delete
   C. ←

4. To delete the character to the right of the insertion point, press:
   A. Bksp
   B. Delete
   C. →

5. Pressing a combination of keys—such as Ctrl + Home to move to the top of the document— is referred to as a:
   A. ScreenTip
   B. Live Preview
   C. Keyboard shortcut

6. A potential contextual spelling error is indicated by a wavy underline of this color:
   A. Red
   B. Green
   C. Blue

7. To select a sentence, hold down this key, and then click anywhere in the sentence.
   A. Alt
   B. Ctrl
   C. Shift

8. A thesaurus provides:
   A. Correct word usage
   B. Words with similar meanings
   C. Reading level of the document

9. To change Proofing tool settings, first display the:
   A. References tab
   B. Home tab
   C. Backstage

10. A reserved area for text and graphics that displays at the bottom of each page in a document is a:
    A. Footer
    B. Header
    C. Margin

Topics for Discussion

1. What kind of information do you commonly see in the headers and footers of textbooks and magazines? Why do you think publishers include this type of information? In a report, what other type of information might you put in a header or footer?

2. When you check the spelling in a document, one of the options is to add unrecognized words to the dictionary. If you were working for a large company, what types of words do you think you would add to your dictionary?

Skill Check

To complete this project, you will need the following files:

- New blank Word document
- w01_Donation_Opportunities
- w01_Donation_Photo

You will save your file as:

- Lastname_Firstname_w01_Donation

1. **Start** Word. On the **Home tab**, click the **Show/Hide** button until it displays in gold. In all uppercase letters, type ASPEN FALLS PUBLIC LIBRARY and press Enter. Type 255 Elm Street and press Enter. Type Aspen Falls, CA 93463 and press Enter two times. Complete the beginning of the letter as follows with the information shown in **Figure 1**. ———

2. Press Enter and type Thank you so much for your interest in making a donation to the Aspen Falls Public Library. You asked about potential projects for which we need additional resources, so I have attached a list of possible projects. Press Enter and type In answer to your question, our library does not have 501c3 status. However, our Friends of the Library group is a 501c3 organization, and all donations to the library through the Friends group are fully tax deductible. Press Enter two times.

3. Type Sincerely, and press Enter two times. Type Douglas Hopkins, Director and then move to the top of the document. Select the first two lines of the letterhead. On the **Home tab**, in the **Styles group**, click the **No Spacing** button. Repeat this procedure with the first two lines of the inside address.

4. In the paragraph that begins *Thank you*, use Bksp to delete *so much*. In the same paragraph, double-click *potential*, press Delete, and then compare your screen with **Figure 2**. ———

5. Press Ctrl + End, and then press Ctrl + Enter to insert a manual page break.

6. Click the **Insert tab**, and then in the **Text group**, click the **Object button arrow**. Click **Text from File**, and then locate and insert the file **w01_Donation_Opportunities**. Press Bksp to remove the blank paragraph.

■ **Continue to the next page to complete this Skill Check** ▶

May 17, 2012

Mr. Thomas Aldridge

2279 Shoreline Dr.

Aspen Heights, CA 93449

Dear Mr. Aldridge:

Subject: Donation to the Library

Figure 1

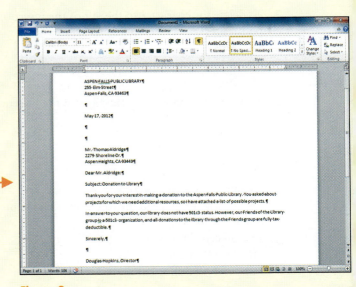

Figure 2

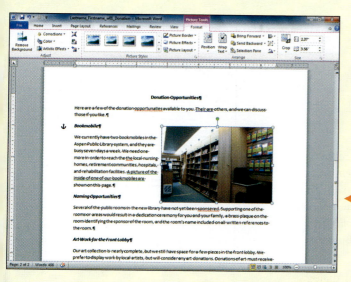

Figure 3

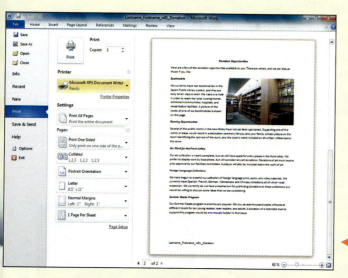

Figure 4

7. Press <kbd>Ctrl</kbd> + <kbd>A</kbd>. On the **Home tab**, in the **Font group**, change the **Font Size** to **11** and change the **Font** to **Calibri**. At the top of the document, select the library name. On the Mini toolbar, change the **Font** to **Arial Black**, the **Font Size** to **16**, and then click **Bold**.

8. **Save** the document in your **Word Chapter 1** folder as Lastname_Firstname_w01_ Donation Display the top of Page 2. Select the heading *Donation Opportunities*, and then on the Mini toolbar, click **Bold** and **Center**.

9. Select the heading *Bookmobile* and from the Mini toolbar, click **Bold**. Select the next heading—*Naming Opportunities*—hold down <kbd>Ctrl</kbd>, and then select the rest of the headings displayed in italic. On the Mini toolbar, click **Bold**.

10. Click to the left of the first *B* in the heading *Bookmobile*. From your student files, insert the picture **w01_Donation_Photo**. With the picture selected, on the **Format tab**, in the **Arrange group**, click the **Wrap Text** button, and then click **Square**. Drag the picture to the right, aligning the right edge at approximately **6.5 inches** on the horizontal ruler and the top edge at approximately **1 inch** on the vertical ruler. Compare your screen with **Figure 3**.

11. Right-click the word, *opportunaties*, that has a wavy red underline, and then click **opportunities**. In the same sentence, right-click *Their are* that displays a wavy blue line, and then click **There are**. Move the insertion point to the top of Page 2.

12. On the **Review tab**, in the **Proofing group**, click the **Spelling & Grammar** button. Make the following corrections—your marked errors may differ: For the repeated word *the*, delete the word. In the sentence that begins *A picture*, change to the suggested correction that ends with the word *is*. Correct the misspelled word *sponsored*, change *too* to *to*, and change *languge* to *language*. Ignore any other changes except words you might have mistyped on Page 1.

13. On the **Insert tab**, in the **Header & Footer** group, click the **Footer** button, and then click **Edit Footer**. On the **Design tab**, in the **Insert group**, click the **Quick Parts** button, and then click **Field**. Under **Field names**, scroll down and click **FileName**. Click **OK**, and then on the **Design tab**, click **Close Header and Footer**.

14. Click **Save**. Click the **File tab**, and then click **Print**. Compare your document with **Figure 4**. Print or submit the file as directed by your instructor. **Exit** Word.

Done! You have completed the Skill Check

Assess Your Skills 1

To complete this document, you will need the following files:

- w01_Meadows
- w01_Meadows_Improvements
- w01_Meadows_Research

You will save your file as:

- Lastname_Firstname_w01_Meadows

1. **Start** Word and display the formatting marks. Click the **File tab**, and then click **Open**. Navigate to your student files. **Open** the file **w01_Meadows**, save it in your **Word Chapter 1** folder as Lastname_Firstname_w01_Meadows and then add the file name to the footer.

2. In the letterhead, select the first line of text and change the **Font** to **Arial Black** and the **Font Size** to **16**. Select the remaining three lines of the letterhead and add **Bold** emphasis.

3. Press Ctrl + End. Type Dear Ms. Jefferson: and press Enter. Type Subject: Aspen Meadows Branch Improvements and press Enter. Type the following paragraph: Thank you for your letter of concern about the Aspen Meadows Branch of the Aspen Falls Public Library. This is our smallest branch, and we are working hard to improve the collection and the services offered to our patrons. We have just completed some improvements, which I have detailed on the attached page. We hope these changes will answer some of your concerns. Press Enter, type Sincerely, and then press Enter two times. Type Douglas Hopkins, Director and then insert a manual page break.

4. On Page 2, insert the file **w01_Meadows_Improvements**. Select all of the text in the new page and change the **Font** to **Calibri**

and the **Font Size** to **11**. Select the report heading that begins *Recent Improvements*, apply **Bold**, change the **Font Size** to **14**, and **Center** the text. Select the three headings on the page—*Collection, Children's Collection,* and *Research Stations*—and apply **Bold** and **Italic** emphasis.

5. Display the **Spelling and Grammar** dialog box and on Page 2, fix the following problems: Remove the duplicate *to*, change *a* to *an*, and correct the spelling of *severel* to *several* and *suatable* to *suitable*. Ignore other marked words in the document unless you find typing errors that you made on Page 1.

6. In the first line of the last paragraph that begins *We have added*, double-click to select the word *deliver*. Use the **Thesaurus** to change *deliver* to **provide**.

7. Move to the blank line at the bottom of Page 2. Press Enter, and then insert the picture in the file **w01_Meadows_Research**. On the **Home tab**, in the **Paragraph group**, click the **Center** button to center the picture. **Save** the changes, and then compare your document with **Figure 1**. Preview your document, make any necessary changes, and then print or submit the file as directed by your instructor.

Done! You have completed Assess Your Skills 1

Figure 1

Assess Your Skills 2

Assess Your Skills 3 and 4 can be found at www.pearsonhighered.com/skills.

To complete this document, you will need the following files:

- w01_Tour
- w01_Tour_Topics

You will save your files as:

- Lastname_Firstname_w01_Tour

MEMORANDUM

TO:	Jamie McArthur, Special Services
FROM:	Douglas Hopkins, Director
DATE:	June 21, 2012
RE:	Virtual Tour of the Library

Jamie:

I have been thinking about the suggestion made at the Board of Trustees meeting the other night that we hire an outside company to design a virtual tour of the library. The virtual tour might consist of several modules featuring different topics. I have listed some of the topics on the next page.

Let me know what you think.

Doug

Lastname_Firstname_w01_Tour

Topics for the Virtual Tour of the New Library

Here is a list I put together of topics I would like to see included if we go ahead with the virtual tour for the Internet:

The Building Exterior

The new building is very striking, and we should have a 360-degree tour of the exterior, including the grounds and the pond. We should also mention the Alvarado architectural firm that we employed to design the building.

The Building Interior

Shots of the interior should include a panorama of our wonderful lobby, and then should move inside to show the collections, the kids' area, the community room, the computer labs, the genealogy room, the office suite, and the board room.

Library Technology

Some of the technology that we show will be physical features, such as computer labs, but some will have to rely on screen shots of technology in action, such as downloading e-books, using the research databases, and some of the adaptive technologies that are available for the disabled. I think it is important that we have a special section that focuses only on the technology. This topic will be of special interest to our youngest and oldest patrons.

Friends of the Aspen Falls Public Library Bookshop

The Friends bookshop is a centerpiece of our new library, and needs to have its own module in the virtual tour.

People

I am not sure we should include any of the staff in the virtual tour. Several of them have already indicated that they do not want to be shown in the tours. If we need one or more people for any of the tour modules, we should probably ask for volunteers.

Lastname_Firstname_w01_Tour

Figure 1

---

1. **Start** Word and display the formatting marks. Open the file **w01_Tour**, save it in your **Word Chapter 1** folder as Lastname_Firstname_w01_Tour and then add the file name to the footer. Select the first line of text and change the **Font** to **Calibri** and the **Font Size** to **36**, and then **Center** and **Bold** the title. Add **Bold** emphasis to the four words on the left side of the memo—TO:, FROM:, DATE:, and RE:.

2. Move to the end of the document, type Jamie:, and then press Enter. Type I have been thinking about the suggestion made at the Board of Trustees meeting the other night that we hire an outside company to design a virtual tour of the library. The virtual tour might consist of several different modules featuring different topics. I have listed some of the more interesting things on the next page. Press Enter, type Let me know what you think. and then press Enter two times. Type Doug and then add a manual page break.

3. In the text you just typed, use Bksp or Delete to remove the phrase *more interesting*. Double-click the next word—*things*—and type topics to replace it. Locate and double-click the first instance of the word *different*— to the left of *modules*—and then press Delete.

4. Position the insertion point at the top of Page 2. Insert the file **w01_Tour_Topics**.

5. On Page 2, select the first line of text, apply **Bold** emphasis, and **Center** the text. Select the five topic titles on the left side of Page 2 and apply **Bold** emphasis. Select all of the text in the document except the title on the first page, and change the **Font Size** to **12**.

6. Move to the top of Page 2. Display the **Spelling and Grammar** dialog box. Delete the repeated word *the*, change *interier* to *interior*, change *databasis* to *databases*, and then change *has* to *have*. Correct any mistakes you made on the first page.

7. Position the insertion point at the bottom of the document. Insert and position the clip art image shown in **Figure 1**. Use *library* as the search term, and search only for **Illustrations**. (Note: If this image is not available, insert the picture in the student file w01_Library_Logo.) **Close** the Clip Art task pane.

8. **Save** the changes and compare your document with **Figure 1**. Preview your document, make any necessary changes, and then print or submit the file as directed by your instructor.

Done! You have completed Assess Your Skills 2

Assess Your Skills Visually

To complete this document, you will need the following file:

- New blank Word document

You will save your document as:

- Lastname_Firstname_w01_Closures

Start Word. Create the document shown in **Figure 1**. **Save** the file as Lastname_Firstname_w01_Closures in your **Word Chapter 1** folder. To complete this document, use Arial Black sized at 24 points for the title and Cambria sized at 12 points for the rest of the document. After the last paragraph, insert the clip art image shown in **Figure 1** by searching for *holidays*. If you do not see the same image, use any other appropriate clip art. Insert the file name in the footer, and then print or submit the file as directed by your instructor.

Done! You have completed Assess Your Skills Visually

MEMORANDUM

TO: All Library Staff

FROM: Douglas Hopkins, Director

DATE: December 15, 2011

RE: Library Closings for the 2012 Calendar Year

I have listed the days we are going to close the library in 2012. I have listed the holidays, the in-service days, and the days we will close early.

Holidays

We will be closed on New Year's Day, Easter, Memorial Day, the Fourth of July, Labor Day, Thanksgiving, and Christmas.

In-Service Days

We will be closed on April 15th for a session on library security, and on November 7th for a session that will focus on streamlining the material handling process.

Close Early

We will close early on New Year's Eve, the day before Easter, the day before Thanksgiving, and Christmas Eve.

HAPPY HOLIDAYS!

Lastname_Firstname_w01_Closures

Figure 1

Skills in Context

To complete this document, you will need the following files:

- New blank Word document
- w01_Trustees_Report

You will save your document as:

- Lastname_Firstname_w01_Trustees

Using the information provided, compose a letter from Douglas Hopkins, the Director of the Aspen Falls Public Library, to Fran Darcy, the Chair of the Library Board of Trustees. Use the current date and the address used in Skill 1. The letter is regarding the attached report on library operations for the previous year, and it should include the purpose of the letter and provide a very brief summary of the attached document. Save the document as

Lastname_Firstname_w01_Trustees On a new page, insert the report **w01_ Trustees_Report** and at an appropriate location in the document, insert a representative clip art image. Format the document appropriately. Check the entire document for grammar and spelling, and then insert the file name in the footer. Submit as directed.

Done! You have completed Skills in Context

Skills and You

To complete this document, you will need the following file:

- New blank Word document

You will save your document as:

- Lastname_Firstname_w01_Careers

Using the skills you have practiced in this chapter, compose either a letter or a memo to the director of your college's Career Center inquiring about the skills needed to find a job. Ask if there are upcoming seminars or workshops that you might attend. If you have a picture of yourself, insert it in the memo as a way of introducing yourself. You should include several instances of text

formatting somewhere in the document. Save the document as Lastname_Firstname_w01_Careers Check the entire document for grammar and spelling, and insert the file name in the footer. Print or submit the file as directed by your instructor.

Done! You have completed Skills and You

CHAPTER 2

Format and Organize Text

▶ Format a document to enhance page layout and improve the readability of the text in the document.
▶ Add bulleted and numbered lists to group related information; add headers and footers to display important information on each page.

Your starting screen will look like this:

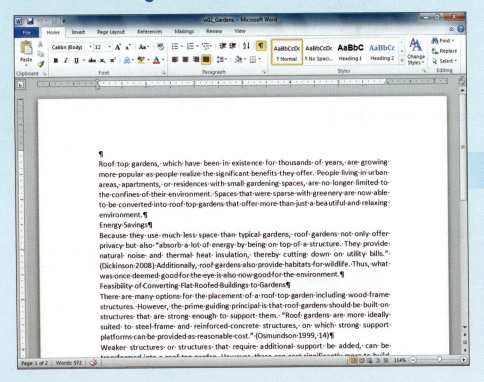

SKILLS

Skills 1-10 Training

At the end of this chapter, you will be able to:

Skill 1   Set Document Margins

Skill 2   Align Text and Set Indents

Skill 3   Modify Line and Paragraph Spacing

Skill 4   Format Text Using Format Painter

Skill 5   Find and Replace Text

Skill 6   Create Bulleted and Numbered Lists

Skill 7   Insert and Format Headers and Footers

Skill 8   Insert and Modify Footnotes

Skill 9   Add Citations

Skill 10   Create Bibliographies

MORE SKILLS

More Skills 11   Record AutoCorrect Entries

More Skills 12   Use AutoFormat to Create Numbered Lists

More Skills 13   Format and Customize Lists

More Skills 14   Manage Document Properties

Outcome

Using the skills listed to the left will enable you to create
a document like this:

Roof Gardens:
Advantages and Potential Problems

By Your Name

March 14, 2012

Roof gardens, which have been in existence for thousands of years, are growing more popular as people realize the significant benefits they offer. People living in urban areas, apartments, or residences with small gardening spaces, are no longer limited to the confines of their environment. Spaces that were sparse with greenery are now able to be converted into roof gardens that offer more than just a beautiful and relaxing environment.

ENERGY SAVINGS

Because they use much less space than typical gardens, roof gardens not only offer privacy but also "absorb a lot of energy by being on top of a structure. They provide natural noise and thermal heat insulation, thereby cutting down on utility bills." (Dickinson 2008) Additionally, roof gardens also provide habitats for wildlife. Thus, what was once deemed good for the eye is also now good for the environment.

FEASIBILITY OF CONVERTING FLAT ROOFED BUILDINGS TO GARDENS

There are many options for the placement of a roof garden including wood-frame structures. However, the primary guiding principal is that roof gardens should be built on structures that are strong enough to support them. "Roof gardens are more ideally suited to steel-frame and reinforced-concrete structures, on which strong support platforms can be provided as reasonable cost." (Osmundson 1999, 14)

Weaker structures or structures that require additional support be added, can be transformed into a roof garden. However, these can cost significantly more to build depending on the initial weight-bearing capability of that structure.[1]

[1] Internal reinforcement is sufficient in most cases.

STRUCTURAL REQUIREMENTS

Developing a roof garden does not need to be limited to the concept of a traditional garden that might be seen on top of a downtown apartment building. Instead, creativity is imperative as other structure-types are considered. Some of these alternatives include:

- Garages and sheds[2]
- Balconies and terraces
- Patios or decks

The main consideration when designing a roof garden is to consider whether the structure can withstand not only the weight of the garden but also the water needed to maintain the garden. "The load-bearing potential of a roof or balcony will determine where beds, containers, and other heavy features can be safely placed." (Stevens 1997, 14) In designing the garden, it will be necessary then to understand the weaknesses and strengths of a particular structure and design accordingly to avoid structural issues.[3]

POSSIBLE PROBLEMS

Before getting started, it is important to understand the potential problems that can impact a roof garden. While there are numerous issues to consider, a few of the more important ones include:

1. Rainwater build-up can sacrifice the structural soundness of the roof. Make sure the structure is slightly angled or has proper drainage to allow for water runoff.
2. The structure may be unable to sustain the weight. Consider container gardens which consist of lower weight but offer the same benefits of in-ground plants.
3. Selecting plants that require too much water can add considerable weight to the garden. The best option is to research and understand which flowers and plants thrive in a given area and do not require a lot of water.

Regardless of the type of roof garden, the final touch is to ensure that it is personalized and contains special touches. Add personal touches by using unique objects that show off the gardener's personality. According to one group of designers, "Keep an eye out. Our favorite sources are salvage yards and antique markets, but garage sales, estate sales, and trash are great places to look." (Zimmeth 2008, 83)

[2] On structurally weaker buildings, potted plants work best.
[3] Heavier materials should be located near load-bearing walls.

Lastname_Firstname_w02_Gardens   DRAFT   4/24/2010 12:30 PM

Bibliography

Dickinson, Marc. *Stunning Roof Gardens Also Have Beautiful Advantages*. 2008. http://www.servicemagic.com/article.show.Stunning-Roof-Gardens-Also-Have-Beautiful-Advantages.13550.html (accessed January 23, 2010).

Osmundson, Theodore H. *Roof Gardens: History, Design and Construction*. New York: W. W. Norton & Company, 1999.

Stevens, David. *Roof Gardens, Balconies & Terraces*. New York: Rizzoli International, 1997.

Zimmeth, Khristi S. "Serenity in the City." *Garden Ideas & Outdoor Living*, Fall 2008: 78-85.

Lastname_Firstname_w02_Gardens   DRAFT   4/24/2010 12:30 PM

You will save this document as:

Lastname_Firstname_w02_Gardens

In this chapter, you will create documents for the Aspen Falls City Hall, which provides essential services for the citizens and visitors of Aspen Falls, California.

Introduction

▶ Document margins are the spaces that display on the outer edges of a printed page. All four page margins can be adjusted independently.

▶ To make paragraphs stand out, add spacing above and below, change the first line indents, and format subheadings. This helps the reader understand the structure of the document, which increases the document's readability.

▶ Lists make information easier to understand. Use numbered lists when information is displayed in a sequence, and use bulleted lists when information can appear in any order.

▶ Informal business reports are often formatted using guidelines in *The Gregg Reference Manual* by William A. Sabin. These guidelines cover the way the text is formatted, the way notes display, and the types of citations used.

**Time to complete all
10 skills – 60 to 90 minutes**

Find your student data files here:

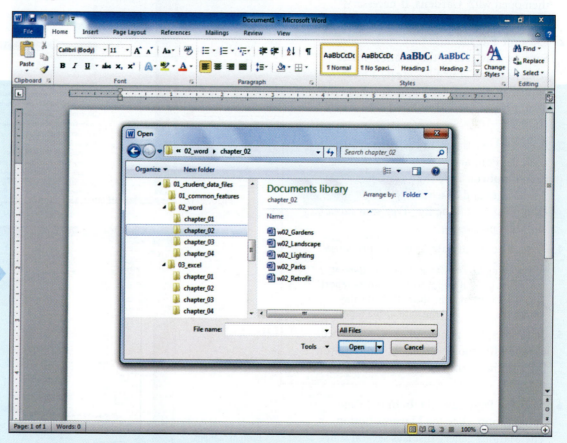

Student data files needed for this chapter:

- New blank Word document
- w02_Gardens

► *Margins* are the spaces between the text and the top, bottom, left, and right edges of the paper.

► Each of the margins can be adjusted independently of the other margins.

1. **Start** 🔵 Word. Click the **File tab**, click **Open**, navigate to your student files, and then open **w02_Gardens**. If necessary, display the formatting marks.

2. Click the **File tab**, and then click **Save As**. Navigate to the location where you are saving your files, create a folder named Word Chapter 2 and then **Save** the document as Lastname_Firstname_w02_Gardens

3. Press Enter five times. In the **Font group**, click the **Font arrow** Calibri (Body) ▾ , and then click **Cambria**. Type Roof Gardens: Advantages and Potential Problems and then press Enter. Type By (*Type your name*), and then press Enter.

4. Type the current date, and then press Enter.

   According to *The Gregg Reference Manual*, the first page of an informal business report uses a 2 inch margin above the title, the author's name, and the date of the report.

5. Select the three paragraphs you just typed. On the Mini toolbar, click the **Bold** button 🄱 , and then compare your screen with **Figure 1.**

6. Click the **Page Layout tab**. In the **Page Setup group**, click the **Margins** button. The Margins gallery displays several standard margin settings and the last custom setting (if any), as shown in **Figure 2.**

■ **Continue to the next page to complete the skill** ▶

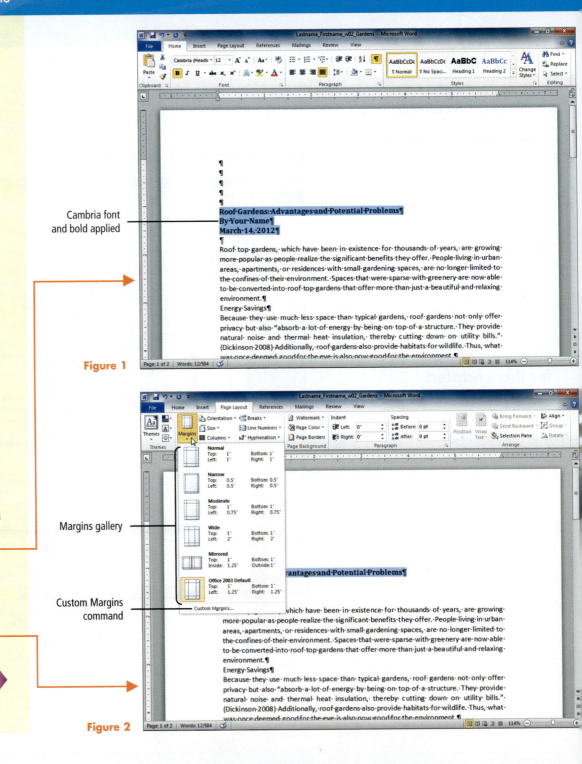

Cambria font and bold applied

Figure 1

Margins gallery

Custom Margins command

Figure 2

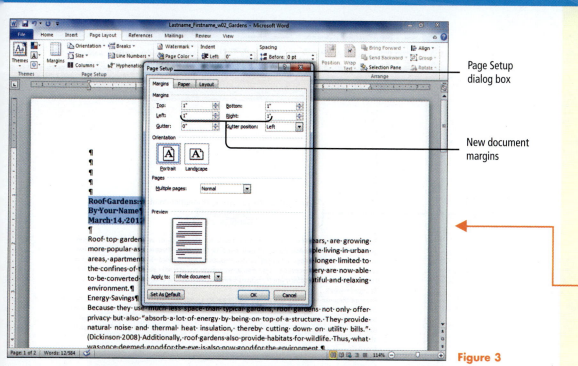

Page Setup dialog box

New document margins

Figure 3

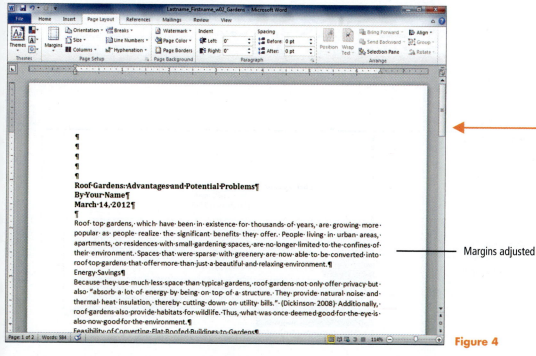

Margins adjusted

Figure 4

7. At the bottom of the **Margins** gallery, click **Custom Margins**.

> The Page Setup dialog box provides you with document formatting options, some of which are not available on the Ribbon.

8. In the **Page Setup** dialog box, be sure the **Margins tab** is selected. Press ⌷Tab⌷ two times. Under **Margins**, in the **Left** box, with *1.25"* selected, click the **down spin arrow** three times to change the left margin to *1"*. Alternately, with the current margin selected, type the new margin in the margin box.

9. Press ⌷Tab⌷, and then repeat this procedure to change the **Right** margin to *1"*. Compare your screen with **Figure 3**.

10. Under **Orientation**, be sure the **Portrait** button is selected. At the bottom of the **Page Setup** dialog box, verify that the **Apply to** box displays *Whole document*, and then click **OK**.

> With *portrait orientation*, the printed page is taller than it is wide; with *landscape orientation*, the printed page width is greater than the page height. Most reports use portrait orientation.

11. Click anywhere in the document to deselect the text. Compare your screen with **Figure 4**, and notice the results of the changes you made to the margins.

12. Save 🖫 the document.

■ **You have completed Skill 1 of 10**

▶ *Indents* are the position of paragraph lines in relation to the page margins.

▶ *Horizontal alignment* is the orientation of the left or right edges of the paragraph— for example, flush with the left or right margins.

1. Position the insertion point anywhere in the first paragraph you typed—the title that begins *Roof Gardens.*

   To align a single paragraph, you need only position the insertion point anywhere in the paragraph.

2. On the **Home tab**, in the **Paragraph group**, click the **Align Right** button to align the title with the right margin.

3. In the **Paragraph** group, click the **Center** button to center the title between the left and right margins.

4. Select the second and third bold title lines. From the Mini toolbar, click the **Center** button, and then compare your screen with **Figure 1**.

5. Below the date title, in the left margin, point to the paragraph that begins *Roof top gardens* and drag down to select that paragraph and the following two paragraphs that begin *Energy Savings* and *Because they use.* Notice that these paragraphs are *justified*—the paragraph text is aligned flush with both the left margin and the right margin.

6. In the **Paragraph** group, click the **Align Left** button. Compare your screen with **Figure 2**, and then click anywhere to deselect the text.

   These paragraphs are no longer justified.

■ **Continue to the next page to complete the skill**

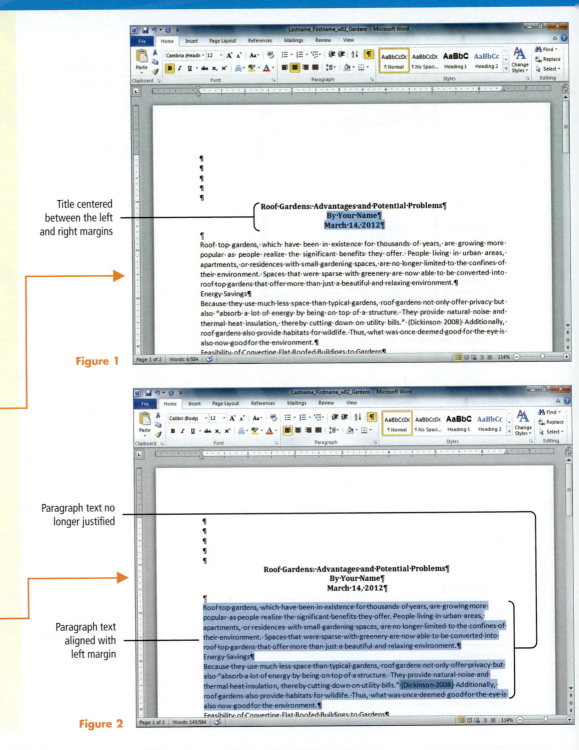

Title centered between the left and right margins

Figure 1

Paragraph text no longer justified

Paragraph text aligned with left margin

Figure 2

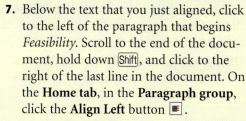

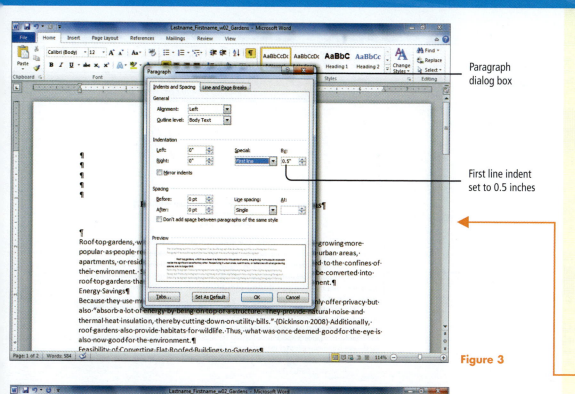

Paragraph
dialog box

First line indent
set to 0.5 inches

Figure 3

7. Below the text that you just aligned, click to the left of the paragraph that begins *Feasibility*. Scroll to the end of the document, hold down ⇧Shift, and click to the right of the last line in the document. On the **Home tab**, in the **Paragraph group**, click the **Align Left** button.

8. Press Ctrl + Home to move to the top of the document. Below the centered titles, click to position the insertion point anywhere in the paragraph that begins *Roof top gardens*.

9. On the **Home tab**, in the **Paragraph group**, click the **Paragraph Dialog Box Launcher**.

    The Paragraph dialog box displays, which includes commands that are not available on the Ribbon.

10. Under **Indentation**, click the **Special box arrow**, and then click **First line**. Compare your screen with **Figure 3**.

    The ***first line indent*** is the location of the beginning of the first line of a paragraph in relationship with the left edge of the remainder of the paragraph. In this case, the *By* box displays *0.5"*, which will indent the first line of the current paragraph one-half inch.

11. Click **OK** to indent the first line of the paragraph.

12. Click anywhere in the paragraph that begins *Because they use*, and repeat the procedure just practiced to indent the first line of the paragraph by 0.5 inches. Compare your screen with **Figure 4**.

13. **Save** the document.

    ■ **You have completed Skill 2 of 10**

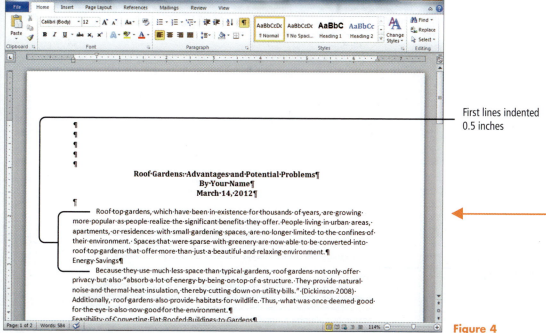

First lines indented
0.5 inches

Figure 4

► *Line spacing* is the vertical distance between lines of text in a paragraph, and can be adjusted for each paragraph.

► *Paragraph spacing* is the vertical distance above and below each paragraph, and can be adjusted for each paragraph.

1. Below the centered titles, click anywhere in the paragraph that begins *Roof top gardens.*

2. On the **Home tab**, in the **Paragraph group**, click the **Line and Paragraph Spacing** button 📇.

   The current setting is *1.0—single-spacing*—which means that no extra space is added between lines of text. Line spacing of 2.0—*double-spacing*—means that the equivalent of a blank line of text displays between each line of text.

3. In the **Line Spacing** list, point to **2.0**, and with Live Preview, notice that the text takes up twice as much space.

4. In the **Line Spacing** list, click **1.15** to change the line spacing, as shown in **Figure 1**.

   Text with a line spacing of 1.15 has been found to be easier to read than single-spaced text.

5. Click the **Page Layout tab**. In the **Paragraph group**, under **Spacing**, click the **After up spin arrow** two times to change the spacing after the paragraph to *12 pt*.

6. In the paragraph that begins *Because they use*, repeat the same procedure to set the line spacing to **1.15** and the spacing after to **12 pt**. Notice the change in the spacing between the paragraphs, as shown in **Figure 2**.

■ **Continue to the next page to complete the skill** ▶

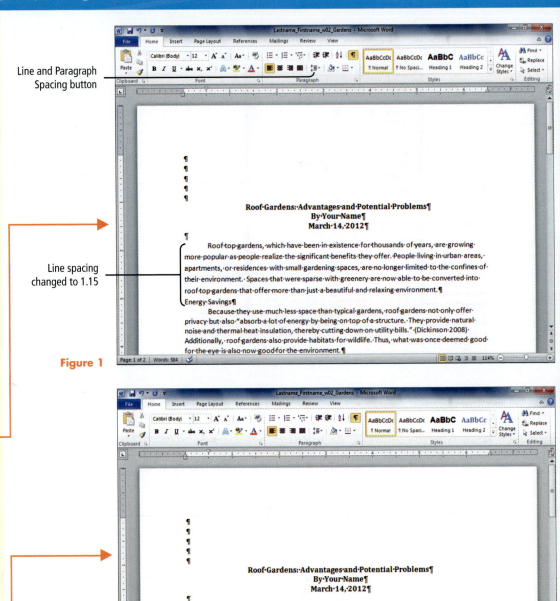

Line and Paragraph Spacing button

Line spacing changed to 1.15

Figure 1

12 point spacing after the paragraph

Figure 2

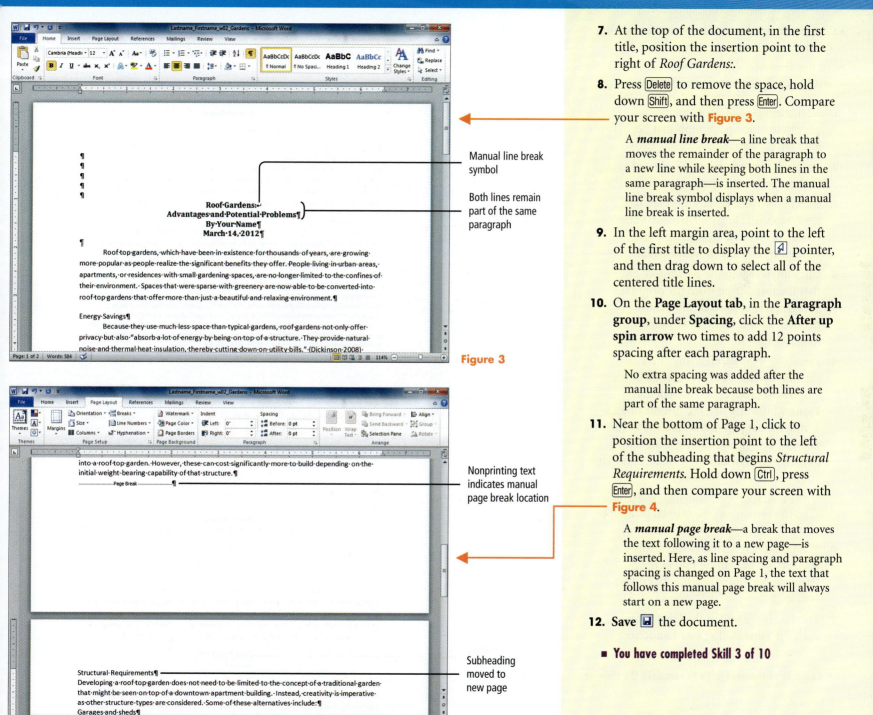

Figure 3

Figure 4

Manual line break symbol

Both lines remain part of the same paragraph

Nonprinting text indicates manual page break location

Subheading moved to new page

7. At the top of the document, in the first title, position the insertion point to the right of *Roof Gardens:*.

8. Press Delete to remove the space, hold down Shift, and then press Enter. Compare your screen with **Figure 3**.

   A ***manual line break***—a line break that moves the remainder of the paragraph to a new line while keeping both lines in the same paragraph—is inserted. The manual line break symbol displays when a manual line break is inserted.

9. In the left margin area, point to the left of the first title to display the ⌐⌐ pointer, and then drag down to select all of the centered title lines.

10. On the **Page Layout tab**, in the **Paragraph group**, under **Spacing**, click the **After up spin arrow** two times to add 12 points spacing after each paragraph.

    No extra spacing was added after the manual line break because both lines are part of the same paragraph.

11. Near the bottom of Page 1, click to position the insertion point to the left of the subheading that begins *Structural Requirements*. Hold down Ctrl, press Enter, and then compare your screen with **Figure 4**.

    A ***manual page break***—a break that moves the text following it to a new page—is inserted. Here, as line spacing and paragraph spacing is changed on Page 1, the text that follows this manual page break will always start on a new page.

12. **Save** 💾 the document.

   ■ **You have completed Skill 3 of 10**

▶ Use *Format Painter* to copy text formatting quickly from one place to another.

▶ To use Format Painter on multiple items, double-click the Format Painter button.

1. Near the top of the document, click anywhere in the paragraph that begins *Roof top gardens.*

2. On the **Home tab**, in the **Clipboard group**, click the **Format Painter** button.

3. Scroll down and point anywhere in the paragraph that begins *There are many.* Notice that the pointer displays. Compare your screen with **Figure 1**.

4. Click anywhere in the paragraph. Notice that the formatting from the original paragraph is applied to the new paragraph, and that the pointer no longer displays.

5. Press Ctrl + Home, click anywhere in the title *By Your Name*, and then in the **Clipboard** group, click the **Format Painter** button. In the middle of Page 1, move the pointer to the left of the *Energy Savings* subheading until the pointer displays, and then click. Compare your screen with **Figure 2**.

    The font, bold style, centering, and paragraph spacing from the original paragraph are all applied to the new paragraph.

6. With the *Energy Savings* subheading selected, on the **Home tab**, in the **Paragraph group**, click the **Align Left** button.

7. On the **Home tab**, in the **Font group**, click the **Font Dialog Box Launcher**.

■ **Continue to the next page to complete the skill**

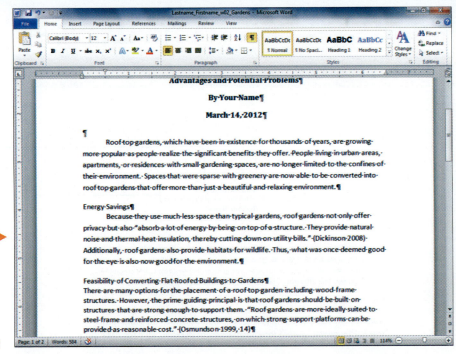

Figure 1

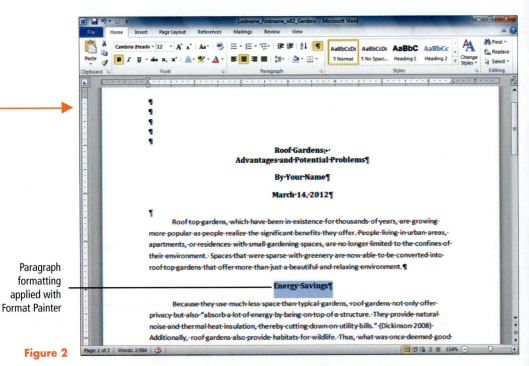

Paragraph formatting applied with Format Painter

Figure 2

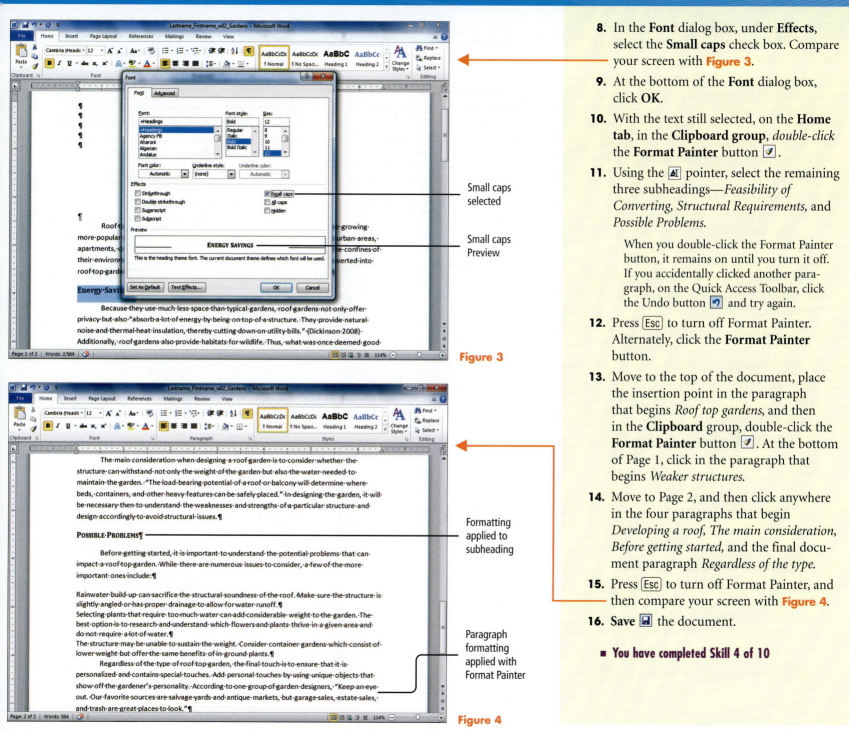

Figure 3

Figure 4

8. In the **Font** dialog box, under **Effects**, select the **Small caps** check box. Compare your screen with **Figure 3**.

9. At the bottom of the **Font** dialog box, click **OK**.

10. With the text still selected, on the **Home tab**, in the **Clipboard group**, *double-click* the **Format Painter** button.

11. Using the pointer, select the remaining three subheadings—*Feasibility of Converting, Structural Requirements,* and *Possible Problems.*

    When you double-click the Format Painter button, it remains on until you turn it off. If you accidentally clicked another paragraph, on the Quick Access Toolbar, click the Undo button and try again.

12. Press Esc to turn off Format Painter. Alternately, click the **Format Painter** button.

13. Move to the top of the document, place the insertion point in the paragraph that begins *Roof top gardens,* and then in the **Clipboard** group, double-click the **Format Painter** button. At the bottom of Page 1, click in the paragraph that begins *Weaker structures.*

14. Move to Page 2, and then click anywhere in the four paragraphs that begin *Developing a roof, The main consideration, Before getting started,* and the final document paragraph *Regardless of the type.*

15. Press Esc to turn off Format Painter, and then compare your screen with **Figure 4**.

16. Save the document.

■ **You have completed Skill 4 of 10**

Callouts on figures:
- Small caps selected
- Small caps Preview
- Formatting applied to subheading
- Paragraph formatting applied with Format Painter

► The Find command is useful if you know a word or phrase is in a document, and you want to locate it quickly.

► Using the Replace command, you can find and then replace words or phrases one at a time, or all at once.

1. Press [Ctrl] + [Home] to move to the top of the document. On the **Home tab**, in the **Editing group**, click the **Find** button.

2. In the **Navigation Pane Search** box, type space Notice that three instances of the word are highlighted, even though two of them are the plural form of the word— *spaces.* If your screen differs, at the top of the **Navigation Pane**, click the **Browse the results from your current search** button ▣.

3. In the **Navigation Pane**, click the third instance of the word, and then compare your screen with **Figure 1**.

4. In the **Search** box, select the existing text, type garden and notice that 24 instances of the word are found.

5. In the **Navigation Pane**, use the vertical scroll bar to scroll down the list of *garden* instances. Scroll to the bottom of the list.

   The located instances include *garden, gardens, gardening,* and *gardener.*

6. Click the last item in the list to scroll down to the location of the selected item.

7. On the **Home tab**, in the **Clipboard group**, click the **Cut** button to remove the selected word. In the Navigation Pane, notice that the search results are removed, as shown in **Figure 2**.

■ **Continue to the next page to complete the skill**

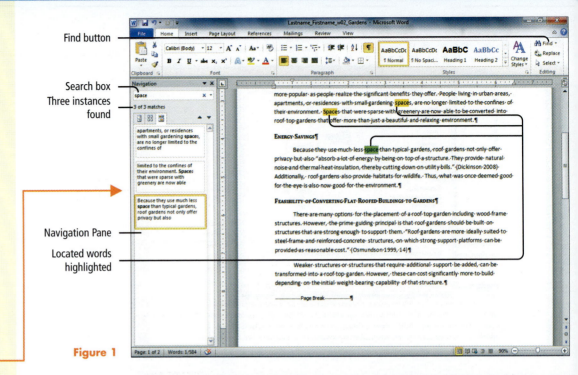

Find button
Search box
Three instances found
Navigation Pane
Located words highlighted

Figure 1

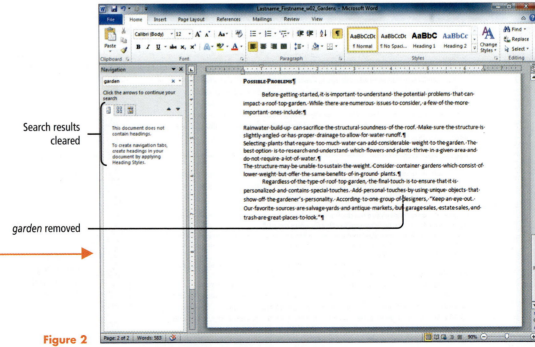

Search results cleared

garden removed

Figure 2

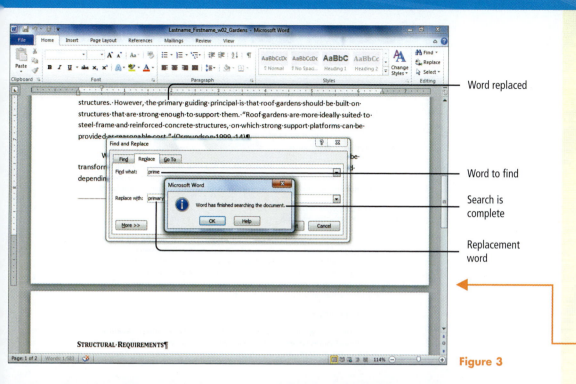

Word replaced

Word to find

Search is
complete

Replacement
word

Figure 3

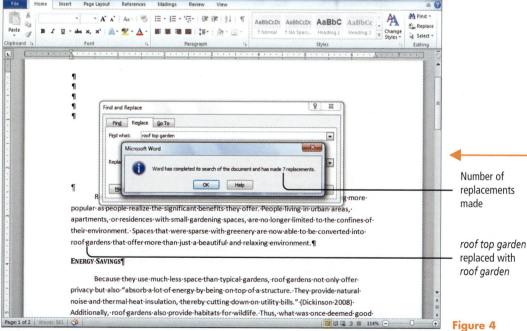

Number of
replacements
made

roof top garden
replaced with
roof garden

Figure 4

8. At the top of the **Navigation Pane**, click the **Close** button ☒.

9. Press Ctrl + Home. On the **Home tab**, in the **Editing group**, click the **Replace** button. Notice that the Find and Replace dialog box displays with the Replace tab active, and that the previous search term—*garden*—displays in the *Find what* box.

10. In the **Find what** box, select the existing text, type prime and press Tab. In the **Replace with** box, type primary

11. Click the **Find Next** button to find the first instance of *prime*, and then click the **Replace** button. Notice that the word is replaced, and a message box displays showing that there are no more instances of *prime* in the document, as shown in **Figure 3**.

12. In the message box, click **OK**. Click anywhere in the text, and notice that the insertion point remains at the beginning of the document.

13. In the **Find and Replace** dialog box, in the **Find what** box, type roof top garden and in the **Replace with** box, type roof garden

14. In the **Find and Replace** dialog box, click the **Replace All** button. Notice that a message box displays, telling you how many replacements were made, as shown in **Figure 4**.

When you do not specify any Find and Replace settings, the replaced text will retain the capitalization used in the original word or phrase.

15. **Close** all open dialog boxes, and then **Save** 🖫 the document.

- **You have completed Skill 5 of 10**

▶ A ***bulleted list*** is a list of items with each item introduced by a symbol—such as a small circle or check mark—in which the list items can be presented in any order.

▶ A ***numbered list*** is a list of items with each item introduced by a consecutive number or letter to indicate definite steps, a sequence of actions, or chronological order.

1. Near the top of Page 2, in the left margin area, display the 🔼 pointer to the left of the paragraph *Garages and sheds*, and then drag down to select the three paragraphs up to and including the paragraph *Patios or decks*.

2. On the **Home tab**, in the **Paragraph group**, click the **Bullets** button ▤▾. Compare your screen with **Figure 1**.

   The symbols used for your bulleted list may vary, depending on the last bullet type used on your computer.

3. With the bulleted list still selected, on the **Home tab**, in the **Paragraph group**, click the **Line and Paragraph Spacing** button ▤▾, and then click **1.15**.

4. In the **Paragraph group**, click the **Increase Indent** button 🔳 one time.

   The list moves 0.25 inches to the right.

5. With the bulleted list still selected, click the **Page Layout tab**, and then in the **Paragraph group**, under **Spacing**, click the **After up spin arrow** two times to increase the spacing after to *12 pt*.

6. Click anywhere in the document, and notice that the space was added after the *last item* in the list only, as shown in **Figure 2**.

■ **Continue to the next page to complete the skill**

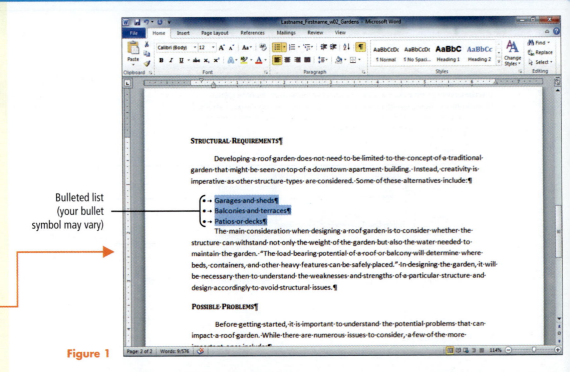

Bulleted list (your bullet symbol may vary)

Figure 1

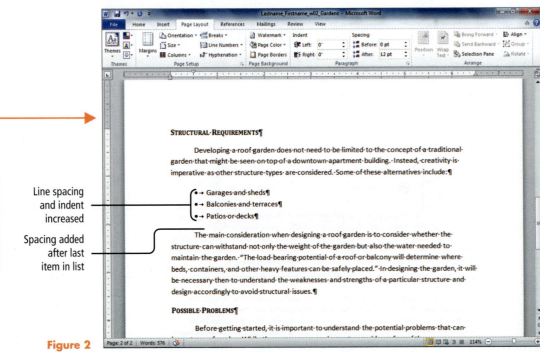

Line spacing and indent increased

Spacing added after last item in list

Figure 2

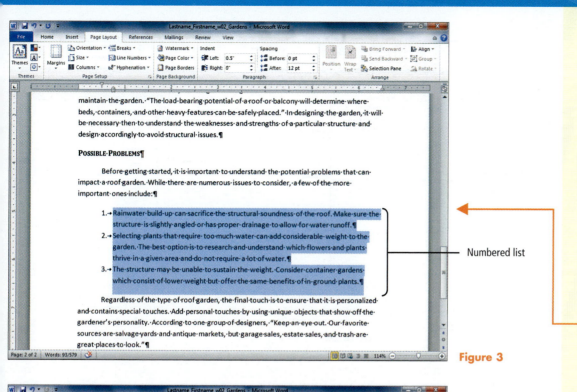

Numbered list

Figure 3

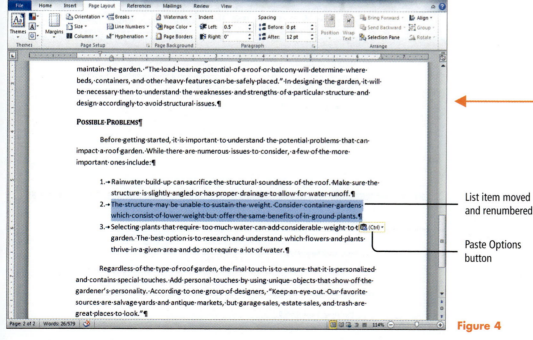

List item moved and renumbered

Paste Options button

Figure 4

7. Scroll to the bottom of Page 2. Select the three paragraphs that begin with *Rainwater build-up* and end with *in-ground plants.*

8. On the **Home tab**, in the **Paragraph group**, click the **Numbering** button. In the **Paragraph group**, click the **Increase Indent** button one time.

9. With the list still selected, in the **Paragraph group**, click the **Line and Paragraph Spacing** button, and then click **1.15**.

10. Click the **Page Layout tab**. In the **Paragraph group**, under **Spacing**, click the **After up spin arrow** two times to change the spacing after the list to *12 pt.* Notice that the space is added only after the last item in the list, as shown in **Figure 3**.

11. In the numbered list, select all of the text in the third item, including the paragraph mark. Do not select the number *3* and, if necessary, press Esc to close the Mini toolbar.

12. Move the pointer over the selected text to display the pointer. Drag the selected text up to the left of *Selecting* in the second item in the list. Compare your screen with **Figure 4**.

    Notice that the step text is moved, the numbering is changed, and the space after the list remains at the bottom of the list. Because dragging text treats the text like it was cut and then pasted, a Paste Options button also displays.

13. Save the document.

■ **You have completed Skill 6 of 10**

► Headers and footers can include not only text, but also graphics and fields—for example, file names and the current date.

► You can turn off the headers and footers on the first page of a document.

1. Press Ctrl + Home to move to the top of the document. Click the **Insert tab**, and then in the **Header & Footer group**, click the **Header** button. Below the **Header** gallery, click **Edit Header**. Notice that the Design contextual tab is added to the Ribbon.

2. On the **Design tab**, in the **Header & Footer** group, click the **Page Number** button, and then point to **Top of Page** to display the Page Number gallery, as shown in **Figure 1**.

3. In the **Page Number** gallery, use the vertical scroll bar to scroll through the page number options. When you are through, scroll to the top of the list. Under **Simple**, click **Plain Number 3** to insert the page number at the right margin.

4. On the **Design tab**, in the **Options group**, select the **Different First Page** check box.

   The page number disappears from the header for Page 1, but will display on all other pages of the document.

5. Double-click anywhere in the document to deactivate the header, and then scroll to the top of Page 2. Notice that the page number displays on Page 2, as shown in **Figure 2**.

   ■ **Continue to the next page to complete the skill**

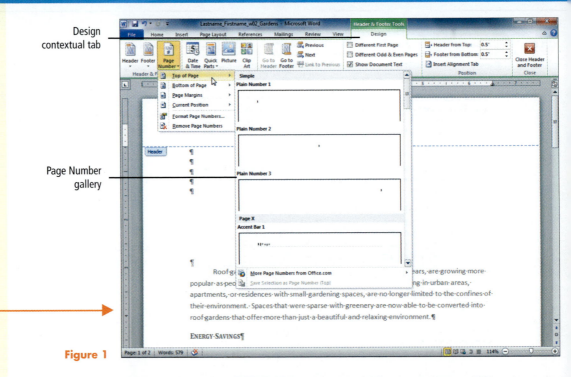

Design contextual tab

Page Number gallery

Figure 1

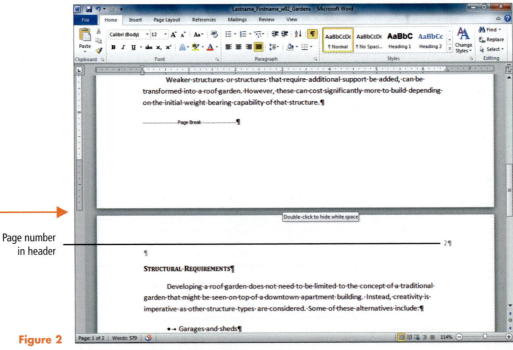

Page number in header

Figure 2

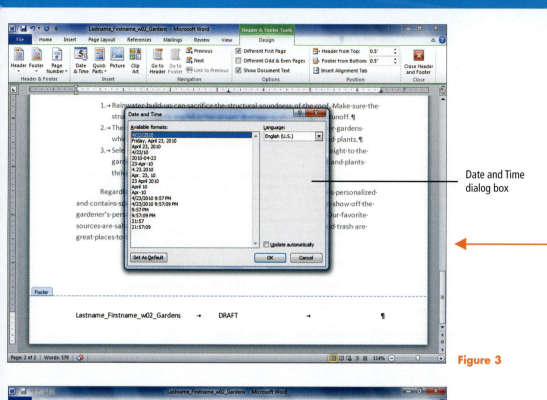

Date and Time dialog box

Figure 3

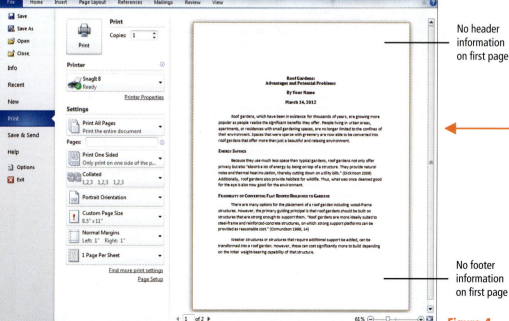

No header information on first page

No footer information on first page

Figure 4

6. Press `Ctrl` + `Home`, and notice that no page number displays on Page 1.

    In most business and research reports, the page number is not included on the first page.

7. Press `Ctrl` + `End` to move to the bottom of Page 2. Below the text, near the bottom edge of the page, right-click, and then from the menu, click **Edit Footer** to make the footer active.

8. In the **Insert group**, click the **Quick Parts** button, and then click **Field**. Under **Field names**, scroll down, click **FileName**, and then click **OK**.

9. Press `Tab`, type DRAFT and then press `Tab`.

10. On the **Design tab**, in the **Insert group**, click the **Date & Time** button. Compare your screen with **Figure 3**.

11. In the **Date and Time** dialog box, under **Available formats**, click the **1/15/2012 4:15 PM** format—your date and time will vary. Select the **Update automatically** check box, and then click **OK**.

    The date and time are added to the footer, and will be updated every time you open this file. In a business setting, the footer information should be removed when the report is finished.

12. Double-click anywhere in the document to deactivate the footer. Press `Ctrl` + `Home`. Click the **File tab**, click **Print**, and notice that the footer text does not display on Page 1, as shown in **Figure 4**.

13. Click the **Home tab**, and then **Save** 🖫 the document.

    ■ **You have completed Skill 7 of 10**

► A **footnote** is a reference placed at the bottom of the page. An **endnote** is a reference placed at the end of a section or a document.

► You can use either numbers or symbols to label footnotes and endnotes.

1. Scroll to the bulleted list near the top of Page 2. At the end of the first bulleted item—*Garages and sheds*—click to position the insertion point.

2. Click the **References tab**, and then in the **Footnotes group**, click the **Insert Footnote** button.

   A footnote displays at the bottom of the page with a number *1* before the insertion point. A line is also inserted above the footnote area to separate it from the document text.

3. Type On structurally weaker buildings, potted plants work best. Compare your screen with **Figure 1**.

   Footnotes are used to provide supplemental information that does not fit well in the document.

4. Scroll up to the paragraph below the bulleted list that begins *The main consideration*. Position the insertion point at the end of the paragraph.

5. In the **Footnotes group**, click the **Insert Footnote** button. Type Heavier materials should be located near load-bearing walls. Compare your screen with **Figure 2**.

   The second footnote displays below the first, and the footnotes are numbered sequentially.

■ **Continue to the next page to complete the skill**

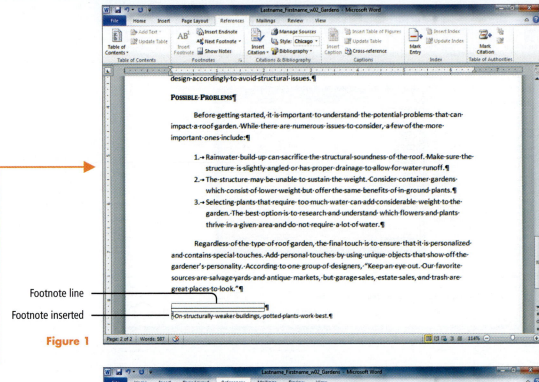

Footnote line
Footnote inserted

Figure 1

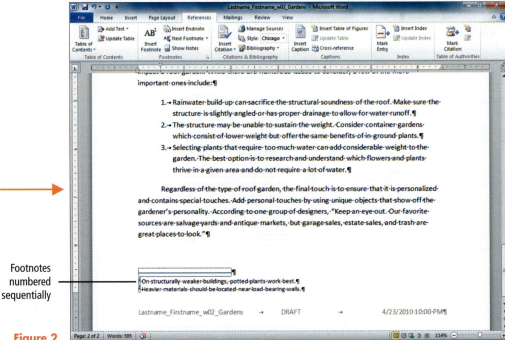

Footnotes numbered sequentially

Figure 2

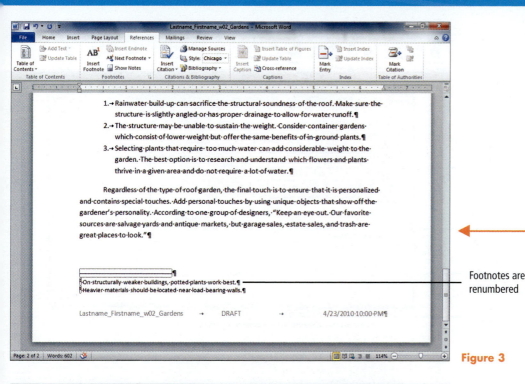

Footnotes are
renumbered

Figure 3

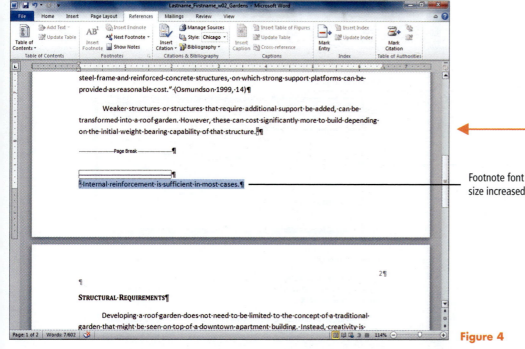

Footnote font
size increased

Figure 4

6. Scroll to the last paragraph on Page 1—the one that begins *Weaker structures or structures*. Position the insertion point at the end of that paragraph.

7. On the **References tab**, in the **Footnotes group**, click the **Footnotes Dialog Box Launcher** 🔲.

    In the Footnote and Endnote dialog box, you can change footnotes to endnotes or label the notes with characters other than numbers.

8. In the **Footnote and Endnote** dialog box, click **Insert**. Notice that the new footnote is number *1*, and then type Internal reinforcement is sufficient in most cases.

9. Scroll to the bottom of Page 2, and then compare your screen with **Figure 3**.

    By default, the footnote font size is smaller than the font size in the rest of the document. Here, the footnote numbers have automatically updated to *2* and *3*.

10. At the bottom of Page 2, select both footnotes. On the Mini toolbar, click the **Font Size arrow** 11 ▾, and then click **12**.

    Most style manuals call for the footer text to be the same size as the document text.

11. Scroll to the bottom of Page 1, select the footnote, and change the **Font Size** to **12**. Compare your screen with **Figure 4**.

12. **Save** 🔲 the document.

    ■ **You have completed Skill 8 of 10**

- ► When you use quotations or detailed information from a reference source, you need to specify the source in the document.

- ► A *citation* is a note in the document that refers the reader to a source in the bibliography.

1. Display the lower half of Page 1. Notice that two citations are displayed in parentheses.

   Many business reports use an abbreviated citation, which contains the author's last name, the year of publication, and the page number.

2. On the **References tab**, in the **Citations & Bibliography group**, click the **Manage Sources** button. Compare your screen with **Figure 1**.

   The sources used in the current document display with a check mark on the right.

3. **Close** the Source Manager dialog box. Near the top of Page 2, in the paragraph that begins *The main*, click to the right of the second quotation mark. On the **References tab**, in the **Citations & Bibliography group**, be sure the **Style** is set to **Chicago**. Click the **Insert Citation** button, and then click **Add New Source**.

4. In the **Create Source** dialog box, if necessary click the **Type of Source arrow**, and then click **Book**. In the **Author** box, type Stevens, David In the **Title** box, type Roof Gardens, Balconies & Terraces

5. For the **Year**, type 1997 and for the **City** type Milan For the **Publisher**, type Rizzoli International and then compare your screen with **Figure 2**.

■ **Continue to the next page to complete the skill**

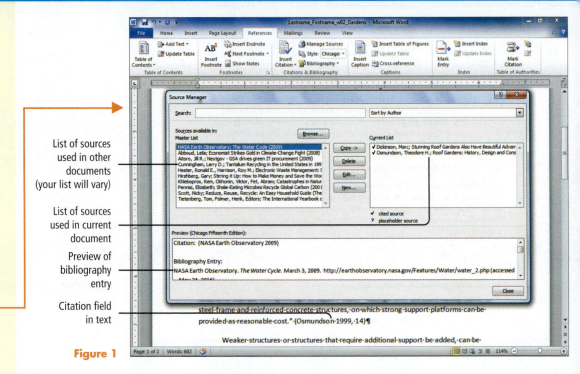

List of sources used in other documents (your list will vary)

List of sources used in current document

Preview of bibliography entry

Citation field in text

Figure 1

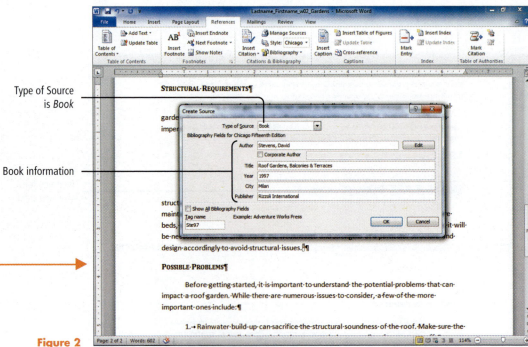

Type of Source is *Book*

Book information

Figure 2

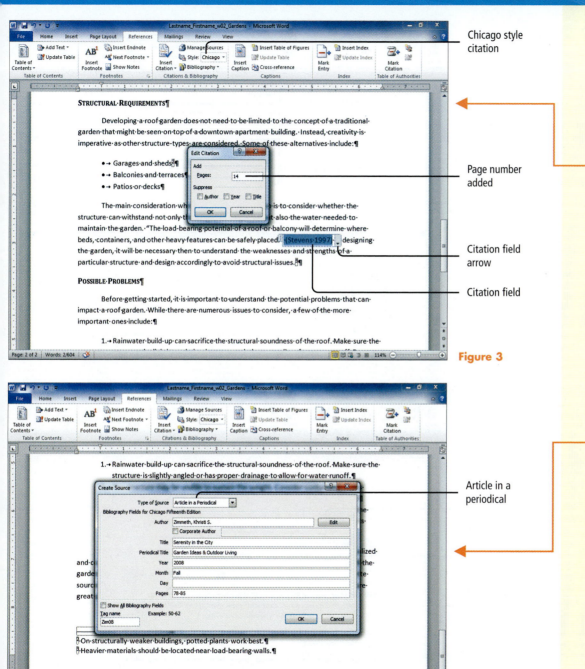

Chicago style citation

Page number added

Citation field arrow

Citation field

Figure 3

Article in a periodical

Figure 4

6. In the **Create Source** dialog box, click **OK** to insert an abbreviated citation. Click the citation one time. On the right side of the field, click the **arrow**, and then from the menu, click **Edit Citation**.

7. In the **Edit Citation** dialog box, under **Add**, in the **Pages** box, type 14 to add the page number to the citation. Compare your screen with **Figure 3**.

8. In the **Edit Citation** dialog box, click **OK**. Press Ctrl + End to move to the end of the document. On the **References tab**, in the **Citations & Bibliography group**, click the **Insert Citation** button, and then click **Add New Source**.

9. In the **Create Source** dialog box, click the **Type of Source arrow**, and then click **Article in a Periodical**. In the **Author** box, type Zimmeth, Khristi S. For the **Title**, type Serenity in the City

10. For the **Periodical Title**, type Garden Ideas & Outdoor Living For the **Year**, type 2008 For the **Month** type Fall For the **Pages**, type 78-85 and then compare your screen with **Figure 4**.

11. In the **Create Source** dialog box, click **OK**. Click the citation, click the **arrow**, and then click **Edit Citation**.

12. In the **Edit Citation** dialog box, in the **Pages** box, type 83 and click **OK**.

13. In the **Citations & Bibliography** group, click the **Manage Sources** button. Notice that your new sources are added to the Source Manager.

14. **Close** the dialog box and **Save** the document.

- **You have completed Skill 9 of 10**

▶ A *bibliography* is a list of sources referenced in a report, and is listed on a separate page at the end of the report.

▶ Different styles use different titles for the sources page, including *Works Cited*, *Bibliography*, *References*, or *Sources*.

1. Press Ctrl + End, and then press Ctrl + Enter to insert a manual page break and start a new page. Press Enter two times.

   The bibliography should begin about two inches from the top of the page.

2. On the **References tab**, in the **Citations & Bibliography group**, click the **Bibliography** button to display two built-in bibliographies, as shown in **Figure 1**.

3. From the gallery, click the **Bibliography** thumbnail to insert a bibliography field. If necessary, scroll up to display the inserted bibliography field. If necessary, close the Navigation pane.

   The bibliography field includes a title and lists the sources cited in the document. The multiple-line references use hanging indents. In a *hanging indent*, the first line extends to the left of the rest of the paragraph.

4. Right-click the **Bibliography** title, and then on the Mini toolbar, click the **Center** button ▣ to center the title on the page.

5. Click to the right of the title, and then press Enter to add a blank line between the title and the sources. Compare your screen with **Figure 2**.

6. If necessary, click the **References** tab. In the **Citations & Bibliography group**, click the **Manage Sources** button.

■ **Continue to the next page to complete the skill** ➤

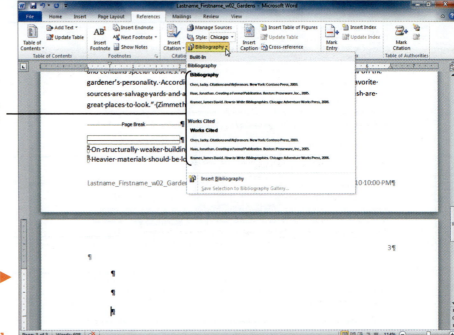

Bibliography gallery

Figure 1

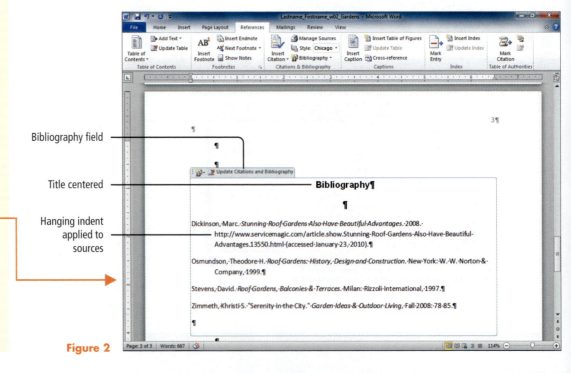

Bibliography field

Title centered

Hanging indent applied to sources

Figure 2

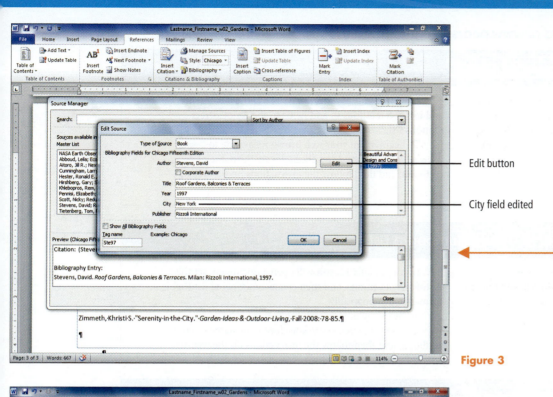

Edit button

City field edited

Figure 3

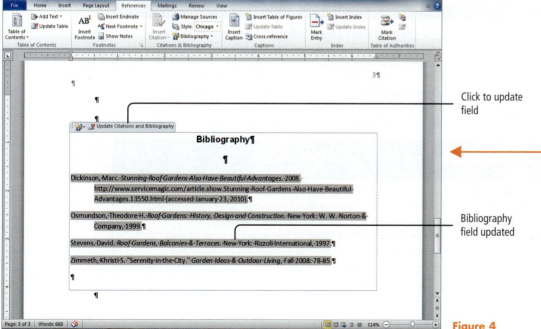

Click to update field

Bibliography field updated

Figure 4

7. In the **Source Manager** dialog box, under **Current List**, select the *Stevens, David* source. At the bottom of the **Source Manager** dialog box, notice the **Preview**, and then click the **Edit** button.

8. In the **Edit Source** dialog box, in the **City** box, select *Milan*. Type New York and then compare your screen with **Figure 3**.

9. Click **OK** to close the dialog box, read the displayed message, and then click **Yes**.

   The change will be made to both the current document and the master list.

10. In the **Source Manager** dialog box, under **Master List**, select the *Stevens, David* source, and then to the right of the Master List, click the **Delete** button. Use the same procedure to remove the *Zimmeth, Khristi S.* source.

   If you are using a computer in a lab or other public area, it is good practice to restore any permanent changes you make to original settings—in this case, remove the sources from the master list.

11. In the **Source Manager** dialog box, click **Close**. Click in the bibliography. Notice that the change from *Milan* to *New York* has not been made—you must manually update fields when you change them.

12. At the top of the bibliography field, click **Update Citations and Bibliography**. Compare your screen with **Figure 4**.

   The bibliography field is updated to include the change you made in the Source Manager.

13. **Save** 🖫 the document. Submit your printout or files electronically as directed by your instructor. **Exit** Word.

Done! You have completed Skill 10 of 10 and your document is complete!

The following More Skills are located at **www.pearsonhighered.com/skills**

More Skills Record AutoCorrect Entries

If you enable the AutoCorrect feature in Word, when you misspell a word that is contained in the AutoCorrect list, the misspelling is corrected automatically. You can add words that you commonly misspell as you type, or you can open a dialog box and add words or phrases that you want to be automatically corrected. This feature can also be used to create shortcuts for phrases that you type regularly.

In More Skills 11, you will open a short document and use two methods to add items to the AutoCorrect Options list.

To begin, open your web browser, navigate to www.pearsonhighered.com/skills, locate the name of your textbook, and then follow the instructions on the website.

More Skills Use AutoFormat to Create Numbered Lists

If you create a lot of numbered lists, Word has an AutoFormat feature that lets you start typing the list, and the program will automatically add numbers and formatting to the list as you type.

In More Skills 12, you will open a document, set the AutoFormat options, and then create a numbered list that is formatted automatically.

To begin, open your web browser, navigate to www.pearsonhighered.com/skills, locate the name of your textbook, and then follow the instructions on the website.

More Skills Format and Customize Lists

In this chapter, you create and format numbered and bulleted lists. There are several other formatting changes you can make to lists. You can change the numbering scheme for numbered lists, and you can change the character used for the bullet symbol. You can also increase or decrease the indent of both types of lists.

In More Skills 13, you will open a document and change the numbering on a numbered list. You will also increase the indent on a bulleted list.

To begin, open your web browser, navigate to www.pearsonhighered.com/skills, locate the name of your textbook, and then follow the instructions on the website.

More Skills Manage Document Properties

Document properties are the detailed information about your document that can help you identify or organize your files, including the name of the author, the title, and keywords. Some document properties are added to the document when you create it. You can add others as necessary.

In More Skills 14, you will open a document, open the Document Properties, and add properties where appropriate.

To begin, open your web browser, navigate to www.pearsonhighered.com/skills, locate the name of your textbook, and then follow the instructions on the website.

Key Terms

Online Help Skills

1. Start 🌐 Word. In the upper right corner of the Word window, click the **Help** button 📷. In the **Help** window, click the **Maximize** 🔲 button.

2. Under **Getting started with Word 2010**, click **Create a document to be used by previous versions of Word**.

3. Read the article's introduction, and then below **Turn on Compatibility Mode**, read the steps required to create a document in an earlier Word format, and then in the last sentence of the introduction, click **Features that behave differently in earlier versions**. Compare your screen with **Figure 1**.

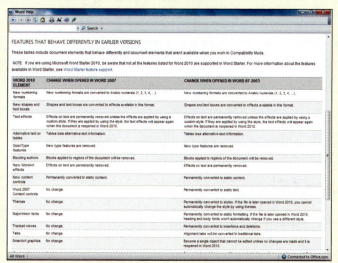

Figure 1

4. Read this information to see if you can answer the following: How do you save a document in an earlier format, such as Word 97-2003? What are three features that work in Word 2010 that do not work properly in Word 97-2003?

Matching

Match each term in the second column with its correct definition in the first column by writing the letter of the term on the blank line in front of the correct definition.

____ **1.** The space between the text and the top, bottom, left, and right edges of the paper when you print the document.

____ **2.** The position of the first line of a paragraph relative to the text in the rest of the paragraph.

____ **3.** The equivalent of a blank line of text displayed between each line of text in a paragraph.

____ **4.** The vertical distance above and below each paragraph in a document.

____ **5.** A command that copies formatting from one place to another.

____ **6.** The command that locates text in a document.

____ **7.** The type of list used for items that are in chronological or sequential order.

____ **8.** A reference added to the end of a section or document.

____ **9.** A list of sources displayed on a separate page at the end of a report.

____ **10.** The command used to display changes made in the Source Manager to a source listed in the bibliography.

A Bibliography

B Double-spacing

C Endnote

D Find

E First line indent

F Format Painter

G Margin

H Numbered

I Paragraph spacing

J Update Field

Multiple Choice

Choose the correct answer.

1. To create your own document margins, use this command at the bottom of the Margins gallery.
   A. Format Paragraph
   B. Document Settings
   C. Custom Margins

2. The placement of paragraph text relative to the left and right document margins is called paragraph:
   A. Alignment
   B. Margins
   C. Orientation

3. The vertical distance between lines in a paragraph is called:
   A. Spacing after
   B. Line spacing
   C. Text wrapping

4. This alignment is used to position paragraph text an equal distance between the left and right margin:
   A. Justify
   B. Center
   C. Middle

5. This type of alignment positions the text so that it is aligned with both the left and right margins.
   A. Justify
   B. Center
   C. Left

6. Hold down [Ctrl] + [Enter] to insert one of these:
   A. Manual line break
   B. Manual paragraph break
   C. Manual page break

7. Items that can be listed in any order are best presented using which of the following?
   A. Bulleted list
   B. Numbered list
   C. Outline list

8. In a bibliography, this type of indent is used for each reference:
   A. Hanging indent
   B. First line indent
   C. Left alignment

9. To place a note on the same page as the reference source, use which of these?
   A. Footnote
   B. Endnote
   C. Citation

10. This refers to an entry in a bibliography.
    A. Footnote
    B. Citation
    C. Endnote

Topics for Discussion

1. You can build and save a list of master sources you have used in research papers and reports and display them using Manage Sources. What are the advantages of storing sources over time?

2. Paragraph text can be left aligned, centered, right aligned, or justified. Left alignment is the most commonly used. In what situations would you use centered text? Justified text? Can you think of any situations where you might want to use right alignment?

Skill Check

To complete this document, you will need the following file:

- w02_Landscape

You will save your document as:

- Lastname_Firstname_w02_Landscape

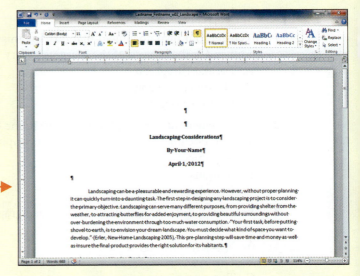

1. **Start** Word. Open **w02_Landscape**. **Save** the document in your **Word Chapter 2** folder as Lastname_Firstname_w02_Landscape

2. On the **Page Layout tab**, in the **Page Setup group**, click the **Margins** button, and then click **Custom Margins**. Under **Margins**, change the **Left** and **Right** margins to **1**, and then click **OK**. In the second title line, to the right of *By*, type your name.

3. Press Ctrl + A. On the **Home tab**, in the **Paragraph group**, change the **Line spacing** to **1.15**. On the **Page Layout tab**, in the **Paragraph group**, change the spacing **After** to **12 pt**.

4. Click in the paragraph that begins *Landscaping can be*. On the **Home tab**, in the **Paragraph group**, change the alignment to **Align Left**. In the **Paragraph group**, display the **Paragraph** dialog box. Under **Indentation**, set the **Special** box to **First line**, and then click **OK**. Compare your screen with **Figure 1**.

Figure 1

5. On the **Home tab**, in the **Clipboard group**, double-click the **Format Painter** button, and then copy the current paragraph formatting to the paragraphs that begin *When designing*, *Landscape garden*, *Time is*, *Landscape design*, and *In addition*; also the last three paragraphs in the document. Press Esc to turn off Format Painter.

6. Near the top of the document, select the subheading *Landscaping as a Weather Barrier*. In the **Font group**, click the **Dialog Box Launcher** to display the **Font** dialog box. Apply **Bold** emphasis and **Small caps**, and then click **OK**. Copy the formatting of this subheading to the other two subheadings: *Landscaping that Attracts Butterflies*, and *Landscaping to Minimize Water Use*.

7. Press Ctrl + Home. On the **Home tab**, in the **Editing group**, click the **Replace** button. In the **Find what** box, type insure In the **Replace with** box, type ensure and then click **Replace All**. **Save** the document, and then compare your screen with **Figure 2**.

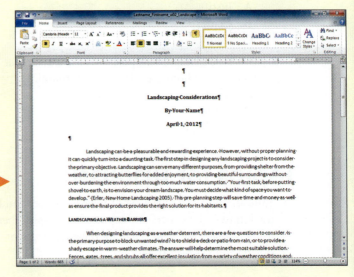

Figure 2

■ **Continue to the next page to complete this Skill Check**

8. Near the bottom of Page 1, locate and select the three tree names, beginning with *Willow hybrid*. In the **Paragraph group**, apply **Bullets**, and then click the **Increase Indent** button.

9. Near the top of Page 2, locate and select the four nonindented paragraphs, beginning with *Planting nectar flowers*. In the **Paragraph group**, apply **Numbering**, and then click the **Increase Indent** button.

10. Press Ctrl + Home. On the **Insert tab**, in the **Header & Footer group**, click **Header**, and then click **Edit Header**. On the **Design tab**, in the **Header & Footer group**, click the **Page Number** button, and then point to **Top of Page**. Under **Simple**, click **Plain Number 3**. Move to the footer. In the **Insert group**, click the **Quick Parts** button, and then click **Field**. Under **Field Names**, click **FileName**, and then click **OK**. In the **Options group**, select the **Different First Page** check box.

11. In the bulleted list, click to the right of *Willow hybrid*. On the **References tab**, in the **Footnotes group**, insert the following footnote: These trees grow quickly but do not live very long. On Page 2, at the end of the second item in the numbered list, insert the following footnote: Local nurseries can help you determine which flowers to use. Compare your screen with **Figure 3**.

12. On the **Home tab**, in the **Editing group**, click the **Find** button. In the **Navigation Pane**, in the search box, type creating and notice that there is only one instance of the word. In the document, double-click the highlighted word, and then type developing to replace the word. **Close** the Navigation Pane.

13. Press Ctrl + Home. In the first paragraph below the title, that begins *Landscaping can be*, locate and click anywhere in the *Erler* citation. Click the citation **arrow**, and then from the menu, click **Edit Citation**. Under **Add**, in the **Pages** box, type 2 and then click **OK**. Click the citation **arrow** again, and then click **Edit Source**. In the **Edit Source** dialog box, change the title of the book from *New Home Landscaping* to New Complete Home Landscaping and then click **OK**.

14. Press Ctrl + End, and then press Ctrl + Enter to add a new page. Press Enter two times.

15. On the **References tab**, in the **Citations & Bibliography group**, click the **Bibliography** button, and then click the **Bibliography** thumbnail. Select the *Bibliography* title. From the Mini toolbar, click the **Center** button. Press End and then press Enter.

16. **Save** the document, and then submit as directed. Compare your document with **Figure 4**.

Done! You have completed the Skill Check

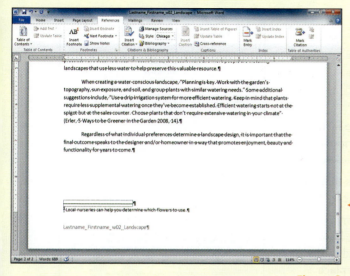

Figure 3

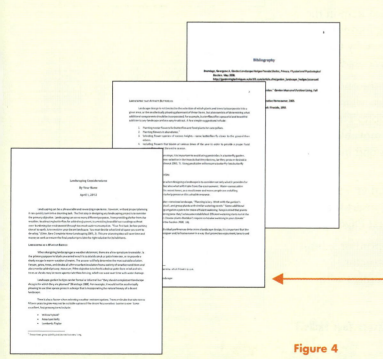

Figure 4

Assess Your Skills 1

To complete this document, you will need the following file:

- w02_Lighting

You will save your document as:

- Lastname_Firstname_w02_Lighting

1. **Start** Word. Locate and open **w02_Lighting**, and then **Save** it in your **Word Chapter 2** folder as Lastname_Firstname_w02_Lighting Set the document's **Top** margin to **1"**, and the **Left** and **Right** margins to **1.3"**.

2. Press ⏎Enter⏎ three times and type Home Lighting For the second title, type By and your name, and then for the third title, type May 25, 2012 Add a blank line following the date.

3. Select *all* of the text in the document. Change the spacing after the paragraphs to *6 pt* and change the **Line Spacing** to **1.15**. Change the paragraph alignment from *Justify* to **Align Left**. **Center** all three titles and change their **Font** to **Arial Black**.

4. Near the top of the document, locate the four questions that begin *What is the function*. Change the four questions to a numbered list, and increase the indent one time. Further down the page, select the four lines starting *provide decorative lighting* and ending *substitute for sunlight* and apply a bulleted list with the indent increased one time. At the bottom of the report, repeat this procedure with the three paragraphs (five lines) that begin *Installing* and *Turning lights* and *Understanding*.

5. Near the top of the document, locate the *Interior Lighting* subheading. Add **Bold** emphasis and **Small Caps**, and change the

Font to **Arial Black**. Apply the same format to the other two subheadings: *Exterior Lighting* and *Lighting for Energy Efficiency*.

6. For the seven remaining paragraphs that are not titles or lists, indent the first line by *0.5"*.

7. Click the **Find** button and search for *lightning*—not *lighting*—and notice how many misuses of the word are found in the document. Display the **Find and Replace** dialog box, and change each instance of *lightning* to *lighting*

8. On Page 1, at the end of the last item in the bulleted list, add the following footnote: The color temperature produced by the lighting units needs to be considered.

9. Near the bottom of Page 1, at the end of the paragraph that begins *Consider what the room*, add the following footnote: These can include both permanent and movable light fixtures. Select both footnotes and increase the **Font Size** to **11** points.

10. On Page 1, insert a **Plain Number 3** page number header. In the footer, insert the file name. Select the **Different First Page** option.

11. **Save** the document, and then print or submit the file as directed by your instructor. Compare your completed document with **Figure 1**.

Done! You have completed Assess Your Skills 1

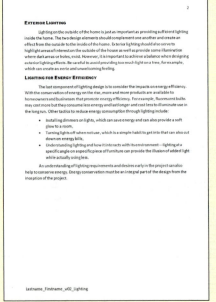

Figure 1

Assess Your Skills 3 and 4 can be found at **www.pearsonhighered.com/skills**.

Assess Your Skills 2

To complete this document, you will need the following file:

- w02_Retrofit

You will save the document as:

- Lastname_Firstname_w02_Retrofit

Figure 1

1. **Start** Word. Locate and open **w02_Retrofit**, and then **Save** it in your **Word Chapter 2** folder as Lastname_Firstname_w02_Retrofit Set the document's **Left** and **Right** margins to *1"*.

2. Type your name in the second title line to the right of *By*.

3. Select all of the text in the document. Change the spacing after all paragraphs to *12 pt* and change the **Line Spacing** to **1.15**. Change the paragraph alignment from *Justify* to **Align Left**. **Center** the three titles and add **Bold** emphasis.

4. For the three subheadings that begin *Evaluating the Energy* and *Simple Ways* and *Energy Savings Does Not*, apply **Bold** emphasis and the **Small Caps** style.

5. On Page 1, select the three paragraphs that begin *Check for drafts*, change them to a numbered list, and then increase the indent one time. Further down the page, select the four paragraphs that begin *Replace light bulbs*, change them to a bulleted list, and then increase the indent one time.

6. At the top of Page 2, click to the right of the quotation mark at the end of the paragraph that ends *credits*. Using the **Chicago** style, insert a new **Article in a Periodical** citation. In the **Author** box, type Connor, Rachel; Stone, Laurie The **Title** is Resource & Energy Efficient Building The **Periodical Title** is Home Power The **Year** is 2008 The **Month** is January The **Pages** are 14 (one-page article). Edit the citation field to include the source's page number.

7. Near the bottom of the report, click at the end of the paragraph that begins *Saving energy*. Insert a new **Book** citation. In the **Author** box, type Clark, William H. The **Title** is Retrofitting for Energy Conservation The **Year** is 1997 The **City** is New York The **Publisher** is McGraw-Hill Edit the citation to add 15 as the page number of the quotation.

8. At the end of the document, use a manual page break to create a new page. At about 2 inches from the top edge of the last page, insert the built-in **Bibliography**. **Center** the title and add a blank line between the title and the sources. Select the title *Bibliography*, change the **Font Size** to **11** and the **Font Color** to **Black**.

9. On Page 1, insert the **Plain Number 3** page number header. In the footer, insert the file name, and then select the **Different First Page** option.

10. **Save** the document, and then print or submit the file as directed by your instructor. Compare your completed document with **Figure 1**.

Done! You have completed Assess Your Skills 2

Assess Your Skills Visually

To complete this document, you will need the following file:

- w02_Parks

You will save your document as:

- Lastname_Firstname_w02_Parks

Open the file **w02_Parks**, and then save it in your **Word Chapter 2** folder as Lastname_ Firstname_w02_Parks Create the document shown in **Figure 1**.

To complete this document, set the left and right margins to 1.3 inches. The first title should start at approximately 2 inches on the vertical ruler. All of the text is 12-point Calibri. The list should align with the first line of the indented paragraphs. Because this is a very short document with only one reference—at the end of the second-to-last paragraph—it is placed in a footnote as shown in **Figure 1**. Line spacing should be 1.15, with six points of spacing after paragraphs. Below the file name in the footer, add the current date field. Print or submit the file as directed by your instructor.

Done! You have completed Assess Your Skills Visually

Park Designs

By Your Name

March 15, 2012

Parks offer numerous benefits, from providing habitats for local animals and plants to serving as a psychological benefit to its occupants. The benefits of open spaces and fresh air have been well documented. Visiting a park can be relaxing and refreshing, and can even help relieve stress. Parks should be designed to accommodate local needs and conditions. Thus, when designing a park, it is important to consider:

- Who will be using the park?
- What kinds of wildlife will live in the park?
- What kinds of plant life are indigenous to the area?

ECOLOGICAL IMPACTS

When considering the ecological aspect of a park, it is critical to understand who will be the natural habitants of the park and what structures or plants would foster their well-being? Gaining a thorough understanding and conduction real world observations are recommended in order to understand the local wildlife and how their presence influences the design of the park.

PARK SIZE

The available space can have a huge impact on the design of a park. Small parks "can provide a place away from but close to home, a place that is not too isolated, and a place that avoids some of the problems that can occur in larger parks, crimes, for example."[1]

One additional step in designing a park is to get the opinions and suggestions of the people living in the community. In doing so, it will help to ensure that the final park is something that they have helped to design and will encourage use.

---

[1] Ann Forsyth and Laura Mussacchio, *Designing Small Parks: A Manual for Addressing Social and Ecological Concerns*, Wiley & Sons, New Jersey, 2005, p. 14.

Lastname_Firstname_w02_Parks
September 12, 2012

Figure 1

Skills in Context

To complete this document, you will need the following file:

- New blank Word document

You will save your document as:

- Lastname_Firstname_w02_National_Parks

The City of Aspen Falls Planning Department is working with the Travel and Tourism Bureau to explore ways to use the city as the base of operation for tourists who want to visit important sites within a day's drive. Using the skills you practiced in this chapter, create a report on the nearby major nature attractions. These could include Yosemite National Park (250 miles), Death Valley National Park (200 miles), Sequoia National Forest (180 miles), and the Channel Islands National Park (40 miles). Research three of these (or other) national sites, and write the highlights of what a visitor might find at each. Your report should include at least two footnotes and two citations, one list for each site, and a bibliography. The lists should contain between three and six items each. Format the report in the style practiced in the chapter.

Save the document as Lastname_Firstname_ w02_National_Parks Insert the file name and current date in the footer, and check the entire document for grammar and spelling. Print or submit the file as directed by your instructor.

Done! You have completed Skills in Context

Skills and You

To complete this document, you will need the following file:

- New blank Word document

You will save your document as:

- Lastname_Firstname_w02_My_Home

Using the skills you have practiced in this chapter, compose a document about your hometown (or county, region, state, or province). The document should include a top margin of two inches; other margins of one inch each, and a title and subtitle appropriately formatted. You should include three paragraphs of text, with appropriate line spacing and spacing after the paragraphs, with the text left aligned and the first lines indented. You should also include a list of things to see or do in the area, and at least three informational footnotes. If you need to use quotations, include references and a bibliography.

Add the file name and date to the footer. Save the document as Lastname_Firstname_w02_My_Home Check the entire document for grammar and spelling. Print or submit the file as directed by your instructor.

Done! You have completed Skills and You

CHAPTER 3

Work with Graphics, Tabs, and Tables

▶ You can add graphics to a document to enhance the effectiveness of your message or to make your document more attractive.

▶ You can use tables to present data in a format of rows and columns, which can make complex information easy to understand at a glance.

Your starting screen will look similar to this:

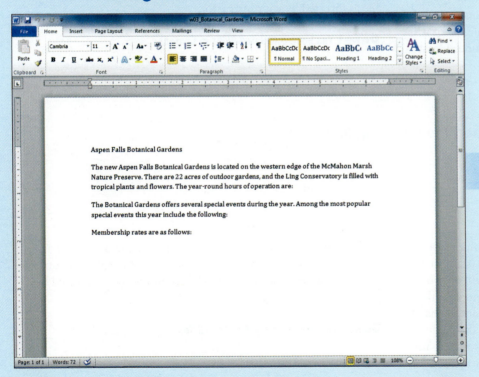

SKILLS

Skills 1-10 Training

At the end of this chapter, you will be able to:

Skill 1	Insert Pictures from Files
Skill 2	Resize and Move Pictures
Skill 3	Format Pictures Using Styles and Artistic Effects
Skill 4	Set Tab Stops
Skill 5	Enter Text with Tab Stops
Skill 6	Apply Table Styles
Skill 7	Create Tables
Skill 8	Add Rows and Columns to Tables
Skill 9	Format Text in Table Cells
Skill 10	Format Tables

MORE SKILLS

More Skills 11	Insert Text Boxes
More Skills 12	Format with WordArt
More Skills 13	Create Tables from Existing Lists
More Skills 14	Insert Drop Caps

Outcome

Using the skills listed to the left will enable you to create a document like this:

Aspen Falls Botanical Gardens

The new Aspen Falls Botanical Gardens is located on the western edge of the McMahon Marsh Nature Preserve. There are 22 acres of outdoor gardens, and the Ling Conservatory is filled with tropical plants and flowers. The year-round hours of operation are:

Day	Hours
Monday-Wednesday	10 to 5
Thursday-Friday	10 to 6
Saturday	8 to 5
Sunday	Noon to 5

The Botanical Gardens offers several special events during the year. Among the most popular special events this year include the following:

Event	Month(s)	Description
Butterflies	May and June	Conservatory display of butterflies from around town and around the world
Rainforest	January to April	Wonders of the rain forests are displayed
Photograph Nature	July and August	Nature photography contest for kids, teens, and adults—photos must be from Aspen Falls area
Holiday Decorations	December	Decorations and model trains

Membership rates are as follows:

Memberships		
Group	Ages	Cost
Children	Under 12	Free
Students	Under 18	$ 8.00
Adults	18 to 60	25.00
Seniors	Over 60	12.50

Lastname_Firstname_w03_Botanical

You will save your file as:

Lastname_Firstname_w03_Botanical

In this chapter, you will create documents for the Aspen Falls City Hall, which provides essential services for the citizens and visitors of Aspen Falls, California.

Introduction

- ▶ Digital images—such as those you have scanned or taken with a digital camera—can be added to a document and formatted using distinctive borders and other interesting and attractive effects.

- ▶ You can organize lists in rows and columns by using tabs.

- ▶ The table feature in Word lets you organize lists and data in columns and rows without needing to create tab settings.

- ▶ You can use tables to summarize and emphasize information in an organized arrangement of rows and columns that are easy to read.

- ▶ You can format tables manually or apply a number of different formats quickly using built-in styles.

**Time to complete all
10 skills – 55 minutes**

Find your student data files here:

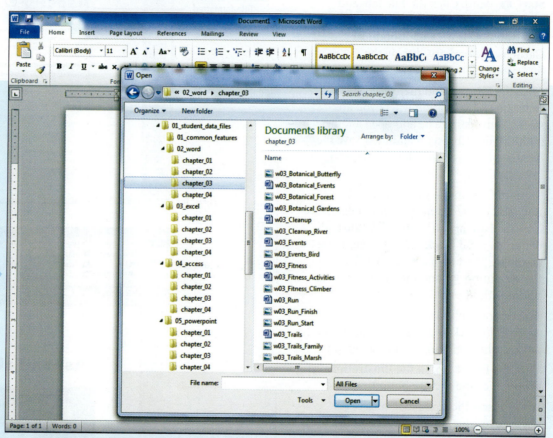

Student data files needed for this chapter:

- w03_Botanical_Gardens
- w03_Botanical_Forest
- w03_Botanical_Butterfly
- w03_Botanical_Events

► Recall that pictures are inserted at the insertion point location and are positioned in the paragraph in the same manner as a letter or a number.

► You can insert pictures that you have scanned or downloaded from the Web, or pictures from your digital camera.

1. **Start** 🌐 Word. Click the **File tab**, and then click **Open**. Navigate to your student files, and then open **w03_Botanical_Gardens**. If necessary, display the formatting marks.

2. Click the **File tab**, and then click **Save As**. Navigate to the location where you are saving your files, create and open a folder named Word Chapter 3 and then **Save** the document as Lastname_Firstname_w03_Botanical

3. Select the document title *Aspen Falls Botanical Gardens*. On the Mini toolbar, click the **Font arrow** `Calibri (Body)`, locate and then click **Arial Black**. Click the **Font Size arrow** `11`, and then click **26**. Click the **Center** button ▤, and then compare your screen with **Figure 1**.

4. In the paragraph that begins *The new Aspen Falls*, click to position the insertion point at the beginning of the paragraph.

5. Click the **Insert tab**. In the **Illustrations group**, click the **Picture** button.

6. In the **Insert Picture** dialog box, navigate to your student files, select **w03_Botanical_Forest**, and then click **Insert**. Compare your screen with **Figure 2**.

■ **Continue to the next page to complete the skill**

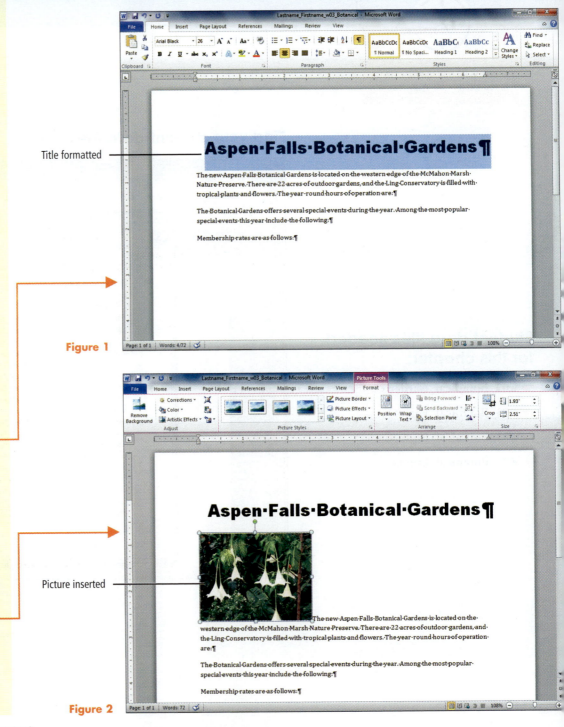

Title formatted

Figure 1

Picture inserted

Figure 2

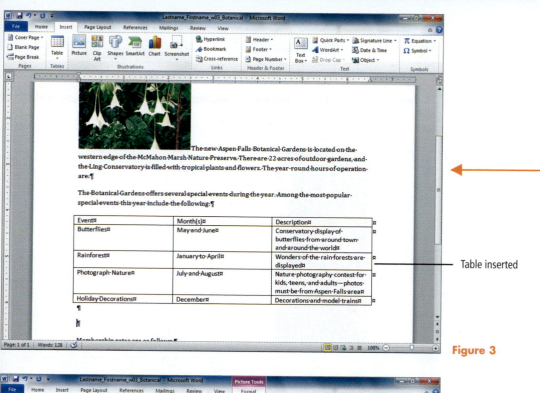

Figure 3

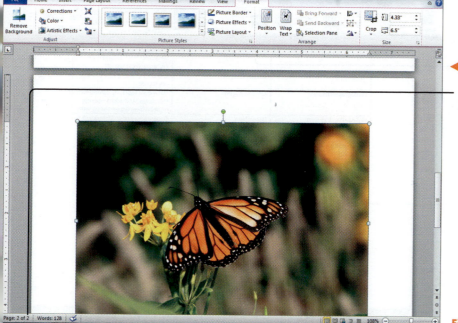

Picture inserted
on new page

Figure 4

7. At the end of the paragraph that begins *The Botanical Gardens offers*, click to position the insertion point to the right of the colon, and then press Enter.

8. On the **Insert tab**, in the **Text group**, click the **Object button arrow**, and then click **Text from File**.

9. In the **Insert File** dialog box, navigate to your student files, select **w03_Botanical_Events**, and then click **Insert** to insert a table. Notice that the insertion point is in the second blank line below the table. Compare your screen with **Figure 3**.

10. With the insertion point still in the second blank paragraph below the inserted table, press Bksp to remove the first blank paragraph.

11. Press Ctrl + End to move to the end of the document, and then press Enter to create a new blank paragraph.

12. On the **Insert tab**, in the **Illustrations group**, click the **Picture** button. Navigate to your student files, select **w03_Botanical_Butterfly**, and then click **Insert**. Compare your screen with **Figure 4**.

   Because the picture is too large to fit in the available space at the bottom of the current page, Word creates a new page.

13. **Save** the document.

■ **You have completed Skill 1 of 10**

► When you select a picture, *sizing handles*—small squares or circles—display around the picture border, and you can drag these handles to resize the picture.

► You can also resize a picture using the Shape Height and Shape Width buttons on the Format tab.

1. At the top of Page 2, be sure the **w03_Botanical** butterfly picture is selected—sizing handles display around the picture border. Notice that a Format tab displays on the Ribbon.

2. If your rulers do not display, on the View tab, in the Show/Hide group, select the Ruler check box.

3. On the right border of the picture, locate the middle—square—sizing handle. Point to the sizing handle to display the ⟷ pointer, and then drag to the left to **2 inches** on the horizontal ruler, as shown in **Figure 1**.

   The picture does not resize proportionally.

4. On the **Quick Access Toolbar**, click the **Undo** button ↺.

5. Scroll to display the bottom of the picture. Point to the sizing handle in the lower right corner of the picture. When the ⤡ pointer displays, drag up and to the left until the right border of the picture aligns at approximately **2.5 inches** on the horizontal ruler.

6. If necessary, scroll to view the bottom of the page, and then compare your screen with **Figure 2**.

   The picture is resized proportionally, and the smaller picture fits at the bottom of the first page of the document.

■ **Continue to the next page to complete the skill**

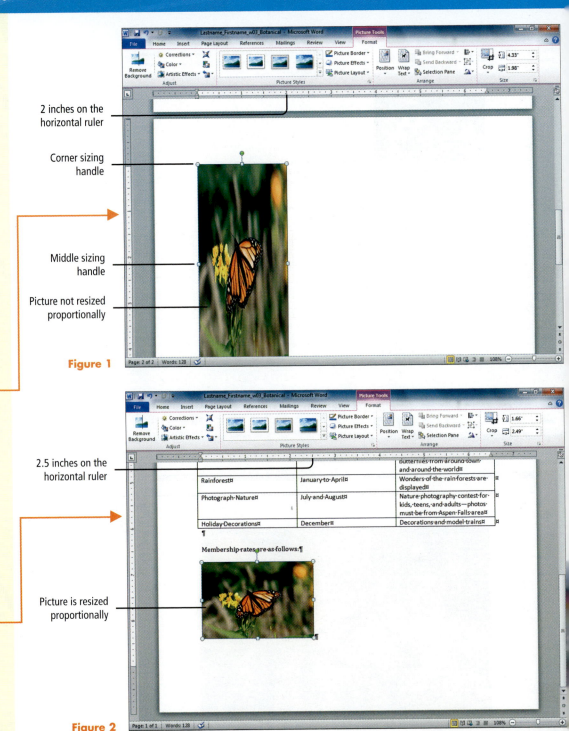

2 inches on the horizontal ruler

Corner sizing handle

Middle sizing handle

Picture not resized proportionally

Figure 1

2.5 inches on the horizontal ruler

Picture is resized proportionally

Figure 2

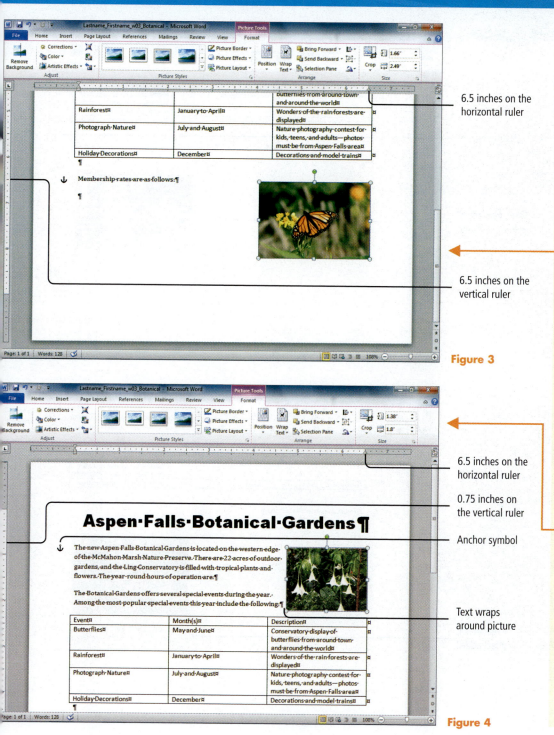

6.5 inches on the horizontal ruler

6.5 inches on the vertical ruler

Figure 3

6.5 inches on the horizontal ruler

0.75 inches on the vertical ruler

Anchor symbol

Text wraps around picture

Figure 4

7. Be sure the picture is still selected. On the **Format tab**, in the **Arrange group**, click the **Wrap Text** button, and then click **Square**.

   This setting changes the picture to a *floating object*, which you can move independently of the surrounding text.

8. Point to the picture to display the ⌖ pointer. Drag the picture to the right so that the right border is aligned approximately at **6.5 inches** on the horizontal ruler and the top border is aligned at approximately **6.5 inches** on the vertical ruler. Compare your screen with **Figure 3**.

9. Press Ctrl + Home, and then click the picture of the gardens. On the **Format tab**, in the **Size group**, click the **Shape Width down spin arrow** 🔲 1.37" ◆ as necessary to change the width of the picture to **1.8"**.

10. On the **Format tab**, in the **Arrange group**, click the **Wrap Text** button, and then click **Square**.

11. Point to the picture to display the ⌖ pointer. Drag the picture to the right, and align the right border at approximately **6.5 inches** on the horizontal ruler. Align the top border at approximately **0.75 inches** on the vertical ruler. Compare your screen with **Figure 4**, and adjust your picture as necessary.

   An *anchor* symbol to the left of the paragraph mark indicates which paragraph the picture is associated with, and the paragraph text wraps around the space filled by the picture.

12. **Save** 💾 the document.

■ **You have completed Skill 2 of 10**

► You can add special effects to the texture of a picture to make it look more like a drawing or a painting.

► You can also apply built-in picture styles, such as borders and frames, and then format those borders.

1. Press `Ctrl` + `End` to move to the bottom of the document, and then click the picture of the butterfly.

2. In the **Size group**, select the value in the **Shape Width** box ![icon](1.37"), type **2.75** and then press `Enter` to change the width of the picture to 2.75 inches. Drag the picture to the left to align the right edge at **6.5 inches** on the horizontal ruler and the top edge at **5.25 inches** on the vertical ruler.

   When you need a size that cannot be entered using spin arrows, type the number in the spin box.

3. On the **Format tab**, in the **Picture Styles group**, click the **Picture Effects** button. Point to **Soft Edges**, and then click **5 Point**. Notice that the edges of the picture fade in, as shown in **Figure 1**.

   A soft edge with a higher number of points will result in a more dramatic fade between the picture and its border.

4. In the **Picture Styles group**, click the **Picture Effects** button, point to **Reflection**, and then under **Reflection Variations**, in the second row, click the first effect—**Tight Reflection, 4 pt offset**.

5. Click anywhere in the text to deselect the picture, and then compare your screen with **Figure 2**.

■ **Continue to the next page to complete the skill** ➤

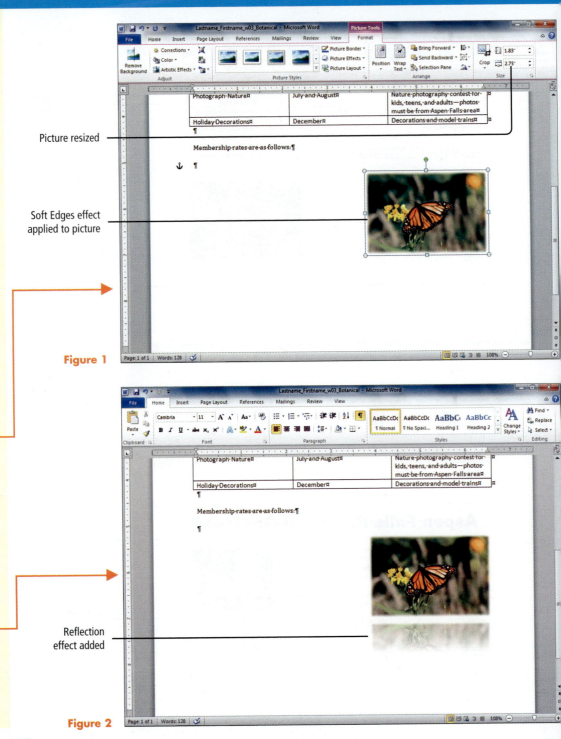

Picture resized

Soft Edges effect applied to picture

Figure 1

Reflection effect added

Figure 2

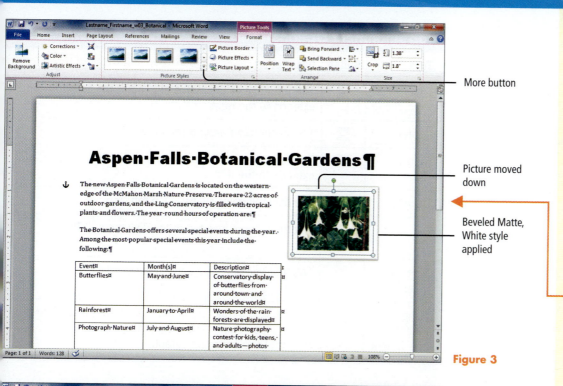

More button

Picture moved down

Beveled Matte, White style applied

Figure 3

6. Press Ctrl + Home to move to the top of the document, and then click the garden picture.

7. With the picture selected, on the **Format tab**, in the **Picture Styles group**, click the **More** button. Point to several of the thumbnails, and watch as Live Preview displays the picture styles.

   Some of the styles add height to the picture and can force the title to the left.

8. In the first row of thumbnails, click the second style—**Beveled Matte, White**.

9. With the picture still selected, press ↓ several times until the document title displays across the screen, as shown in **Figure 3**.

   To move objects in small precise increments, you can *nudge* them in this manner by selecting the object and then pressing one of the arrow keys. Because the new style increased the size of the picture, the table does not stretch across the screen.

10. With the picture still selected, in the **Picture Styles group**, click the **Picture Border** button.

11. Under **Theme Colors**, in the third row of colors, click the seventh color—**Olive Green, Accent 3, Lighter 60%**.

12. In the **Adjust group**, click the **Artistic Effects** button. Point to several thumbnails in the gallery to preview available effects, and then in the fourth row, click the fifth effect—**Plastic Wrap**. Compare your screen with **Figure 4**.

13. **Save** the document.

   ■ **You have completed Skill 3 of 10**

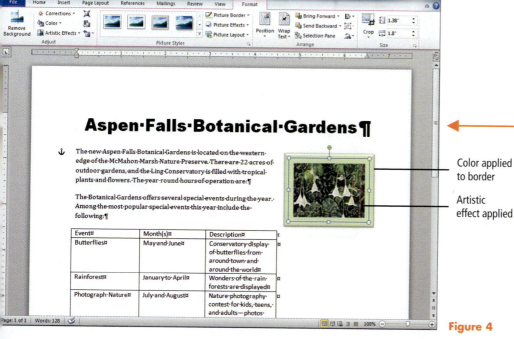

Color applied to border

Artistic effect applied

Figure 4

► A ***tab stop*** is a specific location on a line of text marked on the Word ruler to which you can move the insertion point by pressing Tab. Tabs are used to align and indent text.

► Tab stop types are set when you insert the stop; however, you can change the tab stop type using the Tabs dialog box.

1. Near the top of the document, click at the end of the paragraph that begins *The new Aspen Falls*, and then press Enter. Notice that the table expands to the width of the page.

2. On the left end of the horizontal ruler, notice the **Tab Selector** button ⊡—the icon displayed in your button may vary.

3. Click the button several times to view the various tab types available. Pause at each tab stop type, and view the information in the table in **Figure 1** to see how each of the tab types is used.

   If you have not added any tab stops to a paragraph, default tab stops are placed every half inch on the ruler. These default tab stops are indicated by the small marks at every half inch just below the white area of the ruler.

4. With the insertion point still in the blank paragraph, click the **Tab Selector** button ⊡ until the **Left Tab** icon ⊡ displays.

5. On the horizontal ruler, point to the mark that indicates **0.5 inches**, and then click one time to insert a left tab stop. Compare your screen with **Figure 2**.

■ **Continue to the next page to complete the skill** ➤

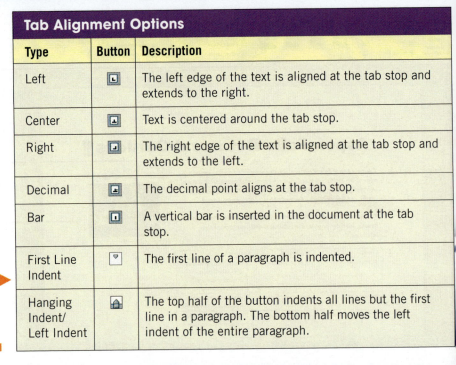

Tab Alignment Options

Type	Button	Description
Left	⊡	The left edge of the text is aligned at the tab stop and extends to the right.
Center	⊡	Text is centered around the tab stop.
Right	⊡	The right edge of the text is aligned at the tab stop and extends to the left.
Decimal	⊡	The decimal point aligns at the tab stop.
Bar	⊡	A vertical bar is inserted in the document at the tab stop.
First Line Indent	▽	The first line of a paragraph is indented.
Hanging Indent/ Left Indent	⌂	The top half of the button indents all lines but the first line in a paragraph. The bottom half moves the left indent of the entire paragraph.

Figure 1

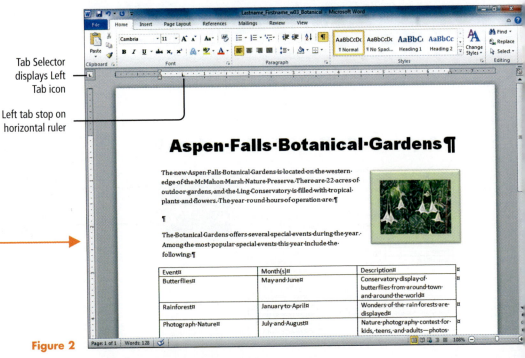

Tab Selector displays Left Tab icon

Left tab stop on horizontal ruler

Figure 2

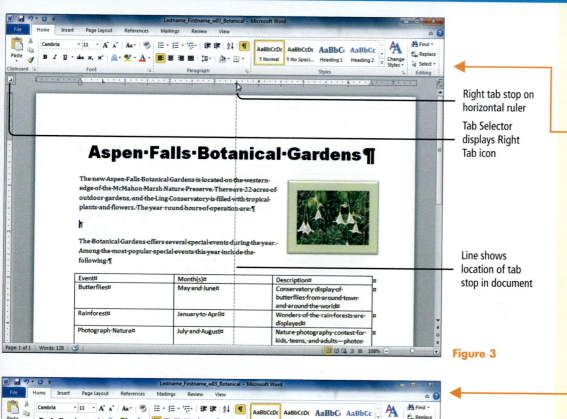

Figure 3

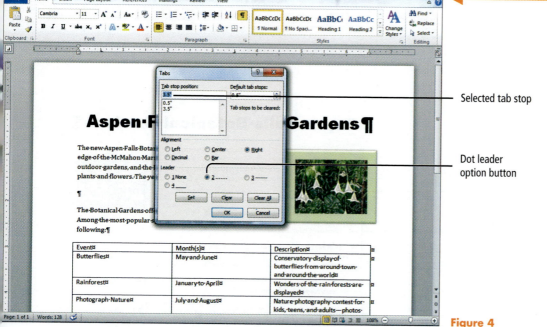

Figure 4

Right tab stop on horizontal ruler

Tab Selector displays Right Tab icon

Line shows location of tab stop in document

Selected tab stop

Dot leader option button

6. Click the **Tab Selector** button 🔲 two times to display the **Right Tab** icon 🔲.

7. On the ruler, point to the mark that indicates **3.5 inches**. Click and hold down the mouse button. Notice that a dotted line indicates the tab location in the document, as shown in **Figure 3**. In this manner, you can determine whether the tab stop is exactly where you want it.

8. Release the mouse button to insert the right tab stop.

9. On the **Home tab**, click the **Paragraph Dialog Box Launcher** 🔲. At the bottom of the displayed **Paragraph** dialog box, click the **Tabs** button.

10. In the **Tabs** dialog box, under **Tab stop position**, select the tab stop at **3.5"**. Under **Leader**, select the **2** option button to add a dot leader to the selected tab stop. Near the bottom of the dialog box, click the **Set** button, and then compare your screen with **Figure 4**.

A *leader* is a series of characters that form a solid, dashed, or dotted line that fills the space preceding a tab stop; a *leader character* is the symbol used to fill the space. A *dot leader* is a series of evenly spaced dots that precede a tab stop.

11. In the **Tabs** dialog box, click **OK**, and then **Save** 🔲 the document.

■ **You have completed Skill 4 of 10**

▶ The Tab key is used to move to the next tab stop in a line of text.

▶ When you want to relocate a tab stop, you can drag the tab stop marker to a new location on the horizontal ruler.

1. Be sure your insertion point is still in the blank paragraph and the tab stops you entered display on the horizontal ruler.

2. Press [Tab] to move the insertion point to the first tab stop you placed on the ruler. Type Day and press [Tab] to move to the right tab with the dot leader that you created.

3. Type Hours and press [Enter]. Compare your screen with **Figure 1**.

   When your insertion point is positioned at a right tab stop and you begin to type, the text moves to the left. When you press [Enter], the new paragraph displays the same tab stop markers on the ruler as the previous paragraph.

4. Press [Tab], type Monday-Wednesday and then press [Tab]. Type 10 to 5 and then press [Enter].

5. Press [Tab], type Thursday-Friday and then press [Tab]. Type 10 to 6 and then press [Enter].

6. Press [Tab], type Saturday and then press [Tab]. Type 8 to 5 and then press [Enter].

7. Press [Tab], type Sunday and then press [Tab]. Type Noon to 5 and compare your screen with **Figure 2**.

8. Select the first line of the tabbed list, and then from the Mini toolbar, click the **Bold** button [B].

■ **Continue to the next page to complete the skill**

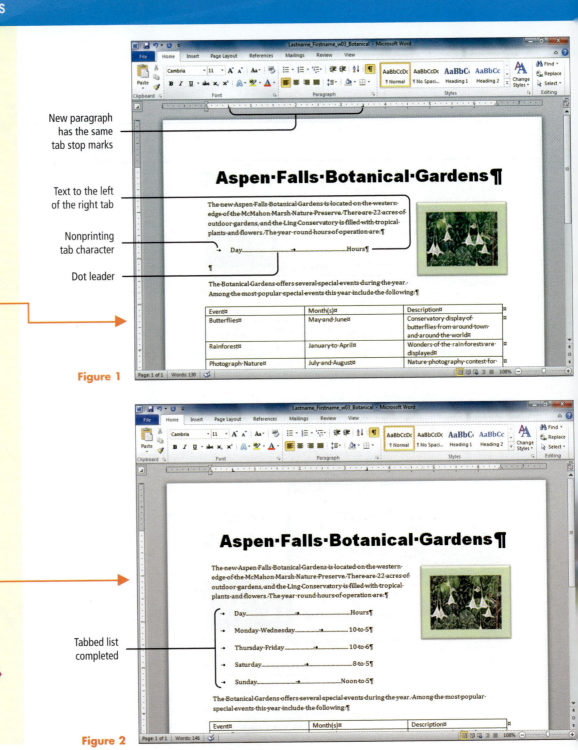

New paragraph has the same tab stop marks

Text to the left of the right tab

Nonprinting tab character

Dot leader

Figure 1

Tabbed list completed

Figure 2

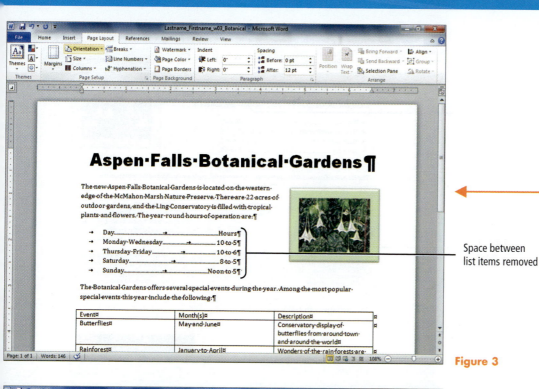

Space between
list items removed

Figure 3

Right tab
stop moved

Left tab
stop moved

Tab stop changes
reflected in Tabs
dialog box

Figure 4

9. Select the first four lines of the tabbed list. Do not select the paragraph that begins *Sunday*.

10. Click the **Page Layout tab**. In the **Paragraph group**, under **Spacing**, click the **After down spin arrow** two times to change the space after the selected paragraphs to **0 pt**. Click anywhere in the document to deselect the text, and then compare your screen with **Figure 3**.

11. To the left of *Day*, point in the margin area to display the 🔼 pointer. Then drag down to select all five items in the tabbed list.

12. On the horizontal ruler, point to the left tab mark at **0.5 inches** on the horizontal ruler. When the ScreenTip *Left Tab* displays, drag left to move the tab mark to **0.25 inches** on the horizontal ruler to move each selected line to the new tab location.

13. With the five lines still selected, on the horizontal ruler, point to the right tab mark at **3.5 inches** on the horizontal ruler. When the ScreenTip *Right Tab* displays, drag left to move the tab mark to **3.25 inches** on the horizontal ruler.

14. On the horizontal ruler, point to the right tab mark again. When the ScreenTip *Right Tab* displays, double-click to display the **Tabs** dialog box. Notice that the new tab stop position values display, as shown in **Figure 4**.

15. Click **Cancel** to close the dialog box, and then **Save** 💾 the document.

■ **You have completed Skill 5 of 10**

► A *table* consists of rows and columns of text or numbers. Tables summarize data effectively and efficiently.

► You can format each table element individually, or you can apply table styles to the entire table.

1. Scroll as needed to display the table.

   The table contains five rows and three columns. Recall that the intersection of a row and a column in a table is called a *cell*.

2. Click in any cell in the table, and then click the **Design tab**. In the **Table Styles group**, notice that a number of predesigned styles are available.

3. Point to the third style—**Light Shading - Accent 1**—to view the Live Preview of that style, as shown in **Figure 1**.

   Because the styles in the first row of the Table Styles gallery display the styles that were used most recently, your first row of thumbnails may vary.

4. In the **Table Styles group**, click the **More** button.

5. In the **Table Styles** gallery, use the vertical scroll bar to scroll to the bottom of the gallery. Locate the **Medium Grid 3 - Accent 3** style, and then point to it, as shown in **Figure 2**.

6. Click one time to apply the **Medium Grid 3 - Accent 3** style.

   You do not have to select the entire table to apply a built-in style.

■ **Continue to the next page to complete the skill**

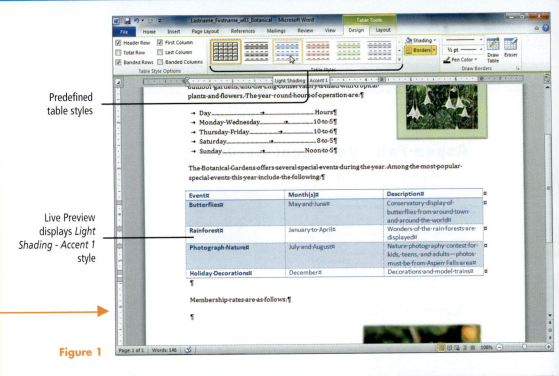

Predefined table styles

Live Preview displays *Light Shading - Accent 1* style

Figure 1

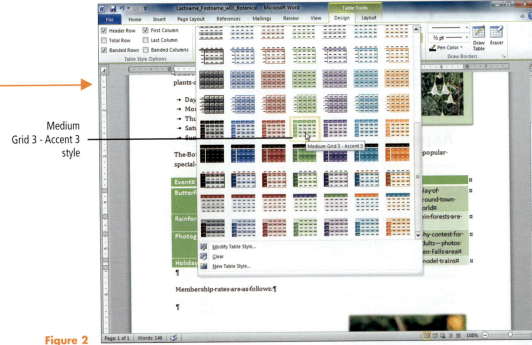

Medium Grid 3 - Accent 3 style

Figure 2

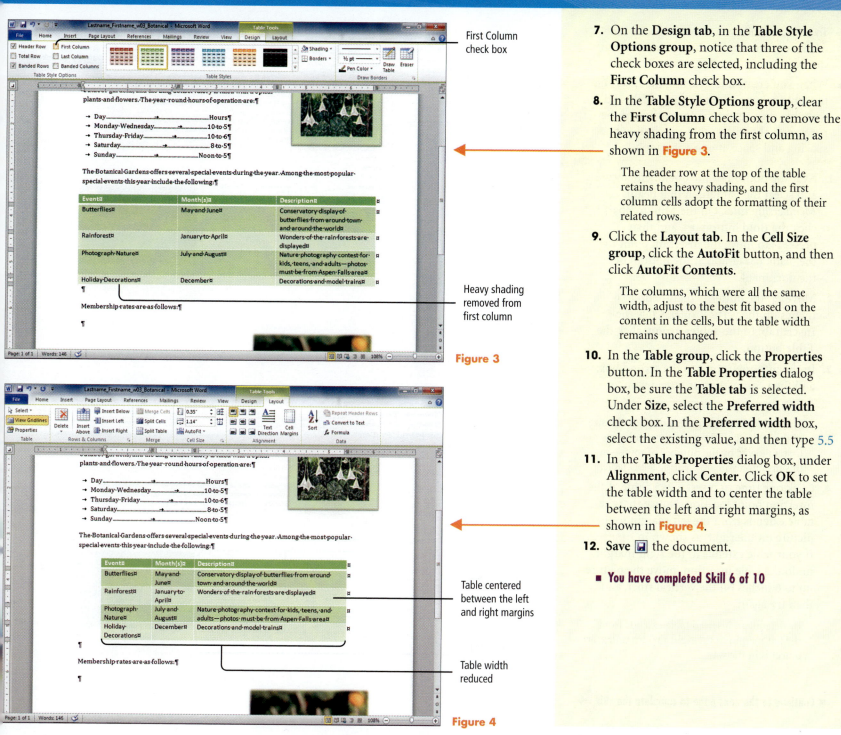

First Column check box

Figure 3

Heavy shading removed from first column

Table centered between the left and right margins

Table width reduced

Figure 4

7. On the **Design tab**, in the **Table Style Options group**, notice that three of the check boxes are selected, including the **First Column** check box.

8. In the **Table Style Options group**, clear the **First Column** check box to remove the heavy shading from the first column, as shown in **Figure 3**.

   The header row at the top of the table retains the heavy shading, and the first column cells adopt the formatting of their related rows.

9. Click the **Layout tab**. In the **Cell Size group**, click the **AutoFit** button, and then click **AutoFit Contents**.

   The columns, which were all the same width, adjust to the best fit based on the content in the cells, but the table width remains unchanged.

10. In the **Table group**, click the **Properties** button. In the **Table Properties** dialog box, be sure the **Table tab** is selected. Under **Size**, select the **Preferred width** check box. In the **Preferred width** box, select the existing value, and then type 5.5

11. In the **Table Properties** dialog box, under **Alignment**, click **Center**. Click **OK** to set the table width and to center the table between the left and right margins, as shown in **Figure 4**.

12. **Save** the document.

   ■ **You have completed Skill 6 of 10**

► To create a table, you need to specify the number of rows and columns you want to start with.

► When you create a table using the Insert tab, the table columns are of equal width, and the table rows retain the formatting of the paragraph above the table—including line spacing and space after a paragraph.

1. Near the bottom of the document, locate and select the paragraph that begins *Membership rates*. On the Mini toolbar, click the **Bold** button ⬛, and then press ⬇ to move the insertion point to the blank paragraph at the bottom of the document.

2. **Move** ⬚ the butterfly picture up to **6 inches** on the vertical ruler. Click the **Insert tab**. In the **Tables group**, click the **Table** button.

3. In the fifth row, point to the second box, and then compare your screen with **Figure 1**.

    The top of the Table gallery displays the size of the table, with the number of columns first, followed by the number of rows—in this instance, you are creating a 2x5 table.

4. Click one time to insert a **2x5 Table** at the insertion point location. Notice that the table extends from the left margin to the picture on the right, as shown in **Figure 2**. If your table extends to the right margin, undo the table insertion, move the picture up to 6 inches on the vertical ruler, and then try again.

    By default, an inserted table extends from the left margin to the right margin unless an object is in the way.

■ **Continue to the next page to complete the skill** ➤

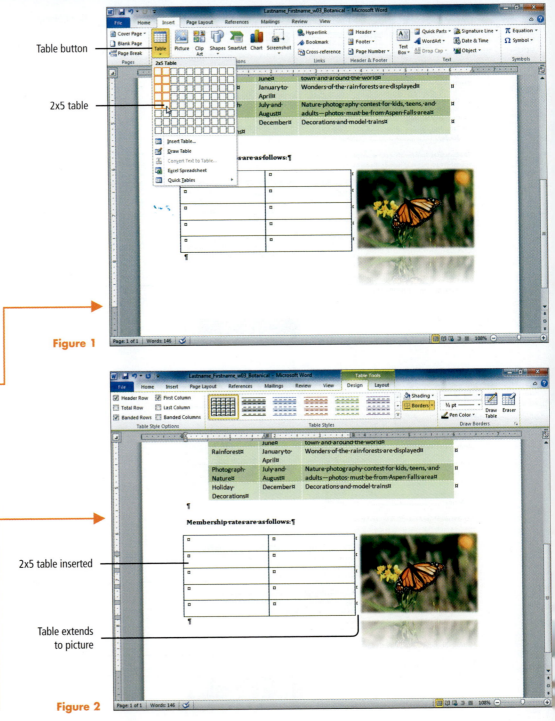

Table button

2x5 table

Figure 1

2x5 table inserted

Table extends to picture

Figure 2

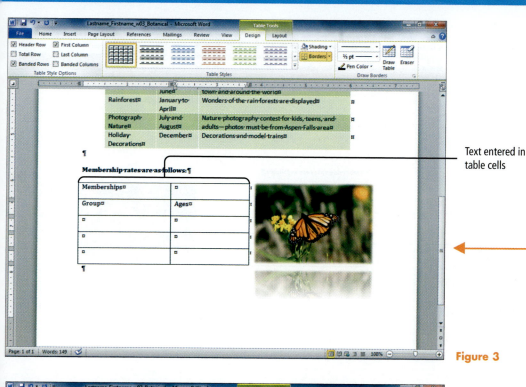

Text entered in table cells

Figure 3

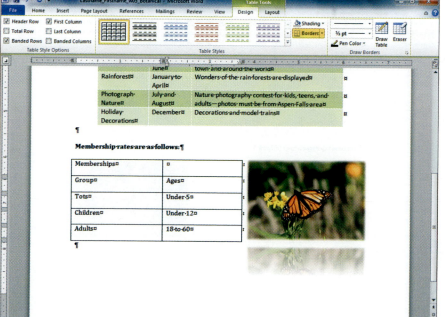

Figure 4

5. Be sure the insertion point is located in the upper left cell of the new table. Type Memberships and then press Tab. Notice that the column widths adjust as you type.

> You can use Tab or the arrow keys to move among cells in a table. When you press Enter, a second line in the same cell is created. If this happens, you can press Bksp or ⟲ to remove the inserted paragraph.

6. Press Tab again to move to the first cell in the second row.

7. Type Group and then press Tab. Type Ages and then press Tab. Compare your screen with Figure 3.

8. With the insertion point in the first cell of the third row, type Tots and then press Tab. Type Under 5 and then press Tab. Do not be concerned if the widths of the columns continue to change while you are typing.

9. In the first cell of the fourth row, type Children and then press Tab. Type Under 12 and then press Tab.

10. In the first cell of the last row, type Adults and then press Tab. Type 18 to 60 and then compare your screen with Figure 4.

11. Save 🖫 the document.

■ **You have completed Skill 7 of 10**

- ► You can add rows to the beginning, middle, or end of a table, and you can delete one or more rows if necessary.
- ► You can add columns to the left or right of the column that contains the insertion point.

1. In the third row of the table, click anywhere in the *Tots* cell.

   To delete a row, you need only position the insertion point anywhere in the row.

2. Click the **Layout tab**, and then in the **Rows & Columns group**, click the **Delete** button. From the displayed list, click **Delete Rows**. If you accidentally click Delete Columns, in the Quick Access Toolbar, click the Undo button 🔄 and try again.

3. Be sure the insertion point is in the *Children* cell. In the **Rows & Columns group**, click the **Insert Below** button. Notice that a blank row is added below the row that contains the insertion point.

4. Type Students and then notice that although the entire row was selected when you started typing, the text was entered into the row's first cell. Press [Tab], and then type Under 18 Press [Tab], and then compare your screen with **Figure 1**.

5. In the last row of the table, in the second column, click to the right of *18 to 60*.

6. Press [Tab] to insert a new row at the bottom of the table.

7. Type Seniors and then press [Tab]. Type Over 60 and then compare your screen with **Figure 2**.

■ **Continue to the next page to complete the skill** ➤

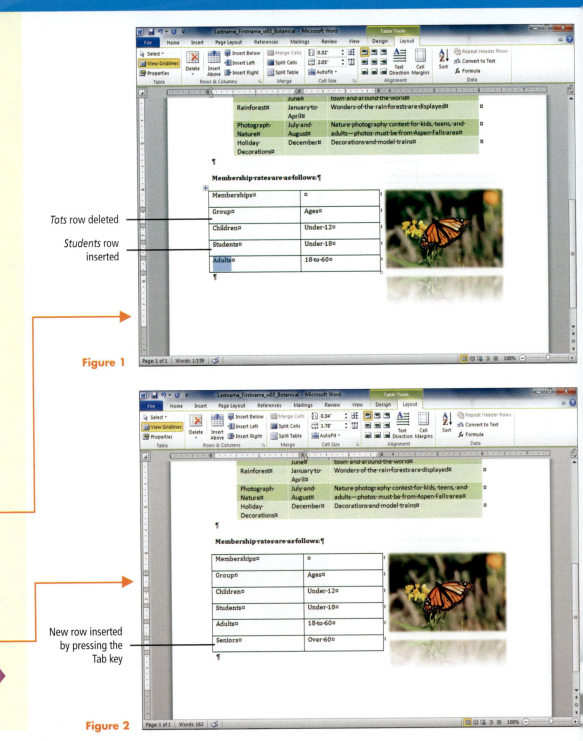

Tots row deleted

Students row inserted

Figure 1

New row inserted by pressing the Tab key

Figure 2

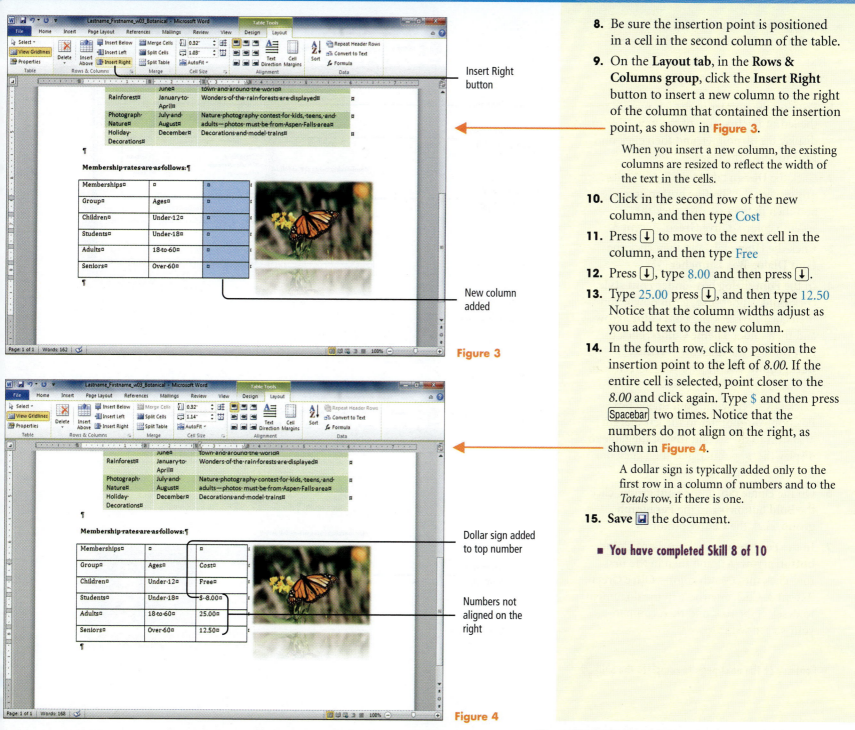

Insert Right button

New column added

Figure 3

Dollar sign added to top number

Numbers not aligned on the right

Figure 4

8. Be sure the insertion point is positioned in a cell in the second column of the table.

9. On the **Layout tab**, in the **Rows & Columns group**, click the **Insert Right** button to insert a new column to the right of the column that contained the insertion point, as shown in **Figure 3**.

   When you insert a new column, the existing columns are resized to reflect the width of the text in the cells.

10. Click in the second row of the new column, and then type Cost

11. Press ↓ to move to the next cell in the column, and then type Free

12. Press ↓, type 8.00 and then press ↓.

13. Type 25.00 press ↓, and then type 12.50 Notice that the column widths adjust as you add text to the new column.

14. In the fourth row, click to position the insertion point to the left of *8.00*. If the entire cell is selected, point closer to the *8.00* and click again. Type $ and then press Spacebar two times. Notice that the numbers do not align on the right, as shown in **Figure 4**.

   A dollar sign is typically added only to the first row in a column of numbers and to the *Totals* row, if there is one.

15. **Save** 💾 the document.

■ **You have completed Skill 8 of 10**

▶ You can format text in tables in the same manner you format text in a document.

▶ Text and numbers can also be aligned in columns.

1. Position the pointer in the left margin to the left of the first row of the new table to display the 🔏 pointer, and then click one time to select the row.

2. Click the **Design tab**. In the **Table Styles group**, click the **Shading button arrow** 🖳▾, and then in the first row, click the seventh color—**Olive Green, Accent 3**.

3. Click the **Home tab**, and then click the **Font Dialog Box Launcher** 🔲.

4. In the **Font** dialog box, under **Font style**, click **Bold**. Under **Size**, scroll down, and then click **14**. Click the **Font color arrow**, and then under **Theme Colors**, click the first color in the first row—**White, Background 1**. Compare your screen with **Figure 1**.

5. Click **OK** to close the Font dialog box. Position your pointer in the left margin area next to the second row of the table to display the 🔏 pointer, and then click one time to select the row.

6. On the **Home tab**, in the **Font group**, click the **Bold** button 🅱. In the **Paragraph group**, click the **Center** button 🔳.

7. In the **Font group**, click the **Font Color button arrow** 🅰▾, and then in the first row, click the seventh color—**Olive Green, Accent 3**. Click anywhere in the document to deselect the row, and then compare your screen with **Figure 2**.

■ **Continue to the next page to complete the skill**

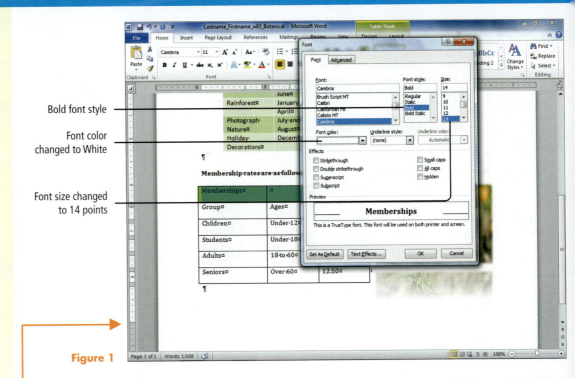

Bold font style

Font color changed to White

Font size changed to 14 points

Figure 1

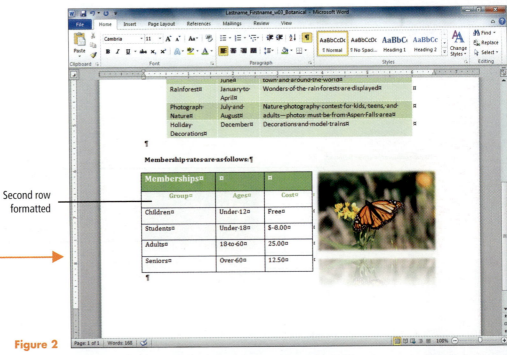

Second row formatted

Figure 2

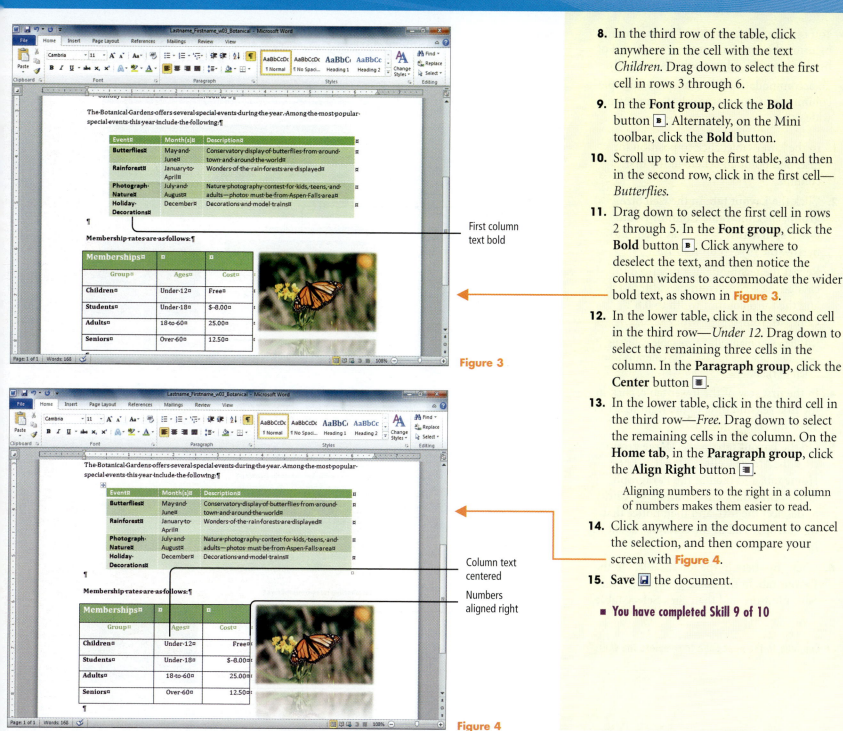

First column text bold

Figure 3

Column text centered

Numbers aligned right

Figure 4

8. In the third row of the table, click anywhere in the cell with the text *Children*. Drag down to select the first cell in rows 3 through 6.

9. In the **Font group**, click the **Bold** button **B**. Alternately, on the Mini toolbar, click the **Bold** button.

10. Scroll up to view the first table, and then in the second row, click in the first cell—*Butterflies*.

11. Drag down to select the first cell in rows 2 through 5. In the **Font group**, click the **Bold** button **B**. Click anywhere to deselect the text, and then notice the column widens to accommodate the wider bold text, as shown in **Figure 3**.

12. In the lower table, click in the second cell in the third row—*Under 12*. Drag down to select the remaining three cells in the column. In the **Paragraph group**, click the **Center** button ▤.

13. In the lower table, click in the third cell in the third row—*Free*. Drag down to select the remaining cells in the column. On the **Home tab**, in the **Paragraph group**, click the **Align Right** button ▤.

    Aligning numbers to the right in a column of numbers makes them easier to read.

14. Click anywhere in the document to cancel the selection, and then compare your screen with **Figure 4**.

15. **Save** 🖫 the document.

■ **You have completed Skill 9 of 10**

▶ You can change the width of table columns by using the AutoFit Contents command or by changing the column widths manually.

▶ To accommodate a title that spans multiple columns, you can merge cells to create one wide cell.

1. In the lower table, click to position the insertion point anywhere in the first column.

2. Click the **Layout tab**. In the **Cell Size group**, click the **Table Column Width down spin arrow** as needed to narrow the first column to **1.5"**.

3. Repeat the technique just practiced to change the second column width to **1.1"** and the third column width to **0.8"**. Compare your screen with **Figure 1**.

   When you manually resize table columns, it is good practice to resize the columns from left to right.

4. In the first row of the lower table, click in the first cell and drag to the right to select all of the cells in the row.

5. On the **Layout tab**, in the **Merge group**, click the **Merge Cells** button. Click the **Home tab**, and then in the **Paragraph group**, click the **Center** button. Click to deselect the text, and then notice that the text spans all of the columns, as shown in **Figure 2**.

6. Click anywhere in the lower table. On the **Layout tab**, in the **Table group**, click the **Select** button, and then click **Select Table**.

■ **Continue to the next page to complete the skill**

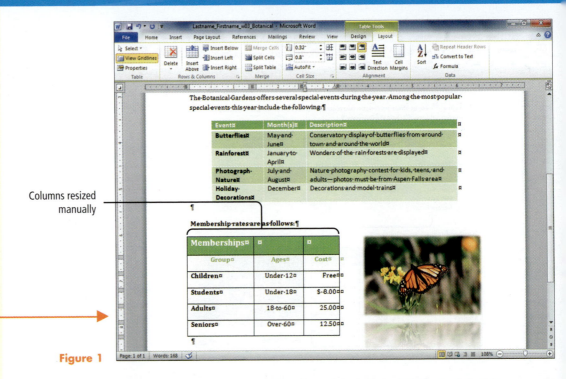

Columns resized manually

Figure 1

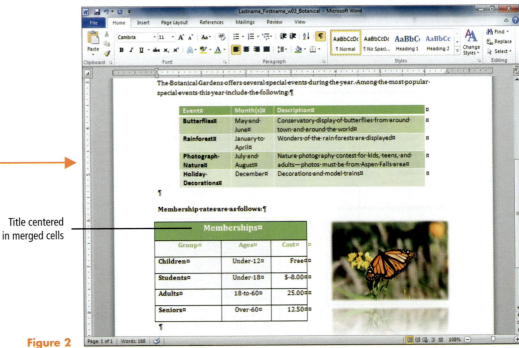

Title centered in merged cells

Figure 2

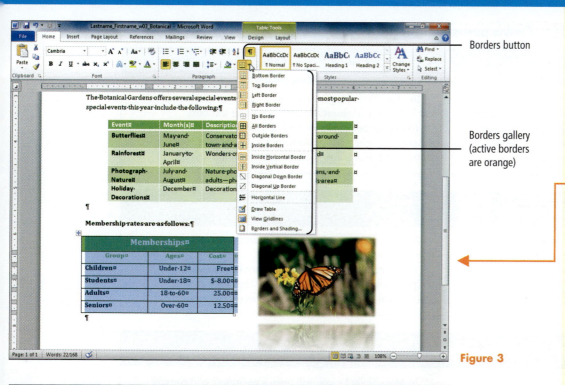

Borders button

Borders gallery
(active borders
are orange)

Figure 3

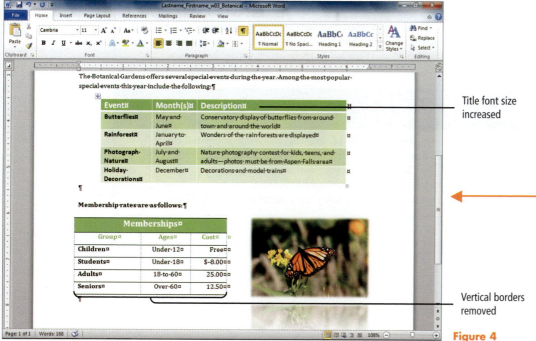

Title font size
increased

Vertical borders
removed

Figure 4

7. With the lower table still selected, on the **Page Layout tab**, in the **Paragraph group**, click the **Spacing After down spin arrow** one time to reduce the spacing after to **6 pt.**

8. On the **Home tab**, in the **Paragraph group**, click the **Borders button arrow**, and then examine the **Borders** gallery. Notice that the borders that are active display in orange, as shown in **Figure 3**.

9. In the **Borders** gallery, click **Left Border**, and notice that the left border is removed from the selected cells.

10. Repeat the same technique to remove the **Right Border** and the **Inside Vertical Border**. Click anywhere in the document to deselect the text.

    Your program may be set to display light, nonprinting grid lines where borders have been removed.

11. In the upper table, select the first row. On the **Home tab**, in the **Font group**, click the **Font Size arrow** [11 ▾], and then click **14**.

    Consistent formatting helps documents look professional. Here, the font size for the two table titles now matches.

12. Click anywhere in the document to deselect the row, and then compare your screen with **Figure 4**.

13. Add the file name to the footer. **Save** 💾 the document. Print or submit the file as directed by your instructor. **Exit** Word.

Done! You have completed Skill 10 of 10 and your document is complete!

More Skills

The following More Skills are located at **www.pearsonhighered.com/skills**

More Skills 11 Insert Text Boxes

Text boxes are floating objects that can be placed anywhere in a document. They are useful when you want to present text in a different orientation from other text. Text boxes function as a document within a document, and they can be resized or moved. Text in a text box wraps in the same manner it wraps in any document.

In More Skills 11, you will open a document and create a text box. You will also resize and format the text box.

To begin, open your web browser, navigate to www.pearsonhighered.com/skills, locate the name of your textbook, and then follow the instructions on the website.

More Skills 12 Format with WordArt

When you create a flyer or a newsletter, you might want to use a distinctive and decorative title. Word provides a feature called WordArt that you can use to change text into a decorative title.

In More Skills 12, you will open a document and create a title that uses WordArt.

To begin, open your web browser, navigate to www.pearsonhighered.com/skills, locate the name of your textbook, and then follow the instructions on the website.

More Skills 13 Create Tables from Existing Lists

You can create a new table by using the Table button on the Insert tab. You can also use the Table button to convert a tabbed list into a table.

In More Skills 13, you will open a document and convert a tabbed list into a table. You will also format the table.

To begin, open your web browser, navigate to www.pearsonhighered.com/skills, locate the name of your textbook, and then follow the instructions on the website.

More Skills 14 Insert Drop Caps

Word provides a number of methods to format text distinctively. To give text the professional look you often see in books and magazines, you can use a large first letter to begin the first paragraph of the document.

In More Skills 14, you will open a document and create a drop cap for the first character of the first paragraph.

To begin, open your web browser, navigate to www.pearsonhighered.com/skills, locate the name of your textbook, and then follow the instructions on the website.

Key Terms

Online Help Skills

1. **Start** 🔵 Word. In the upper right corner of the Word window, click the **Help** button 🔘. In the **Help** window, click the **Maximize** 🔲 button.

2. Click in the search box, type page numbers and then click the **Search** button 🔍. In the search results, click **Add or remove headers, footers, and page numbers**.

3. Read the article's introduction, and then below **What do you want to do?**, click **Add a page number without any other information**. Compare your screen with **Figure 1**.

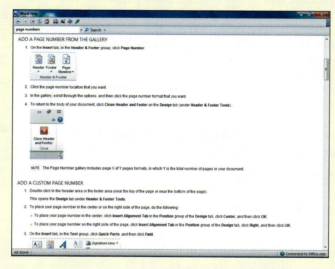

Figure 1

4. Read the section to see if you can answer the following: What is a quick way to open a header or footer? How can you show page numbers in the *Page X of Y* format—for example, *Page 3 of 12*?

Matching

Match each term in the second column with its correct definition in the first column by writing the letter of the term on the blank line in front of the correct definition.

_____ **1.** The feature used to change a picture to a floating object so that it can be moved independently of a paragraph.

_____ **2.** The type of sizing handle used to resize a picture proportionally.

_____ **3.** The formatting feature that makes a picture's edges appear to fade into the picture.

_____ **4.** A specific location in the document, marked on the Word ruler, to which you can move using Tab key.

_____ **5.** A series of characters that form a solid, dashed, or dotted line that fills the space preceding a tab stop.

_____ **6.** Information presented in rows and columns to summarize and present data effectively and efficiently.

_____ **7.** A set of predefined table formats.

_____ **8.** When you create a table using the Insert tab, the table columns will all be of this width.

_____ **9.** With the insertion point in the last cell in the table, the key used to create a new row at the bottom of the table.

_____ **10.** The command used to make the size of the table columns reflect the data in the columns.

A AutoFit Contents

B Corner

C Equal

D Leader

E Soft Edges

F Tab

G Tab Stop

H Table

I Table Styles

J Wrap Text

Multiple Choice

Choose the correct answer.

1. When you select a picture, use these to change the picture height or width.
   A. Arrow keys
   B. Sizing handles
   C. PgUp or PgDn

2. The symbol that indicates which paragraph a picture is associated with.
   A. Anchor
   B. Paragraph mark
   C. Em dash

3. To move a selected picture small distances using an arrow key.
   A. Drag
   B. Bump
   C. Nudge

4. A series of evenly spaced dots that precede a tab.
   A. Ellipsis
   B. Tab stop position
   C. Dot leader

5. When you make a change to a tab stop in the Tabs dialog box, click this button to apply the changes.
   A. Set
   B. Clear
   C. Apply

6. The intersection of a row and column in a table.
   A. Banded row
   B. Cell
   C. Banded column

7. The command used to change a picture to make it look more like a drawing or a painting.
   A. Artistic Effects
   B. Picture Styles
   C. Picture Effects

8. Use this key to move from one part of a table to another.
   A. Alt
   B. Tab
   C. Ctrl

9. How many columns are in a 3x7 table?
   A. 3
   B. 7
   C. 21

10. Numbers in a table are typically aligned this way.
    A. Left
    B. Center
    C. Right

Topics for Discussion

1. Tables have largely taken the place of tabs in most documents. Can you think of any situations where you might want to use tabs instead of tables? What would you have to do to a table to make it look like a tabbed list?

2. Pictures add interest to your documents when used in moderation. What guidelines would you recommend for using pictures—or any other type of graphics—in a document?

Skill Check

To complete this document, you will need the following files:

- w03_Fitness
- w03_Fitness_Activities
- w03_Fitness_Climber

You will save your document as:

- Lastname_Firstname_w03_Fitness

1. **Start** Word. Click the **File tab**, and then click **Open**. Navigate to your student files, and open **w03_Fitness**. Click the **File tab**, click **Save As**, navigate to your **Word Chapter 3** folder, **Save** the document as Lastname_Firstname_w03_Fitness and then add the file name to the footer.

2. In the paragraph that begins *The following*, click to position the insertion point at the beginning of the paragraph. On the **Insert tab**, in the **Text group,** click the **Object button arrow**, and then click **Text from File**. Locate and insert w03_Fitness_Activities.

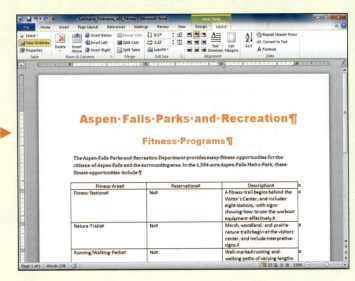

Figure 1

3. Click in the first row of the inserted table. On the **Layout tab**, in the **Rows & Columns group**, click the **Insert Above** button. Right-click the new row. On the Mini toolbar, click the **Center** button. In the first cell, type Fitness Area and press [Tab]. In the second cell, type Reservations and press [Tab]. In the third cell, type Description and then compare your screen with **Figure 1**.

4. Click the **Design tab**. In the **Table Styles group**, click the **More** button, and then under **Built-In**, in the first row, click the last style—**Light Shading - Accent 6**.

5. On the **Layout tab**, in the **Cell Size group**, click the **AutoFit** button, and then click **AutoFit Contents**.

6. In the **Table group**, click the **Properties** button. In the **Table Properties** dialog box, set the **Preferred Width** to 6", and then under **Alignment**, **Center** the table. Click **OK**, and then compare your screen with **Figure 2**. **Save** the document.

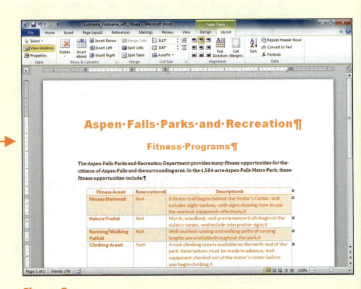

Figure 2

7. At the end of the paragraph that begins *The following*, position the insertion point after the colon, and then press [Enter] to create a blank line.

8. Click the **Insert tab**. In the **Tables group**, click the **Table** button, and then insert a **2x6** table.

> ■ **Continue to the next page to complete this Skill Check**

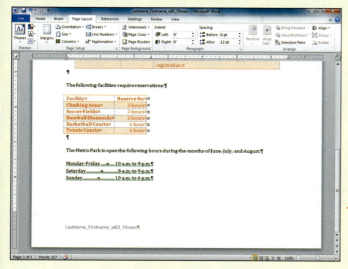

Figure 3

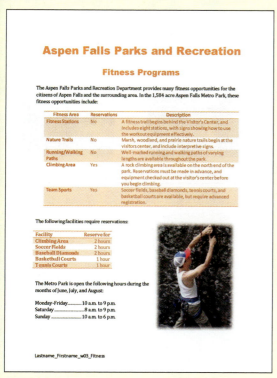

Figure 4

9. Enter the following information in the table:

Facility	Reserve for
Climbing Area	2 hours
Soccer Fields	2 hours
Baseball Diamonds	2 hours
Basketball Courts	1 hour
Tennis Courts	1 hour

10. On the **Design tab**, apply the same table style you applied to the upper table—**Light Shading - Accent 6**. On the **Layout tab**, in the **Cell Size group**, click the **AutoFit** button, and then click **AutoFit Contents**.

11. Select the five cells that contain numbers. On the **Home tab**, in the **Paragraph group**, click the **Align Right** button.

12. Press Ctrl + End to position the insertion point at the end of the document. On the left side of the horizontal ruler, click the **Tab Selector** button to display the Right Tab icon. Insert a right tab at **2.5 inches** on the horizontal ruler.

13. Double-click the tab mark. In the **Tabs** dialog box, under **Leader**, select **2**, click **Set**, and then click **OK**. Type the following tabbed list, pressing Tab before typing the text in the *second* column:

Monday-Friday	10 a.m. to 9 p.m.
Saturday	8 a.m. to 9 p.m.
Sunday	10 a.m. to 6 p.m.

14. Select the first two items in the tabbed list. On the **Page Layout tab**, in the **Paragraph group**, set the **Spacing After** to **0 pt**. Press Ctrl + End, and then compare your screen with **Figure 3**.

15. On the **Insert tab**, in the **Illustrations group**, click the **Picture** button, and then locate and **Insert** the **w03_Fitness_Climber** picture. On the **Format tab**, in the **Size group**, select the number in the **Shape Width** box, type **2.5** and then press Enter. In the **Arrange group**, apply **Square** wrapping.

16. On the **View tab**, in the **Zoom group**, click the **Two Pages** button. Drag the picture to page 1 so that the upper edge aligns at about **5.25 inches** on the vertical ruler and the right edge aligns at about **6.5 inches** on the horizontal ruler. Adjust the picture position as necessary.

17. On the **Format tab**, in the **Picture Styles group**, click the **Picture Effects** button, point to **Soft Edges**, and then click **10 point**. On the **View tab**, in the **Zoom group**, click the **100%** button.

18. Click anywhere to deselect the picture, and then compare your document with **Figure 4**. **Save** the document, and submit it as directed. **Exit** Word.

Done! You have completed the Skill Check

Assess Your Skills 1

To complete this document, you will need the following files:

- w03_Run
- w03_Run_Start
- w03_Run_Finish

You will save your document as:

- Lastname_Firstname_w03_Run

1. **Start** Word. Locate and open **w03_Run**, and then save it in your **Word Chapter 3** folder as Lastname_Firstname_w03_Run

2. Add a new third column to the table. In the first cell of the new column, type Start Time and then complete the column with the following:

10:00 a.m.	11:30 a.m.	1:00 p.m.
10:30 a.m.	12:00 p.m.	
11:00 a.m.	12:30 p.m.	

3. Click in the first row of the table, and add a new row above the first row. In the first cell of the new row, type Waves for 10K Run

4. Select the table, and then apply the **Light Shading - Accent 6** table style. Apply **AutoFit Contents** formatting. **Align Right** all of the cells in the third column. Apply **Bold** formatting to the titles in row 2.

5. **Merge** the cells in the first row of the table, and then **Center** the text. Select the table, and increase the **Font Size** to **14** points. **Center** the table.

6. Move to the end of the document, and press Enter. Type: There are several requirements for registration in Waves A through E, and these can be found on the attached registration form. Each participant will receive a T-shirt package after the race. Press Enter.

7. Insert a left tab stop at **2 inches** and a right tab stop at **4.5 inches** on the horizontal ruler. Add a dot leader to the right tab stop. Enter the following text to create a tabbed list. *Be sure to press* Tab *before the first item in each row.*

Category	Cost
Men	$40
Women	40
Children (12 & under)	20
Seniors (62 & older)	25

8. In the first row of the list, **Bold** the titles. For the first four rows in the list, change the **Spacing After** to **0 pt**.

9. Insert the **w03_Run_Start** picture, apply **Square** text wrapping, change the **Width** to **2.8"**, and then position the left edge of the picture at the left margin and the top of the picture at **7 inches** on the vertical ruler. Repeat this procedure with the **w03_Run_Finish** picture, except position the picture at the right margin.

10. Add the file name to the footer. **Save** the document, and then print or submit the file as directed by your instructor. Compare your completed document with **Figure 1**.

Done! You have completed Assess Your Skills 1

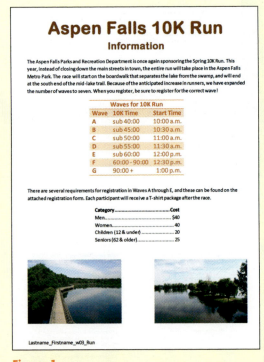

Figure 1

Assessment

Assess Your Skills 3 and 4 can be found at
www.pearsonhighered.com/skills.

Assess Your Skills 2

To complete this document, you will need the following files:

- w03_Cleanup
- w03_Cleanup_River

You will save your document as:

- Lastname_Firstname_w03_Cleanup

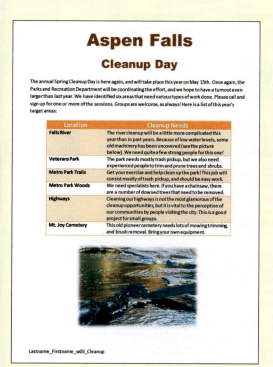

Figure 1

1. **Start** Word. Locate and open **w03_Cleanup**, and then save it in your **Word Chapter 3** folder as Lastname_Firstname_w03_Cleanup **Center** both document titles, change the **Font** to **Arial Black**, and then change the **Font Color** to the last color under Theme Colors—**Orange, Accent 6, Darker 50%**. Change the **Font Size** of the first title to **36** points and the **Font Size** of the second title to **24** points. Change the **Spacing After** the first title to **0 pt**.

2. Select the table, and then apply the last table style in the fourth row—**Medium Shading 1 - Accent 6**. Insert a new row at the bottom of the table, and in the new row, type Mt. Joy Cemetery Press ⬚Tab⬚, and then type This old pioneer cemetery needs lots of mowing, trimming, and brush removal. Bring your own equipment.

3. Set the **Width** of the first column to **1.5"**. Use the **Table Properties** dialog box to set the **Preferred Width** of the table to **5.5 inches** and to **Center** the table.

4. In the first row of the table, change the **Font Size** to **14** points, and then **Center** the table titles.

5. At the end of the document, insert the picture **w03_Cleanup_River**. Change the height of the picture to **2.5"**. Apply **Square** text wrapping, and then drag the picture so that it is centered under the table and the top edge is about 0.25 inches below the table. If you accidentally drag the picture into the table, click the Undo button and try again. If the picture moves to the second page, switch to Two Pages view.

6. With the picture still selected, apply a **Soft Edges** picture effect of **10 Points**, and then apply the second artistic effect in the fourth row—**Texturizer Artistic Effect**.

7. Add the file name to the footer. **Save** the document, and then print or submit the file as directed by your instructor. Compare your completed document with **Figure 1**.

Done! You have completed Assess Your Skills 2

Assess Your Skills Visually

To complete this document, you will need the following files:

- New blank Word document
- w03_Trails
- w03_Trails_Family
- w03_Trails_Marsh

You will save your document as:

- Lastname_Firstname_w03_Trails

Open a new Word document, and then save it in your **Word Chapter 3** folder as Lastname_Firstname_w03_Trails Create the document shown in **Figure 1**.

To complete this document, add the titles and opening paragraph. The titles are in **Arial Rounded MT Bold 24** point and **16** point, and the space between the titles is **0 pt**. Insert the table from the **w03_Trails** file, and format it as shown, with the **Header Row** formatting removed, the width of the first column set at **1.6"**, and the table width **6"**. The font colors are **Automatic**, and the titles are the last color in the last column under Theme Colors—**Orange, Accent 6, Darker 50%**. Add the **w03_Trails_Family** and **w03_Trails_Marsh** pictures, and then size and position the pictures as shown in **Figure 1**. The Marsh picture has the **Paint Brush** Artistic Effect applied. Add the file name to the footer, **Save** the document, and then print or submit the file as directed by your instructor.

Done! You have completed Assess Your Skills Visually

City of Aspen Falls
Self-Guided Tours

The Aspen Falls Parks and Recreation Department has created several self-guided tours that cover the history of the city and the local environment. Brochures for each of the tours are available at City Hall, all of the park offices, all local schools, and the area libraries.

Historic Houses	Take a walking tour through the historic district of Aspen Falls. Use the self-guided tour guide to learn about the history and architecture of some of our more interesting buildings.
Flower Gardens	Take a tour through the houses in the older part of town, and see some spectacular flower gardens. Because these gardens are on private property, the tours are open only on Sunday afternoons from 1 to 4 p.m.
Bird Watching	Both the nature trails in the Metro Park and the shoreline trails along the ocean offer you plenty of opportunity for birding. The best time of the day is the very early morning.
Marsh Life	A meandering boardwalk trail through the marsh area in the Metro Park gives you the opportunity to see the wide varieties of plant, animal, and insect life in the marsh.
Waterfalls and Rapids	There are actually two trails, along the Falls River and Aspen Creek, that can be walked individually or together, passing a number of small waterfalls and rapids—great for pictures!
Geological Formations	Take a look at the physical evidence of the strike-slip zone between the North American Plate and the Pacific Plate. Interpretive signs are placed at interesting locations along this shoreline trail.

Lastname_Firstname_w03_Trails

Figure 1

Skills in Context

To complete this document, you will need the following files:

- New blank Word document
- w03_Events
- w03_Events_Bird

You will save your document as:

- Lastname_Firstname_w03_Events

Each month, the City of Aspen Falls Parks and Recreation Department hosts events throughout the city. Using the information in the file **w03_Events**, create a flyer that describes and lists the events that will be held during the month of May. Begin with a title and a subtitle, followed by a short descriptive paragraph about the events. Then create the table of events that are going to take place during the specified month. You will need to determine the appropriate number of columns. In the table, include column headings; at the top of the table, include a table title that spans all of the columns. Use an appropriate table style

to make the table attractive. Locate and insert a picture or a clip art image that is related to one of the events in some way; you can use the included w03_Events_Bird picture if you want. Format the picture using appropriate picture styles.

Save the document as Lastname_Firstname_w03_Events Insert the file name in the footer, and be sure to check the entire document for grammar and spelling. Print or submit the file as directed by your instructor.

Done! You have completed Skills in Context

Skills and You

To complete this project, you will need the following file:

- New blank Word document

You will save your document as:

- Lastname_Firstname_w03_Resume

Using the skills you have practiced in this chapter, create a resume using a table for the structure. To find information on what to include in a resume, find a book in your library or search for *resume* on the web. To complete your resume, you will need to hide most, if not all, of the table borders. (Hint: In this chapter, you merged cells across a row. In the resume, you will probably want to merge cells in a column several times.)

Save the document as Lastname_Firstname_w03_Resume Check the entire document for grammar and spelling. Add the file name to the footer. Print or submit electronically as directed by your instructor.

Done! You have completed Skills and You

CHAPTER 4

Apply Special Text, Paragraph, and Document Formats

- ▶ Text used in a flyer is commonly displayed in two or three columns.
- ▶ Clip art is included with Microsoft Office and is treated in much the same way as pictures are.
- ▶ You can use the mail merge feature in Word to create mailing labels to distribute flyers or brochures.

Your starting screen will look like this:

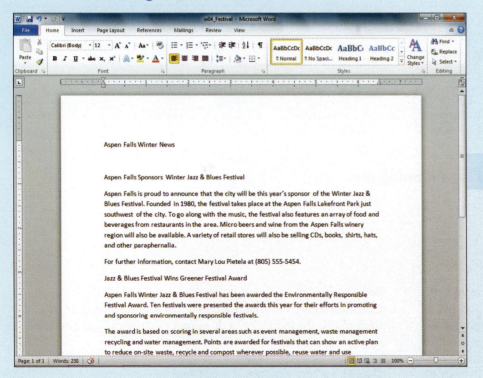

SKILLS
Skills 1–10 Training

At the end of this chapter, you will be able to:

Skill 1 Create Multiple-Column Text
Skill 2 Insert a Column Break
Skill 3 Apply and Format Text Effects
Skill 4 Use and Create Quick Styles
Skill 5 Add Borders and Shading to Paragraphs and Pages
Skill 6 Insert and Format Clip Art Graphics
Skill 7 Insert SmartArt Graphics
Skill 8 Format SmartArt Graphics
Skill 9 Create Labels Using Mail Merge
Skill 10 Preview and Print Mail Merge Documents

MORE SKILLS

More Skills 11 Create Resumes from Templates
More Skills 12 Create Outlines
More Skills 13 Prepare Documents for Distribution
More Skills 14 Preview and Save Documents as Web Pages

Outcome

Using the skills listed to the left will enable you to create documents like this:

First Name	Last Name	Address 1	Address 2	City	State	Zip	Phone
Leslie	Spurgeon	1187 Ripple Street		Aspen Falls	CA	93463	(805) 555-0194
Carrol	Bruno	161 Bel Meadow Drive		Aspen Falls	CA	93464	(805) 555-4909
Irma	Knowles	173 New Street		Aspen Falls	CA	93464	(805) 555-1821
Mark	Cole	803 Jett Lane	#320	Aspen Falls	CA	93464	(805) 555-7209
		703 Willison Street	#8	Aspen Falls	CA	93464	(805) 555-0277
		358 Maryland Avenue		Aspen Falls	CA	93463	(805) 555-8182
		892 Lightning Point Drive		Aspen Falls	CA	93463	(805) 555-6360
		646 School House Road	#352	Aspen Falls	CA	93463	(805) 555-6201
		626 Desert Broom Court	#320	Aspen Falls	CA	93464	(805) 555-2625
		936 Losh Lane	#1550	Aspen Falls	CA	93464	(805) 555-2713
		40 Turkey Pen Lane		Aspen Falls	CA	93463	(805) 555-2737
		808 Oakridge Farm Lane		Aspen Falls	CA	93464	(805) 555-3419
		311 Gore Street		Aspen Falls	CA	93464	(805) 555-7152
		934 Davisson Street		Aspen Falls	CA	93463	(805) 555-4049
		078 Raccoon Run		Aspen Falls	CA	93463	(805) 555-6926
		333 Conference Center Way		Aspen Falls	CA	93464	(805) 555-6645
		36 Saint Clair Street	#D	Aspen Falls	CA	93464	(805) 555-2835
		442 Ingram Road	#G	Aspen Falls	CA	93463	(805) 555-6814
		571 Lucy Lane		Aspen Falls	CA	93463	(805) 555-5391
		514 Public Works Drive	#1442	Aspen Falls	CA	93464	(805) 555-8206
		772 Patterson Road		Aspen Falls	CA	93464	(805) 555-7333
		1 Green Acres Road		Aspen Falls	CA	93463	(805) 555-4261
		401 Buena Vista Avenue	#D	Aspen Falls	CA	93464	(805) 555-0185
		98 Spring Street		Aspen Falls	CA	93464	(805) 555-4550
		894 Bullpen Road		Aspen Falls	CA	93464	(805) 555-1853

Aspen Falls Winter News

ASPEN FALLS SPONSORS WINTER JAZZ & BLUES FESTIVAL

Aspen Falls is proud to announce that the city will be this year's sponsor of the Winter Jazz & Blues Festival. Founded in 1980, the festival takes place at the Aspen Falls Lakefront Park just southwest of the city. To go along with the music, the festival also features an array of food and beverages from restaurants in the area. Micro beers and wine from the Aspen Falls winery region will also be available. A variety of retail stores will also be selling CDs, books, shirts, hats, and other paraphernalia.

The award is based on scoring in several areas such as event management, waste management recycling and water management. Points are awarded for festivals that can show an active plan to reduce on-site waste, recycle and compost wherever possible, reuse water and use sustainable power.

Some of the Jazz & Blues Festival efforts include the promotion of Refuse, Reuse, Reduce, Recycle, only allow recyclable materials within the festival site, observing the 'leave no trace' program and using parking income to help protect the nearby wetlands.

For further information, contact Mary Lou Pietela at (805) 555-5454.

JAZZ & BLUES FESTIVAL WINS GREENER FESTIVAL AWARD

Aspen Falls Winter Jazz & Blues Festival has been awarded the Environmentally Responsible Festival Award. Ten festivals were presented the awards this year for their efforts in promoting and sponsoring environmentally responsible festivals.

Refuse

Reuse

Reduce

Recycle

Lastname_Firstname_w04_Festival

Kristin Arnold
740 Turkey Pen Lane
Aspen Falls, CA 93463

Robert Bingham
536 Saint Clair Street
#D
Aspen Falls, CA 93464

Dessie Broadnay
4808 Oakridge Farm Lane
Aspen Falls, CA 93464

Bruno
Meadow Drive
ls, CA 93464

Mark Cole
803 Jett Lane
#320
Aspen Falls, CA 93464

Bryan Crum
1078 Raccoon Run
Aspen Falls, CA 93463

ugley
lic Works Drive
ls, CA 93463

Abraham Garza
1626 Desert Broom Court
#320
Aspen Falls, CA 93464

Michael Hammonds
1936 Losh Lane
#1550
Aspen Falls, CA 93464

Howard
Acres Road
ls, CA 93463

Marsha Keelin
2934 Davisson Street
Aspen Falls, CA 93463

Irma Knowles
173 New Street
Aspen Falls, CA 93464

McArthur
pen Road
ls, CA 93464

Willie Mench
4442 Ingram Road
#G
Aspen Falls, CA 93463

Tracy Michael
4311 Gore Street
Aspen Falls, CA 93464

kirk
ool House Road
ls, CA 93463

Margaret Peavey
4571 Lucy Lane
Aspen Falls, CA 93463

Ilda Pinto
198 Spring Street
Aspen Falls, CA 93464

mirez
htning Point Drive
ls, CA 93463

Cassie Simpson
1333 Conference Center Way
Aspen Falls, CA 93464

Leslie Spurgeon
1187 Ripple Street
Aspen Falls, CA 93463

Stevenson
ryland Avenue
ls, CA 93463

William Tapper
1703 Willison Street
#8
Aspen Falls, CA 93464

James Tomlinson
1772 Patterson Road
Aspen Falls, CA 93464

Vincent
ena Vista Avenue

ls, CA 93464

Firstname_w04_Festival_Merged

stival_Addresses

You will save your files as:

Lastname_Firstname_w04_Festival
Lastname_Firstname_w04_Festival_Addresses
Lastname_Firstname_w04_Festival_Labels
Lastname_Firstname_w04_Festival_Merged

In this chapter, you will create documents for the Aspen Falls City Hall, which provides essential services for the citizens and visitors of Aspen Falls, California.

Introduction

▶ You can convert text from one column to two or three columns, which in a newsletter or flyer is often easier to read.

▶ Clip art and SmartArt graphics display information visually and can add a professional look to a document.

▶ To draw attention to a small amount of text, you can add a border and shading to the paragraph.

▶ You can take an existing list of names and addresses from any Office application and use the mail merge feature in Word to create mailing labels.

Time to complete all
10 skills – 60 minutes

Find your student data files here:

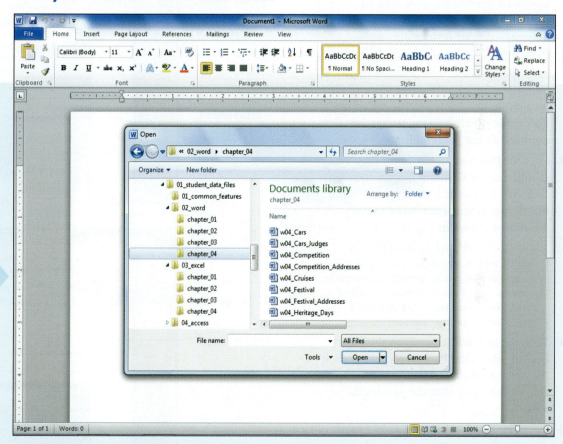

Student data files needed for this chapter:

- New blank Word document
- w04_Festival
- w04_Festival_Addresses

► In a brochure or flyer, using multiple columns make text easier to read.

► Two or three columns are typically used on a standard 8 1/2" x 11" page.

1. **Start** 🟦 Word. Open **w04_Festival**, create a folder named Word Chapter 4 and then **Save** the document as Lastname_Firstname_w04_Festival Add the file name to the footer. If necessary, display formatting marks.

2. Locate the paragraph that begins *Aspen Falls Sponsors*, and then position the 🔼 pointer to the left of the first word in the paragraph. Drag down to the end of the document—including the paragraph mark in the last paragraph.

3. Click the **Page Layout tab**. In the **Page Setup group**, click the **Columns** button, and then click **Two**. If necessary, scroll up, and notice that the text is formatted in two uneven columns, as shown in **Figure 1**.

   A section break displays above the two-column text. A *section* is a portion of a document that can be formatted differently from the rest of the document. A *section break* marks the end of one section and the beginning of another section.

4. With the text still selected, on the **Page Layout tab**, in the **Paragraph group**, click the **After down spin arrow** one time to change the space after the paragraphs to **6 pt.**

5. Click the **Home tab**. In the **Font group**, click the **Font arrow** Calibri (Body), and then scroll down and select **Comic Sans MS**. Click the **Font Size arrow** 11, and then click **11**. Compare your screen with **Figure 2**.

■ **Continue to the next page to complete the skill**

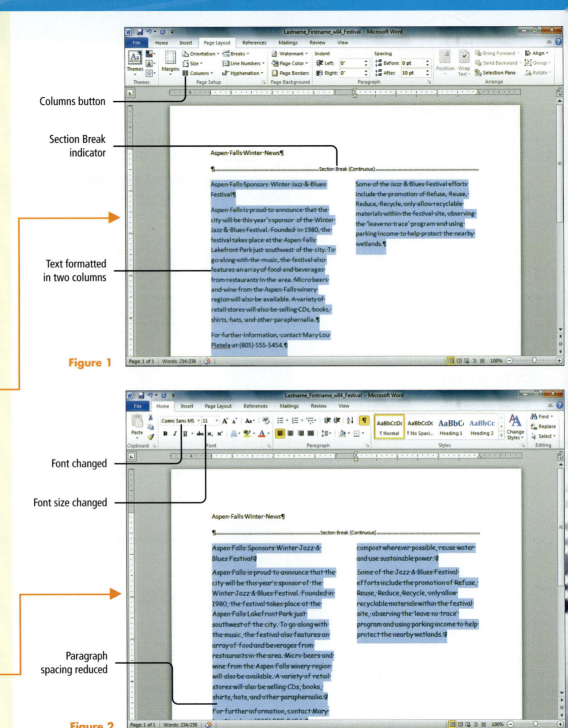

Columns button

Section Break indicator

Text formatted in two columns

Figure 1

Font changed

Font size changed

Paragraph spacing reduced

Figure 2

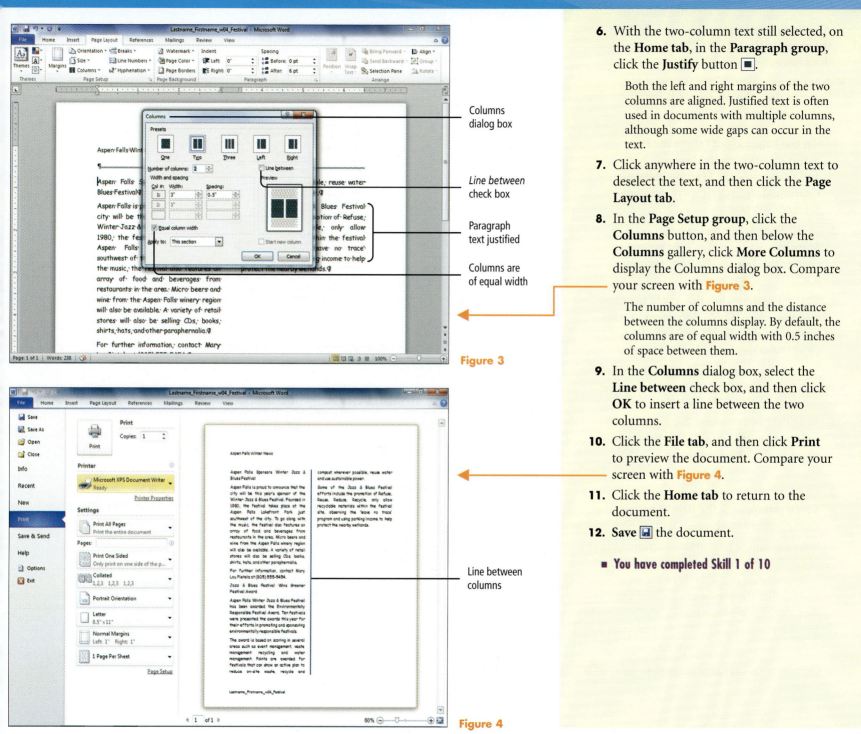

Figure 3

Figure 4

Columns dialog box

Line between check box

Paragraph text justified

Columns are of equal width

Line between columns

6. With the two-column text still selected, on the **Home tab**, in the **Paragraph group**, click the **Justify** button ▣.

> Both the left and right margins of the two columns are aligned. Justified text is often used in documents with multiple columns, although some wide gaps can occur in the text.

7. Click anywhere in the two-column text to deselect the text, and then click the **Page Layout tab**.

8. In the **Page Setup group**, click the **Columns** button, and then below the **Columns** gallery, click **More Columns** to display the Columns dialog box. Compare your screen with **Figure 3**.

> The number of columns and the distance between the columns display. By default, the columns are of equal width with 0.5 inches of space between them.

9. In the **Columns** dialog box, select the **Line between** check box, and then click **OK** to insert a line between the two columns.

10. Click the **File tab**, and then click **Print** to preview the document. Compare your screen with **Figure 4**.

11. Click the **Home tab** to return to the document.

12. Save 🖫 the document.

■ **You have completed Skill 1 of 10**

► A *column break* forces the text following the break to the top of the next column but does not automatically create a new page.

► You can increase or decrease the space between the columns to adjust the document layout.

1. On the **Page Layout tab**, in the **Page Setup group**, click the **Margins** button, and then below the **Margins** gallery, click **Custom Margins** to display the Page Setup dialog box.

2. In the **Page Setup** dialog box, under **Margins**, use the **down spin arrows** to change the **Top** and **Bottom** margins to **0.8"**.

3. Under **Preview**, click the **Apply to arrow**, and then click **Whole document**. At the bottom of the dialog box, click **OK** to close the dialog box.

   If the document has multiple sections, by default actions from the Page Setup dialog box apply only to the current section.

4. Near the bottom of the document, in the left column, click to position the insertion point to the left of the paragraph that begins *The award is based*.

5. On the **Page Layout tab**, in the **Page Setup group**, click the **Breaks** button, and then compare your screen with **Figure 1**.

6. Take a moment to examine common types of breaks displayed in the Breaks gallery and described in the table in **Figure 2**. Notice that the breaks are divided into two categories—Page Breaks and Section Breaks.

■ **Continue to the next page to complete the skill**

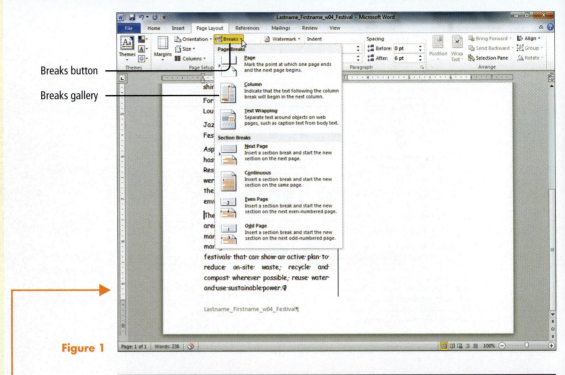

Breaks button

Breaks gallery

Figure 1

Common Types of Breaks	
Type	**Description**
Page break	Moves the text following the break to a new page; does not create a new section.
Column break	Moves the text following the break to the top of the next column, which will create a new page only if the break is made in the right column of a page.
Next Page section break	Moves the text following the break to a new page and creates a new section.
Continuous section break	Creates a new section following the break but does not move the text to the next page.

Figure 2

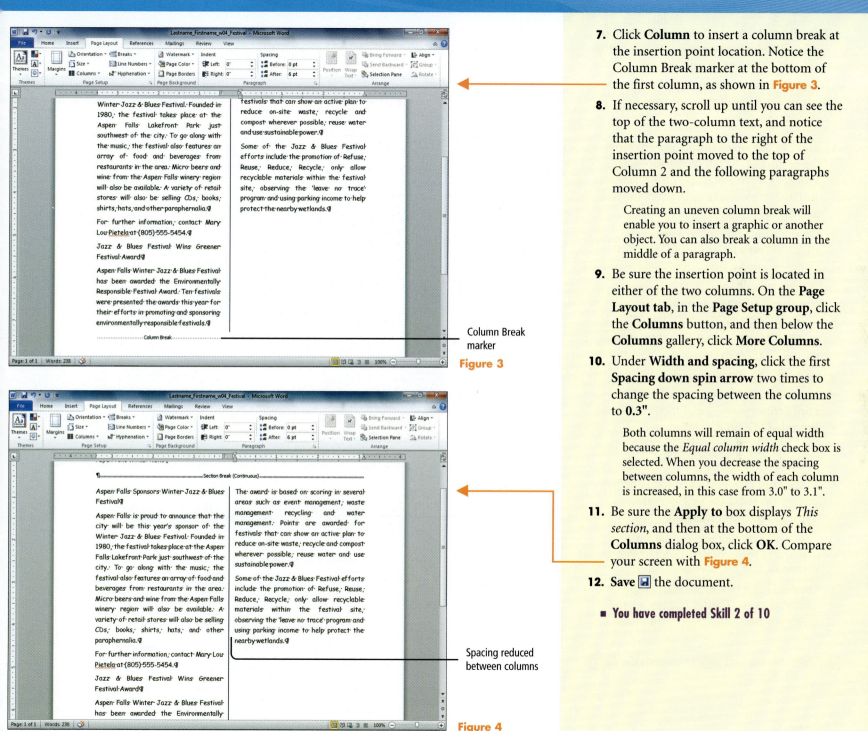

Column Break marker

Figure 3

Section Break (Continuous)

Spacing reduced between columns

Figure 4

7. Click **Column** to insert a column break at the insertion point location. Notice the Column Break marker at the bottom of the first column, as shown in **Figure 3**.

8. If necessary, scroll up until you can see the top of the two-column text, and notice that the paragraph to the right of the insertion point moved to the top of Column 2 and the following paragraphs moved down.

   Creating an uneven column break will enable you to insert a graphic or another object. You can also break a column in the middle of a paragraph.

9. Be sure the insertion point is located in either of the two columns. On the **Page Layout tab**, in the **Page Setup group**, click the **Columns** button, and then below the **Columns** gallery, click **More Columns**.

10. Under **Width and spacing**, click the first **Spacing down spin arrow** two times to change the spacing between the columns to **0.3"**.

    Both columns will remain of equal width because the *Equal column width* check box is selected. When you decrease the spacing between columns, the width of each column is increased, in this case from 3.0" to 3.1".

11. Be sure the **Apply to** box displays *This section*, and then at the bottom of the **Columns** dialog box, click **OK**. Compare your screen with **Figure 4**.

12. **Save** ☐ the document.

    ■ **You have completed Skill 2 of 10**

► **Text effects** are decorative formats, such as outlines, shadows, text glow, and colors, that make text stand out in a document.

► You should use text effects sparingly in a document, typically just for titles or subtitles.

1. Move to the top of the document. Move the pointer to the left of the *Aspen Falls Winter News* title to display the 🖈 pointer, and then click one time to select the title and the paragraph mark.

2. On the **Home tab**, in the **Font group**, click the **Text Effects** button 🄰▾. Compare your screen with **Figure 1**.

   A Text Effects gallery displays as well as several other text formatting options.

3. In the **Text Effects** gallery, in the first row, click the fourth thumbnail—**Fill - White, Outline - Accent 1**.

4. With the title text still selected, on the **Home tab**, in the **Font group**, click the **Font arrow** Calibri (Body) , and then click **Arial Rounded MT Bold**.

   The font changes, but the text effect is still applied.

5. In the **Font group**, click in the **Font Size** box 11 ▾ to select the existing value. Type 38 and then press Enter.

   By typing the font size, you are not restricted to the displayed sizes when you click the Font Size arrow.

6. On the **Home tab**, in the **Paragraph group**, click the **Center** button ▤, and then compare your screen with **Figure 2**.

■ **Continue to the next page to complete the skill** ➤

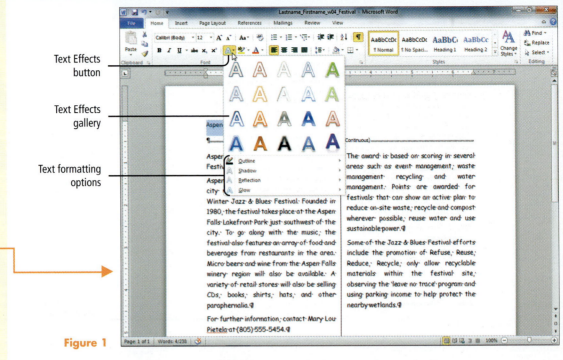

Text Effects button
Text Effects gallery
Text formatting options

Figure 1

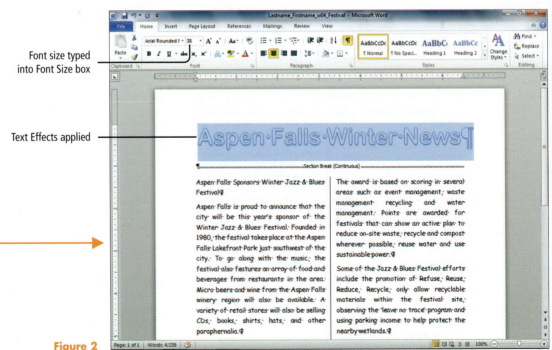

Font size typed into Font Size box

Text Effects applied

Figure 2

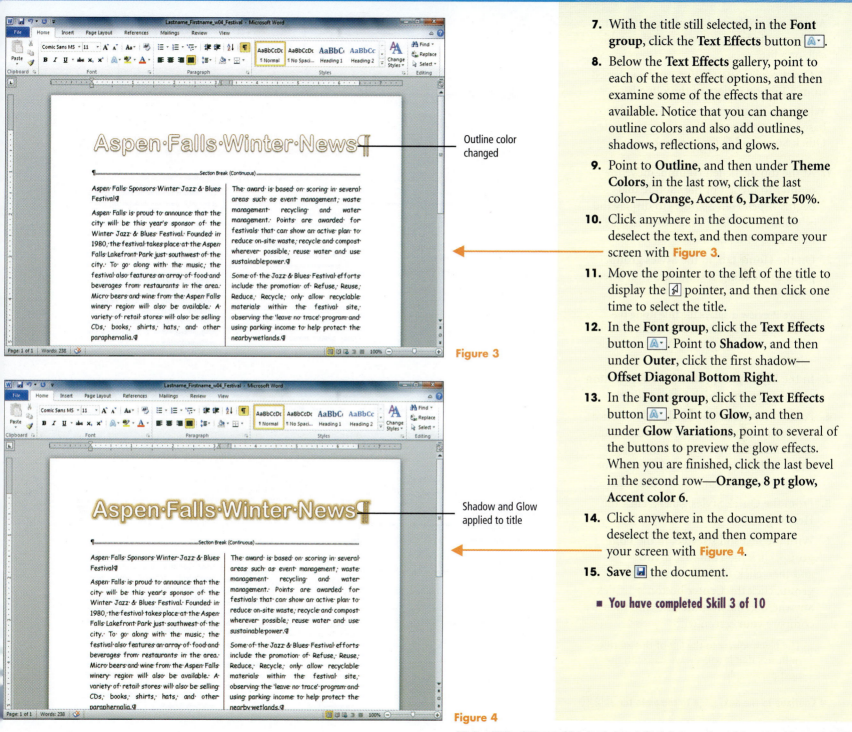

Outline color changed

Figure 3

Shadow and Glow applied to title

Figure 4

7. With the title still selected, in the **Font group**, click the **Text Effects** button.

8. Below the **Text Effects** gallery, point to each of the text effect options, and then examine some of the effects that are available. Notice that you can change outline colors and also add outlines, shadows, reflections, and glows.

9. Point to **Outline**, and then under **Theme Colors**, in the last row, click the last color—**Orange, Accent 6, Darker 50%**.

10. Click anywhere in the document to deselect the text, and then compare your screen with **Figure 3**.

11. Move the pointer to the left of the title to display the pointer, and then click one time to select the title.

12. In the **Font group**, click the **Text Effects** button. Point to **Shadow**, and then under **Outer**, click the first shadow—**Offset Diagonal Bottom Right**.

13. In the **Font group**, click the **Text Effects** button. Point to **Glow**, and then under **Glow Variations**, point to several of the buttons to preview the glow effects. When you are finished, click the last bevel in the second row—**Orange, 8 pt glow, Accent color 6**.

14. Click anywhere in the document to deselect the text, and then compare your screen with **Figure 4**.

15. **Save** the document.

■ **You have completed Skill 3 of 10**

► A *style* is a predefined set of formats that can be applied to text, a paragraph, a table cell, or a list.

► A *Quick Style* is a style that can be accessed from a Ribbon gallery of thumbnails.

► When you create your own Quick Style based on existing text formatting, the new Quick Style is added to the Ribbon.

1. At the top of the left column, move the pointer to the left of the subtitle that begins *Aspen Falls Sponsors* to display the ⬛ pointer, and then drag down to select both lines of text.

2. On the **Home tab**, in the **Styles group**, point to **Heading 1**. Compare your screen with **Figure 1**.

   Live Preview displays the title using the Heading 1 Quick Style. The Quick Style is not applied until you click the Quick Style button.

3. In the **Styles group**, click the **More** button ⬛ to display the **Quick Styles** gallery.

4. Point to several of the Quick Styles. Notice the different formats that are available, and also notice that the subtitle font changes with the different styles but the text in the rest of the document remains the same.

5. From the **Quick Styles** gallery, click the **Heading 2** style.

6. With the text still selected, in the **Font group**, click the **Font Size arrow** ⬛, and then click **16**. In the **Paragraph group**, click the **Center** button ⬛. Click anywhere to deselect the title, and then compare your screen with **Figure 2**.

   The black square to the left of the subtitle indicates that it will always stay with the next paragraph.

■ **Continue to the next page to complete the skill**

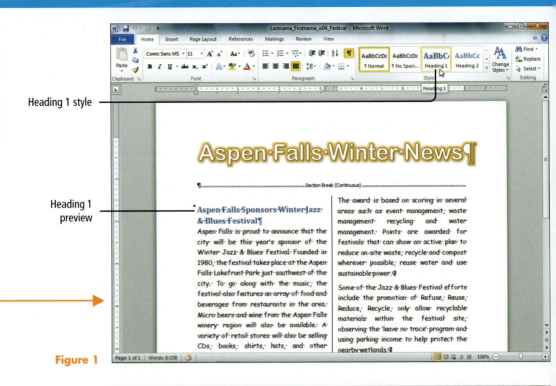

Heading 1 style

Heading 1 preview

Figure 1

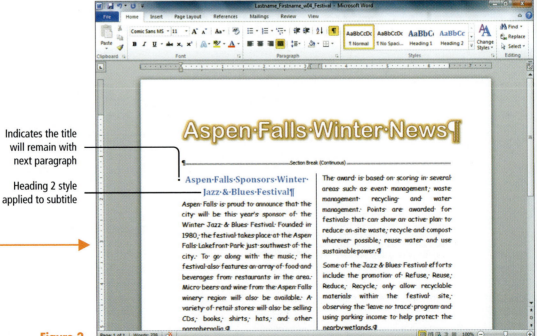

Indicates the title will remain with next paragraph

Heading 2 style applied to subtitle

Figure 2

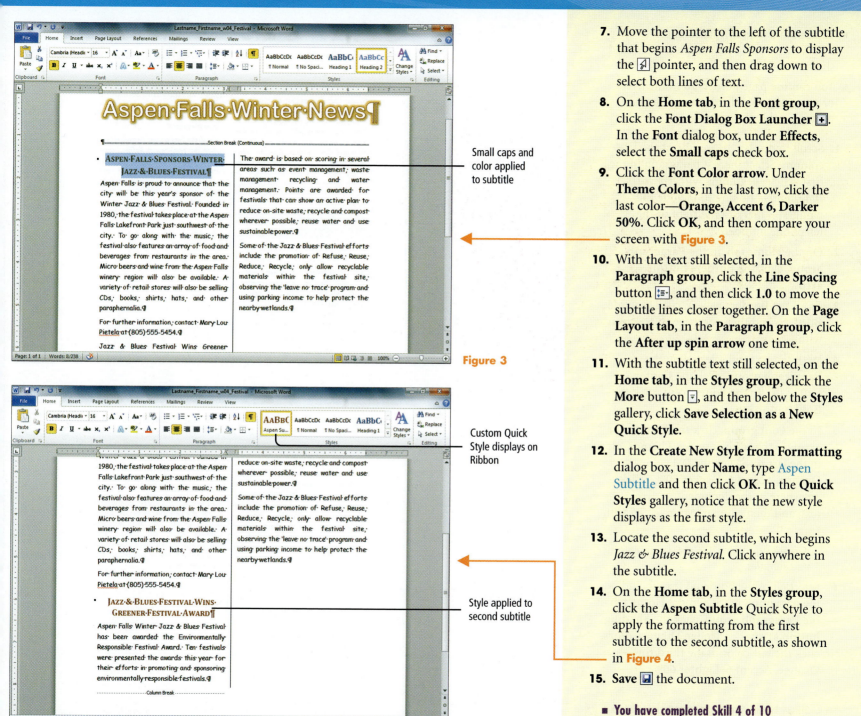

Small caps and color applied to subtitle

Figure 3

Custom Quick Style displays on Ribbon

Style applied to second subtitle

Figure 4

7. Move the pointer to the left of the subtitle that begins *Aspen Falls Sponsors* to display the 🔧 pointer, and then drag down to select both lines of text.

8. On the **Home tab**, in the **Font group**, click the **Font Dialog Box Launcher** ➕. In the **Font** dialog box, under **Effects**, select the **Small caps** check box.

9. Click the **Font Color arrow**. Under **Theme Colors**, in the last row, click the last color—**Orange, Accent 6, Darker 50%**. Click **OK**, and then compare your screen with **Figure 3**.

10. With the text still selected, in the **Paragraph group**, click the **Line Spacing** button 📏, and then click **1.0** to move the subtitle lines closer together. On the **Page Layout tab**, in the **Paragraph group**, click the **After up spin arrow** one time.

11. With the subtitle text still selected, on the **Home tab**, in the **Styles group**, click the **More** button ⯆, and then below the **Styles** gallery, click **Save Selection as a New Quick Style**.

12. In the **Create New Style from Formatting** dialog box, under **Name**, type Aspen Subtitle and then click **OK**. In the **Quick Styles** gallery, notice that the new style displays as the first style.

13. Locate the second subtitle, which begins *Jazz & Blues Festival*. Click anywhere in the subtitle.

14. On the **Home tab**, in the **Styles group**, click the **Aspen Subtitle** Quick Style to apply the formatting from the first subtitle to the second subtitle, as shown in **Figure 4**.

15. **Save** 💾 the document.

■ **You have completed Skill 4 of 10**

► To make a paragraph stand out in a document, add a paragraph border. Add shading and color for even more impact.

► You can use page borders to frame flyers or posters, giving the document a more professional look.

1. Scroll to display the middle of the first column. Select the last paragraph in the first article, beginning with *For further information.* Be sure to include the paragraph mark to the right of the telephone number.

2. On the **Home tab**, in the **Paragraph group**, click the **Borders button arrow** .

3. From the **Borders** gallery, click **Outside Borders**, and then compare your screen with **Figure 1.** ——

4. With the text still selected, in the **Paragraph group**, click the **Center** button . In the **Font group**, click the **Bold** button .

5. In the **Font group**, click the **Font Color arrow** , and then under **Theme Colors**, in the last row, click the last color— **Orange, Accent 6, Darker 50%.** Click anywhere in the document to deselect the text, and then compare your screen with **Figure 2.** ——

   The font color matches the document title and subtitles.

6. Select all of the bordered text, including the paragraph mark. On the **Home tab**, in the **Paragraph group**, click the **Shading button arrow** . Under **Theme Colors**, click the last color in the third row— **Orange, Accent 6, Lighter 60%.**

■ **Continue to the next page to complete the skill** ►

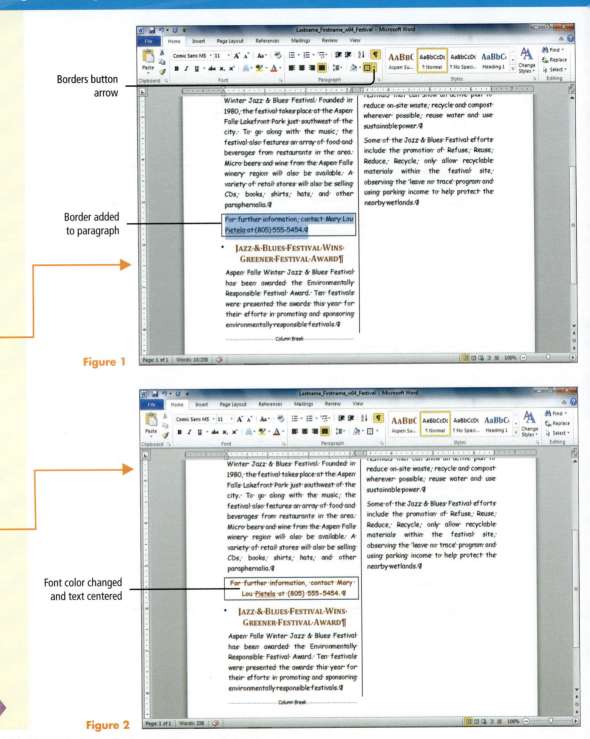

Borders button arrow

Border added to paragraph

Figure 1

Font color changed and text centered

Figure 2

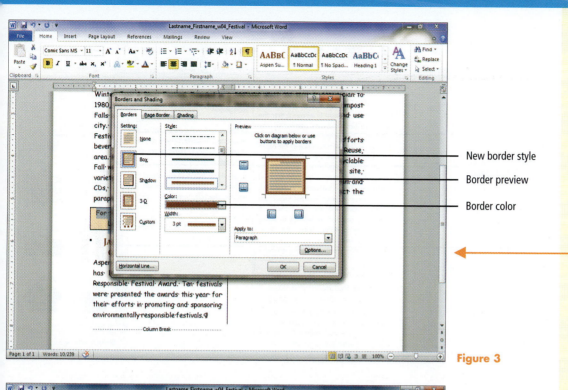

New border style

Border preview

Border color

Figure 3

Page border applied

Shading added

Border formatted

Figure 4

7. With the text still selected, in the **Paragraph group**, click the **Borders button arrow** ▦ ▾, and below the **Borders** gallery, click **Borders and Shading**.

8. In the **Borders and Shading** dialog box, be sure the **Borders tab** is active. Under **Style**, scroll down and select the first line style with a thick upper line and a thin bottom line.

9. Click the **Color arrow**, and then under **Theme Colors**, click the last color in the last row—**Orange, Accent 6, Darker 50%**. Notice that a preview of the box displays in the Preview area, as shown in **Figure 3**.

10. At the bottom of the **Borders and Shading** dialog box, click **OK**. Click anywhere in the document to deselect the text.

11. In the **Paragraph group**, click the **Borders button arrow** ▦ ▾, and then click **Borders and Shading**.

12. In the **Borders and Shading** dialog box, click the **Page Border tab**. Under **Setting**, click **Box**. Click the **Color arrow**, and then under **Theme Colors**, click the last color in the last row—**Orange, Accent 6, Darker 50%**. Click the **Width arrow**, and then click **1¹⁄₂ pt**.

13. Click **OK** to close the dialog box, and then compare your screen with **Figure 4**.

14. **Save** 💾 the document.

- **You have completed Skill 5 of 10**

▶ *Clip art* is a set of images, drawings, photographs, videos, and sound included with Microsoft Office or accessed from Microsoft Office Online.

▶ You insert clip art from the Clip Art task pane.

1. Near the top of the first column, in the paragraph that begins *Aspen Falls is proud*, click to position the insertion point at the beginning of the paragraph.

2. Click the **Insert tab**. In the **Illustrations group**, click the **Clip Art** button.

   The Clip Art task pane displays on the side of the screen.

3. In the **Clip Art** task pane, in the **Search for** box, type jazz Click the **Results should be arrow**, select the **Illustrations** check box, and then clear all of the other check boxes.

4. Click anywhere in the **Clip Art** task pane, and then be sure the **Include Office.com content** check box is selected. Near the top of the **Clip Art** task pane, click **Go**. Compare your screen with **Figure 1**.

   The position of your clip art images may vary.

5. Locate the *Jazz & Blues* image identified in **Figure 1**. Point to the image, and then click the image arrow. If you do not have access to Microsoft Office Online, choose another image and adjust it as necessary.

6. From the menu, click **Insert**, and then compare your screen with **Figure 2**. **Close** ☒ the Clip Art task pane.

   The image is placed at the insertion point as an *inline* image—as if it were a character from the keyboard.

■ Continue to the next page to complete the skill

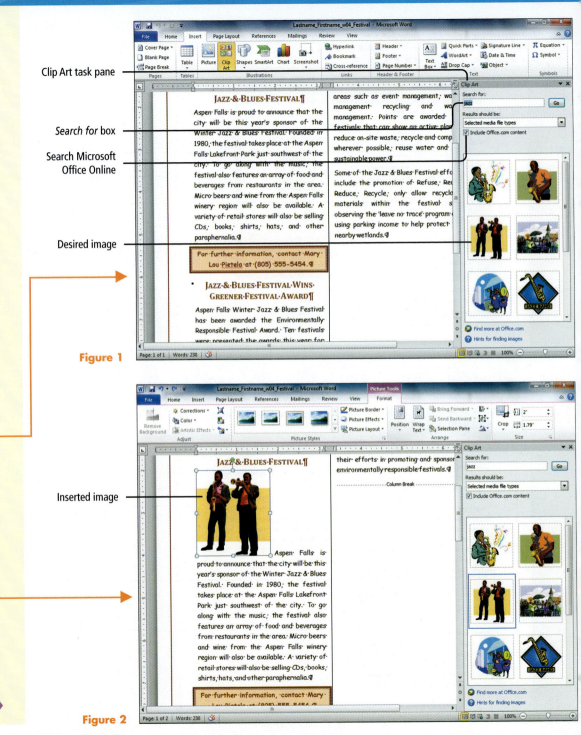

Clip Art task pane

Search for box

Search Microsoft Office Online

Desired image

Figure 1

Inserted image

Figure 2

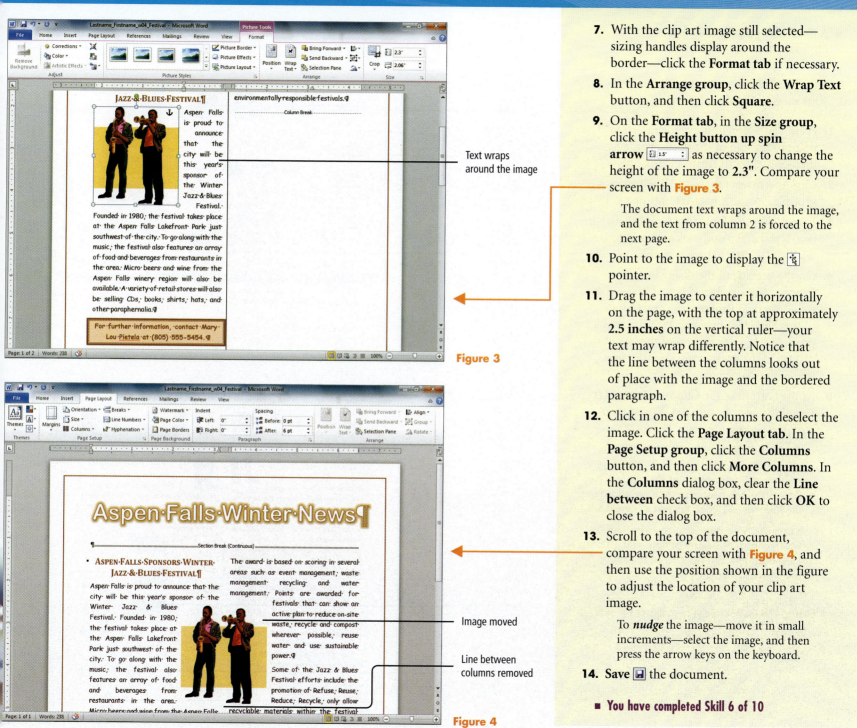

Text wraps around the image

Figure 3

Image moved

Line between columns removed

Figure 4

7. With the clip art image still selected—sizing handles display around the border—click the **Format tab** if necessary.

8. In the **Arrange group**, click the **Wrap Text** button, and then click **Square**.

9. On the **Format tab**, in the **Size group**, click the **Height button up spin arrow** as necessary to change the height of the image to **2.3"**. Compare your screen with **Figure 3**.

   The document text wraps around the image, and the text from column 2 is forced to the next page.

10. Point to the image to display the pointer.

11. Drag the image to center it horizontally on the page, with the top at approximately **2.5 inches** on the vertical ruler—your text may wrap differently. Notice that the line between the columns looks out of place with the image and the bordered paragraph.

12. Click in one of the columns to deselect the image. Click the **Page Layout tab**. In the **Page Setup group**, click the **Columns** button, and then click **More Columns**. In the **Columns** dialog box, clear the **Line between** check box, and then click **OK** to close the dialog box.

13. Scroll to the top of the document, compare your screen with **Figure 4**, and then use the position shown in the figure to adjust the location of your clip art image.

   To *nudge* the image—move it in small increments—select the image, and then press the arrow keys on the keyboard.

14. **Save** the document.

- **You have completed Skill 6 of 10**

► A *SmartArt graphic* is a visual representation of information.

► You can choose from many different SmartArt layouts to communicate your message or ideas.

1. Press [Ctrl] + [End] to move the insertion point to the end of the document, and then press [Enter] to create a blank line.

2. Click the **Insert tab**. In the **Illustrations group**, click the **SmartArt** button.

3. In the **Choose a SmartArt Graphic** dialog box, scroll down and look at the various types of layouts that are available.

4. On the left side of the dialog box, click **Process**. Click the third layout in the sixth row—**Vertical Process** (the exact location of this SmartArt may vary). Notice that a preview and a description of the layout display in the preview area on the right side of the dialog box, as shown in **Figure 1**.

5. At the bottom of the **Choose a SmartArt Graphic** dialog box, click **OK**, and then compare your screen with **Figure 2**.

The Vertical Process SmartArt graphic displays at the insertion point, with the graphic width equal to the width of the column. Two SmartArt Tools contextual tabs are added to the Ribbon—a Design tab and a Format tab.

The SmartArt outline displays sizing handles, which consist of a series of dots, and a Text Pane button, which displays on the left of the SmartArt border.

■ **Continue to the next page to complete the skill**

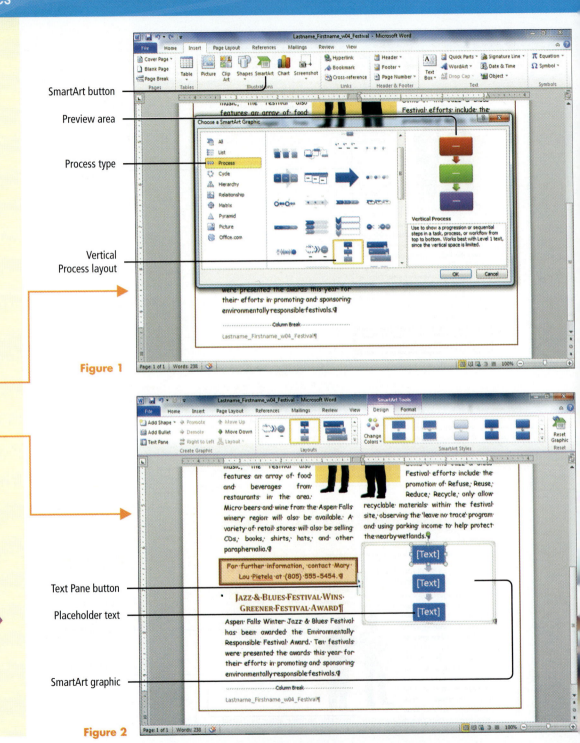

SmartArt button

Preview area

Process type

Vertical Process layout

Figure 1

Text Pane button

Placeholder text

SmartArt graphic

Figure 2

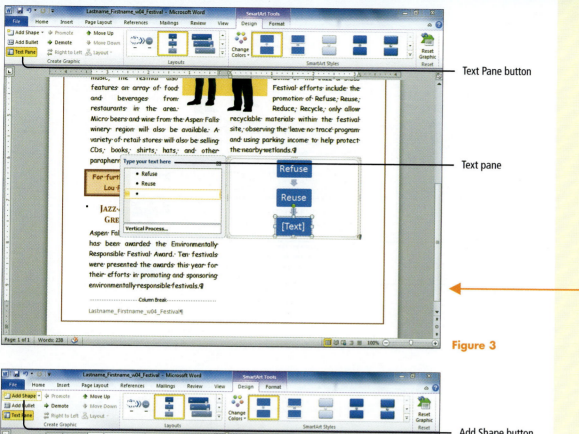

Text Pane button

Text pane

Figure 3

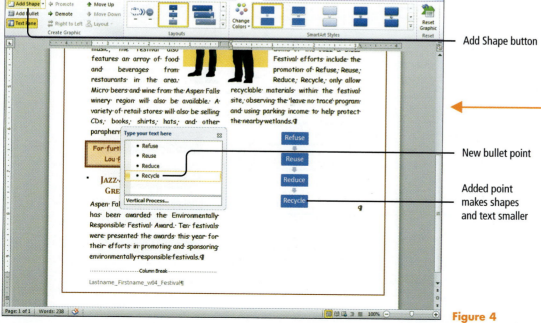

Add Shape button

New bullet point

Added point makes shapes and text smaller

Figure 4

6. Click in the top [**Text**] shape, type Refuse and then notice that the shape resizes as you type. The font size also adjusts automatically.

[*Text*] is ***placeholder text***—reserved space in shapes into which you enter your own text. If no text is entered, the placeholder text will not print.

7. In the second shape, click the [**Text**] placeholder, and then type Reuse

To move to the next [Text] shape, you must click in the shape—you cannot use Tab to move from one shape to the next.

8. On the **Design tab**, in the **Create Graphic group**, click the **Text Pane** button. Notice that the items in the shapes are displayed as a bulleted list, as shown in **Figure 3**.

9. In the **Text** pane, if necessary, click in the third [**Text**] placeholder, and then type Reduce Notice that while you type in the bulleted list, the text also displays in the third SmartArt shape.

To move to the next [Text] shape in the Text pane, you can also press ↑ or ↓.

10. On the **Design tab**, in the **Create Graphic group**, click the **Add Shape** button to display another bullet point. Type Recycle and then compare your screen with **Figure 4**. Notice that the shapes and the text in the shapes became smaller when you added an item to the list.

11. **Close** ⊠ the Text pane, and then **Save** 🖫 the document.

■ **You have completed Skill 7 of 10**

► When you change the height or width of a SmartArt graphic, the shapes and the text will automatically adjust to fit the available space.

► In a SmartArt graphic, you can also format the text, the backgrounds, and the borders of the shapes.

1. Click the border of the SmartArt graphic to select it. On the **Format tab**, click the **Size** button.

2. In the displayed list, click the **Height box up spin arrow** as necessary to increase the height of the graphic to **3"**. Compare your screen with **Figure 1**.

   When you change the height or width of a SmartArt graphic, the graphic width is not resized proportionally; however, the text font size increases to fit the new shape size.

3. Click anywhere on the border of the top shape—*Refuse*. Hold down Ctrl, and then click the other three shapes to select all four shapes in the SmartArt graphic.

4. With all four shapes selected, click the **Size** button. Click the **Width box up spin arrow** as necessary to increase the width of the graphic to **2.5"**.

5. In the **Shape Styles group**, click the **Shape Fill** button. Under **Theme Colors**, click the last color in the last row—**Orange, Accent 6, Darker 50%**.

6. In the **WordArt Styles group**, click the **Text Fill** button. Under **Theme Colors**, click the last color in the third row—**Orange, Accent 6, Lighter 60%**. Compare your screen with **Figure 2**.

■ **Continue to the next page to complete the skill** ▶

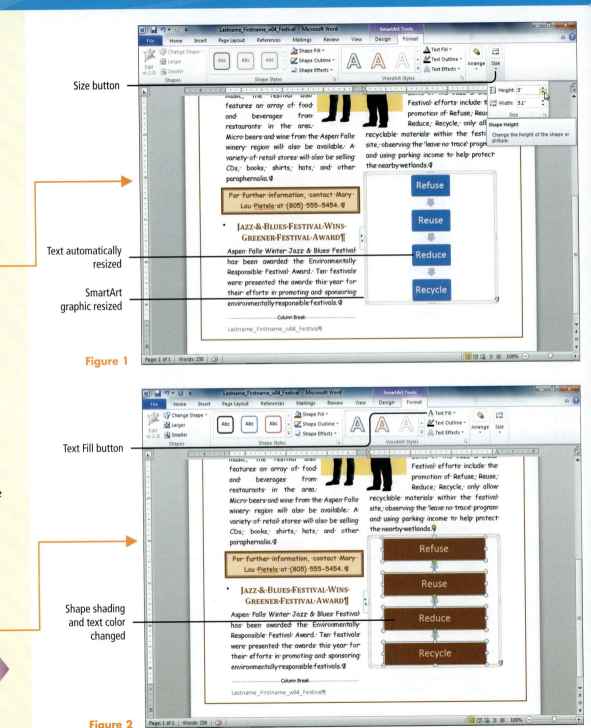

Size button

Text automatically resized

SmartArt graphic resized

Figure 1

Text Fill button

Shape shading and text color changed

Figure 2

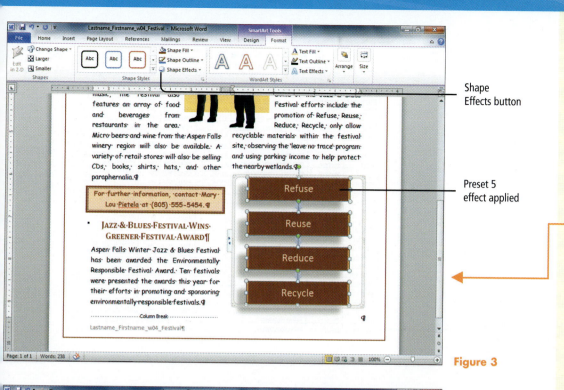

Shape Effects button

Preset 5 effect applied

Figure 3

7. With all four shapes still selected, in the **Shape Styles group**, click the **Shape Effects** button.

8. Take a moment to point to several of the categories, and then point to some of the effects and watch as Live Preview shows you what your layout would look like using each effect.

9. Point to **Preset**, and then under **Presets**, click the first effect in the second row— **Preset 5**. Compare your screen with **Figure 3**.

10. With all four shapes still selected, in the **WordArt Styles group**, click the **Text Effects** button. Point to **Reflection**, and then under **Reflection Variations**, click the first effect in the first row—**Tight Reflection, touching**.

11. Click anywhere in the text in one of the columns to deselect the SmartArt graphic.

12. On the **View tab**, in the **Zoom group**, click the **One Page** button. Compare your screen with **Figure 4**. If necessary, adjust the location of the clip art image and the size of the SmartArt graphic to match the ones in the figure.

13. In the **Zoom group**, click the **100%** button. **Save** 🔲 the document.

14. Print or submit the file as directed by your instructor, and then **Exit** Word.

■ **You have completed Skill 8 of 10**

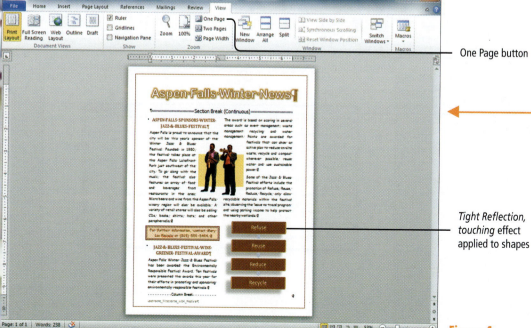

One Page button

Tight Reflection, touching effect applied to shapes

Figure 4

► The *mail merge* feature in Word is used to customize letters or labels by combining a main document with a data source.

► The *main document* contains the text that remains constant; the *data source* contains the information—such as names and addresses—that changes with each letter or label.

1. **Start** ◉ Word. Click the **File tab**, **Open** the document **w04_Festival_Addresses**, and then **Save** the document in your **Word Chapter 4** folder as Lastname_Firstname_w04_Festival_Addresses Add the file name to the footer.

2. Take a moment to examine the table of names and addresses.

   This table will be the data source for the mailing labels you will create to use with the festival flyer you created earlier in this chapter.

3. Scroll to the bottom of the table. Right-click in the bottom row of the table. From the shortcut menu, point to **Insert**, and then click **Insert Rows Below**. Enter the information for Duncan McArthur 1894 Bullpen Road Aspen Falls CA 93464 (805) 555-1853 and then compare your screen with **Figure 1**. **Save** 🖫 the document and **Exit** Word.

4. **Start** Word. **Save** the document in your **Word Chapter 4** folder as Lastname_Firstname_w04_Festival_Labels If necessary, display formatting marks.

5. Click the **Mailings tab**. In the **Start Mail Merge group**, click the **Start Mail Merge** button, and then click **Labels** to open the Label Options dialog box, as shown in **Figure 2**.

■ **Continue to the next page to complete the skill**

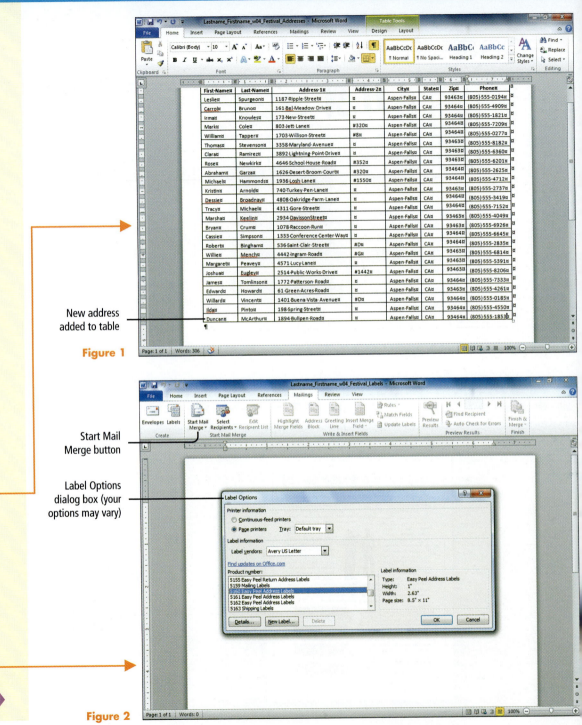

New address added to table

Figure 1

Start Mail Merge button

Label Options dialog box (your options may vary)

Figure 2

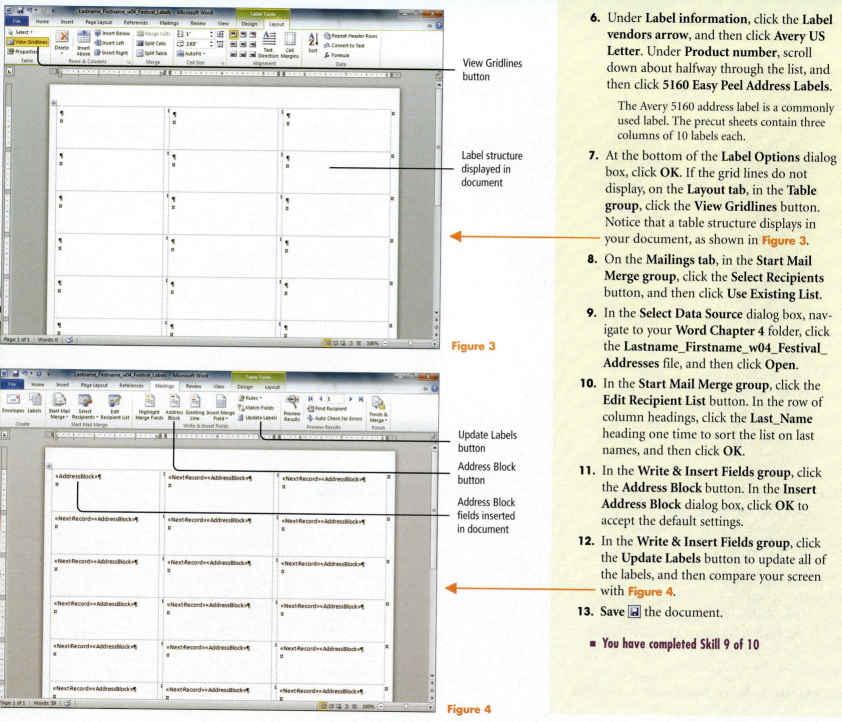

View Gridlines button

Label structure displayed in document

Figure 3

Update Labels button

Address Block button

Address Block fields inserted in document

Figure 4

6. Under **Label information**, click the **Label vendors arrow**, and then click **Avery US Letter**. Under **Product number**, scroll down about halfway through the list, and then click **5160 Easy Peel Address Labels**.

   The Avery 5160 address label is a commonly used label. The precut sheets contain three columns of 10 labels each.

7. At the bottom of the **Label Options** dialog box, click **OK**. If the grid lines do not display, on the **Layout tab**, in the **Table group**, click the **View Gridlines** button. Notice that a table structure displays in your document, as shown in **Figure 3**.

8. On the **Mailings tab**, in the **Start Mail Merge group**, click the **Select Recipients** button, and then click **Use Existing List**.

9. In the **Select Data Source** dialog box, navigate to your **Word Chapter 4** folder, click the **Lastname_Firstname_w04_Festival_ Addresses** file, and then click **Open**.

10. In the **Start Mail Merge group**, click the **Edit Recipient List** button. In the row of column headings, click the **Last_Name** heading one time to sort the list on last names, and then click **OK**.

11. In the **Write & Insert Fields group**, click the **Address Block** button. In the **Insert Address Block** dialog box, click **OK** to accept the default settings.

12. In the **Write & Insert Fields group**, click the **Update Labels** button to update all of the labels, and then compare your screen with **Figure 4**.

13. Save 💾 the document.

■ **You have completed Skill 9 of 10**

► It is good practice to preview your labels before printing them so you can see whether formatting changes are necessary.

► You can check the final results of your mail merge by printing first to plain paper instead of the more expensive preprinted label sheets.

1. On the **Mailings tab**, in the **Preview Results group**, click the **Preview Results** button. Verify that the Address Block fields display actual data. Notice that there is a large space between the lines of each label and that the bottoms of the labels that have two address lines—those with apartment numbers—are cut off, as shown in **Figure 1**.

2. In the first label, move the insertion point to the left of the first line of text, and drag down to select all three paragraphs of the address label.

3. Click the **Page Layout tab**. In the **Paragraph group**, click the **Spacing Before down spin arrow** to change the spacing before each paragraph to **0 pt**. Notice that the spacing changes only for the first label; the rest of the labels remain unchanged.

4. On the **Home tab**, in the **Font group**, click the **Font arrow** Calibri (Body), and then click **Cambria**. Click the **Font Size arrow** 11, and then click **12**. Compare your screen with **Figure 2**.

5. Scroll to the bottom of the document and click anywhere in the bottom row. On the **Layout tab**, in the **Rows & Columns group**, click the **Delete** button, and then click **Delete Rows**. Move to the top of the document.

■ **Continue to the next page to complete the skill**

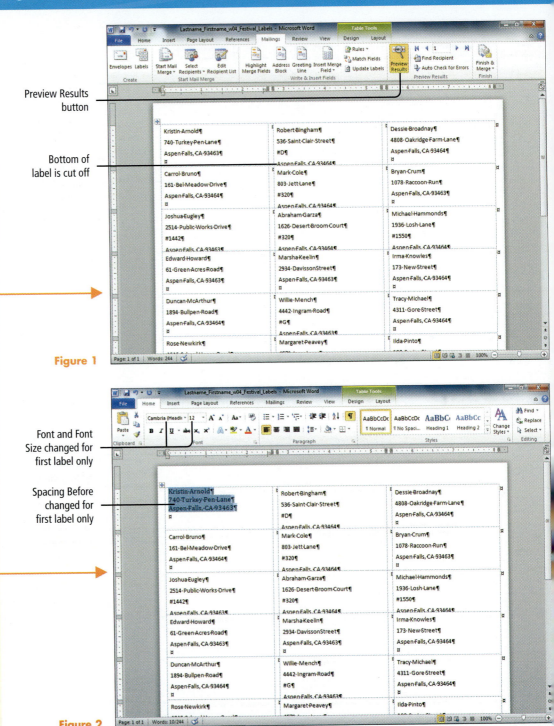

Preview Results button

Bottom of label is cut off

Figure 1

Font and Font Size changed for first label only

Spacing Before changed for first label only

Figure 2

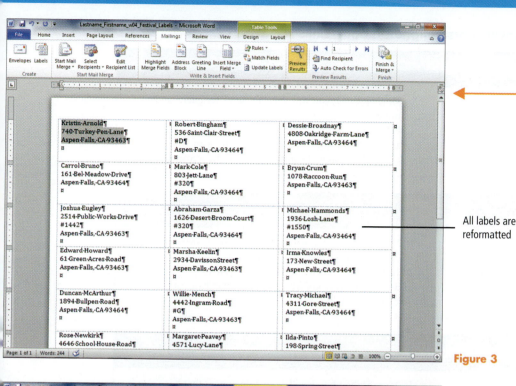

All labels are reformatted

Figure 3

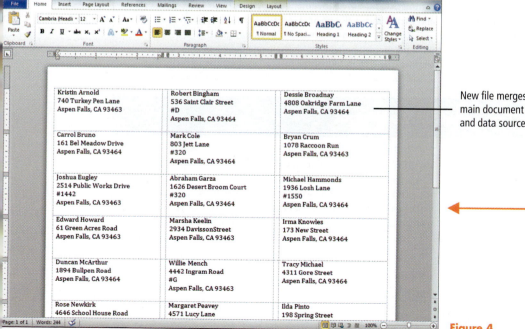

New file merges main document and data source

Figure 4

6. On the **Mailings tab**, in the **Write & Insert Fields group**, click the **Update Labels** button to apply the formatting of the original address block to all of the labels, as shown in **Figure 3**.

   To reformat labels, you can first change the *original* address block, and then update the remaining labels in this manner, or you can select all of the labels and make the changes.

7. On the **Mailings tab**, in the **Finish group**, click the **Finish & Merge** button, and then click **Edit Individual Documents**. In the **Merge to New Document** dialog box, click **OK**. Notice that a new document named *Labels1* is created.

   The *Labels1* document has merged two documents—the main document and the data source. Combining the two enables you to work in a single document.

8. Click the **Save** button 🖫, and then save the document in your **Word Chapter 4** folder as Lastname_Firstname_w04_ Festival_Merged Add the file name to the footer.

9. On the **Home tab**, in the **Paragraph group**, click the **Show/Hide** button ¶ to turn off the formatting marks. Press [Ctrl] + [Home], and then compare your screen with **Figure 4**.

10. **Save** 🖫, and then **Close** ⊠ the merged document. **Close** ⊠ **Lastname_ Firstname_w04_Festival_Labels** but do not save or submit. Print or submit the files as directed by your instructor. **Exit** Word.

Done! You have completed Skill 10 of 10 and your document is complete!

More Skills

The following More Skills are located at **www.pearsonhighered.com/skills**

More Skills Create Resumes from Templates

Templates are predesigned document structures that enable you to create a new document quickly. Word templates are available for many document types, including memos, letters, business cards, and fax cover sheets. Several different resume templates are also available.

In More Skills 11, you will open a resume template, and then complete the resume.

To begin, open your web browser, navigate to www.pearsonhighered.com/skills, locate the name of your textbook, and then follow the instructions on the website.

More Skills Create Outlines

When you work with a document, assigning outline levels to various parts of the text can be helpful. When you use outline levels, you can move blocks of text around in a document just by moving an outline item—all associated text moves with the outline item.

In More Skills 12, you will open a document, switch to Outline view, create outline levels, and move outline text.

To begin, open your web browser, navigate to www.pearsonhighered.com/skills, locate the name of your textbook, and then follow the instructions on the website.

More Skills Prepare Documents for Distribution

Before sharing a document with colleagues, it is good practice to remove any hidden data or personal information embedded in the document. Word can inspect your document and remove any features that you do not want to share.

In More Skills 13, you will open a document that has comments and other document properties, inspect the document, and then remove all personal information.

To begin, open your web browser, navigate to www.pearsonhighered.com/skills, locate the name of your textbook, and then follow the instructions on the website.

More Skills Preview and Save Documents as Web Pages

You can preview a document to see what it would look like as a web page. When you have the document formatted the way you want, you can save the document in a format that can be used on the web.

In More Skills 14, you will open a document, add a hyperlink to text in the document, preview the document as a web page, and finally save the document as a web page.

To begin, open your web browser, navigate to www.pearsonhighered.com/skills, locate the name of your textbook, and then follow the instructions on the website.

Key Terms

Online Help Skills

1. **Start** 🪟 Word. In the upper right corner of the Word window, click the **Help** button 🔘. In the **Help** window, click the **Maximize** 🔲 button.

2. Click in the search box, type mail merge and then click the **Search** button 🔍. In the search results, click **Use mail merge to create and print letters and other documents**.

3. Read the article's introduction, and then click the blue text in step. **Add placeholders**. Compare your screen with **Figure 1**.

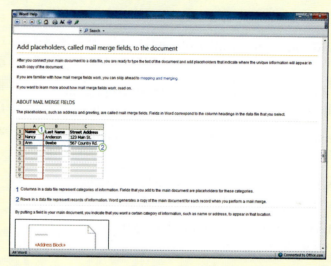

Figure 1

4. Read the section to see if you can answer the following: What fields are included in an address block? How would you add individual fields, such as a first name or last name, to a form letter?

Matching

Match each term in the second column with its correct definition in the first column by writing the letter of the term on the blank line in front of the correct definition.

____ **1.** In mail merge, the command used to modify all labels based on changes made to the original label.

____ **2.** In the Columns gallery, the command that displays the Columns dialog box.

____ **3.** A style displayed on the Ribbon.

____ **4.** A set of decorative formats that make text stand out in a document.

____ **5.** A portion of a document that can be formatted differently from the rest of the document.

____ **6.** A format that makes a paragraph stand out from the rest of the text.

____ **7.** A set of images, photographs, videos, and sound provided by Microsoft that is available on your computer or online.

____ **8.** To move an object in small increments by selecting the object, and then pressing one of the arrow keys.

____ **9.** Text that reserves space in a SmartArt shape but does not print.

____ **10.** A feature that combines a main document and a data source to create customized letters or tables.

A Border

B Clip art

C Mail merge

D More Columns

E Nudge

F Placeholder

G Quick Style

H Section

I Text effects

J Update Labels

Multiple Choice

Choose the correct answer.

1. The default width assigned to columns.
   - **A.** Proportional
   - **B.** Equal
   - **C.** Unbalanced

2. A predefined set of text formats that can be applied from the Ribbon.
   - **A.** Quick Style
   - **B.** SmartArt
   - **C.** Clip art

3. A picture is inserted into a document using this format.
   - **A.** Centered
   - **B.** Text wrapped
   - **C.** Inline

4. Moves the text to the right of the insertion point to the top of the next column.
   - **A.** Page break
   - **B.** Column break
   - **C.** Continuous break

5. A type of break that is used to create a new section that can be formatted differently from the rest of the document.
   - **A.** Page
   - **B.** Column
   - **C.** Continuous

6. To change the color of the background in a paragraph, add this to the text background.
   - **A.** Shading
   - **B.** A border
   - **C.** Text emphasis

7. Reserved spaces in shapes into which you enter your own text.
   - **A.** Text effects
   - **B.** Placeholder text
   - **C.** Data sources

8. A graphic visual representation of information.
   - **A.** Text effects
   - **B.** Clip art
   - **C.** SmartArt

9. Used by a mail merge document, this file contains information such as names and addresses.
   - **A.** Data source
   - **B.** Main document
   - **C.** Merge document

10. In a mail merge document, this document contains the text that remains constant.
    - **A.** Data source
    - **B.** Main document
    - **C.** Merge document

Topics for Discussion

1. In this chapter, you practiced inserting a clip art image in a document. When do you think clip art images are most appropriate, and in what kind of documents might clip art images be inappropriate. If you had to create a set of rules for using clip art in a document, what would the top three rules be?

2. In this chapter, you used the mail merge feature in Word to create labels and name tags. With mail merge, you can also insert one field at a time—and the fields do not have to be just names and addresses. Can you think of any situations where you might want to insert fields in a letter or another document?

Skill Check

To complete this document, you will need the following files:

- w04_Cars
- w04_Cars_Judges

You will save your documents as:

- Lastname_Firstname_w04_Cars
- Lastname_Firstname_w04_Cars_Labels

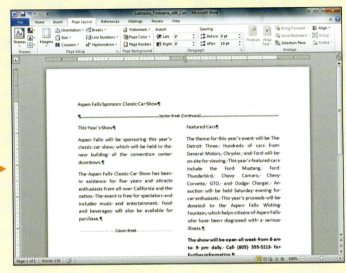

Figure 1

1. **Start** Word, and open **w04_Cars**. **Save** the document in your **Word Chapter 4** folder as Lastname_Firstname_w04_Cars Add the file name to the footer.

2. Locate the paragraph *This Year's Show*, and then select the document text from that point to the end of the document. On the **Home tab**, in the **Paragraph group**, **Justify** the text. On the **Page Layout tab**, in the **Page Setup group**, click the **Columns** button, and then click **Two**.

3. Position the insertion point at the beginning of the paragraph *Featured Cars*. On the **Page Layout tab**, in the **Page Setup group**, click the **Breaks** button, and then click **Column**. Compare your screen with **Figure 1**.

4. Select the document title. On the **Home tab**, in the **Styles group**, click the **More** button, and then click **Title**.

5. In the **Font group**, click the **Text Effects** button, and then in the fourth row of the gallery, click the first thumbnail—**Gradient Fill - Blue, Accent 1, Outline - White, Glow - Accent 2**. **Center** the title, and then change the **Font Size** to **42** pt.

6. Select the subtitle *This Year's Show*. In the **Font group**, click the **Dialog Box Launcher**. Under **Font style**, click **Bold**. Under **Size**, click **16**. Click the **Font Color arrow**, and then under **Theme Colors**, click the sixth color in the first row—**Red Accent 2**. Under **Effects**, select the **Small caps** check box, and then click **OK**. In the **Paragraph group**, click the **Center** button.

7. In the **Styles group**, click the **More** button, and then click **Save selection as a New Quick Style**. In the **Create New Style from Formatting** dialog box, under **Name**, type Cars Subtitle and then press Enter.

8. Select the second subtitle—*Featured Cars*. On the **Home tab**, in the **Styles group**, click the **Cars Subtitle** Quick Style. Compare your screen with **Figure 2**.

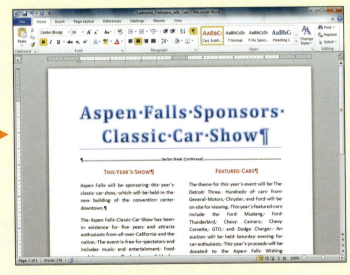

Figure 2

- Continue to the next page to complete this Skill Check

9. Click anywhere in the document. On the **Insert tab**, in the **Illustrations group**, click the **Clip Art** button.

10. In the **Clip Art** task pane, in the **Search for** box, type sports car and then click **Go**. Click the image shown in **Figure 3** (or a similar image if this one is not available). Close the **Clip Art** pane. On the **Format tab**, in the **Arrange group**, click the **Wrap Text** button, and then click **Tight**. On the **Format tab**, in the **Size group**, change the **Width** to 2.5". Move the image to the position shown in **Figure 3**.

11. Select the last paragraph in the document. In the **Paragraph group**, click the **Borders button arrow**, and then click **Outside Borders**. In the **Paragraph group**, click the **Shading button arrow**. Under **Theme Colors**, click the second color in the sixth column—**Red, Accent 2, Lighter 80%**.

12. Click anywhere in the document. On the **Insert tab**, in the **Illustrations group**, click the **SmartArt** button. Click **Process**, click the **Funnel** layout—the fourth layout in the tenth row—and then click **OK**. Click the border of the SmartArt image. On the **Format tab**, click the **Arrange** button. Click the **Position** button, and then under **With Text Wrapping**, in the third row, click the second button. Click the **Size** button, and increase the **Height** to 2.2".

13. On the **Design tab**, in the **SmartArt Styles group**, click the **More** button, and then click the first style under **3-D**—Polished. In the **Create Graphic group**, click the **Text Pane** button. For the four bullets, type Chevy and Chrysler and Ford and Classic Cars and then **Close** the Text pane. Deselect the SmartArt graphic, and then compare your document with **Figure 3**. **Save** and **Exit** Word.

14. **Start** Word. On the **Mailings tab**, in the **Start Mail Merge group**, click the **Start Mail Merge** button, and then click **Labels**. Under **Label information**, select **Avery US Letter**. Under **Product number**, click **5160**, and then click **OK**. In the **Start Mail Merge group**, click **Select Recipients**, click **Use Existing List**, and then locate and open **w04_Cars_Judges**.

15. In the **Write & Insert Fields** group, click the **Address Block** button, and then click **OK**. In the **Write & Insert Fields group**, click the **Update Labels** button.

16. In the **Preview Results group**, click the **Preview Results** button. In the **Finish group**, click the **Finish & Merge** button, click **Edit Individual Documents**, and then click **OK**. Delete the last row in the table. **Save** the document in your **Word Chapter 4** folder as Lastname_Firstname_w04_Cars_Labels and add the file name to the footer. Compare your document with **Figure 4**.

17. **Save** and then submit your documents as directed. **Exit** Word but do not save changes to any other documents.

Done! You have completed the Skill Check

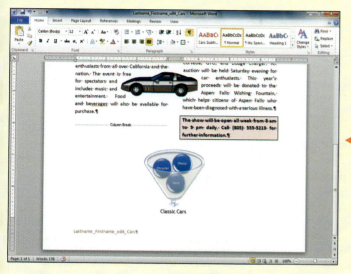

Figure 3

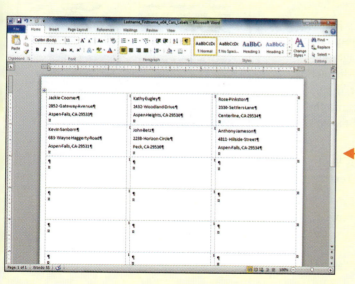

Figure 4

Assess Your Skills 1

To complete this document, you will need the following file:

- w04_Cruises

You will save your document as:

- Lastname_Firstname_w04_Cruises

1. **Start** Word. Locate and open **w04_Cruises**, save it in your **Word Chapter 4** folder as Lastname_Firstname_w04_Cruises and then add the file name to the footer. Select the title *Aspen Lake Cruises*—including the paragraph mark—and then on the **Home tab**, apply the **Intense Quote** Quick Style.

2. With the title still selected, change the title font size to **36** points. Apply the **Gradient Fill - Blue, Accent 1** text effect—the fourth effect in the third row. Then apply an **Offset Diagonal Bottom Left** text effect shadow— under **Outer**, the third effect in the first row.

3. Starting with the *Aspen Lake Nature Cruise* subtitle, select all of the text to the end of the document, and then change it to a two-column format. **Justify** the two-column text. Display the **Columns** dialog box, and then change the **Spacing** between the columns to **0.3"**. At the left side of the *Valentine's Day Cruise!* subtitle, insert a column break.

4. Select the *Aspen Lake Nature Cruise* subtitle, and then apply **Bold, Italic,** and **Center** alignment. Change the font size to **16** points, the font color to **Blue, Accent 1,** and then apply the **Small Caps** effect.

5. Create a new **Quick Style** named Cruise Subtitle based on the subtitle you just formatted. Apply the **Cruise Subtitle** Quick Style to the *Valentine's Day Cruise!* subtitle.

6. Position the insertion point at the beginning of the last paragraph, which begins *Book online or call.* Use the **Clip Art** task pane to search the Clip Art media type for cruise ship and then insert the image shown in **Figure 1**.

7. Change the width of the clip art image to **2.5"**. Change the **Wrap Text** to **Top and Bottom**, and then center the image horizontally in the column, as shown in **Figure 1**.

8. At the bottom of the first column, select the last paragraph, including the paragraph mark. Add an **Outside Border** to the paragraph. Display the **Borders and Shading** dialog box. Change the border width to **1½ pt**, the border color to **Dark Blue, Text 2**, and the shading fill to **Blue, Accent 1, Lighter 80%**— the fifth color in the second row.

9. Add a **Box** style page border that is **½ pt** wide, with a **Color** of **Dark Blue, Text 2**.

10. Compare your document with **Figure 1**. **Save** your document, and then submit it as directed.

Done! You have completed Assess Your Skills 1

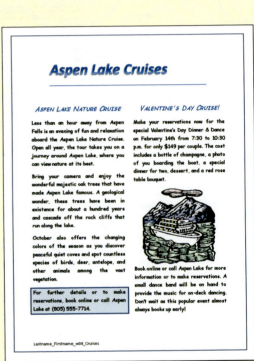

Figure 1

Assess Your Skills 2

Assess Your Skills 3 and 4 can be found at www.pearsonhighered.com/skills.

To complete this document, you will need the following files:

- w04_Competition
- w04_Competition_Addresses

You will save your documents as:

- Lastname_Firstname_w04_Competition
- Lastname_Firstname_w04_Competition_Labels

1. **Start** Word. Locate and open **w04_Competition**, save it in your **Word Chapter 4** folder as Lastname_Firstname_w04_Competition and then add the file name to the footer.

2. Select the document title. Change the title text to **Arial Black**, **42** points, and **Center** the text. Change the *title* **Line Spacing** to **1.0**, and the **Spacing After** to **0 pt**. With the title still selected, apply the **Gradient Fill - Orange, Accent 6, Inner Shadow** text effect—the second effect in the fourth row. Apply an **Orange, 5 pt glow, Accent color 6 Glow** text effect—the last Glow effect in the first row.

3. Press Ctrl + End to move to the end of the document. Insert a **Cycle** SmartArt graphic using the **Radial Cycle** layout—the first style in the third row. In the center circle, type Best in Show

4. Display the **Text Pane**, and then fill in the empty bullet points with the following text:

   Vintage
   Classic
   Hot Rod
   Custom

5. **Close** the Text pane. Change the SmartArt **Height** to 3" and the **Width** to 6.5". On the **Design tab**, apply the **Cartoon SmartArt Style**—the third style under 3-D.

6. With the SmartArt graphic still selected, **Change Colors** to **Colorful - Accent Colors**—the first style under Colorful.

7. Insert a **Shadow** page border with the **Orange, Accent 6, Darker 50%** color and a width of **3 pt**. **Save** your document, and then **Exit** Word.

8. Create a new blank document. Start the mail merge process to create **Labels** using **Avery US Letter, Product number 5160**. Use the **w04_Competition_Addresses** document as the data source. Add an **Address Block**, and accept all address block defaults, and then **Update Labels**. In the first label, remove the spacing before the address block. **Update Labels** and then preview the results. Merge all the labels into a single document. Delete the two bottom rows of the table.

9. **Save** the mail merge document in your **Word Chapter 4** folder as Lastname_Firstname_w04_Competition_Labels and then add the file name to the footer. Compare your completed documents with **Figure 1**. **Exit** Word—do not save the original mail merge document. Print or submit your documents as directed.

Figure 1

Done! You have completed Assess Your Skills 2

Assess Your Skills Visually

To complete this document, you will need the following file:

- w04_Heritage_Days

You will save your document as:

- Lastname_Firstname_w04_Heritage_Days

Start Word, and open **w04_Heritage_Days**. Create a flyer as shown in **Figure 1**. **Save** the file as Lastname_Firstname_w04_Heritage_Days in your **Word Chapter 4** folder.

To complete this document, apply the **Title** Quick Style, with a font size of **26 pt**. Break the column as indicated. In the bordered text, apply the **Dark Blue, Text 2** text and border colors, and **Blue, Accent 1, Lighter 80%** shading. Use the same border color for the page border. Set all border widths to **3 pt**. Insert the **Clip Art** image shown in **Figure 1** using old west as the search term, and change its **Height** to 2".

For the subtitles, use an **18** point font size, **Small caps**, and **Center** the titles. Use the same color you used for the borders. For the SmartArt graphic, in the **Relationship** category, apply the **Converging Radial** layout. Adjust the graphic to **6.5"** wide and **3"** high, and then apply the **White Outline** SmartArt style. Insert the file name in the footer, and then print or submit it electronically as directed.

Done! You have completed Assess Your Skills Visually

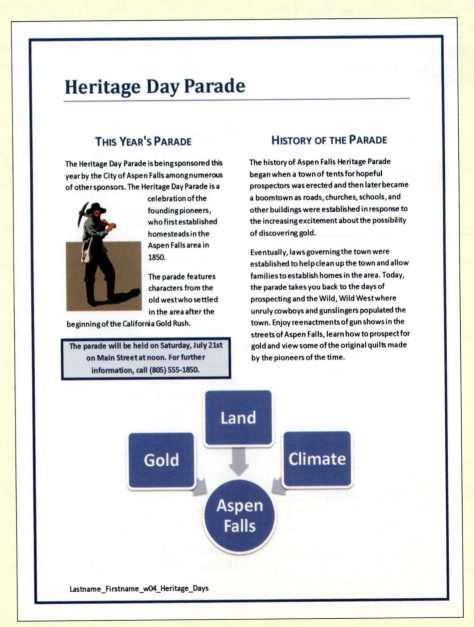

Figure 1

Skills in Context

To complete this document, you will need the following file:

- New blank Word document

You will save your document as:

- Lastname_Firstname_w04_Attractions

Create a flyer about the attractions around Aspen Falls. Use the web to research northern California for ideas—you could research attractions such as sailing, nature trails, bird watching, waterfalls, wineries, and so on. The flyer should have a formatted title and a subtitle, and then two-column text describing the area's attractions. Your completed document should include a page border, a paragraph or paragraphs with a paragraph border and shading, a clip art image, and a SmartArt graphic of your choice. You can include a picture if you would like to do so.

Save the document as Lastname_Firstname_w04_Attractions Insert the file name in the footer, and be sure to check the entire document for grammar and spelling. Print or submit the file electronically as directed.

Done! You have completed Skills in Context

Skills and You

To complete this document, you will need the following file:

- New blank Word document

You will save your document as:

- Lastname_Firstname_w04_Family

Using the skills you have practiced in this chapter, create a flyer to send to family members about family events coming up during the next year. The flyer should have a formatted title and a subtitle, and then two-column text describing the various events. Your completed document should include a page border, a paragraph with a paragraph border and shading, a clip art image, and a SmartArt graphic of your choice.

Save the document as Lastname_Firstname_w04_Family Check the entire document for grammar and spelling. Print or submit the file electronically as directed.

Done! You have completed Skills and You

CHAPTER 5

Apply Advanced Formatting and Layout Settings

▶ Documents can be formatted and enhanced by including elements such as symbol characters, OpenType features, section breaks, custom margins, horizontal lines, highlighting, tabs, and tables with formulas.

▶ Quick Part entries and objects can be created, modified, and inserted into documents to save time.

Your starting screen will look like this:

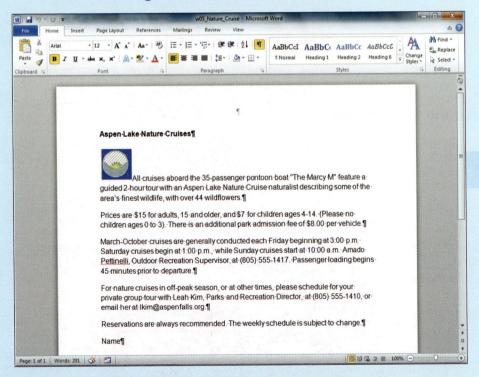

SKILLS
Skills 1-10 Training

At the end of this chapter, you will be able to:

Skill 1 Insert Symbols
Skill 2 Use OpenType Features
Skill 3 Insert Continuous Section Breaks and Apply Custom Margins
Skill 4 Create Horizontal Lines, Use Paste Options, and Highlight Text
Skill 5 Modify Tab Settings Using the Ruler
Skill 6 Remove Backgrounds from Pictures and Modify Text-Wrap Points
Skill 7 Create Quick Parts
Skill 8 Modify and Insert Quick Parts
Skill 9 Insert Formulas into Tables
Skill 10 Update Table Formulas

MORE SKILLS

More Skills 11 Draw Tables and Convert Tables to Text
More Skills 12 Convert Pictures to SmartArt
More Skills 13 Copy Content from Web Pages Using Paste Options
More Skills 14 Use Master and Subdocuments

Outcome

Using the skills listed to the left will enable you to create documents like these:

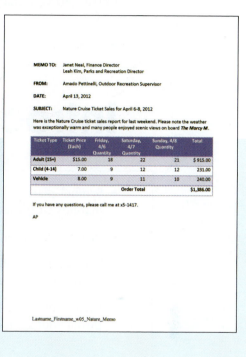

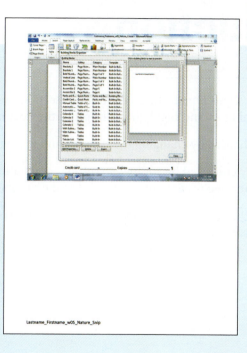

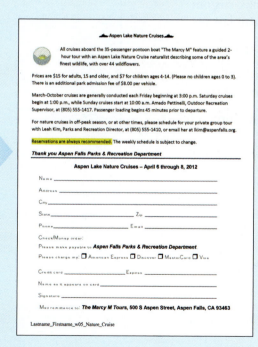

You will save your files as:

Lastname_Firstname_w05_Nature_Cruise
Lastname_Firstname_w05_Nature_Snip
Lastname_Firstname_w05_Nature_Memo

In this chapter, you will create documents for the Aspen Falls City Hall, which provides essential services for the citizens and visitors of Aspen Falls, California.

Introduction

- Symbol characters, OpenType features, continuous section breaks, custom margins, horizontal lines, and highlighting improve the document layouts.

- Pictures can be enhanced by changing the skewing and text-wrap points.

- Text can be visually enhanced by adding tab settings and tables. Tables can include formulas and the results can be updated as the numbers change.

- Saving your own Quick Part entries saves time and ensures continuity throughout all documents.

Time to complete all
10 skills – 50 to 90 minutes

Find your student data files here:

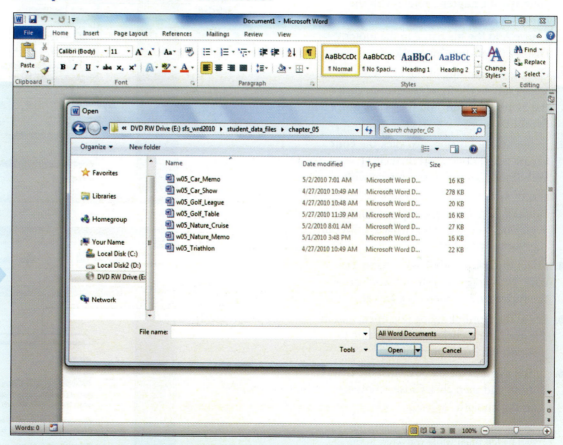

Student data files needed for this chapter:

- w05_Nature_Cruise
- w05_Nature_Memo

▶ Recall that a symbol is a character not found on most keyboards and includes the copyright symbol and special bullet characters.

▶ Most fonts include commonly-used symbols, while some fonts include only symbols.

1. **Start** ⊕ Word and open the student data file **w05_Nature_Cruise**. Save the file in your **Word Chapter 5** folder with the name Lastname_Firstname_w05_Nature_ Cruise Add the file name to the footer. Display the formatting marks.

2. Click the beginning of the title. On the **Insert tab**, in the **Symbols group**, click the **Symbol** button, and then click **More Symbols**.

3. In the **Symbol** dialog box, click the **Font arrow**, scroll down, and then click **Webdings**. Compare your screen with **Figure 1**.

   Webdings is a font that displays *character graphic*—small graphic characters that can be formatted as text.

4. Select the boat symbol ⬓—character code 111—located in the last column of the fifth row, and then click **Insert**.

5. Leave the **Symbol** dialog box open, and in the document, click right of the title to position the insertion point.

6. In the **Symbol** dialog box, click the **Insert** button, and then click **Close**. Compare your screen with **Figure 2**.

   In this manner, the Symbol dialog box can be left open while you work in the document. This enables you to insert symbols in different locations without opening and closing the Symbol dialog box.

▪ **Continue to the next page to complete the skill** ➤

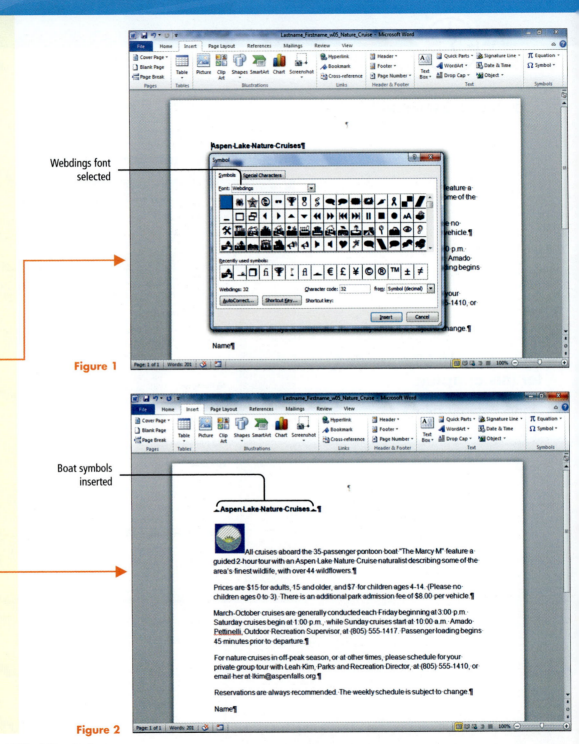

Webdings font selected

Figure 1

Boat symbols inserted

Figure 2

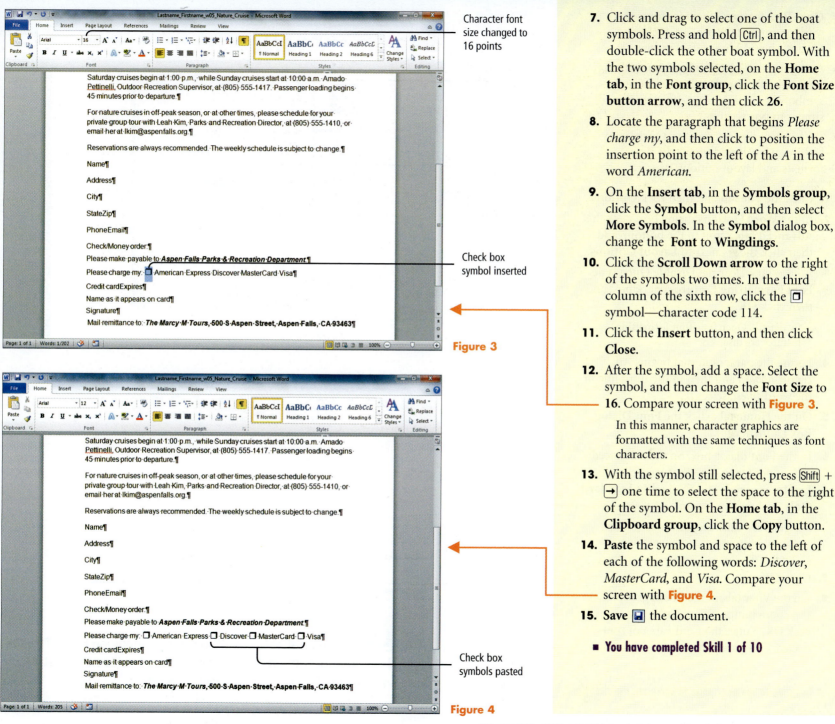

Character font size changed to 16 points

Check box symbol inserted

Figure 3

Check box symbols pasted

Figure 4

7. Click and drag to select one of the boat symbols. Press and hold [Ctrl], and then double-click the other boat symbol. With the two symbols selected, on the **Home tab**, in the **Font group**, click the **Font Size button arrow**, and then click **26**.

8. Locate the paragraph that begins *Please charge my*, and then click to position the insertion point to the left of the *A* in the word *American*.

9. On the **Insert tab**, in the **Symbols group**, click the **Symbol** button, and then select **More Symbols**. In the **Symbol** dialog box, change the **Font** to **Wingdings**.

10. Click the **Scroll Down arrow** to the right of the symbols two times. In the third column of the sixth row, click the ▢ symbol—character code 114.

11. Click the **Insert** button, and then click **Close**.

12. After the symbol, add a space. Select the symbol, and then change the **Font Size** to **16**. Compare your screen with **Figure 3**.

   In this manner, character graphics are formatted with the same techniques as font characters.

13. With the symbol still selected, press [Shift] + [→] one time to select the space to the right of the symbol. On the **Home tab**, in the **Clipboard group**, click the **Copy** button.

14. **Paste** the symbol and space to the left of each of the following words: *Discover*, *MasterCard*, and *Visa*. Compare your screen with **Figure 4**.

15. **Save** 🖫 the document.

■ **You have completed Skill 1 of 10**

► *OpenType feature*—includes fonts that work on multiple platforms, including Macintosh and Microsoft Windows.

► An example of an *OpenType font* is the ⓕ symbol in the Font list. Two or more symbols or characters are often combined; similar to typesetting.

► When preparing documents, OpenType features provide additional character formats and layout options.

1. Click the **File tab** and then click **Options**.

2. In the **Word Options** dialog box, click the **Advanced tab**, scroll to the bottom, and then click the ▷ next to **Layout Options**.

3. If necessary, clear the **Disable OpenType Font Formatting Features** check box, and then click **OK**.

    By default, OpenType font formatting features are disabled.

4. Locate the paragraph that begins *All cruises aboard* and then in the third line in the word *finest*, select *fi*.

5. On the **Home tab**, click the **Font Dialog Box Launcher** 🔲.

6. In the **Font** dialog box, on the **Advanced tab**, under **OpenType Features**, click the **Ligatures arrow**, and then select **Standard Only** as shown in **Figure 1**.

    Ligatures—small graphic characters that display when two or more symbols are combined.

7. Click **OK**.

8. On the **View tab**, in the **Zoom group**, click the **Zoom** button, select **200%**, and then click **OK**. Notice the *f* and *i* are not connected. Compare your screen with **Figure 2**.

■ **Continue to the next page to complete the skill**

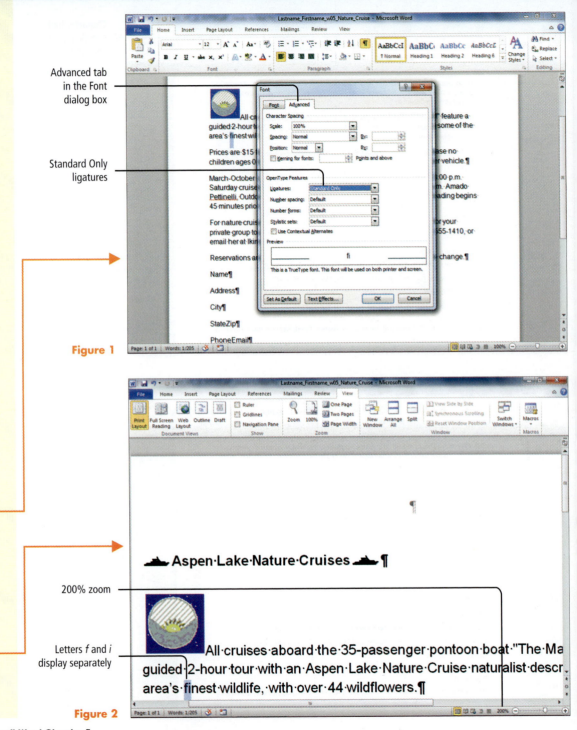

Advanced tab in the Font dialog box

Standard Only ligatures

Figure 1

200% zoom

Letters *f* and *i* display separately

Figure 2

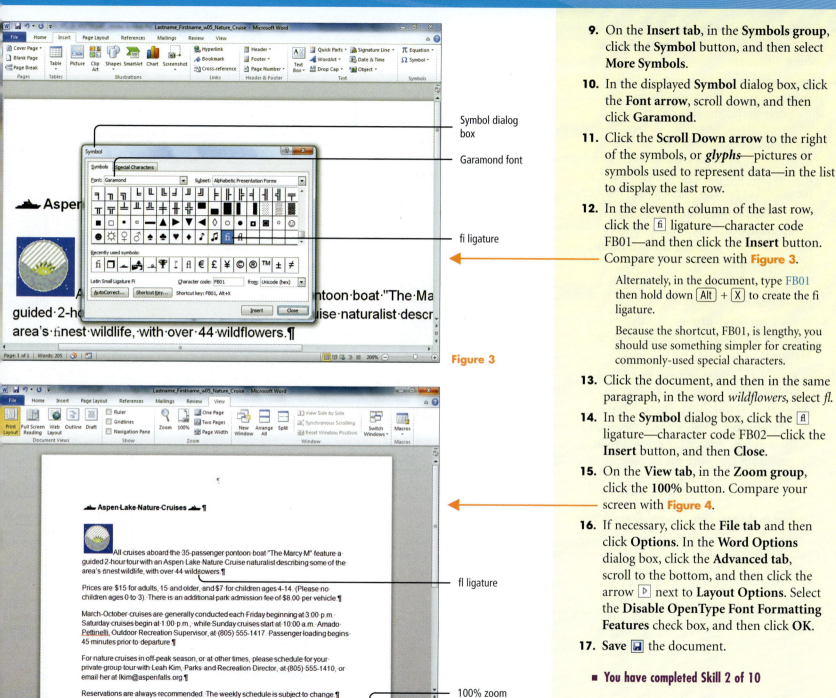

Symbol dialog box

Garamond font

fi ligature

Figure 3

fl ligature

100% zoom

Figure 4

9. On the **Insert tab**, in the **Symbols group**, click the **Symbol** button, and then select **More Symbols**.

10. In the displayed **Symbol** dialog box, click the **Font arrow**, scroll down, and then click **Garamond**.

11. Click the **Scroll Down arrow** to the right of the symbols, or *glyphs*—pictures or symbols used to represent data—in the list to display the last row.

12. In the eleventh column of the last row, click the ⨍i ligature—character code FB01—and then click the **Insert** button. Compare your screen with **Figure 3**.

> Alternately, in the document, type FB01 then hold down Alt + X to create the fi ligature.

> Because the shortcut, FB01, is lengthy, you should use something simpler for creating commonly-used special characters.

13. Click the document, and then in the same paragraph, in the word *wildflowers*, select *fl*.

14. In the **Symbol** dialog box, click the ⨍l ligature—character code FB02—click the **Insert** button, and then **Close**.

15. On the **View tab**, in the **Zoom group**, click the **100%** button. Compare your screen with **Figure 4**.

16. If necessary, click the **File tab** and then click **Options**. In the **Word Options** dialog box, click the **Advanced tab**, scroll to the bottom, and then click the arrow ▷ next to **Layout Options**. Select the **Disable OpenType Font Formatting Features** check box, and then click **OK**.

17. Save 🖫 the document.

- **You have completed Skill 2 of 10**

► *Continuous section breaks* are inserted into a document when you want to format each section differently.

► Margin settings can be customized when you need margins that are different from the choices in the Margins gallery.

1. Locate the paragraph that begins *Reservations are always,* and then click to position the insertion point to the right of the period at the end of the paragraph.

2. On the **Page Layout tab**, in the **Page Setup group**, click the **Breaks** button as shown in **Figure 1**. Under **Section Breaks**, select **Continuous**.

3. Press Ctrl + Home to move to the beginning of the document.

4. In the **Page Setup group**, click the **Margins** button, and then click **Custom Margins**.

   Alternately, in the Page Setup group, click the Page Setup Dialog Box Launcher ⌐.

5. In the **Page Setup** dialog box, verify that the **Margins tab** displays. Under **Margins**, in the **Top** box, replace the existing value by typing .75 Compare your screen with **Figure 2**.

■ **Continue to the next page to complete the skill**

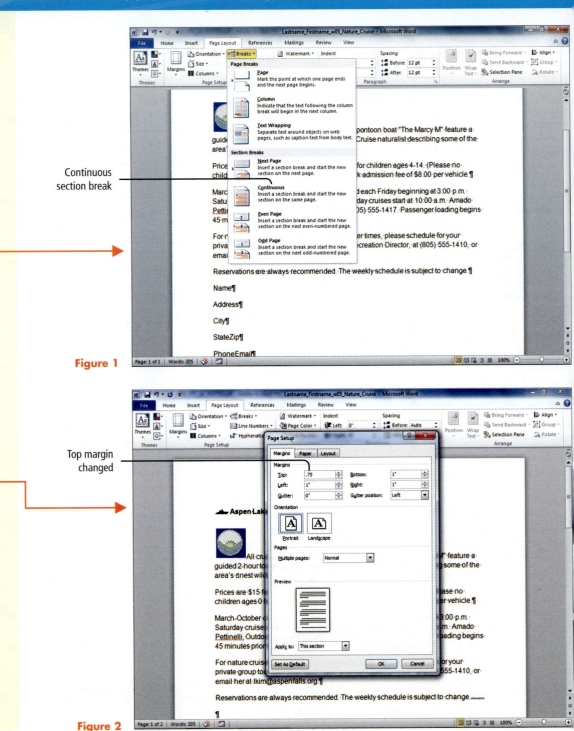

Continuous section break

Figure 1

Top margin changed

Figure 2

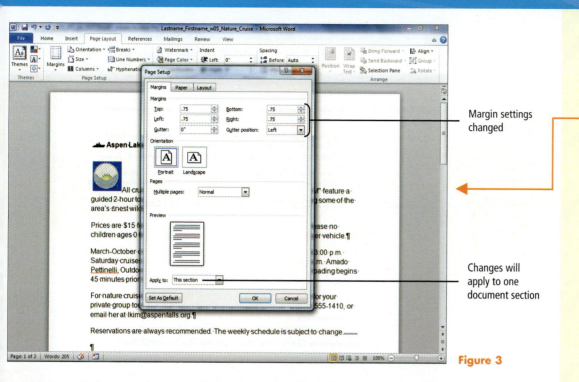

Margin settings changed

Changes will apply to one document section

Figure 3

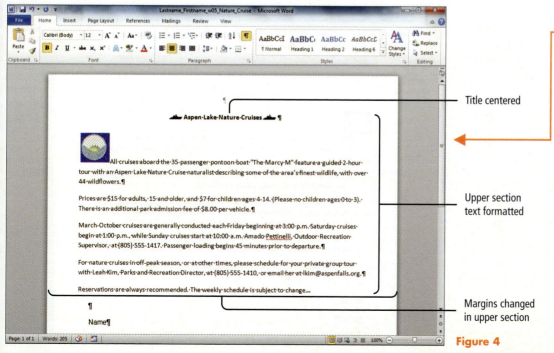

Title centered

Upper section text formatted

Margins changed in upper section

Figure 4

6. In the **Bottom** box, replace the existing text with .75 Repeat this technique to change the **Left** and **Right** margins to .75

7. At the bottom of the **Page Setup** dialog box, verify that the **Apply to** box displays *This section* as shown in **Figure 3**, and then click **OK**.

8. If necessary, display the formatting marks. In the top section of the document, verify that the margins have changed above the section break but not in the section below it.

   The screen displays a section break, which separates the document into two sections that can be formatted separately.

9. Select all the text above the section break. On the **Home tab**, in the **Font group**, click the **Font button arrow** and then click **Calibri**.

10. Click anywhere in the title. On the **Home tab**, in the **Paragraph group**, click the **Center** button. Compare your screen with **Figure 4**.

11. Save 🖫 the document.

■ **You have completed Skill 3 of 10**

▶ Inserting *horizontal lines* separates document text so that it is easier to read.

▶ *Paste Options* provide formatting choices when pasting text into the current document.

▶ Text can be highlighted to make it stand out in the document.

1. Click the beginning of the blank paragraph between the section break and the paragraph that begins with *Name*.

2. Press and hold [Shift] while pressing [-] five times. Press [Enter]. Compare your screen with **Figure 1**.

When you press and hold [Shift] while pressing [-] five times, five underlines display in the document. Pressing [Enter] converts the underlines to a horizontal line above the blank paragraph.

3. Locate the title *Aspen Lake Nature Cruises* and select the text—be sure that the symbols and the paragraph mark are not selected—and then click the **Copy** button.

4. Click the beginning of the blank paragraph below the horizontal line. Click the **Paste button arrow**. Compare your screen with **Figure 2** and then click **Merge Formatting** 🔳.

Paste Options include *Keep Source Formatting*—pastes text with the formatting from the original location—*Merge Formatting*—pastes text and applies the formatting in use in the new location—and *Keep Text Only*—pastes text with all formatting removed.

■ **Continue to the next page to complete the skill** ▶

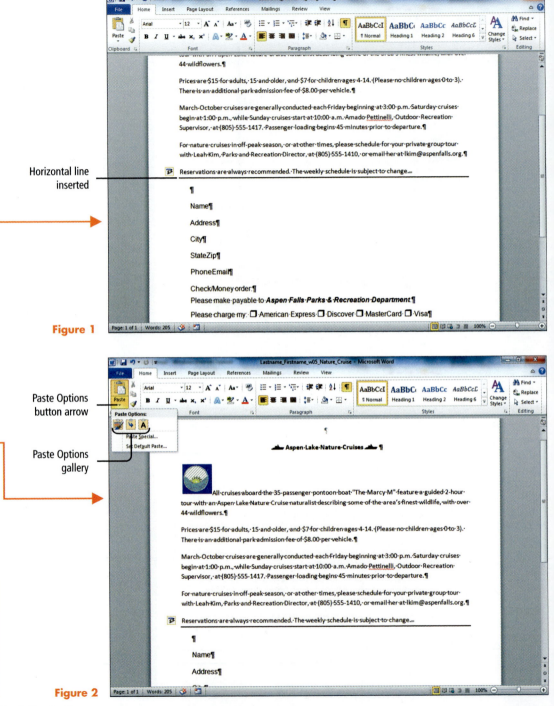

Horizontal line inserted

Figure 1

Paste Options button arrow

Paste Options gallery

Figure 2

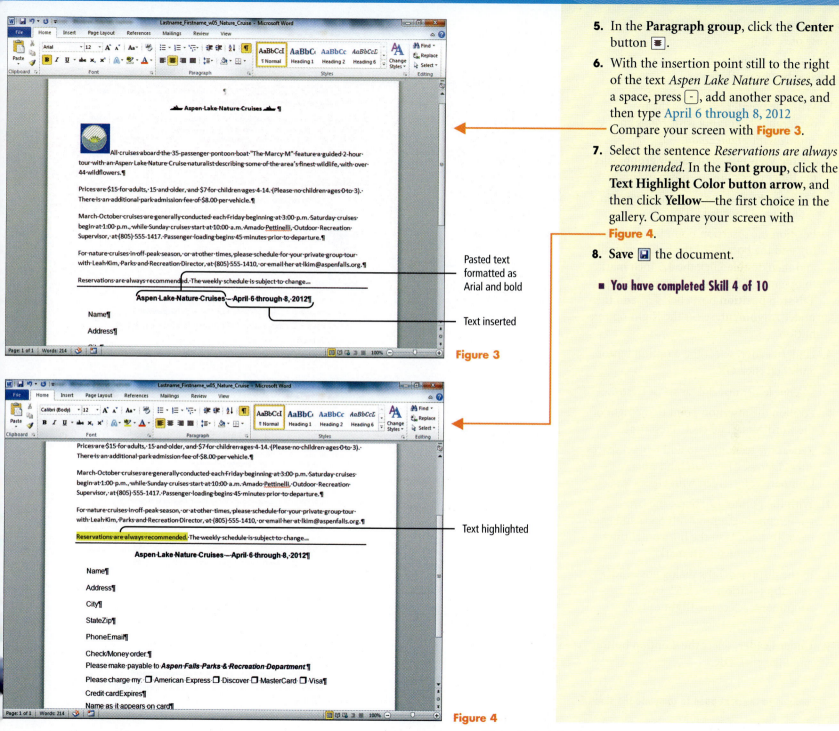

Pasted text formatted as Arial and bold

Text inserted

Figure 3

Text highlighted

Figure 4

5. In the **Paragraph group**, click the **Center** button ⊞.

6. With the insertion point still to the right of the text *Aspen Lake Nature Cruises*, add a space, press ⊟, add another space, and then type April 6 through 8, 2012 Compare your screen with **Figure 3**.

7. Select the sentence *Reservations are always recommended*. In the **Font group**, click the **Text Highlight Color button arrow**, and then click **Yellow**—the first choice in the gallery. Compare your screen with **Figure 4**.

8. **Save** 🖫 the document.

■ **You have completed Skill 4 of 10**

► Tab settings can be used to align text for ease of reading.

► Tab settings may be changed in the Tabs dialog box or on the ruler.

1. With the pointer 🔏, select the five paragraphs beginning with *Name* and ending with *PhoneEmail*.

2. On the **View tab**, in the **Show group**, select the **Ruler** check box as shown in **Figure 1**.

   Alternately, click the View Ruler button in the vertical scroll bar.

3. Position the insertion point between the top and the bottom of the horizontal ruler and then double-click the **4.5** inch mark to open the **Tabs** dialog box. In the large **Tab stop position** box, click *4.5"* and then under **Alignment**, select the **Right** option button.

4. Under **Leader**, select the **4** option button and then click **OK**.

   A line leader that ends at 4.5" is created.

5. Position the insertion point to the right of the word *Name* and click. Press Tab.

6. Repeat the technique to add tabbed spaces after *Address*, *City*, *State*, and *Phone*. Compare your screen with **Figure 2**.

7. With the pointer 🔏, select the two paragraphs beginning with *State* and ending with *Email*. On the horizontal ruler, double-click the **6** inch mark.

8. In the displayed **Tabs** dialog box, under **Tab stop position**, click **6"**. Under **Alignment**, select the **Right** option button.

9. Under **Leader**, select the **4** option button and then click **OK**.

■ **Continue to the next page to complete the skill**

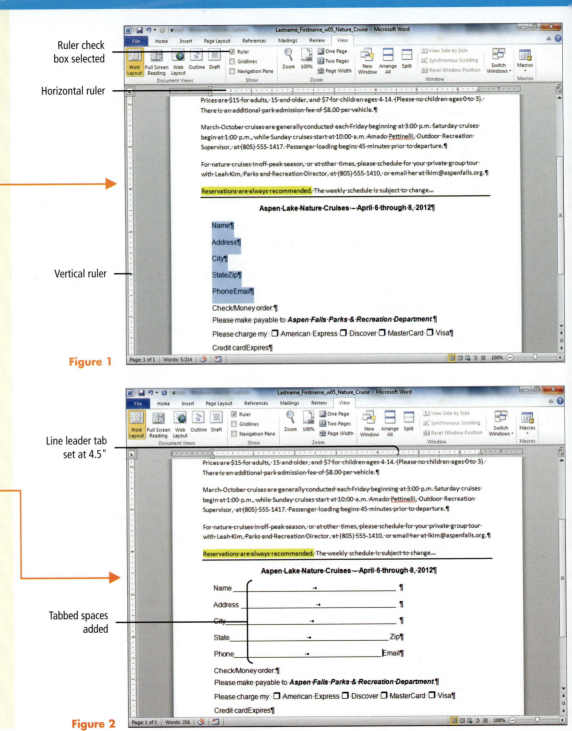

Ruler check box selected

Horizontal ruler

Vertical ruler

Figure 1

Line leader tab set at 4.5"

Tabbed spaces added

Figure 2

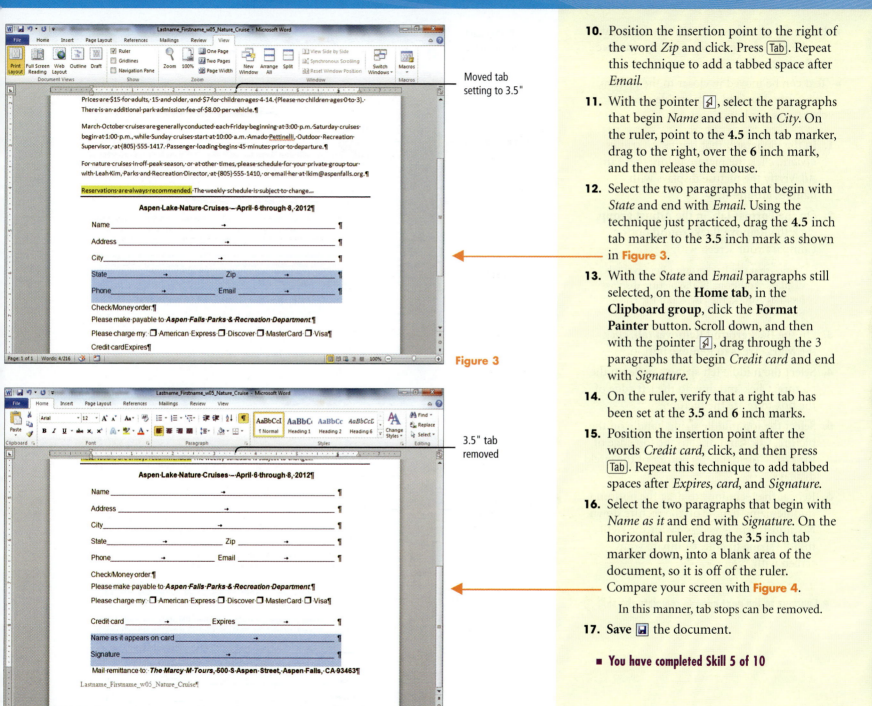

Moved tab setting to 3.5"

Figure 3

3.5" tab removed

Figure 4

10. Position the insertion point to the right of the word *Zip* and click. Press Tab. Repeat this technique to add a tabbed space after *Email*.

11. With the pointer [cursor icon], select the paragraphs that begin *Name* and end with *City*. On the ruler, point to the **4.5** inch tab marker, drag to the right, over the **6** inch mark, and then release the mouse.

12. Select the two paragraphs that begin with *State* and end with *Email*. Using the technique just practiced, drag the **4.5** inch tab marker to the **3.5** inch mark as shown in **Figure 3**.

13. With the *State* and *Email* paragraphs still selected, on the **Home tab**, in the **Clipboard group**, click the **Format Painter** button. Scroll down, and then with the pointer [cursor icon], drag through the 3 paragraphs that begin *Credit card* and end with *Signature*.

14. On the ruler, verify that a right tab has been set at the **3.5** and **6** inch marks.

15. Position the insertion point after the words *Credit card*, click, and then press Tab. Repeat this technique to add tabbed spaces after *Expires*, *card*, and *Signature*.

16. Select the two paragraphs that begin with *Name as it* and end with *Signature*. On the horizontal ruler, drag the **3.5** inch tab marker down, into a blank area of the document, so it is off of the ruler. Compare your screen with **Figure 4**.

   In this manner, tab stops can be removed.

17. **Save** [save icon] the document.

■ **You have completed Skill 5 of 10**

- Parts of a picture, such as the background, can be adjusted to improve the appearance of the picture.

- Text can be moved in closer to the picture, or wrapped around it, to enable more characters per line.

1. In the paragraph that begins *All cruises aboard*, click the picture before the *A* in *All*. Verify the picture displays with handles around it.

2. On the **Format tab**, in the **Adjust group**, click the **Remove Background** button. Compare your screen with **Figure 1**.

   Notice that the Background Removal tab displays. Additionally, the picture displays handles around the circle, not the entire box.

3. On the **Background Removal tab**, click the **Mark Areas to Remove** button.

4. Select the middle left sizing handle on the picture. Click and drag to the left edge of the box to resize the picture.

5. Select the top middle sizing handle on the picture. Click and drag to the top edge of the box. Notice the top border of the circle displays.

6. Repeat the technique to drag the bottom middle sizing handle on the picture down. No adjustment is necessary for the right middle sizing handle. Compare your screen with **Figure 2**.

■ **Continue to the next page to complete the skill**

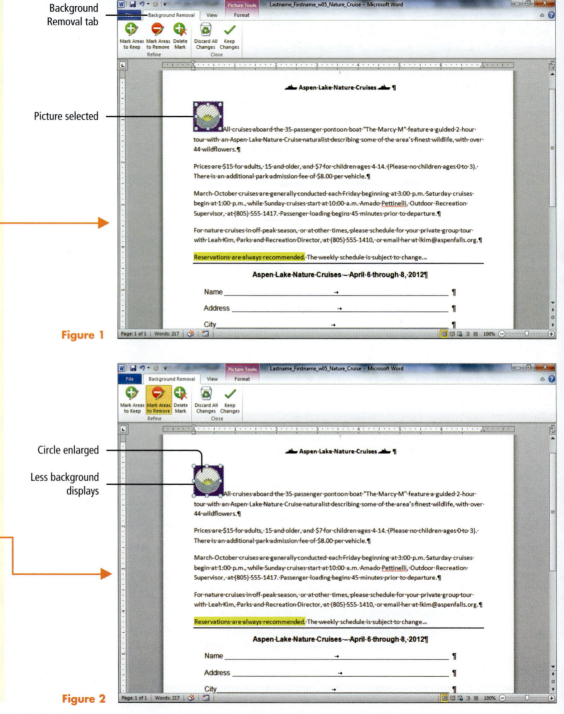

Figure 1

Figure 2

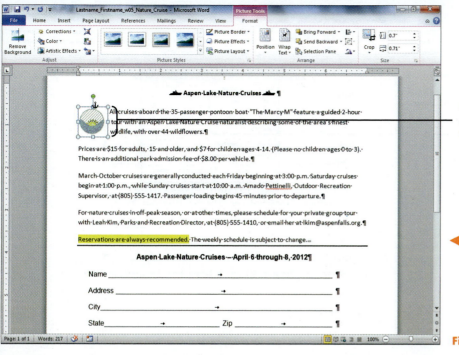

Paragraph text aligned tightly with picture

Figure 3

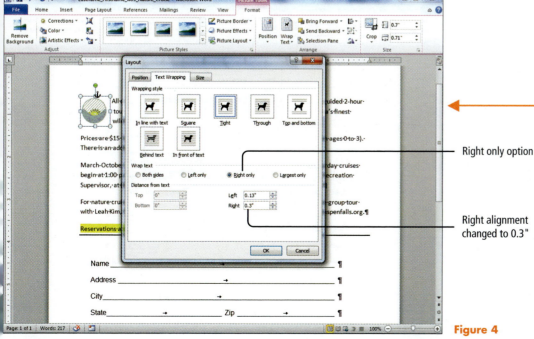

Right only option

Right alignment changed to 0.3"

Figure 4

7. On the **Background Removal tab**, click the **Delete Mark** button.

8. Click anywhere in the document to deselect the picture. Verify the blue background no longer displays around the picture.

   Notice the paragraph text that begins *All cruises aboard* aligns closely with the bottom edge of the picture.

9. Click the picture to select it. On the **Format tab**, in the **Arrange group**, click the **Wrap Text** button.

10. Click **Tight** and then compare your screen with **Figure 3**.

    The Tight option places the text closer to the picture. In this case, the text on the first and third lines of the paragraph moves closer in line with the picture. The second line is not as close because the picture is wider next to this line.

11. In the **Arrange group**, click the **Wrap Text** button, and then click **More Layout Options**.

12. In the **Layout** dialog box, on the **Text Wrapping tab**, under **Wrap text**, select the **Right only** option button.

13. In the dialog box, under **Distance from text**, click the **Right up spin arrow** two times to display **0.3"**, and then compare your screen with **Figure 4**.

14. Click **OK**. Deselect the picture.

15. Save the document.

   ▪ **You have completed Skill 6 of 10**

► *Quick parts* are saved text and objects that can be retrieved from the Quick Parts gallery.

► Quick parts help ensure accuracy and consistency of items shared by multiple users.

1. Locate the paragraph that begins *Please make payable to* and then select the text *Aspen Falls Parks & Recreation Department* and the period. Be careful not to select the period or the paragraph mark.

2. On the **Insert tab**, in the **Text group**, click the **Quick Parts** button, and then click **Save Selection to Quick Part Gallery**.

3. In the **Name** box, verify the text *Aspen Falls* displays as shown in **Figure 1**.

   The Create New Building Block dialog box is used to name and set options for quick parts. A ***building block*** is any object or group of objects in a Word document that can be saved for later retrieval. The Quick Parts gallery acts as a library of building blocks that can be inserted into documents.

4. Click the **Category arrow**, and then click **Create New Category**.

5. In the displayed **Create New Category** dialog box, type Parks and Recreation and then click **OK**. Compare your screen with **Figure 2**.

■ **Continue to the next page to complete the skill**

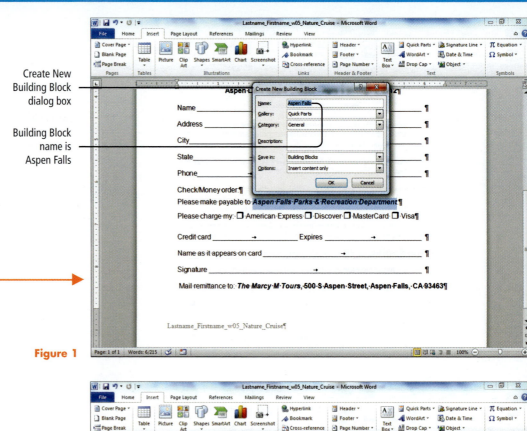

Create New Building Block dialog box

Building Block name is Aspen Falls

Figure 1

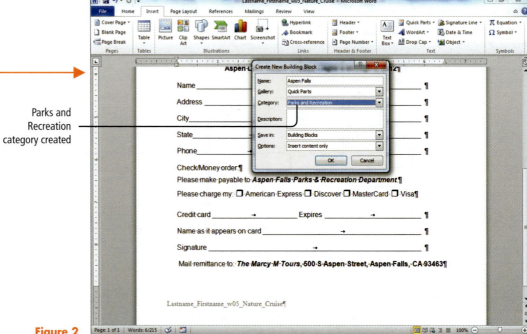

Parks and Recreation category created

Figure 2

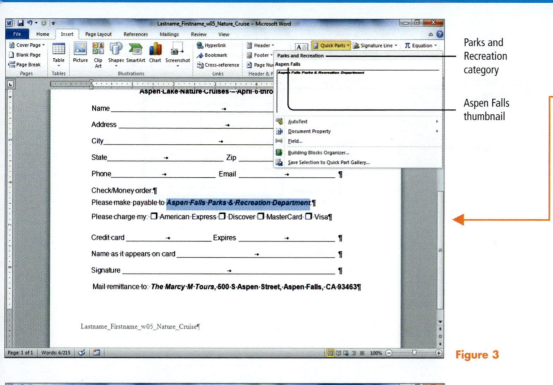

Figure 3

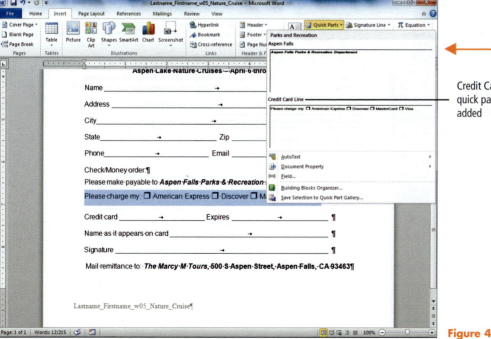

Credit Card Line quick parts added

Figure 4

6. In the **Create New Building Block** dialog box, click **OK**.

7. In the **Text group**, click the **Quick Parts** button, and then compare your screen with **Figure 3**.

   Quick parts display as thumbnails in the Quick Parts gallery. Here, the Aspen Falls Parks & Recreation Department thumbnail displays under the Parks and Recreation category.

8. Click anywhere in the document to close the **Quick Parts** gallery.

9. Select the text in the paragraph that begins with *Please charge* and ends with *Visa*. Be careful not to select the paragraph mark.

10. Use the technique just practiced to create a new quick parts entry named Credit Card Line and place it in the **Parks and Recreation** category. Click **OK**.

11. In the **Text group**, click the **Quick Parts** button, and then verify that the two thumbnails display as shown in **Figure 4**.

12. Click anywhere in the document to close the **Quick Parts** gallery. Deselect the text.

13. **Save** 🖫 the document.

■ **You have completed Skill 7 of 10**

► Building blocks created as quick parts are inserted into a document using the Quick Parts gallery.

► Quick parts can be renamed, modified, or deleted.

1. On the **Insert tab**, in the **Text group**, click the **Quick Parts** button.

2. Right-click the **Aspen Falls** thumbnail, and then in the displayed shortcut menu, click **Edit Properties**.

3. In the **Modify Building Block** dialog box, in the **Name** box, replace the text with Parks and Recreation Department Compare your screen with **Figure 1**.

4. Click **OK**, read the displayed message, and then click **Yes**.

5. Locate the paragraph that begins *Reservations are always recommended* and then click the end of the paragraph, to the right of the period after the word *change*.

6. Press Enter one time to display a paragraph mark at the end of the line.

7. In the **Text group**, click the **Quick Parts** button, and then click the **Parks and Recreation Department** thumbnail. Compare your screen with **Figure 2**.

8. Locate the paragraph that begins *Aspen Falls Parks &*. Click to position the insertion point at the beginning of the paragraph. Type Thank you and then add a space.

■ **Continue to the next page to complete the skill**

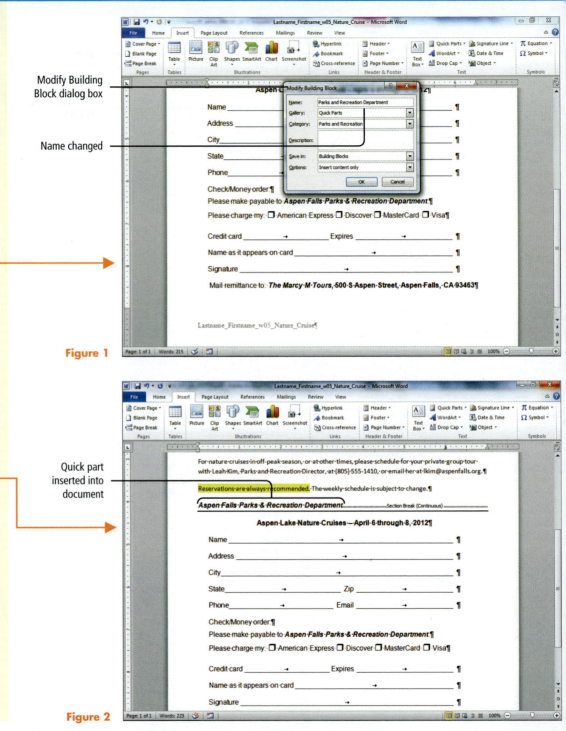

Modify Building Block dialog box

Name changed

Figure 1

Quick part inserted into document

Figure 2

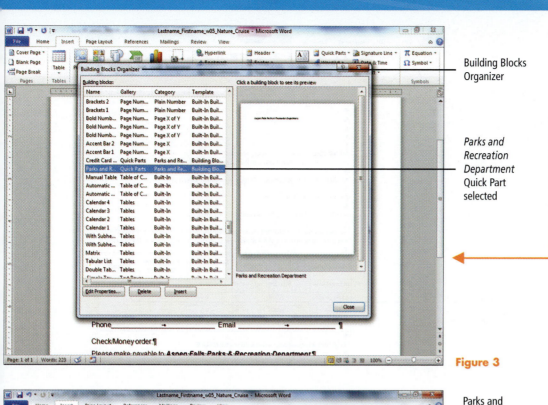

Building Blocks Organizer

Parks and Recreation Department Quick Part selected

Figure 3

Parks and Recreation Department thumbnail deleted

Credit Card Line thumbnail deleted

Figure 4

9. In the **Text group**, click **Quick Parts**.

10. Right-click the **Parks and Recreation Department** thumbnail, and then in the displayed shortcut menu, click **Organize and Delete**. Compare your screen with **Figure 3**.

11. Click Start ⊞ , click **All Programs**, and then open the **Accessories** folder. Click **Snipping Tool**, click the **New button arrow**, and then click **Full-screen Snip**.

12. Click the **Save Snip** button ⊟. In the **Save As** dialog box, navigate to your **Word Chapter 5** folder, **Save** the file as Lastname_Firstname_w05_Nature_Snip and then **Close** ⊠ the Snipping Tool window.

13. Print the snip or submit the file as directed by your instructor.

14. In the displayed **Building Blocks Organizer** dialog box, click the **Delete** button. Read the displayed message, and then click **Yes**.

15. Repeat the technique just practiced to delete the *Credit Card Line* building block. **Close** the dialog box.

16. On the **Insert tab**, in the **Text group**, click the **Quick Parts** button, and verify the two thumbnails have been deleted. Compare your document with **Figure 4**.

17. **Save** ⊟ the document. If you are printing your work for this project, print the document.

18. **Close** the Word document.

19. If necessary, click **Don't Save** to the message about saving "Building Blocks."

■ **You have completed Skill 8 of 10**

► Tables visually enhance documents and make data easier to read.

► Formulas can be inserted into tables to provide totals, count rows, or perform other calculations.

1. Open the student data file **w05_Nature_ Memo**. Save the file in your **Word Chapter 5** folder with the name Lastname_ Firstname_w05_Nature_ Memo If necessary, display the formatting marks.

2. Add the file name to the footer.

3. In the second row of the table, click the blank cell below the word *Total*, and before the end-of-cell marker—similar to a paragraph mark for a cell. Compare your screen with **Figure 1**.

4. On the **Layout tab**, in the **Data group**, click the **Formula** button. In the displayed **Formula** dialog box, under **Formula**, replace the existing formula with =b2*(c2+d2+e2) as shown in **Figure 2**.

   Table formulas refer to table cells by their position in the table. For A1, the *A* represents the first column, and the *1* represents the first row.

   Here, the formula will first add the values for Friday, Saturday, and Sunday— (c2+d2+e2), then, multiply the sum by the ticket price in b2.

■ **Continue to the next page to complete the skill**

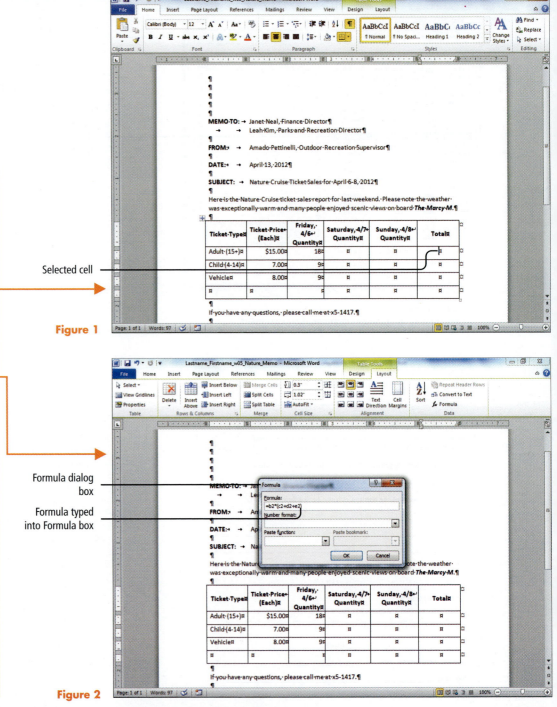

Selected cell

Figure 1

Formula dialog box

Formula typed into Formula box

Figure 2

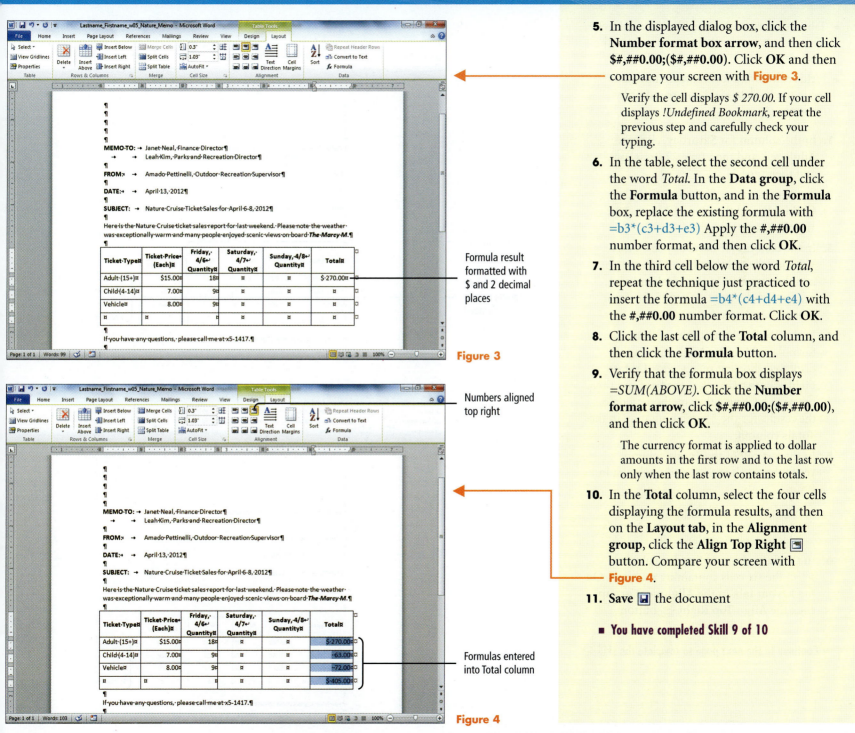

Formula result formatted with $ and 2 decimal places

Figure 3

Numbers aligned top right

Formulas entered into Total column

Figure 4

5. In the displayed dialog box, click the **Number format box arrow**, and then click **$#,##0.00;($#,##0.00)**. Click **OK** and then compare your screen with **Figure 3**.

> Verify the cell displays *$ 270.00*. If your cell displays *!Undefined Bookmark*, repeat the previous step and carefully check your typing.

6. In the table, select the second cell under the word *Total*. In the **Data group**, click the **Formula** button, and in the **Formula** box, replace the existing formula with =b3*(c3+d3+e3) Apply the **#,##0.00** number format, and then click **OK**.

7. In the third cell below the word *Total*, repeat the technique just practiced to insert the formula =b4*(c4+d4+e4) with the **#,##0.00** number format. Click **OK**.

8. Click the last cell of the **Total** column, and then click the **Formula** button.

9. Verify that the formula box displays *=SUM(ABOVE)*. Click the **Number format arrow**, click **$#,##0.00;($#,##0.00)**, and then click **OK**.

> The currency format is applied to dollar amounts in the first row and to the last row only when the last row contains totals.

10. In the **Total** column, select the four cells displaying the formula results, and then on the **Layout tab**, in the **Alignment group**, click the **Align Top Right** button. Compare your screen with **Figure 4**.

11. **Save** the document

■ **You have completed Skill 9 of 10**

► Table cell formulas are fields that need to be updated whenever changes are made to the table data.

► Fields containing formulas are updated using the Update Field command or by pressing F9.

1. In the column for **Saturday**, click the **Adult** cell, and then type 22 Press Tab, and then type 21

2. In the column for **Saturday**, click the **Child** cell, and then type 12 Press Tab, and then type 12

3. In the column for **Saturday**, click the **Vehicle** cell, and then type 11 Press Tab, and then type 10 In the **Totals** column, notice that the formula results have not changed as shown in **Figure 1**.

4. In the **Total** column, right-click the formula field in the **Adult** row. In the displayed shortcut menu, click **Update Field**. Alternately, select the field and then press F9. Using either method, update the results for the 3 remaining rows in the **Totals** column.

5. In the last cell of the **Totals** column, verify the result is *$1,386.00* as shown in **Figure 2**.

   Whenever table cell data is changed, you need to remember to update any formula fields that reference those cells.

6. In the **Saturday** and **Sunday** columns, select the six cells containing numbers. On the **Layout tab**, in the **Alignment group**, click the **Align Top Right** button.

■ **Continue to the next page to complete the skill**

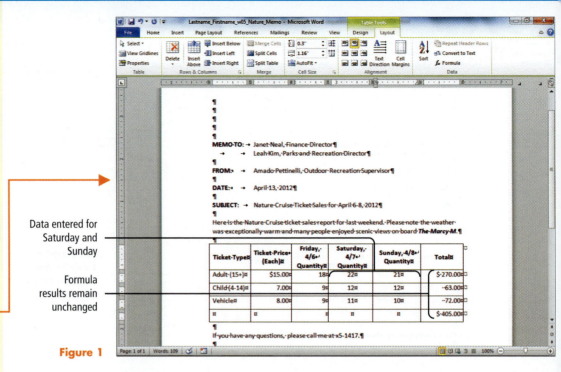

Data entered for Saturday and Sunday

Formula results remain unchanged

Figure 1

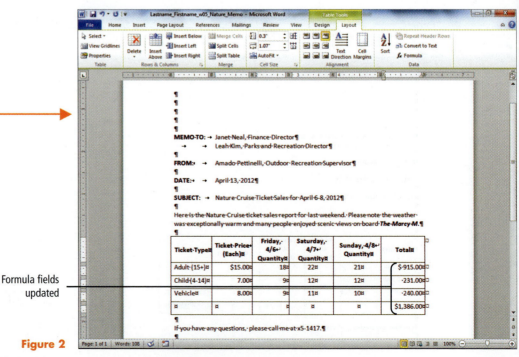

Formula fields updated

Figure 2

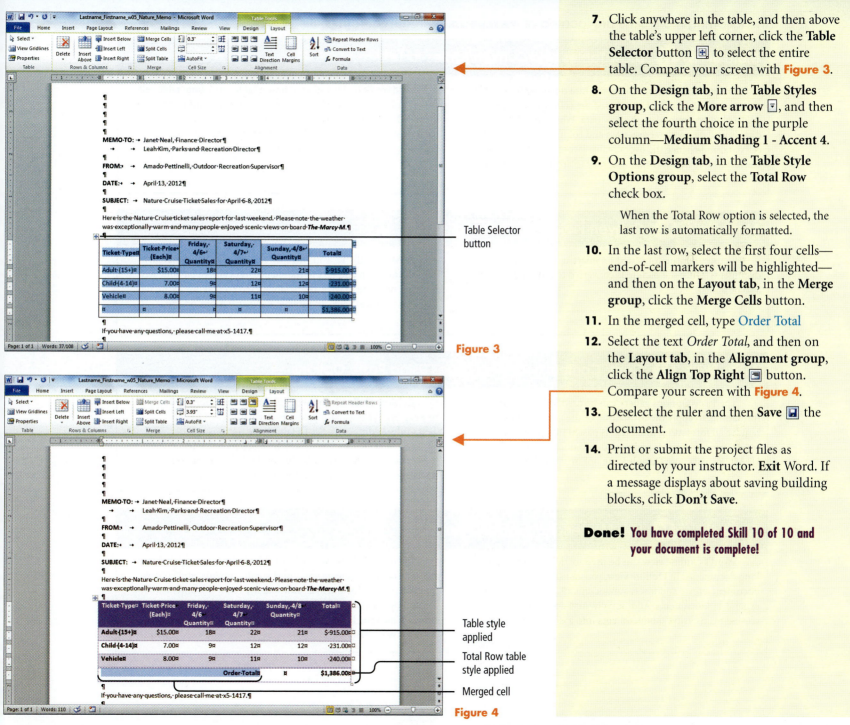

Figure 3

Table Selector
button

Figure 4

Table style
applied

Total Row table
style applied

Merged cell

7. Click anywhere in the table, and then above the table's upper left corner, click the **Table Selector** button ⊞ to select the entire table. Compare your screen with **Figure 3**.

8. On the **Design tab**, in the **Table Styles group**, click the **More arrow** ▾, and then select the fourth choice in the purple column—**Medium Shading 1 - Accent 4**.

9. On the **Design tab**, in the **Table Style Options group**, select the **Total Row** check box.

When the Total Row option is selected, the last row is automatically formatted.

10. In the last row, select the first four cells— end-of-cell markers will be highlighted— and then on the **Layout tab**, in the **Merge group**, click the **Merge Cells** button.

11. In the merged cell, type Order Total

12. Select the text *Order Total*, and then on the **Layout tab**, in the **Alignment group**, click the **Align Top Right** ⊟ button. Compare your screen with **Figure 4**.

13. Deselect the ruler and then **Save** 🖫 the document.

14. Print or submit the project files as directed by your instructor. **Exit** Word. If a message displays about saving building blocks, click **Don't Save**.

Done! You have completed Skill 10 of 10 and your document is complete!

More Skills

The following More Skills are located at **www.pearsonhighered.com/skills**

More Skills 11 — Draw Tables and Convert Tables to Text

Tables can be drawn or inserted into documents. As tables are created and modified, the size of the columns may need to be adjusted to accommodate the new data. Word provides tools that distribute data evenly across rows and columns, split cells, align cell data, and change the overall table layout. Word can also convert a table into text that uses tabs to arrange the data into columns.

In More Skills 11, you will draw a table, distribute table cell data evenly, split table cells, and convert table data into a text format. To begin, open your web browser, navigate to www.pearsonhighered.com/skills, locate the name of your textbook, and follow the instructions on the website.

More Skills 12 — Convert Pictures to SmartArt

Pictures may be converted to SmartArt to enhance documents. Once the picture is converted to SmartArt, text can also be added.

In More Skills 12, you will convert a picture to a SmartArt graphic and then add text to the shape. To begin, open your web browser, navigate to www.pearsonhighered.com/skills, locate the name of your textbook, and follow the instructions on the website.

More Skills 13 — Copy Content from Web Pages Using Paste Options

The Paste Options gallery can be used to keep the original formatting, to apply the formatting of the new location, or to remove all formatting when text is pasted into documents. Text copied from web pages and pasted into documents can include all HTML formats, too. Default Paste options can also be set.

In More Skills 13, you will use the Paste Options gallery to Keep Source Formatting, Merge Formatting, and Keep Text Only. Additionally, Set Default Paste options will be applied. To begin, open your web browser, navigate to www.pearsonhighered.com/skills, locate the name of your textbook, and follow the instructions on the website.

More Skills 14 — Use Master and Subdocuments

Word's Outline view can be used to view and organize long documents. In Outline view, you can show the master document, create and insert subdocuments, and collapse and expand subdocuments. Additionally, new documents can be created by inserting subdocuments into a document.

In More Skills 14, you will use the Outline view to show the master document, create and insert subdocuments, and collapse and expand subdocuments. Additionally, a new document will be created by inserting subdocuments. To begin, open your web browser, navigate to www.pearsonhighered.com/skills, locate the name of your textbook, and follow the instructions on the website.

Key Terms

Online Help Skills

1. **Start** ![Start] Word. In the upper right corner of the Word window, click the **Help** button ![Help]. In the **Help** window, click the **Maximize** ![Maximize] button.

2. Click in the search box, type Quick Parts and then click the **Search** button ![Search]. In the search results, click **Quick Parts**.

3. Read the article's introduction, and then below **In this article**, click **AutoText**. Compare your screen with **Figure 1**.

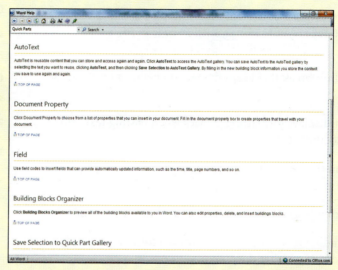

Figure 1

4. Read the section to see if you can answer the following: What is AutoText? Why might you save something to the AutoText Gallery?

Matching

Match each term in the second column with its correct definition in the first column by writing the letter of the term on the blank line in front of the correct definition.

____ **1.** The name of a font that displays character graphics.

____ **2.** A graphic character that displays when two or more characters are combined.

____ **3.** This is used to divide a document into multiple parts that can have different page layout settings, such as page borders and margins.

____ **4.** A type of section break that keeps the section below it on the same page.

____ **5.** A button that displays formatting choices when pasting text into the current document.

____ **6.** A paste option that copies text and applies the formatting in use in the new location.

____ **7.** A line that extends from the beginning of a tab to its tab stop.

____ **8.** A custom building block that can be retrieved for later use in the same document or another document.

____ **9.** The dialog box that allows users to select, modify, and delete quick parts.

____ **10.** The keyboard shortcut that updates a selected formula field.

A Building Blocks Organizer

B Continuous

C F9

D Leader

E Ligature

F Merge Formatting

G Paste Options

H Quick parts

I Section break

J Wingdings

Multiple Choice

Choose the correct answer.

1. A type of font that will work on multiple platforms.
   A. OpenType
   B. PrinterType
   C. TrueType

2. An example of an OpenType font.
   A. Courier
   B. Euro Sign
   C. Garamond

3. The tab location in the Word Options dialog box with the check box to Disable OpenType Font Formatting Features.
   A. Advanced
   B. Display
   C. General

4. An OpenType picture or symbol used to represent data.
   A. Cell
   B. Glyph
   C. Special Character

5. The type of section break that divides the same page.
   A. Continuous
   B. Even Page
   C. Odd Page

6. The type of line that displays when five underscore characters are typed followed by the Enter key.
   A. Diagonal
   B. Horizontal
   C. Vertical

7. The Paste Option that removes all formatting from the text.
   A. Keep Source Formatting
   B. Keep Text Only
   C. Merge Formatting

8. The feature that will take away parts of the selected picture.
   A. Background Removal
   B. SmartArt
   C. Wrap Text

9. A collection of rows and columns used to represent data.
   A. Cell
   B. Tab
   C. Table

10. The function that will add all the cells in the previous rows in a table column.
    A. =SUM
    B. =TOTAL(ROWS)
    C. =SUM(ABOVE)

Topics for Discussion

1. Imagine that you work for a small business. What types of quick parts could be created for the business?

2. Imagine that you work for a small business. What types of subdocuments would a typical small business need to create?

Skill Check

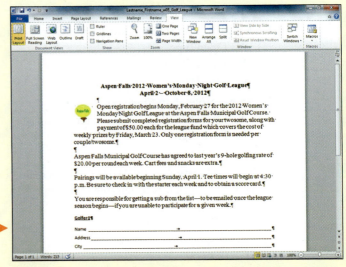

Figure 1

To complete this project, you will need the following files:

- w05_Golf_League
- w05_Golf_Table

You will save your files as:

- Lastname_Firstname_w05_Golf_League
- Lastname_Firstname_w05_Golf_Table

1. **Start** Word and open **w05_Golf_League**. Save the file in your **Word Chapter 5** folder as Lastname_Firstname_w05_Golf_League Add the file name to the footer.

2. Select the picture. On the **Format tab**, in the **Adjust group**, click the **Remove Background** button. On the **Background Removal tab**, in the **Refine group**, click the **Mark Areas to Remove** button. Drag each middle sizing handle out to the edge of the solid square. Click the **Delete Mark** button.

3. On the **Format tab**, in the **Arrange group**, click the **Wrap Text** button, and then click **Square**. Deselect the picture and then compare with **Figure 1**.

4. In the title, select *Aspen Falls 2012*. On the **Insert tab**, in the **Text group**, click the **Quick Parts** button, and then click **Save Selection to Quick Part Gallery**. Click **OK**.

5. Turn on the ruler and then click the first occurrence of *Email*. On the horizontal ruler, drag the right tab mark at **3.13** inches down.

6. Click the beginning of the *Golfer 1* line. Press and hold [Shift] while pressing [-] five times. Press [Enter] one time.

7. On the **Page Layout tab**, in the **Page Setup group**, click the **Breaks** button, and then click **Continuous**.

8. Locate and select *Golfer 1*. Press and hold [Ctrl] and then select *Golfer 2*. On the **Home tab**, in the **Font group**, click the **Text Highlight Color button** arrow, and then click **Bright Green**. Compare with **Figure 2**.

9. In the paragraph that begins *When paying* add a space after *to*.

10. On the **Insert tab**, in the **Text group**, click the **Quick Parts** button, and then click the **Aspen Falls 2012** thumbnail.

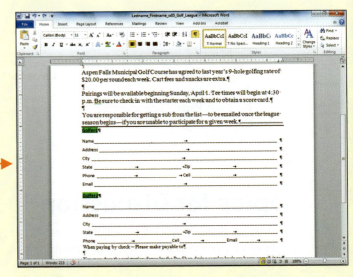

Figure 2

■ **Continue to the next page to complete this Skill Check** ▶

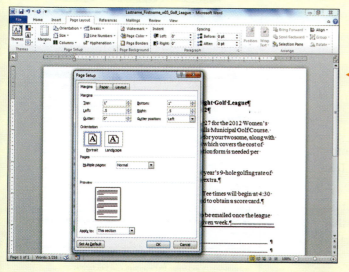

Figure 3

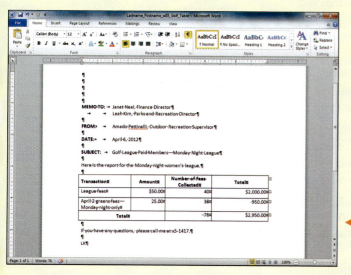

Figure 4

11. In the **Text group**, click the **Quick Parts** button. Right-click *Aspen Falls 2012*, and then click **Organize and Delete**.

12. With *Aspen Falls* selected, click **Delete**. Click **Yes**, and then click **Close**.

13. Click anywhere in the bottom section. On the **Page Layout tab**, in the **Page Setup group**, click the **Margins** button, and then click **Custom Margins**. Change the left and right margins in the top section only to **.5"** Compare with **Figure 3** and then click **OK**.

14. On the **File tab**, click **Options**. In the **Word Options** dialog box, click the **Advanced tab**. Expand the **Layout Options**, and then clear the **Disable OpenType Font Formatting Features** check box. Click **OK**.

15. On the **Home tab**, click the **Font Dialog Box Launcher**. On the **Advanced tab**, under **OpenType Features**, click the **Ligatures arrow**, and then select **Standard Only**. Click **OK**.

16. In the paragraph that begins *Aspen Falls Municipal*, locate the word *golfing*, and select *fi*. Type FB01 and then press Alt + X.

17. Move to the beginning of the document. On the **Insert tab**, in the **Symbols group**, click the **Symbol** button, and then click **More Symbols**. Click the **Font arrow**, and then click **Webdings**. Insert the ☞ symbol (character code 119) and then click **Close**. Select the symbol. Change the **Font Size** to **18**. Copy the ☞ and then apply the **Keep Source Formatting Paste Option** to the end of the line.

18. On the **File tab**, click **Options**. Click the **Advanced tab**. Expand the **Layout Options**, and then select the **Disable OpenType Font Formatting Features** check box. Click **OK**. Turn the ruler off. **Save** your work, and then **Close** the document.

19. Locate and open **w05_Golf_Table**, and then save it in your **Word Chapter 5** folder as Lastname_Firstname_w05_Golf_Table Add the filename to the footer.

20. Click the table's first blank cell in the **Total** column. On the **Layout tab**, in the **Data group**, click the **Formula** button. Insert a formula that multiplies the *Amount* by the *Number of Fees Collected* =b2*c2 In the formula, apply the **$#,##0.00; ($#,##0.00)** format.

21. In the table's third row **Total** column, repeat the technique to insert a similar formula with the **#,##0.00** format.

22. In the table's last cell, insert a formula that calculates the column total. In the formula, apply the **$#,##0.00;($#,##0.00)** format. In the table, select *20*. Replace it with 25 Update the formulas. Compare with **Figure 4**.

23. **Save** and then print or submit the files as directed by your instructor. **Exit** Word.

Done! You have completed the Skill Check

Assess Your Skills 1

To complete this project, you will need the following files:

- w05_Car_Show
- w05_Car_Memo

You will save your files as:

- Lastname_Firstname_w05_Car_Show
- Lastname_Firstname_w05_Car_Memo

1. **Start** Word. Locate and open **w05_Car_Show**, and then save it in your **Word Chapter 5** folder as Lastname_Firstname_w05_Car_Show Add the file name to the footer. Display the ruler.

2. Insert the ♣ symbol (character code 37) from the **Webdings** font to the left of the *V* in *Vintage* in the title. Change the symbol's **Font Color** to **Dark Blue**. Copy the ♣ and then apply the **Keep Source Formatting Paste Option** to the end of the line.

3. In the paragraph that begins *2012*, at the beginning, insert a **Continuous** section break. In the bottom section, change the bottom margin to .9 and the left and right margins to .5

4. Select the paragraphs that begin with *WHEN* and end with *parking lot*. Move the tab marker to **1** on the horizontal ruler.

5. Before the section break, use the keyboard method to insert a horizontal line. Repeat this technique to insert a horizontal line above the paragraph that begins *Check/Money order*.

6. In the paragraph that begins *FEE*, locate and select the *fi* in the word *first* and apply the *fi* glyphs from the **Garamond** font.

7. Select the text that begins *Space is* through *cars*, and then apply the **Turquoise Text Highlight Color**.

8. Locate and select the paragraph that begins *Name*, drag through the paragraph that begins *Amount enclosed*. Move the tab at 6 to **7** inches. Turn off the ruler.

9. **Save** your work, and then **Close** the document. Locate and open **w05_Car_Memo**, and then save it in your **Word Chapter 5** folder as Lastname_Firstname_w05_Car_Memo Add the file name to the footer.

10. In the first blank cell in the table's **Total** column, insert a formula that multiplies the *Price* by the *Number of Entries*. Apply the **$#,##0.00;($#,##0.00)** number format.

11. In the table's third row, in the **Total** column, repeat the previous technique to insert a similar formula with the **#,##0.00** number format.

12. Insert a formula in the last cell that calculates the column total. Apply the **$#,##0.00; ($#,##0.00)** number format. **Align Top Right** all numbers in the **Total** column.

13. In the table, select *35*. Replace it with 50 Update the formulas.

14. **Save** and then print or submit the project files as directed by your instructor. **Exit** Word.

Done! You have completed Assess Your Skills 1

Figure 1

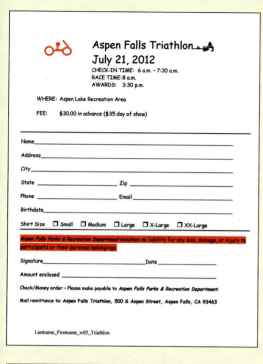

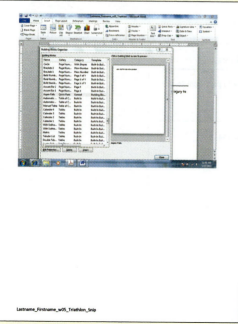

Figure 1

Assess Your Skills 2

To complete this project, you will need the following file:

- w05_Triathlon

You will save your files as:

- Lastname_Firstname_w05_Triathlon
- Lastname_Firstname_w05_Triathlon_Snip

1. **Start** Word. Locate and open **w05_Triathlon**, and then save it in your **Word Chapter 5** folder as Lastname_Firstname_ w05_ Triathlon Add the file name to the footer. Display the ruler.

2. Insert the ☐ symbol (Wingdings character code 114) before the word *Small*. Add a space, and then change symbol's **Font Size** to **16**.

3. Copy the symbol and the space. **Paste** using the **Keep Source Formatting Paste Option** to the left of: *Medium, Large, X-Large,* and *XX-Large.*

4. Click the end of the paragraph that begins *FEE*, and insert a **Continuous** section break. In the bottom section, adjust the margins to **Narrow.**

5. Click left of *Name*, and use the keyboard method to insert a horizontal line above the paragraph. Repeat this technique to insert a horizontal line above the paragraph that begins *Aspen Falls Triathlon assumes.*

6. Move to the beginning of the document. At the end of the first paragraph, insert each of the following symbols from the **Webdings** font: ⛵—code 138—and 🏊—code 80.

7. Select the picture and remove the background.

8. Apply square wrap to the picture.

9. Locate the paragraph that begins *Check/Money* and select the text *Aspen Falls Parks & Recreation Department.* Save the selection to the **Quick Parts** gallery. In the **Create New Building Block** dialog box, accept all default options.

10. In the bottom section, locate the paragraph that begins *Aspen Falls Triathlon* and select the text *Aspen Falls Triathlon.* Replace the selected text with the *Aspen Falls* quick parts.

11. Open the **Building Blocks Organizer**, and then locate the *Aspen Falls* building block.

12. Create a full-screen snip, **Save** it in your **Word Chapter 5** folder as Lastname_ Firstname_w05_Triathlon_Snip and then close the Snipping Tool window.

13. Delete the *Aspen Falls* thumbnail.

14. Select the paragraphs that begin *Name* through *Birthdate* and then move the tab setting from 6.5" to **7"** on the horizontal ruler.

15. Apply the **Red Text Highlight Color** to the paragraph that begins *Aspen Falls Parks.*

16. **Save** and then print or submit the project as directed by your instructor. **Exit** Word.

Done! You have completed Assess Your Skills 2

Assess Your Skills Visually

To complete this project, you will need the following file:

- New, blank Word document

You will save your file as:

- Lastname_Firstname_w05_Library_Registration

Re-create the registration form shown in **Figure 1**. Insert the ⬇ symbol—code 168—from the Webdings font before and after the first paragraph of the document. Insert a continuous section break after the paragraph(s) related to *Fees*, and then in the lower section, change the top, bottom, left, and right margins to .80 Insert the horizontal lines shown, and in the *Shirt size* line, insert the ☐ symbol—code 114 from the Wingdings font. For the form lines, apply right leader tabs set at 4.5 and 7 inches.

Save the file as Lastname_Firstname_w05_Library_Registration in your **Word Chapter 5** folder. Insert the file name in the footer and then print or submit the project as directed by your instructor. **Exit** Word.

Done! You have completed Assess Your Skills Visually

Aspen Falls Library Summer Program
Children's Registration
June 4 – July 13, 2012

CHECK-IN:	Any time prior to 1:00 p.m. on June 4.
WEEKLY PROGRAM:	Mondays, 1:00 p.m. – 2:30, Resource Center
AWARDS:	Party on July 13, 1:00 - 3:30 p.m., Resource Center
WHERE:	Aspen Falls Library - Resource Center
FEES:	None as long as you reside in the City of Aspen Falls Outside of Aspen Falls, please check with librarian

Name _____

Address _____

City _____

Phone _____ Email _____

Birth date _____

Shirt Size ☐ Small ☐ Medium ☐ Large ☐ X-Large ☐ XX-Large

Aspen Falls Library assumes no liability for any loss, damage, or injury to participants or their personal belongings.

Signature _____ Date _____

Mail form to: Aspen Falls Library, 500 S Aspen Street, Aspen Falls, CA 93463

Lastname_Firstname_w05_Library_Registration

Figure 1

Skills in Context

To complete this project, you will need the following file:

- New blank Word document

You will save your file as:

- Lastname_Firstname_w05_Local_Event

Choose a school or local event, and then create a registration form for the event. Insert at least one symbol into the document. Divide the form into at least two sections using a continuous section break, and then customize the margins for each section. Add at least one horizontal line. Include tab settings for right leader tabs that are used to collect information such as name, address, city, state, zip code, phone, email, and so on. Insert at least one table with formulas.

Save the file as Lastname_Firstname_ w05_Event in your **Word Chapter 5** folder. Print or submit the project as directed by your instructor. **Exit** Word.

Done! You have completed Skills in Context

Skills and You

To complete this project, you will need the following file:

- New blank Word document

You will save your file as:

- Lastname_Firstname_w05_Family_Event

Prepare a sign-up sheet for an upcoming family reunion or family party/holiday gathering that includes at least one symbol. Use the form to collect written information such as name, address, city, state, zip code, phone, email address, and news to share from the past year. Include right leader tab settings to gather the information. Create a continuous section break, custom margins, and a horizontal line.

Save the file as Lastname_Firstname_w05_Family_ Event in your **Word Chapter 5** folder. Print or submit the project as directed by your instructor. **Exit** Word.

Done! You have completed Skills and You

CHAPTER 6

Create a Document with Visual Elements

► Newsletters can be enhanced by adjusting column settings, inserting built-in text boxes, linking text boxes, changing text direction, inserting and modifying shapes, removing picture backgrounds, cropping pictures to shapes, and hiding and reordering pictures.

► Data from Excel can be linked to Word documents. Charts can also be created and modified in the Word document.

Your starting screen will look like this:

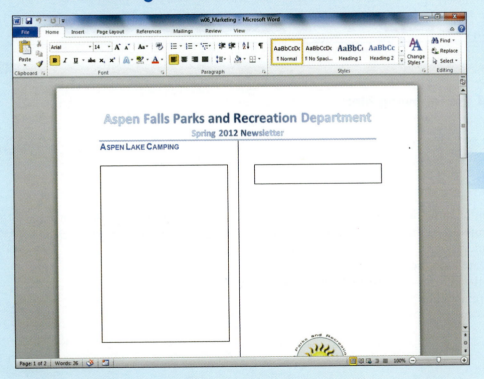

SKILLS
Skills 1-10 Training

At the end of this chapter, you will be able to:

Skill 1 Work with Template Files

Skill 2 Insert Built-in Text Boxes

Skill 3 Link Text Boxes

Skill 4 Change Text Direction

Skill 5 Link to Excel Worksheet Data

Skill 6 Insert Charts

Skill 7 Modify Charts

Skill 8 Insert and Modify Shapes

Skill 9 Crop Pictures to Shapes

Skill 10 Use the Selection and Visibility Pane

MORE SKILLS

More Skills 11 Work with Page Number Building Blocks

More Skills 12 Insert Equations

More Skills 13 Insert Quick Tables

More Skills 14 Create Watermark Building Blocks

Outcome

Using the skills listed to the left will enable you to create documents like these:

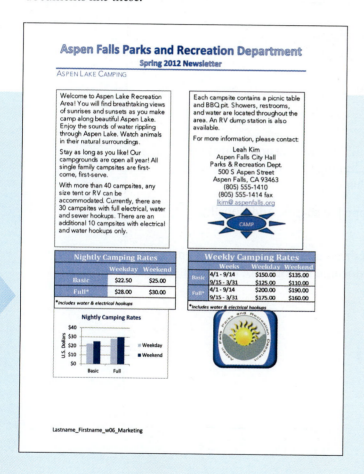

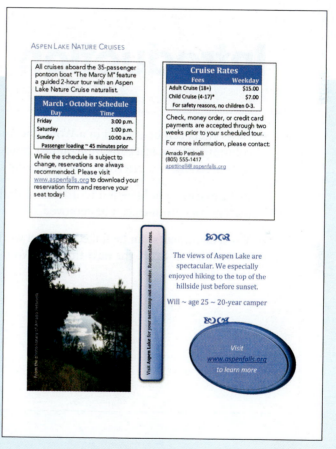

You will save your file as:

Lastname_Firstname_w06_Marketing

In this chapter, you will create documents for the Aspen Falls City Hall, which provides essential services for the citizens and visitors of Aspen Falls, California.

Introduction

▶ Newsletters can be created in a Word document by inserting and adjusting column settings, inserting built-in text boxes, linking text boxes, changing text direction, and inserting and modifying shapes.

▶ Pictures can be hidden and reordered or cropped to shapes. Additionally, picture backgrounds can be removed.

▶ Word documents can be linked to Excel worksheets and charts. When an item is modified in Excel, the next time the Word document is opened, the object is updated.

Time to complete all
10 skills – 50 to 90 minutes

Find your student data files here:

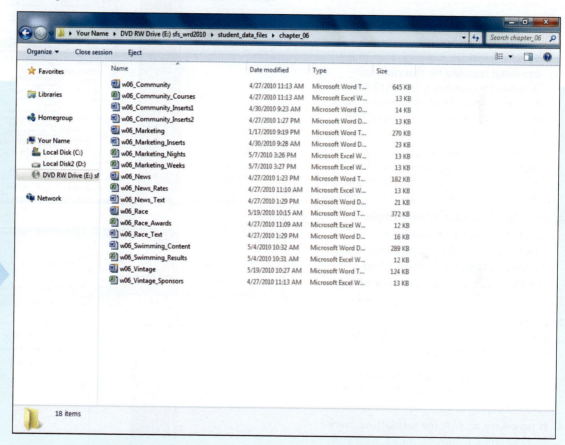

Student data files needed for this chapter:

- w06_Marketing
- w06_Marketing_Inserts
- w06_Marketing_Nights
- w06_Marketing_Weeks

► A *template*—is a prebuilt document with placeholders and formatting already in place into which you insert your own text and objects.

► Recall that a newsletter created in Word is often separated into columns. The column width and the spacing between columns can be adjusted.

1. **Start** ⊕ Word and open the student data file **w06_Marketing**.

   The document is a two-page, two-column, newsletter template file that contains formatted text, pictures, and text boxes. This file can be opened and used as many times as desired to create monthly Aspen Falls newsletters.

   To view the default templates that are available in Word by category, on the File tab, click New. Additionally, other templates are available online at Office.com/templates.

2. Save the file in your **Word Chapter 6** folder with the name Lastname_ Firstname_w06_Marketing Observe that the **Save as type** list displays **Word Template**. Click the **Save as type arrow** as shown in **Figure 1**.

3. In the displayed list, click **Word Document**, and then click **Save**. Add the file name to the footer.

   The Word template file is now saved as a Word document with some text and formats already in place.

4. If necessary, display the formatting marks and the ruler. Compare your screen with **Figure 2**.

■ **Continue to the next page to complete the skill**

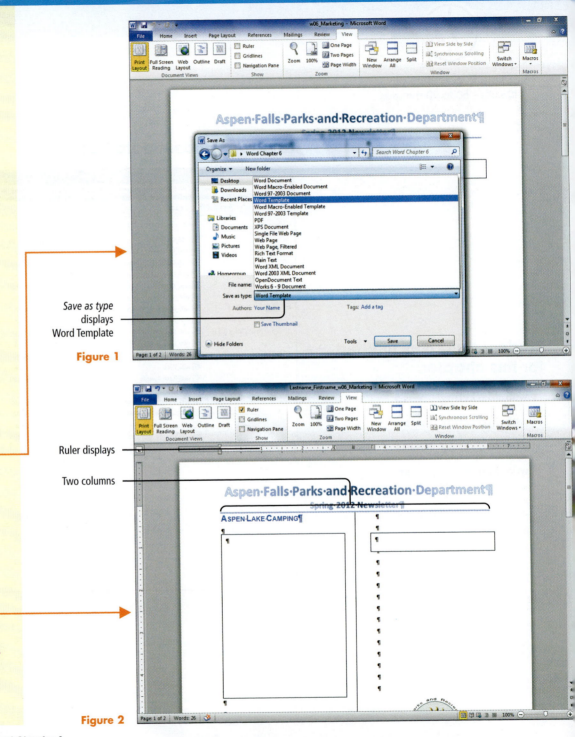

Save as type displays Word Template

Figure 1

Ruler displays

Two columns

Figure 2

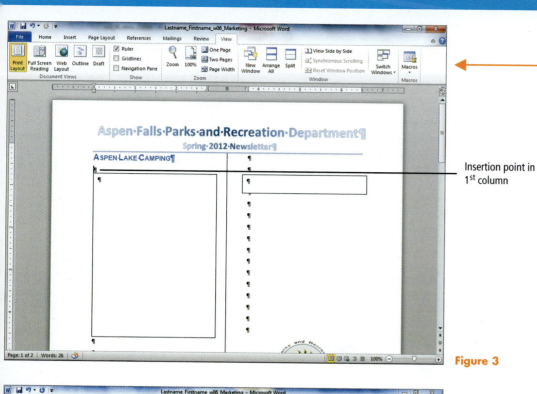

Insertion point in 1st column

Figure 3

5. Locate and then click the first blank paragraph below *Aspen Lake Camping* as shown in **Figure 3**.

> Because the insertion point is positioned at the left side of the document, the first column is active. The ruler displays the left and right margin settings for the first column.

6. On the **Page Layout tab**, in the **Page Setup group**, click the **Columns** button, and then click **More Columns**.

7. In the **Columns** dialog box, under **Presets**, click **Two**. Verify the column width changes to 3".

> The spacing between columns changes to 0.5". The equal column width check box is selected.

8. Clear the **Line between** check box and observe the **Preview**.

9. Click the **Apply to arrow** and then click **Whole document**. Compare your screen with **Figure 4**.

> The Preview displays how the changes will look in your document once the dialog box is closed.

10. Click **OK**.

11. Save 🖫 the document.

- **You have completed Skill 1 of 10**

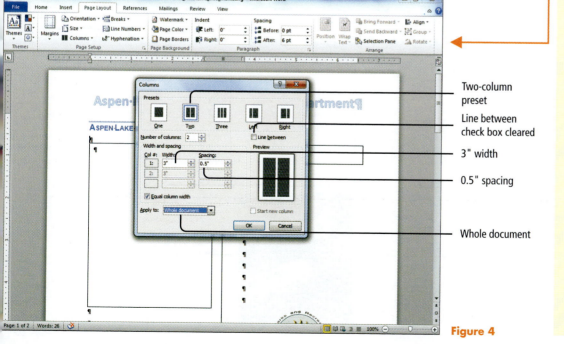

Two-column preset

Line between check box cleared

3" width

0.5" spacing

Whole document

Figure 4

► Word has several built-in text boxes with predefined styles that you can insert without having to draw and format a plain text box.

► After inserting a built-in text box, you can replace the text and graphics as needed.

1. On Page 2, below the text box in the right column, click the first blank paragraph.

2. On the **Insert tab**, in the **Text group**, click the **Text Box** button.

3. In the **Built-In** gallery, scroll to locate and then select the **Decorative Quote** thumbnail. Compare your screen with **Figure 1**.

   Built-in text boxes provide decorative effects and a formatted placeholder in which you can enter your own text.

4. Click the built-in text box border, and then with the ⊞ pointer, drag the text box in the right column on Page 2 down. The top edge of the text box should be positioned even with the top edge of the picture in the first column and aligned with the left edge of column 2.

   The paragraph symbol moves to the right of the text box so that text can be inserted next to the text box if desired.

5. In the built-in text box, click the field that begins *Type a quote*, and then type The views of Aspen Lake are spectacular. We especially enjoyed hiking to the top of the hillside just before sunset. Press Enter, and then type Will ~ age 25 ~ 20-year camper Compare your screen with **Figure 2**.

■ **Continue to the next page to complete the skill**

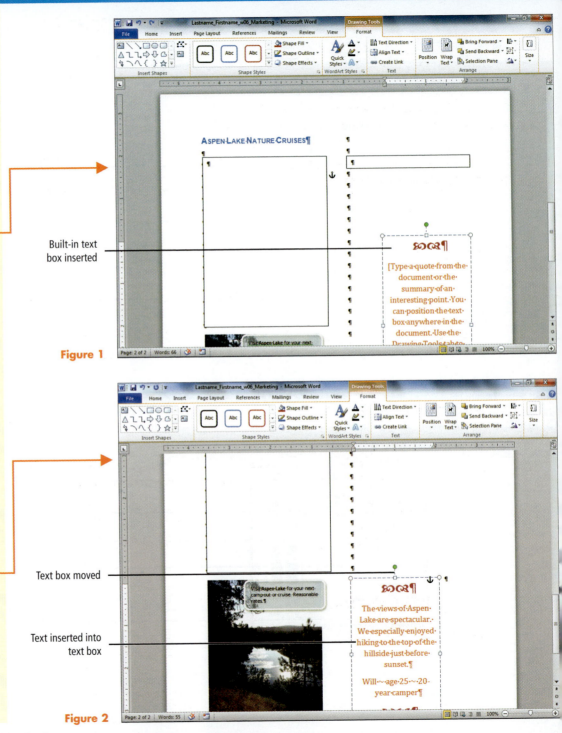

Built-in text box inserted

Figure 1

Text box moved

Text inserted into text box

Figure 2

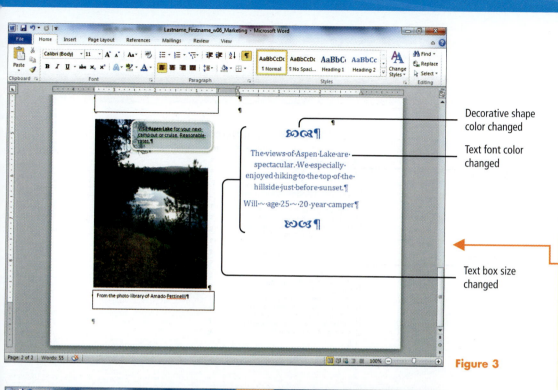

Decorative shape color changed

Text font color changed

Text box size changed

Figure 3

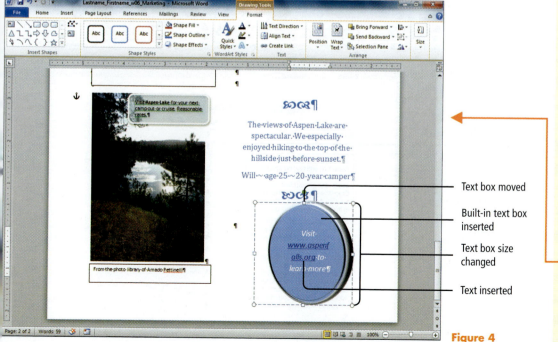

Text box moved

Built-in text box inserted

Text box size changed

Text inserted

Figure 4

6. Click the quote text box border that begins *The views of* to select everything inside the text box.

7. On the **Home tab**, in the **Font group**, click the **Font Color button arrow**. Click the fifth color in the first row—**Blue, Accent 1**.

8. With the text box still selected, on the **Format tab**, if necessary, click the **Size** button and then change the **Shape Height** 1.5″ to 3 and the **Shape Width** 1.37″ to 3 If necessary, press Enter.

9. Deselect the text box on Page 2, and then compare your screen with **Figure 3**.

10. On the **Insert tab**, in the **Text group**, click the **Text Box** button. In the **Built-In** gallery, scroll to locate and select the **Mod Quote** thumbnail.

    The text box displays in the middle of Page 2.

11. Position the insertion point over the bottom border of the Mod Quote built-in text box border and click to select it.

12. On the **Format tab**, if necessary, click the **Size** button, and then change the **Shape Height** 1.5″ to 2.4 Press Enter.

13. With the text box still selected, point to the top border and then drag the text box down to position it right below the decorative shape in the text box that begins *The views of.* Center the text box object horizontally between the right column.

14. In the built-in text box, click the field that begins *Type a quote,* and then type Visit www.aspenfalls.org to learn more as shown in **Figure 4**.

15. **Save** the document.

- **You have completed Skill 2 of 10**

► The contents of two or more text boxes can be linked. **Linked text boxes** are used so that text automatically flows between one or more text boxes. For example, when there is no longer room to display text in the first text box, the remaining text is automatically placed in the second, linked text box.

1. Open the student data file **w06_Marketing_Inserts** and then select the paragraph that begins *Welcome to Aspen* through the blank paragraph below *lkim@aspenfalls.org*

2. On the **Home tab**, in the **Clipboard group**, click the **Copy** button.

3. Switch to the **Lastname_Firstname_w06_Marketing** window. Press [Ctrl] + [Home].

4. Below *ASPEN LAKE CAMPING*, click the border of the empty text box. On the **Home tab**, in the **Clipboard group**, click the **Paste button arrow**. In the **Paste Options** gallery, click the first button, **Keep Source Formatting** 🔲. Compare your screen with **Figure 1**.

   The first three paragraphs display in the text box. There is no room to display the remaining text without resizing the box or adjusting the font size.

5. On the **Format tab**, in the **Text group**, click the **Create Link** button. Position the 🖐 in the empty text box in the right column on Page 1 and click. Compare with **Figure 2**.

   The remaining text copied from the file displays in the second text box. The text is linked to the first text box.

■ Continue to the next page to complete the skill ▶

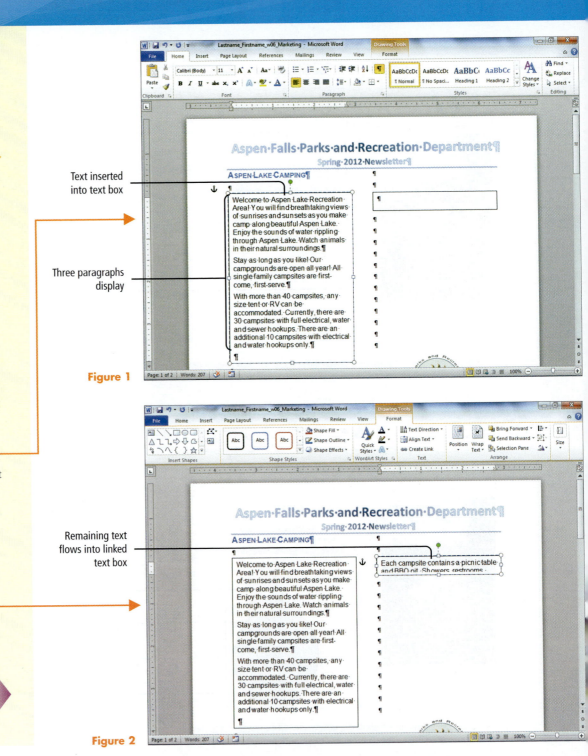

Text inserted into text box

Three paragraphs display

Figure 1

Remaining text flows into linked text box

Figure 2

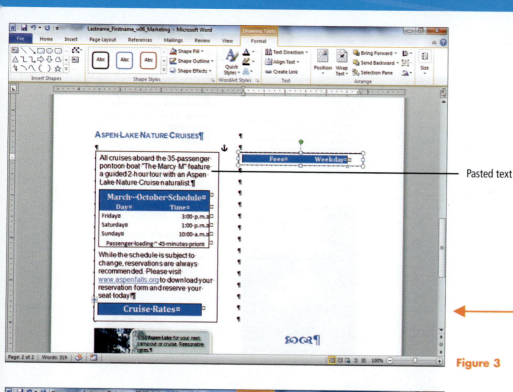

Pasted text

Figure 3

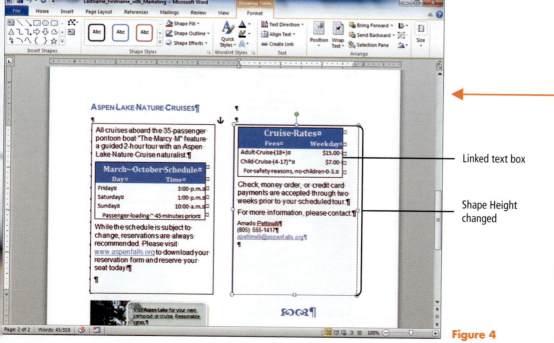

Linked text box

Shape Height changed

Figure 4

6. Switch to the **w06_Marketing_Inserts** window. Select the paragraph that begins *All cruises aboard* through the paragraph that ends *apettinelli@aspenfalls.org*. **Copy** the text. **Close w06_Marketing_Inserts.**

7. In the **Lastname_Firstname_w06_ Marketing** window, on Page 2, click the border of the first empty text box in column 1.

8. On the **Home tab**, in the **Clipboard group**, click the **Paste button arrow**. In the **Paste Options** gallery, click the first button, **Keep Source Formatting**.

9. On the **Format tab**, in the **Text group**, click the **Create Link** button. On Page 2, click the empty text box in the top-right column. Compare with **Figure 3**.

10. On Page 2, click the border of the first text box in column 2, if necessary. On the **Format tab**, if necessary, click the **Size** button, change the **Shape Height** to 4 and then, if necessary, press Enter.

11. On Page 2, column 1, inside the first text box, locate the paragraph that begins *While the schedule*. Click the end of the paragraph and then press Enter. Compare with **Figure 4**.

   The title Cruise Rates moves above the table in column 2.

12. On Page 1, click the border of the first text box in column 2. On the **Format tab**, if necessary, click the **Size** button, change the **Shape Height** to 4 and then, if necessary, press Enter.

13. **Save** the document.

- **You have completed Skill 3 of 10**

► In a text box, the text can be rotated to face a different direction—sideways or upside down, for example.

► Sometimes the direction of the text in a placeholder must be changed to fit the desired area or for ease of reading.

1. On Page 2, locate and select the border of the text box in the left column that begins *Visit Aspen Lake.*

   The text displays horizontally.

2. On the **Format tab**, in the **Text group**, click the **Text Direction** button, and then click **Rotate all text 270°**. Compare your screen with **Figure 1**.

   Text direction button choices include horizontal, rotate all text 90°, and rotate all text 270°.

3. Verify the text box that begins *Visit Aspen Lake* is selected. Click the lower-left handle and then drag down and to the right to position the lower-left corner so that it is even with the bottom border of the picture.

   The left edge of the text box will be aligned with the last *i* in *Pettinelli* in the text box below.

4. Click the border of the text box and then drag it over to the right of the picture so that the text box is positioned in between the two columns and so that it is not touching any other text boxes. Compare your screen with **Figure 2**.

■ **Continue to the next page to complete the skill**

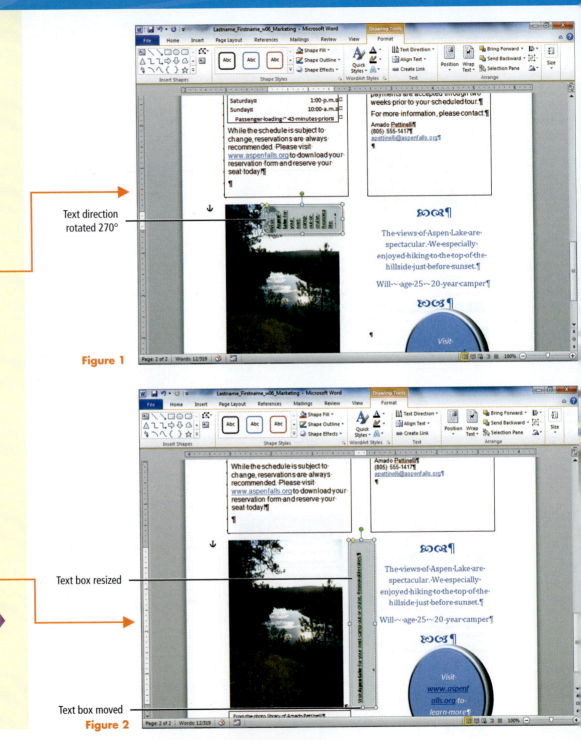

Text direction rotated 270°

Figure 1

Text box resized

Text box moved

Figure 2

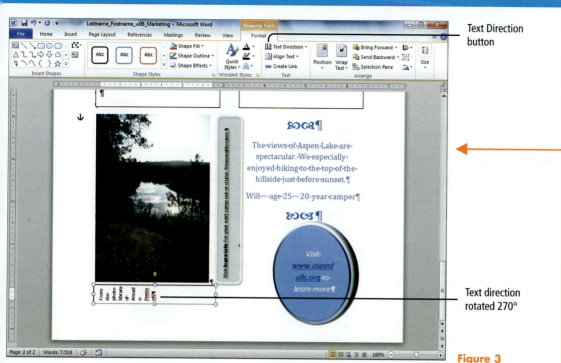

Text Direction button

Text direction rotated 270°

Figure 3

Text box resized and positioned

Border and fill color removed from text box

Font color changed

Figure 4

5. On Page 2, at the bottom of the left column, click the border of the text box that begins *From the photo* to select the text box.

6. On the **Format tab**, in the **Text group**, click the **Text Direction** button, and then click **Rotate all text 270°**. Compare your screen with **Figure 3**.

7. Verify the text box that begins *From the photo* is selected. On the **Format tab**, if necessary, click the **Size** button, change the **Shape Height** ⊞ 1.5" ↕ to **2.5** Change the **Shape Width** ⊟ 1.37" ↕ to **0.4** and then press Enter.

8. On the **Format tab**, in the **Shape Styles group**, click the **Shape Outline** button, and then click **No Outline**.

9. Verify the text box that begins *From the photo* is selected. In the **Shape Styles group**, click the **Shape Fill** button and then click **No Fill**.

10. Verify the text box that begins *From the photo* is selected. On the **Home tab**, in the **Font group**, click the **Font Color button arrow**, and then click the first button in the first row—**White, Background 1**.

    Text in the selected text box will not be visible momentarily.

11. With the text box that begins *From the photo* selected, drag to position the upper left corner inside the landscape photograph so that the bottom-left edge of the text box touches the bottom and left corners of the landscape photograph as shown in **Figure 4**.

12. **Save** 🖫 the document.

■ **You have completed Skill 4 of 10**

▶ An *object* is text, a chart, SmartArt, or a picture that can be added to an Office document.

▶ Objects created in other programs can be inserted, positioned, and linked to the original document.

1. Scroll to Page 1. In the left column, click the first empty paragraph below the text box.

2. On the **Insert tab**, in the **Text group**, click the **Object** button.

3. In the **Object** dialog box, click the **Create from File tab**, and then click **Browse**. Navigate to the student files, select **w06_Marketing_Nights**, and then, if necessary, click **Insert**.

4. In the **Object** dialog box, select the **Link to file** check box. Compare your screen with **Figure 1**.

   Selecting the Link to file check box will create a shortcut to the object in the file selected in step 3.

5. Click **OK** to insert the Excel worksheet.

6. In the right column, click to position the insertion point in the first blank paragraph before the section break. Press Enter.

7. Repeat the technique just practiced to insert **w06_Marketing_Weeks** as a linked object.

8. Click the border of the *Aspen Falls* figure, and drag it down to Page 1, below the *Weekly Camping Rates* object in column 2 as shown in **Figure 2**.

9. Double-click the Excel object that begins *Nightly Camping Rates* to open an Excel worksheet.

▪ **Continue to the next page to complete the skill** ▶

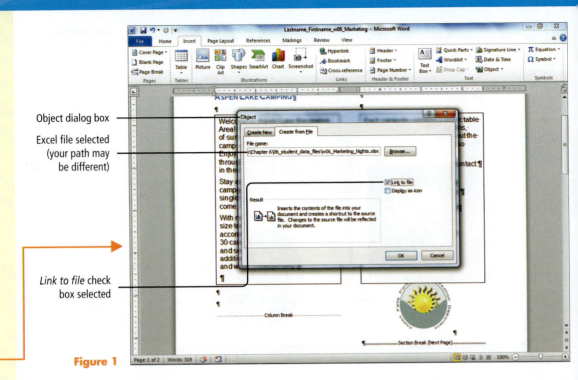

Object dialog box

Excel file selected (your path may be different)

Link to file check box selected

Figure 1

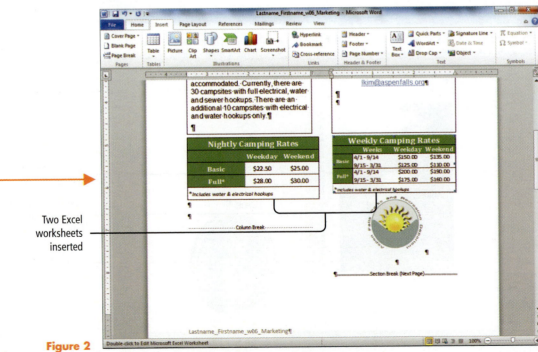

Two Excel worksheets inserted

Figure 2

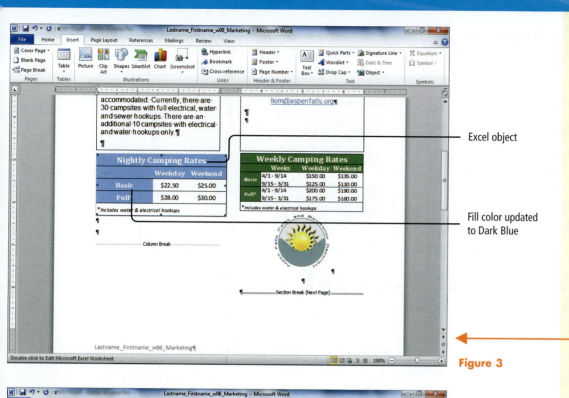

Figure 3

Excel object

Fill color updated to Dark Blue

Link color updated in Word

Figure 4

In the destination file, double-clicking a *linked object*—an object that is updated whenever the original source file is updated—opens it in the application that created the original source file.

10. In Excel, click the **Maximize** button.

11. In Excel, drag to select cells **A1** through **C2**, press the Ctrl key and then click cells **A3** and **A4**. On the **Home tab**, in the **Font group**, click the **Fill Color button arrow**. In the gallery, click the fourth color in the third row—**Dark Blue, Text 2, Lighter 60%**.

12. Click **Save** and then **Close** the Excel file. Click the Word document.

13. In the left column, right-click the Excel object, and then click **Update Link**. Compare your Word document with **Figure 3**.

   Any changes made to the source file will also be reflected in the destination file.

   Because the object is linked, the Word document—the destination file—displays the changes made in Excel—the source file.

14. For the Excel object in the right column, repeat the techniques just practiced to open the object in Excel. In cells **A1** through **D2** and **A3** through **A6**, change the **Fill Color** to **Dark Blue, Text 2, Lighter 60%** and then **Save** and **Close** Excel.

15. Click the Word document. For the Excel object in the right column, update the link. Compare your screen with **Figure 4**.

16. **Save** the document.

■ **You have completed Skill 5 of 10**

► A *chart* is a graphic representation of the data in a worksheet or table. A chart can be created in Excel using a datasheet and then inserted into a Word document.

► Charts can be inserted into Word documents to enhance the text.

1. In Word, position the insertion point in the first blank paragraph below the *Nightly Camping Rates* object.

2. On the **Insert tab**, in the **Illustrations group**, click the **Chart** button.

3. In the **Insert Chart** dialog box, under **Column**, verify the **Clustered Column** button is selected and then click **OK**. Compare your screen with **Figure 1**.

    When you insert a chart, the screen splits between Word and Excel. The Word window displays the chart, and the Excel window displays the underlying data used to create the chart. The Excel datasheet is edited to create a chart that reflects your own labels and data.

4. In Excel, click cell **B1**—*Series 1*, the cell in the intersection of column **B** and row **1**—and then type Weekday Press [Tab] and then type Weekend

    As you type in the Excel worksheet, the chart in the Word document is updated.

5. Click cell **A2**—*Category 1*, type Basic and then press [Enter]. Type Full and then press [Enter]. Compare your screen with **Figure 2**.

6. Click cell **B2** and then type 22.5 Press [Enter]. Type 28 and then press [Enter].

■ **Continue to the next page to complete the skill**

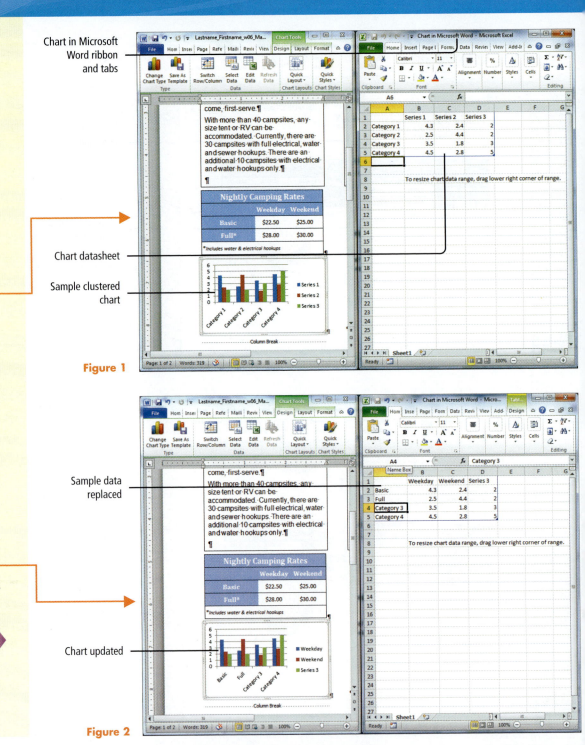

Chart in Microsoft Word ribbon and tabs

Chart datasheet

Sample clustered chart

Figure 1

Sample data replaced

Chart updated

Figure 2

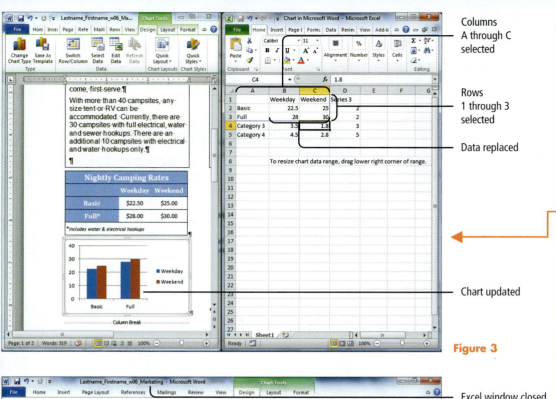

Columns
A through C
selected

Rows
1 through 3
selected

Data replaced

Chart updated

Figure 3

7. In cell **C2**, type 25 and then press Enter. In cell **C3**, type 30 and then press Enter.

8. In the Excel window, point to the lower right corner of the blue box surrounding the data in the bottom of cell **D5**. With the ⬉ pointer, drag to the left so that the blue box surrounds the range **A1** to **C5**.

9. Point to the lower right corner of the blue box surrounding the data in the bottom of cell **C5**. With the ⬉ pointer, drag up so that the blue box surrounds the range **A1** to **C3**. Compare your screen with **Figure 3**.

   A *range* is two or more cells that are adjacent or nonadjacent.

   Observe the chart in the Word window at the left. The chart includes data from the selected range in Excel.

   In the Excel window, each of the four cells bordered in blue is referred to as a *data point*, a value that originates in a datasheet cell. Data points that are related to one another form a *data series*.

10. **Close** ❌ the Excel window to return to the Word window.

11. If necessary, point to the border of the chart to display the 🔀 pointer. Right-click the border of the chart object. In the displayed shortcut menu, point to **Wrap Text** and then click **Square**. Drag the chart down the first column of Page 1, positioning the upper left corner below the *Nightly Camping Rates* data. Compare your screen with **Figure 4**.

12. **Save** 💾 the document.

   ■ **You have completed Skill 6 of 10**

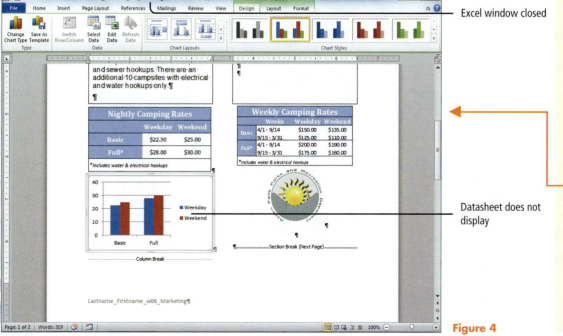

Excel window closed

Datasheet does not display

Figure 4

► Charts can be formatted using Chart Tools—the Design, Layout, and Format tabs.

► You can change colors, insert chart titles, and format values on the chart axis.

1. Click the chart to select it and to display the Chart Tools tabs.

2. Click one of the blue bars to select the *Weekday* data series as shown in **Figure 1**.

3. On the **Format tab**, in the **Current Selection group**, click the **Format Selection** button.

4. In the displayed **Format Data Series** dialog box, click **Fill**.

5. Select the **Solid fill** option, click the **Color** button, select the fifth color in the third row—**Blue, Accent 1, Lighter 60%**—and then click **Close**.

6. In the chart, click either red bar to select the *Weekend* data series. Repeat the technique just learned to change the **Fill Color** to the fourth color—**Dark Blue, Text 2**—and then click **Close**.

7. If necessary, click the border of the chart. On the **Layout tab**, in the **Labels group**, click the **Chart Title** button, and then click **Above Chart**.

8. In the *Chart Title* text box, type Nightly Camping Rates

   If necessary, right-click anywhere in the Chart Title text box and then in the shortcut menu, click Edit Text.

9. Click the border of the chart title to exit text-editing mode. On the **Home tab**, in the **Font group**, click the **Font Size** button, and then click **12**. Compare your screen with **Figure 2**.

■ Continue to the next page to complete the skill ➤

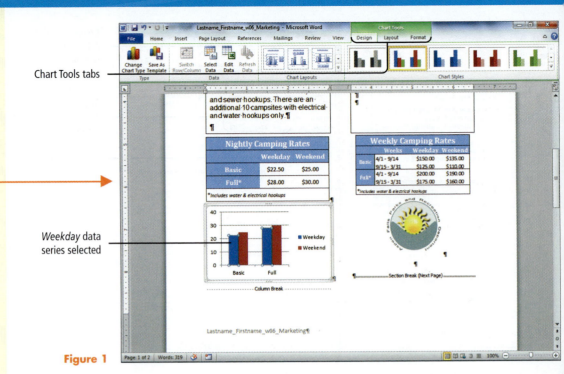

Chart Tools tabs

Weekday data series selected

Figure 1

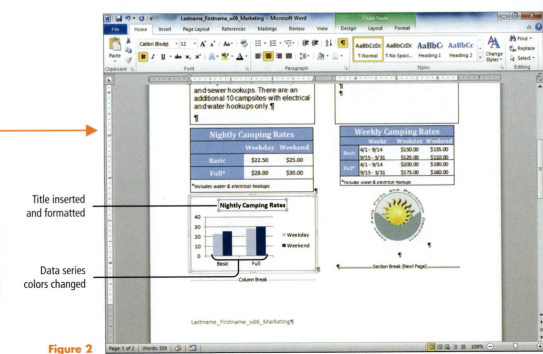

Title inserted and formatted

Data series colors changed

Figure 2

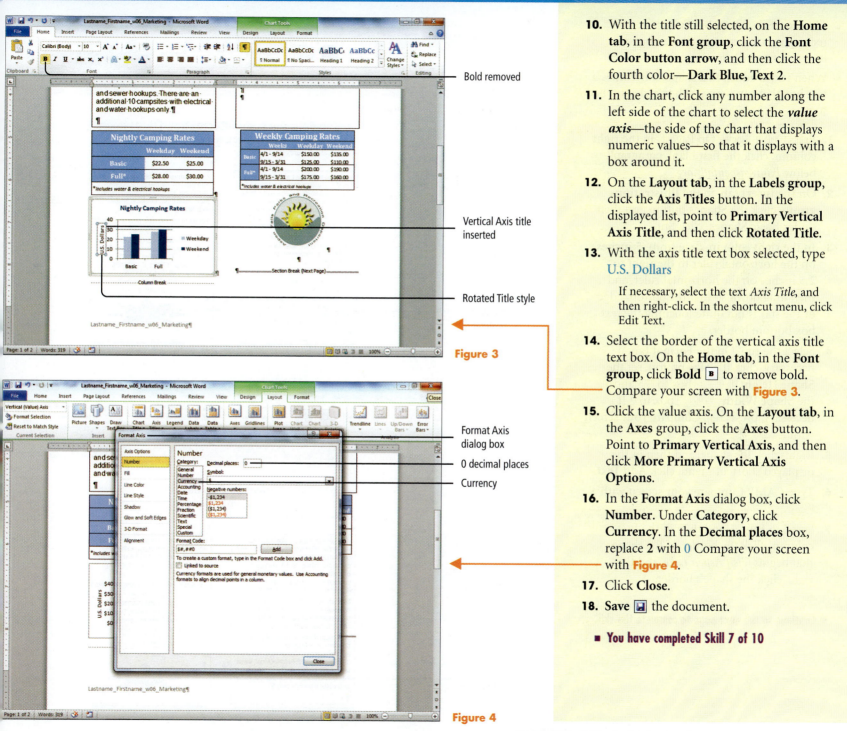

Bold removed

Vertical Axis title inserted

Rotated Title style

Figure 3

Format Axis dialog box

0 decimal places

Currency

Figure 4

10. With the title still selected, on the **Home tab**, in the **Font group**, click the **Font Color button arrow**, and then click the fourth color—**Dark Blue, Text 2**.

11. In the chart, click any number along the left side of the chart to select the *value axis*—the side of the chart that displays numeric values—so that it displays with a box around it.

12. On the **Layout tab**, in the **Labels group**, click the **Axis Titles** button. In the displayed list, point to **Primary Vertical Axis Title**, and then click **Rotated Title**.

13. With the axis title text box selected, type **U.S. Dollars**

    If necessary, select the text *Axis Title*, and then right-click. In the shortcut menu, click Edit Text.

14. Select the border of the vertical axis title text box. On the **Home tab**, in the **Font group**, click **Bold** ⓑ to remove bold. Compare your screen with **Figure 3**.

15. Click the value axis. On the **Layout tab**, in the **Axes** group, click the **Axes** button. Point to **Primary Vertical Axis**, and then click **More Primary Vertical Axis Options**.

16. In the **Format Axis** dialog box, click **Number**. Under **Category**, click **Currency**. In the **Decimal places** box, replace **2** with **0** Compare your screen with **Figure 4**.

17. Click **Close**.

18. Save 🖫 the document.

- **You have completed Skill 7 of 10**

► *Shapes* are drawing objects such as rectangles, arrows, and callouts that are inserted into a document.

► When text is added to a shape, it becomes a text box that can have text box styles applied to it.

1. Press Ctrl + Home. On Page 1, in the right column, click the first blank paragraph below *lkim@aspenfalls.org*.

2. On the **Insert tab**, in the **Illustrations group**, click the **Shapes** button and then under **Basic Shapes**, click **Sun**.

3. In the right column, drag from **.5 inches** on the horizontal ruler to the right to **2.5 inches** on the horizontal ruler, and then drag down so that the bottom edge of the star is not quite touching the text box bottom border.

4. Select the sun. On the **Format tab**, if necessary, click the **Size** button, set the **Shape Height** box to **.75** and the **Shape Width** box to **2** If necessary, press Enter. Compare your screen with **Figure 1**.

5. Right-click the shape, and then in the displayed shortcut menu, click **Add Text**.

6. Type CAMP Compare your screen with **Figure 2**.

7. Scroll to Page 2, and then in the first column, click the border of the shape that begins *Visit Aspen Lake*, and then right-click the shape's border.

■ **Continue to the next page to complete the skill**

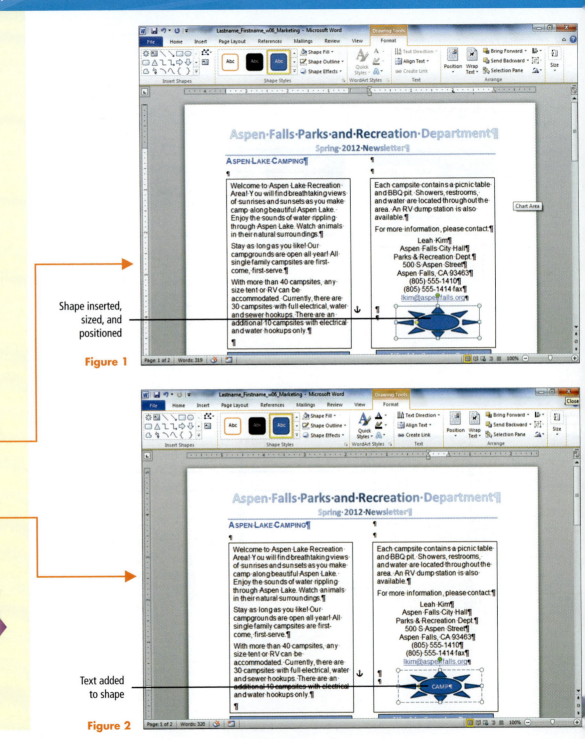

Shape inserted, sized, and positioned

Figure 1

Text added to shape

Figure 2

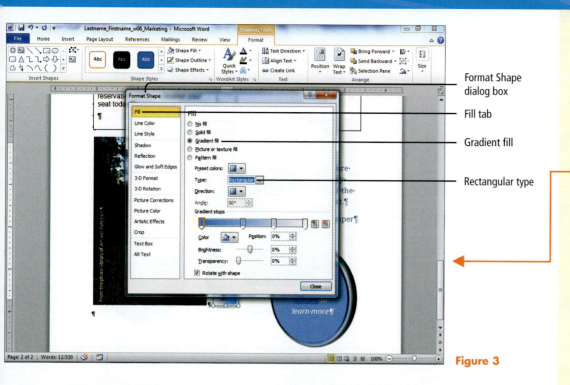

Format Shape dialog box

Fill tab

Gradient fill

Rectangular type

Figure 3

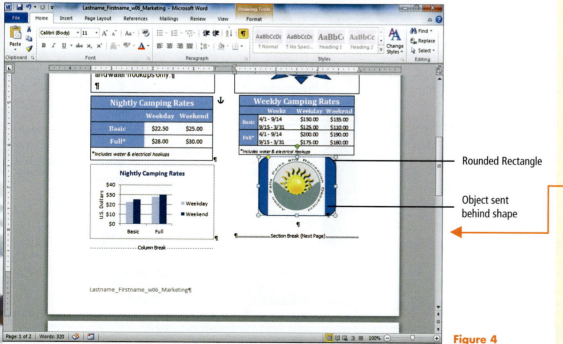

Rounded Rectangle

Object sent behind shape

Figure 4

8. In the displayed shortcut menu, click **Format Shape**. In the **Format Shape** dialog box, under **Fill**, select the **Gradient fill** option button.

9. Click the **Preset colors** button, and then select the fourth color in the first row—**Daybreak**.

10. Click the **Type arrow**, and then click **Rectangular** as shown in **Figure 3**. Click **Close**.

11. Verify the border of the text box that begins *Visit Aspen Lake* is selected. On the **Format tab**, in the **Shape Styles group**, click the **Shape Outline** button, and then click the second color in the first row—**Black, Text 1**.

12. Scroll to view the bottom of Page 1. On the **Insert tab**, in the **Illustrations group**, click the **Shapes** button, and then under **Rectangles**, click **Rounded Rectangle**.

13. Position the ⊞ pointer above and to the left of the *Aspen Falls Parks and Recreation Department* logo. Click and then drag down and to the right a little past the first blank paragraph symbol to the right of the logo object.

14. With the blue rounded rectangle covering the logo object, on the **Format tab**, in the **Arrange group**, click the **Send Backward button arrow**, and then click **Send Behind Text**. Compare your screen with **Figure 4**.

15. **Save** 🖫 the document.

   ■ **You have completed Skill 8 of 10**

► When you need to display only a portion of a picture, you can **crop** the picture—to reduce the size of a picture by removing unwanted vertical or horizontal edges.

1. Scroll to the bottom of Page 2, and then select the landscape photograph.

2. On the **Format tab**, in the **Size group**, click the **Crop** button to frame the picture with cropping handles.

3. Point to the bottom middle cropping handle. With the pointer, drag up so that the cropping handle is aligned with the bottom of the rightmost pine tree and then release the mouse button. Compare your screen with **Figure 1**.

4. Press Enter to turn off Crop.

5. Click the photograph to select it. On the **Format tab**, in the **Size group**, click the **Size Dialog Box Launcher** .

6. In the **Layout** dialog box, on the **Size tab**, under **Scale**, clear the **Lock aspect ratio** check box.

> **Aspect ratio** keeps the height and width of an object proportionate. For example, if the height is 3" and the width is 2", a change in height would result in the width automatically increasing to a size determined by Word.

> When the lock aspect ratio check box is deselected, or unlocked, the height and width of the object can be changed independently of one another.

7. On the **Size tab**, under **Height**, change **Absolute** to 4 Compare your screen with **Figure 2**.

8. Click **OK**.

■ **Continue to the next page to complete the skill**

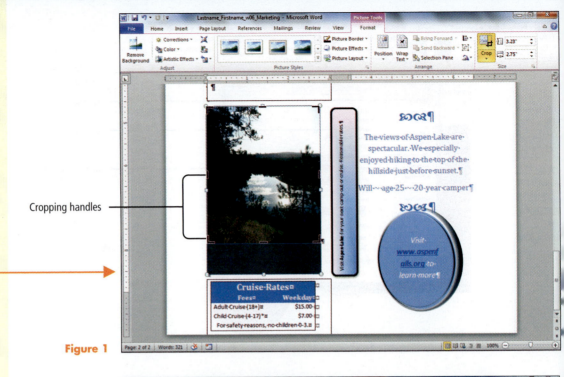

Cropping handles

Figure 1

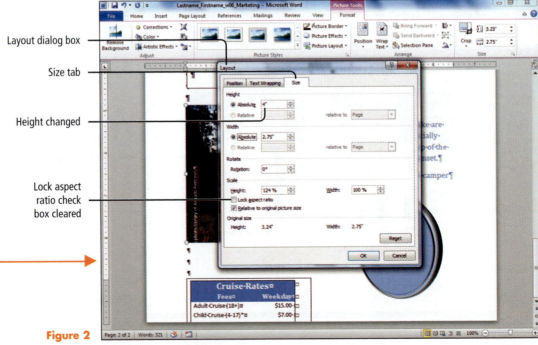

Layout dialog box

Size tab

Height changed

Lock aspect ratio check box cleared

Figure 2

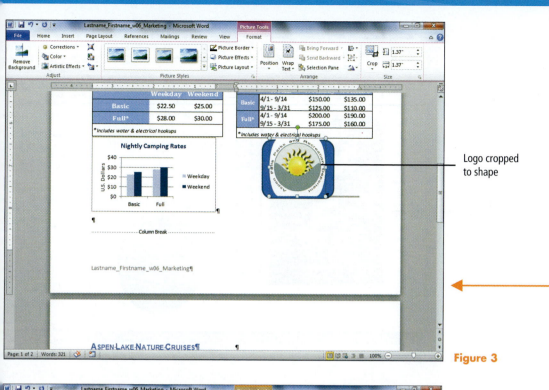

Logo cropped to shape

Figure 3

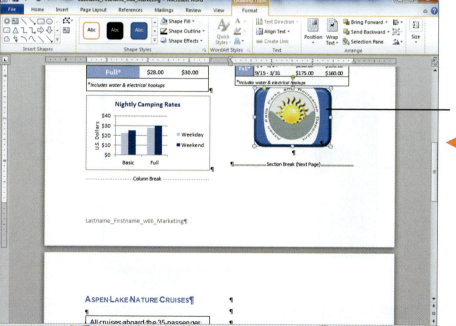

Bevel effect applied

Figure 4

9. With the photograph still selected, on the **Format tab**, in the **Size group**, click the **Crop button arrow**, and then point to **Crop to Shape**. Under **Rectangles**, click the sixth thumbnail—**Snip and Round Single Corner Rectangle**.

10. On Page 1, at the bottom of column 2, click the *Aspen Falls* logo shape, not the blue rounded rectangle.

11. On the **Format tab**, in the **Size group**, click the **Crop button arrow**, and then point to **Crop to Shape**. Under **Flowchart**, click the third thumbnail in the third row—**Flowchart: Direct Access Storage** button. Compare your screen with **Figure 3**.

12. Behind the *Aspen Falls* logo, click the rounded rectangle until the sizing handles display.

13. On the **Format tab**, in the **Shape Styles group**, click the **Shape Effects** button. Point to **Bevel**, and then under **Bevel**, click the last thumbnail in the first row—**Cool Slant**. Compare your screen with **Figure 4**.

14. If necessary, select the rectangle object, point to the border, and then click and hold to drag up so that top edge is aligned with the top edge of the Aspen Falls logo.

15. If necessary, on Page 2, column 2, select the first text box border, and then drag up so the top edge is aligned with the top edge of the text box at the left.

16. Save the document.

- **You have completed Skill 9 of 10**

▶ The *Selection and Visibility pane* displays a list of shapes, including pictures and text boxes, located on the current page.

▶ The Selection and Visibility pane is used to manage documents with several objects. Individual objects can be organized, named, or hidden so that you can select only desired objects.

1. Press Ctrl + End. On the **Home tab**, in the **Editing group**, click the **Select** button, and then click **Selection Pane**.

2. In the **Selection and Visibility** pane, click the first shape—Text Box 2, or similar number—and then verify the text box that begins *The views of* is selected.

3. On the **Format tab**, if necessary, click the **Size** button. Change the **Height** to 2.5 Press Enter. Compare with **Figure 1**.

4. Click the oval shape with text that begins *Visit www.aspenfalls. org.*

5. In the **Selection and Visibility** pane, double-click *Oval 400*, or similar number, select the text, type Website Reference and then press Enter.

   When multiple shapes are included in a document, it is useful to name the shapes to correctly identify them in the Selection and Visibility pane.

6. With the oval still selected, on the **Format tab**, in the **Shape Styles group**, click the **Shape Effects** button. Point to **3-D Rotation**, and then click **3-D Rotation Options**.

7. In the **Format Shape** dialog box, click **Line Color** as shown in **Figure 2**.

■ **Continue to the next page to complete the skill**

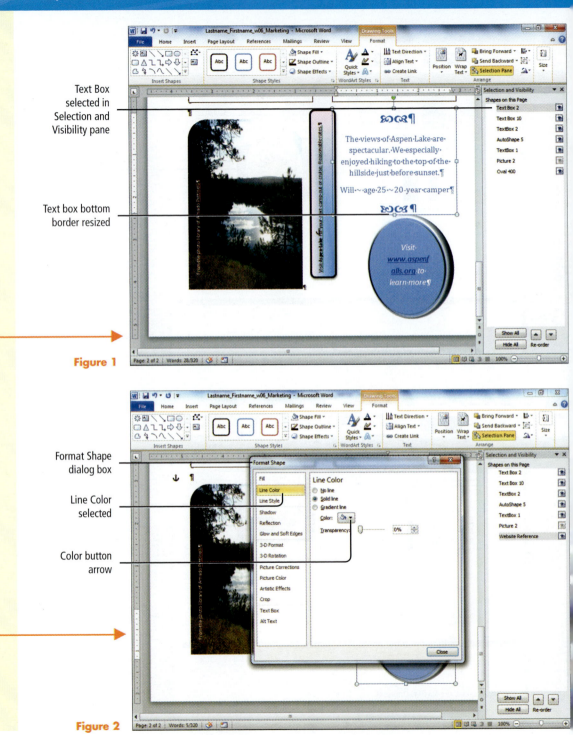

Text Box selected in Selection and Visibility pane

Text box bottom border resized

Figure 1

Format Shape dialog box

Line Color selected

Color button arrow

Figure 2

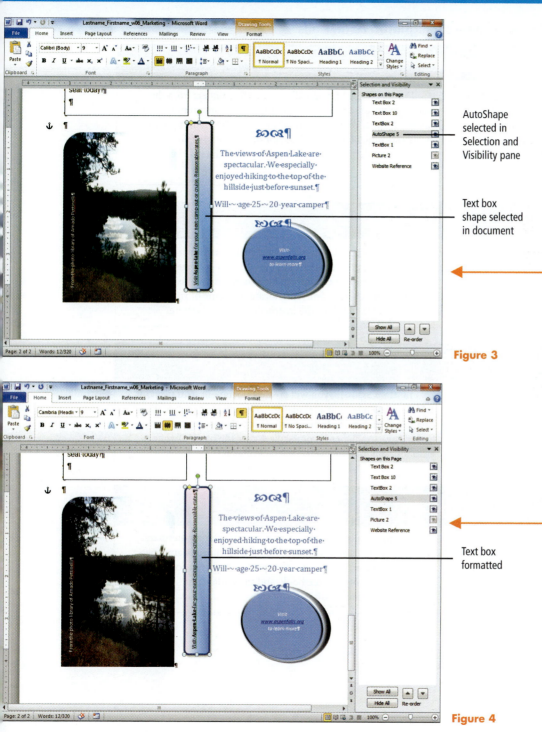

AutoShape selected in Selection and Visibility pane

Text box shape selected in document

Figure 3

Text box formatted

Figure 4

8. Under **Line Color**, click the **Color** button, and then click the fifth color in the first row—**Blue, Accent 1**. Click **Close**.

9. In the **Selection and Visibility** pane, verify **Website Reference** is selected. On the **Format tab**, if necessary, click the **Size** button, and then change the **Shape Height** ⬚ 1.5" to 1.75 Press Enter.

10. On the **Home tab**, in the **Font group**, change the **Font Size** to **9**.

11. If necessary, select the **Website Reference** shape, point to the right-middle handle, and then click and drag to the right so the website displays on one line.

12. In the **Selection and Visibility** pane, click **AutoShape 5** or similar number, to select the rounded rectangle that begins *Visit Aspen Lake* as shown in **Figure 3**.

13. On the **Format tab**, in the **Shape Styles group**, click the **Shape Outline** button, and then click the fourth color in the first row—**Dark Blue, Text 2**.

14. On the **Home tab**, in the **Paragraph group**, click the **Middle Align** button ⬛.

15. In the **Font group**, click the **Font** button, and then click **Cambria**. Compare your screen with **Figure 4**.

16. **Close** ⬚ the **Selection and Visibility** pane.

17. On the **View tab**, in the **Show group**, clear the **Ruler** check box.

18. **Save** ⬚ the document. Print or submit the file as directed by our instructor. **Exit** Word.

Done! You have completed Skill 10 of 10 and your document is complete!

More Skills

The following More Skills are located at **www.pearsonhighered.com/skills**

More Skills Work with Page Number Building Blocks

Page numbers can be inserted by selecting a building block from the Page Number gallery. When a page number is selected from the gallery, it is automatically inserted into a header or footer. Page numbers can then be modified. For example, the starting number can be increased and the number format can be changed.

In More Skills 11, you will insert page numbers from the Page Number gallery and then modify the starting number and number format. To begin, open your web browser, navigate to www.pearsonhighered.com/skills, locate the name of your textbook, and then follow the instructions on the website.

More Skills Insert Equations

Word has several built-in equations that can be used to insert common equations into documents. When other types of equations are needed, they can be typed and modified using the Equation Tools tab.

In More Skills 12, you will open a memo and then insert several built-in equations and build your own custom equation. To begin, open your web browser, navigate to www.pearsonhighered.com/skills, locate the name of your textbook, and then follow the instructions on the website.

More Skills Insert Quick Tables

Word provides built-in tables known as Quick Tables. These include formatted calendars, matrixes, and tabular lists. After a Quick Table is inserted, the data needs to be changed.

In More Skills 13, you will create a document with two Quick Tables—a calendar and a tabular list. You will then replace the data in both tables. To begin, open your web browser, navigate to www.pearsonhighered.com/skills, locate the name of your textbook, and then follow the instructions on the website.

More Skills Create Watermark Building Blocks

A watermark typically displays in the background of a document. Watermarks can be text or images that are faded and moved to the back of the text. You may have seen a "Confidential" watermark notation on a document. Watermarks can be saved as building blocks so that they can be accessed in the Watermark gallery.

In More Skills 14, you will insert and format a watermark. You will save the watermark as a building block. To begin, open your web browser, navigate to www.pearsonhighered.com/skills, locate the name of your textbook, and then follow the instructions on the website.

Key Terms

Online Help Skills

1. **Start** 🟠 Word. In the upper right corner of the Word window, click the **Help** button 🔵. In the **Help** window, click the **Maximize** 🔲 button.

2. Click in the search box, type watermarks and then click the **Search** button 🔍. In the search results, click **Add a watermark or remove a watermark**.

3. Read the article's introduction, and then below **What do you want to do?**, click **Learn about watermarks**. Compare your screen with **Figure 1**.

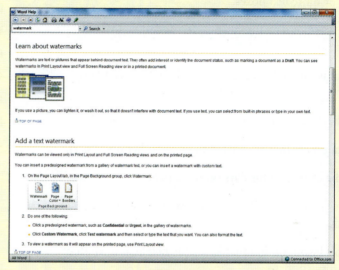

Figure 1

4. Read the section to see if you can answer the following: What is a watermark? What is the purpose of the washout feature?

Matching

Match each term in the second column with its correct definition in the first column by writing the letter of the term on the blank line in front of the correct definition.

____ **1.** A prebuilt document with placeholders and formatting already in place into which you insert your own text and objects.

____ **2.** A Word feature that is used so that text automatically flows between one or more text boxes.

____ **3.** A chart, SmartArt, or a picture that can be added to a Word document.

____ **4.** An object that is updated whenever the original source file is updated.

____ **5.** A numeric chart value that originates in a datasheet cell.

____ **6.** Contains data points that are related to one another on a chart.

____ **7.** The side of the chart that displays numeric data.

____ **8.** To reduce the size of a picture by removing unwanted vertical or horizontal edges.

____ **9.** A picture tools layout option that keeps the height and width of the objects proportionate.

____ **10.** A view that displays a list of shapes, including pictures and text boxes, located on the current page.

A Aspect ratio

B Crop

C Data point

D Data series

E Linked object

F Linked text box

G Object

H Selection and Visibility

I Template

J Value axis

Multiple Choice

Choose the correct answer.

1. The type of line that can be inserted between columns.
   A. Diagonal line
   B. Horizontal line
   C. Vertical line

2. In a blank document, the default number of columns.
   A. One
   B. Two
   C. Three

3. A built-in feature of Word that includes sidebars and pull quotes in which text can be inserted.
   A. Object
   B. Text box
   C. WordArt

4. The type of text box where the text that does not fit in one text box can be flowed into a second text box.
   A. Aligned
   B. Cropped
   C. Linked

5. The text box option used to display text vertically in a text box.
   A. Horizontal
   B. Rotate all text 270°
   C. Vertical

6. The type of chart used to show comparisons among related data.
   A. Bubble
   B. Clustered column
   C. Line

7. The file that contains the linked object that can be updated is called this type of file.
   A. Destination
   B. Matching
   C. Original

8. A chart value that originates in a worksheet cell or table cell.
   A. Axis
   B. Data point
   C. Legend

9. The type of data displayed in a value axis.
   A. Numeric
   B. Pie chart
   C. Text

10. The sizing feature where the horizontal and vertical edges of a picture can be removed.
    A. Crop
    B. Crop aspect
    C. Crop to shape

Topics for Discussion

1. Imagine you are the office manager for a small insurance agency who has been asked to prepare a newsletter to market the services provided by the insurance agency. What types of text would you include in the newsletter? What images would you include?

2. Imagine you are preparing a marketing newsletter for a nonprofit organization. You just held your annual fundraising campaign and have been asked to prepare a newsletter with two charts that highlight the age groups of the people you will be assisting and the percentages of your top 5–7 largest expenses (for example, employee, rent, office supplies, training, and so on). What types of text, images, and charts would you include?

Skill Check

To complete this project, you will need the following files:

- w06_News
- w06_News_Rates
- w06_News_Text

You will save your file as:

- Lastname_Firstname_w06_News

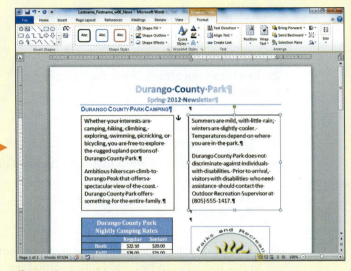

1. **Start** Word. Open the student data file **w06_News**. Save the file in your **Word Chapter 6** folder with the name Lastname_Firstname_w06_News Click the **Save as type** list. Click **Word Document**. Add the file name to the footer. Display the formatting marks and the ruler.

2. Locate and open the student data file **w06_News_Text**. Select the paragraphs that begin *Whether* through *(805) 555-1417*. On the **Home tab**, in the **Clipboard group**, click **Copy**.

3. In the **Lastname_Firstname_w06_News** file, on Page 1, column 1, click the text box border, and then on the **Home tab**, click the **Paste button arrow**. Click **Keep Source Formatting**.

Figure 1

4. On the **Format tab**, in the **Text group**, click **Create Link**. In column 2, click the text box. If a message box displays, click **Close**, and then click the text box again.

5. On Page 1, in column 2, above the picture, click the first text box border. On the **Format tab**, if necessary, click the **Size** button. If necessary, change the **Shape Height** to 3 Press Enter. Compare with **Figure 1**.

6. On Page 1, in column 2, above the logo, click the blank paragraph. On the **Insert tab**, in the **Text group**, click the **Object** button. In the **Object** dialog box, click the **Create from File tab**, and then click **Browse**. Navigate to the student files, select **w06_News_Rates**. Click **Insert**. In the **Object** dialog box, select the **Link to file** check box. Click **OK**. Compare your screen with **Figure 2**.

7. On Page 1, in column 1, click the second blank paragraph below the *Nightly Camping Rates* table. On the **Insert tab**, in the **Illustrations group**, click the **Chart** button. Verify **Clustered Column** is selected and click **OK**.

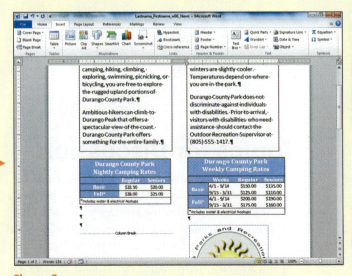

Figure 2

■ Continue to the next page to complete this Skill Check

8. In Excel, click **Series 1**. Type Regular Add the chart text shown in **Figure 3**. Point to the lower-right corner of cell D5, click and drag left to column C. Point to the lower-right corner of cell C5, click and drag up to cell C3. **Exit** Excel.

9. Click the border of the chart. On the **Layout tab**, in the **Labels group**, click the **Chart Title** button, and then click **Above Chart**. Type Nightly Camping Rates Select the chart title border. Change the **Font Size** to **12**.

10. On the **Insert tab**, in the **Illustrations group**, click the **Shapes** button. Under **Rectangles**, click **Rounded Rectangle**. On Page 2, column 1, click the first blank paragraph.

11. On the **Format tab**, if necessary, click the **Size** button. Change the **Shape Height** to **5** and the **Shape Width** to **2.5** Press Enter.

12. In the **w06_News_Text** file, select the paragraphs that begins with *Fun Activities* and end with **Bicycling**. On the **Home tab**, in the **Clipboard group**, click **Copy**. **Close** the window.

13. In the Word document, on Page 2, right-click the **Rounded Rectangle**. Click **Add Text**. On the **Home tab**, in the **Clipboard group**, click **Paste**.

14. On Page 2, select the picture. On the **Format tab**, in the **Size group**, click the **Crop button arrow**. Click **Crop to Shape**, and then under **Basic Shapes**, select the third shape in the second row—**Teardrop**.

15. On the **Home tab**, in the **Editing group**, click the **Select** button and then click **Selection Pane**. In the **Selection and Visibility** pane, click **TextBox 2**, or similar number.

16. On the **Format tab**, in the **Text group**, click the **Text direction arrow**, and then click **Rotate all text 270°**. If necessary, click the **Size** button and then change the **Shape Height** to **3** and the **Shape Width** to **0.4** Drag the text box up. Position the text box to the left of the photo, with the top edge aligned with the roof.

17. At the top of Page 2, click the blank paragraph. On the **Insert tab**, in the **Text group**, click the **Text Box** button. Click the **Austere Quote** button. Drag the quote text box below the rounded rectangle. Click the quote text box and then type Open all year! Select the text box border. Change the **Font Size** to **26** points. On the **Format tab**, in the **Shape Styles group**, change the **Shape Fill** to the fifth one in the second row—**Blue, Accent 1, Lighter 80%** as shown in **Figure 4**.

18. Clear the ruler check box. **Save** and then print or submit the file as directed by your instructor. **Exit** Word.

Done! You have completed the Skill Check

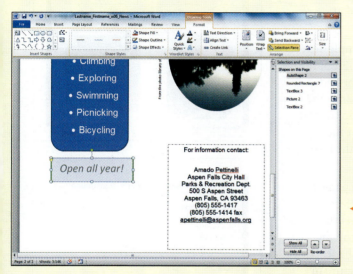

	A	B	C
1		Regular	Seniors
2	Basic	22.5	20
3	Full	28	25

Figure 3

Figure 4

Assess Your Skills 1

To complete this project, you will need the following files:

- w06_Race
- w06_Race_Text
- w06_Race_Awards

You will save your file as:

- Lastname_Firstname_w06_Race

1. **Start** Word and then open the student data file **w06_Race**. **Save** the file in your **Word Chapter 6** folder with the name Lastname_Firstname_w06_Race Change the **Save as type** to **Word Document**. Add the file name to the footer. Display the formatting marks and the ruler.

2. Copy all the text from **w06_Race_Text**. **Close w06_Race_Text**. On Page 1, click the first text box border and **Paste**. Create a link and then click the border of the first text box in column 2.

3. Select the first text box in column 2 and change the **Shape Height** to 3

4. On Page 2, in column 1, in the blank paragraph below the table insert the Excel worksheet object **w06_Race_Awards** with a link to the file.

5. Double-click the Excel object to open **w06_Race_Awards**. Select cells **A2** through **B7**. **Copy** the cells. **Exit** Excel. Click the blank paragraph to the right of the Excel object and then press Enter two times.

6. In Word, insert a **Clustered Column chart**. In the **Excel** datasheet, click cell **A1** and then **Paste** the **w06_Race_Awards** data. Use the range selector to select cells **A1** through **B6**. **Exit** Excel.

7. Select the chart and change the **Shape Height** to 2 and the **Shape Width** to 3

8. Use the **Layout tab** to **Show Legend at Bottom**.

9. At the bottom of Page 1, insert a **Simple Text Box** between the two pictures. Type From the Aspen Falls photo library. Change the text direction to **Rotate all text 270°**. Change the text box **Shape Height** to 2.5 Position the text box between the two pictures so that the top edge of the text box is aligned with the top edges of the pictures.

10. Display the **Selection and Visibility** pane. In the **Selection and Visibility** pane, select **Picture 9**, or similar number, to select the picture of the couple in the pool. Crop the picture to the **Rounded Rectangle** shape. For **Picture 8**, or similar number, the picture of the girl running, crop the picture to the **Rounded Rectangle** shape, and then close the **Selection and Visibility** pane. Clear the **Ruler** check box. Compare your screen with **Figure 1**.

11. **Save** and then print or submit the file as directed by your instructor. **Exit** Word.

Done! You have completed Assess Your Skills 1

Figure 1

Assess Your Skills 2

To complete this project, you will need the following files:

- w06_Community
- w06_Community_Courses
- w06_Community_Insert1
- w06_Community_Insert2

You will save your file as:

- Lastname_Firstname_w06_Community

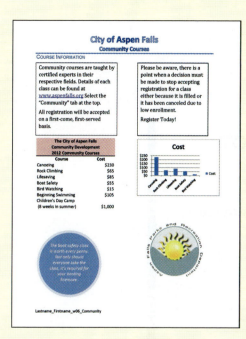

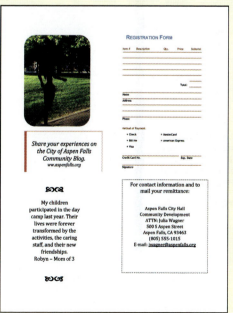

Figure 1

1. **Start** Word and then open the student data file **w06_Community**. Save the file in your **Word Chapter 6** folder with the name Lastname_Firstname_w06_Community Change the **Save as type** to **Word document**. Add the file name to the footer. Display the formatting marks and the ruler.

2. Locate and open the student data file **w06_Community_Inserts1**. **Copy** all the text and then **Close** the file. **Paste** into the first text box in **Lastname_Firstname_w06_Community**. Create a link from the first text box in column 1 to the first text box in column 2.

3. Select both text boxes and then change the **Shape Height** to 2.6

4. On Page 1, in column 1, in the first blank paragraph below the text box, insert the Excel worksheet **w06_Community_Courses** with a link to the file.

5. Double-click the Excel object to open **w06_Community_Courses**. Select cells **A4** through **B9**. **Copy** the cells. **Exit** Excel.

6. On Page 1, in column 2, in the blank paragraph below the text box, insert a **Clustered Column** chart. In **Excel**, **Paste** the copied content into cell **A1**. Use the range selector to drag left to **B6**. **Exit** Excel. Adjust the **Shape Height** to 2 and the **Shape Width** to 3 Click *Canoeing* and use the **Home tab** to change the **Font Size** to **8**.

7. On Page 2, click the first blank paragraph in column 1. Insert a **Decorative Quote** built-in text box. Align the top left edge of the quote with the second blank paragraph below the text box that begins *Share your*. Locate and open the student data file **w06_Community_Inserts2**. **Copy** all the text and **Close** the file. Select the text in the quote, and then **Paste** into the quote. Select the border of the quote text box and then change the **Font Color** to **Automatic**.

8. Use the **Selection and Visibility** pane to select **Picture 0**, or similar number—the image of the sculpture, and then crop the picture to the **Rounded Rectangle** shape.

9. **Close** the **Selection and Visibility** pane. Deselect the **Ruler** check box. Compare your screen with **Figure 1**.

10. **Save** and then print or submit the file as directed by your instructor. **Exit** Word.

Done! You have completed Assess Your Skills 2

Assess Your Skills Visually

To complete this project, you will need the following files:

- w06_Vintage
- w06_Vintage_Sponsors

You will save your file as:

- Lastname_Firstname_w06_Vintage

Start Word, and then open the **w06_Vintage** template file. Save the template as a document in your **Word Chapter 6** folder as Lastname_Firstname_w06_Vintage and then add the file name to the footer. Display the formatting marks and the ruler. Create the newsletter for the City of Aspen Falls annual vintage car show shown in **Figure 1**.

On Page 1, below the Event Sponsors text box, double-click and then insert the Excel worksheet object, **w06_Vintage_ Sponsors** as a linked file. In the text box above the car that begins *The 2012 30th*, format the text box using the third Shape Style in the second row—**Colored Fill – Red, Accent 2**. Insert the **Decorative Quote** text box. Move it below the *Early Registration* table, and then type the text as shown in **Figure 1**. Change the text box **Shape Width** to **3.25"** and the **Font Color** to **Red, Accent 2**, and make any other formatting changes.

Compare your screen with **Figure 1**. Print or submit the file as directed by your instructor.

Done! You have completed Assess Your Skills Visually

Figure 1

Skills in Context

To complete this project, you will need the following files:

- w06_Swimming_Content
- w06_Swimming_Results

You will save your file as:

- Lastname_Firstname_w06_Swimming

Prepare a newsletter for the City of Aspen Falls summer swim team. Your newsletter should include all of the items found in **w06_Swimming_Content**. In the newsletter, insert the linked Excel worksheet object, **w06_Swimming_Results** into a text box at the bottom left corner of Page 1. If desired, crop and size the picture(s). Format and arrange the newsletter content to create an effective newsletter.

Save the blank document in your **Word Chapter 6** folder as Lastname_Firstname_w06_Swimming and then add the file name to the footer. Print or submit the file as directed by your instructor.

Done! You have completed Skills in Context

Skills and You

To complete this project, you will need the following file:

- New blank Word document

You will save your file as:

- Lastname_Firstname_w06_Club

Prepare a newsletter to market a student organization on your campus to which you belong.

Save your newsletter as Lastname_Firstname_w06_Club Add the file name to the footer. Print or submit the project electronically as directed.

Be sure to include a chart, at least one shape, at least three pictures, and a built-in text box. Crop at least one of the pictures.

Done! You have completed Skills and You

CHAPTER 7

Prepare a Document with References

▶ Long Word documents should include references—cover pages, table of contents, table of figures, and indexes, for example—to help the reader locate information.

▶ Long documents can also include bookmarks so that you can use the Select Browse Object toolbar to locate specific areas in the document or locate objects such as figures.

Your starting screen will look like this:

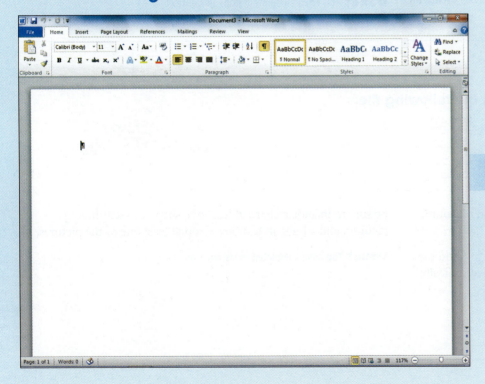

SKILLS

Skills 1-10 Training

At the end of this chapter, you will be able to:

Skill 1 Mark Items for Indexes
Skill 2 Create Cross-References
Skill 3 Insert and Modify Indexes
Skill 4 Prepare a Table of Figures
Skill 5 Update a Table of Figures
Skill 6 Insert Page Numbers for Odd and Even Pages
Skill 7 Create Table of Contents
Skill 8 Insert Bookmarks
Skill 9 Insert Cover Pages
Skill 10 Use the Navigation Pane and the Select Browse Object Toolbar

MORE SKILLS

More Skills 11 Navigate Footnotes and Convert Footnotes to Endnotes
More Skills 12 Add Citations in the APA Style
More Skills 13 Manage Versions
More Skills 14 Create Table of Authorities

Outcome

Using the skills listed to the left will enable you to create documents like these:

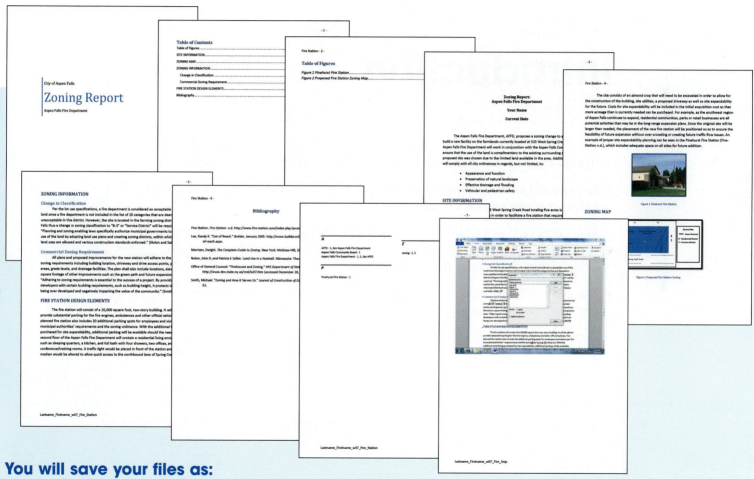

You will save your files as:

Lastname_Firstname_w07_Fire_Station

Lastname_Firstname_w07_Fire_Snip

In this chapter, you will create documents for the Aspen Falls City Hall, which provides essential services for the citizens and visitors of Aspen Falls, California.

Introduction

▶ Long Word documents often need a cover page, a table of contents, a table of figures, and odd and even page numbers to help readers locate information.

▶ You can add an index with cross-references that identifies the page numbers of entries that you mark for inclusion.

▶ References such as a table of contents or an index use fields to list entries and their page numbers. When you change a document, you should update these fields so that they display the correct information.

▶ You can add bookmarks to long documents so that you can use the Select Browse Object toolbar to quickly move to that bookmark.

**Time to complete all
10 skills – 50 to 90 minutes**

Find your student data files here:

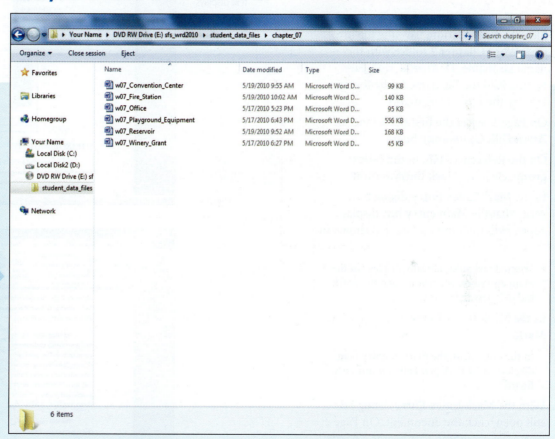

**Student data file needed
for this chapter:**

- w07_Fire_Station

► An *index* displays a list of words and phrases found in a document along with their corresponding page numbers.

► An *index entry field* identifies words, phrases, or cross-references that will go in the index. By marking index entries with index entry fields, you provide the information needed for Word to build the index.

1. **Start** 🪟 Word, and open the student data file **w07_Fire_Station**. Save the file in your **Word Chapter 7** folder with the name Lastname_Firstname_w07_Fire_ Station Add the file name to the footer. Display the formatting marks.

2. On Page 1, select the first occurrence of *Aspen Falls Community Board*.

3. On the **References tab**, in the **Index group**, click the **Mark Entry** button.

4. In the **Mark Index Entry** dialog box, verify that the **Main entry** box displays *Aspen Falls Community Board* as shown in **Figure 1**.

   Selected text automatically displays in the Main entry box when you open the Mark Index Entry dialog box.

5. In the **Mark Index Entry** dialog box, click **Mark**.

   In the document, the marked entry field displays as { XE "Aspen Falls Community Board" }.

6. With the **Mark Index Entry** dialog box still open, click the document. On Page 2, locate the paragraph that begins *The site consists*. Select the text *Pinehurst Fire Station* as shown in **Figure 2**.

7. Click the **Mark Index Entry** dialog box, and then verify that *Pinehurst Fire Station* displays.

■ **Continue to the next page to complete the skill**

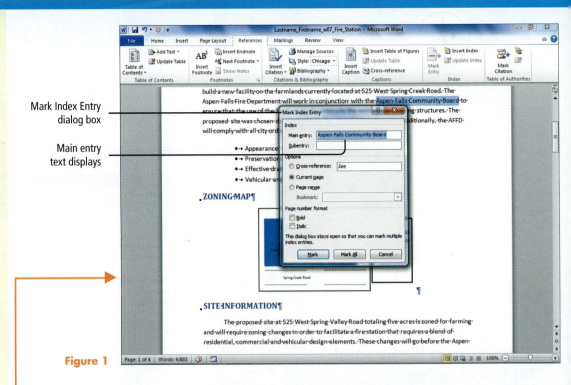

Mark Index Entry dialog box

Main entry text displays

Figure 1

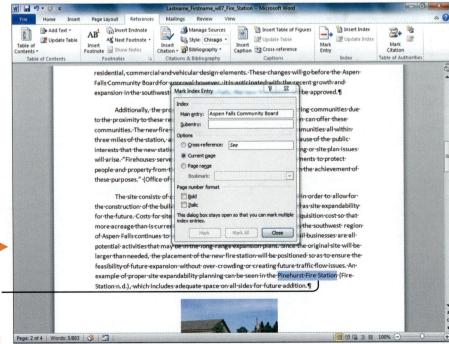

Selected text

Figure 2

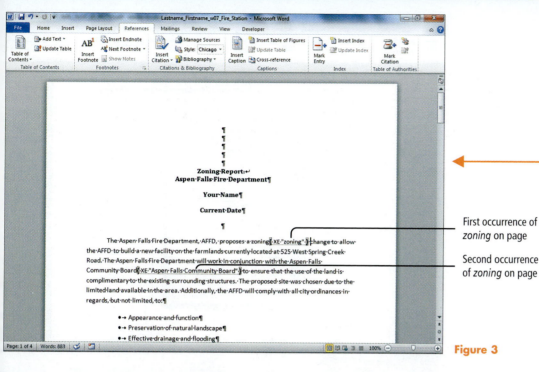

First occurrence of *zoning* on page

Second occurrence of *zoning* on page

Figure 3

Index entries do not display

Figure 4

8. Click **Mark**, and then click the document. On Page 1, locate the paragraph that begins *The Aspen Falls* and then select the first *zoning* occurrence.

9. Click the **Mark Index Entry** dialog box, verify that the **Main entry** box displays *zoning* and then click **Mark All**.

10. Click **Close**. Deselect *zoning* Compare your screen with **Figure 3**.

    The first occurrence of the word *zoning* in each section has been marked on the page. Only the first occurrence in each paragraph is marked because the page number is what is referenced. In this manner, the Mark All feature locates and inserts index entry fields for the selected word or phrase.

11. On the **Home tab**, in the **Editing group**, click the **Find** button, and then in the displayed **Navigation Pane**, verify that *zoning* displays.

    The word *zoning* displays in the Navigation Pane and displays with a yellow highlight throughout the document.

    Zoning is not marked in headings or citations.

12. Click the **Next Search Results** button, and continue moving through the document. Verify that the Mark All command performed correctly.

13. **Close** ☒ the **Navigation Pane**.

14. Turn off the formatting marks. Compare your screen with **Figure 4**.

    Index entries are no longer visible because they are nonprinting characters.

15. Display formatting marks. **Save** 🖫 the document.

    ■ **You have completed Skill 1 of 10**

► A *cross-reference* is an index entry associated with a different word or phrase that is similar in context to the original index entry.

► A cross-reference is created in the Mark Index Entry dialog box and is identified as a cross-reference in the index entry field.

1. On Page 1, locate the paragraph that begins *The Aspen Falls Fire Department* and then select the first occurrence of *Aspen Falls Fire Department*.

2. On the **References tab**, in the **Index group**, click the **Mark Entry** button.

3. In the **Mark Index Entry** dialog box, in the **Main entry** box, verify that *Aspen Falls Fire Department* displays, and then click **Mark**. Compare your screen with **Figure 1**.

4. With the **Mark Index Entry** dialog box still open, click the document. In the paragraph that begins *The Aspen Falls Fire Department* select the first occurrence of *AFFD*.

5. Click the displayed **Mark Index Entry** dialog box, verify that *AFFD* shows in the first box, and then click **Mark**. Compare your screen with **Figure 2**.

■ **Continue to the next page to complete the skill**

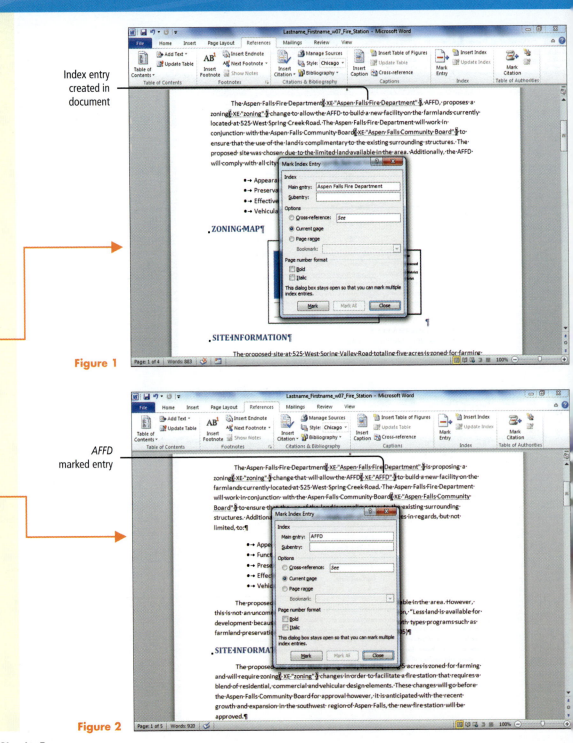

Index entry created in document

Figure 1

AFFD marked entry

Figure 2

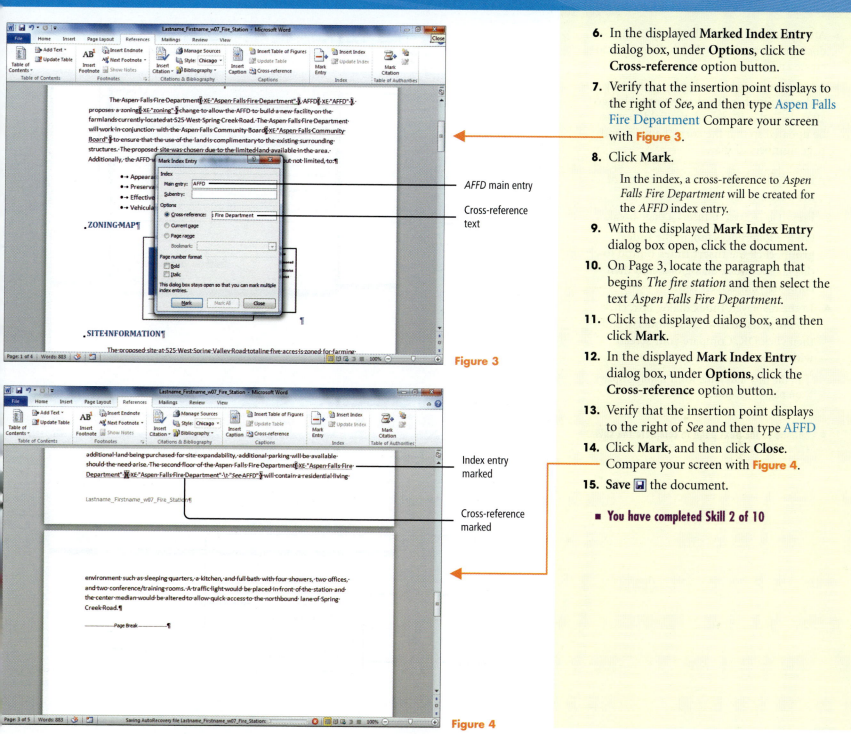

AFFD main entry

Cross-reference text

Figure 3

Index entry marked

Cross-reference marked

Figure 4

6. In the displayed **Marked Index Entry** dialog box, under **Options**, click the **Cross-reference** option button.

7. Verify that the insertion point displays to the right of *See*, and then type Aspen Falls Fire Department Compare your screen with **Figure 3**.

8. Click **Mark**.

   In the index, a cross-reference to *Aspen Falls Fire Department* will be created for the *AFFD* index entry.

9. With the displayed **Mark Index Entry** dialog box open, click the document.

10. On Page 3, locate the paragraph that begins *The fire station* and then select the text *Aspen Falls Fire Department*.

11. Click the displayed dialog box, and then click **Mark**.

12. In the displayed **Mark Index Entry** dialog box, under **Options**, click the **Cross-reference** option button.

13. Verify that the insertion point displays to the right of *See* and then type AFFD

14. Click **Mark**, and then click **Close**. Compare your screen with **Figure 4**.

15. Save 💾 the document.

■ **You have completed Skill 2 of 10**

▶ After you mark each index entry in the document, you use the Index dialog box to create and format the index.

▶ An index uses fields to display each entry and page number. If a document is changed after the index is created, the field(s) must be updated so that the correct entries and page numbers display.

1. Press Ctrl + End to move to the end of the document.

2. Press Ctrl + Enter to insert a page break.

3. On the **References tab**, in the **Index group**, click the **Insert Index** button to display the **Index** dialog box, and then compare your screen with **Figure 1**.

4. In the displayed **Index** dialog box, click the **Formats arrow**, click **Modern**, and then click **OK**. Compare your screen with **Figure 2**.

In the new index, the word *zoning* displays on pages 1, 2, and 3.

■ **Continue to the next page to complete the skill**

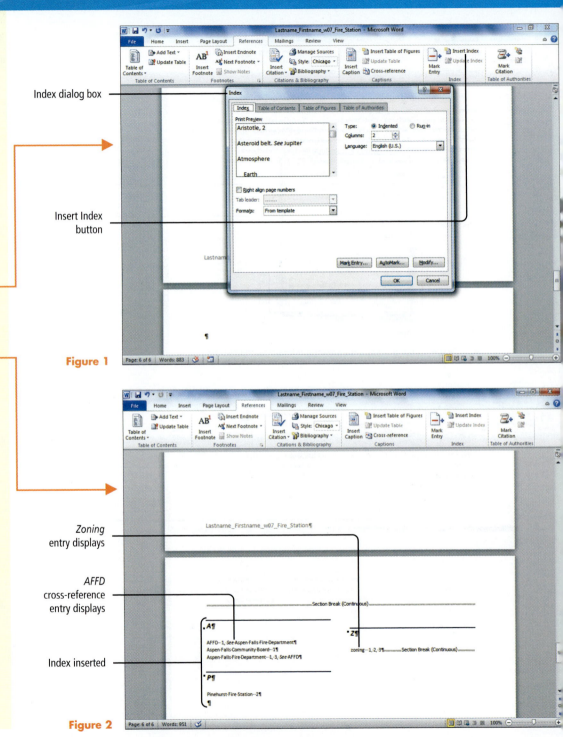

Index dialog box

Insert Index button

Figure 1

Zoning entry displays

AFFD cross-reference entry displays

Index inserted

Figure 2

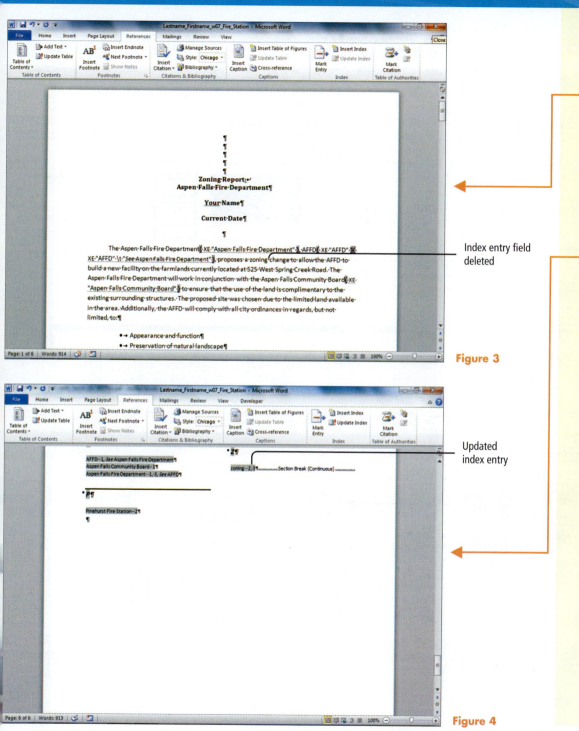

Index entry field deleted

Figure 3

Updated index entry

Figure 4

5. On Page 1, locate the paragraph that begins *The Aspen Falls,* select the index entry field { XE "zoning" }, and then press Del to remove the index reference. Compare your screen with **Figure 3**.

6. Press Ctrl + End to move to the end of the document. At the end of the document, locate the index, and notice that the *zoning* index entry still lists Page 1.

7. Click the word *Pinehurst* to select the entire index.

8. On the **References tab**, in the **Index group**, click the **Update Index** button, and then compare your screen with **Figure 4**.

The *zoning* index entry no longer displays a reference to Page 2. Each time an item is added or removed from the index or content is added to or deleted from the document, you need to update the index to reflect current page numbers.

9. Save 🖫 the document.

■ **You have completed Skill 3 of 10**

► A *table of figures* contains references to figures, equations, and tables in the document. It usually includes the caption text and page number of each figure, equation, and table.

► In a report, the table of figures usually follows the table of contents.

1. On Page 3, select the picture of the fire station, and then on the **References tab**, in the **Captions group**, click the **Insert Caption** button. In the displayed **Caption** dialog box, with the insertion point in the **Caption** box, add a space after *Figure 1* and then type Pinehurst Fire Station Click **OK**.

2. On Page 1, select the Zoning Map figure, and then on the **References tab**, in the **Captions group**, click the **Insert Caption** button.

3. In the **Caption** dialog box, with the insertion point after *Figure 1* add a space, and then type Proposed Fire Station Zoning Map Click **OK**, and then compare your screen with **Figure 1**.

4. Press Ctrl + Home.

5. Press Ctrl + Enter to insert a page break.

6. Press Ctrl + Home to move to the new Page 1. If necessary, position the insertion point to the left of the page break. Type Table of Figures Press Enter, and then compare your screen with **Figure 2**.

■ **Continue to the next page to complete the skill**

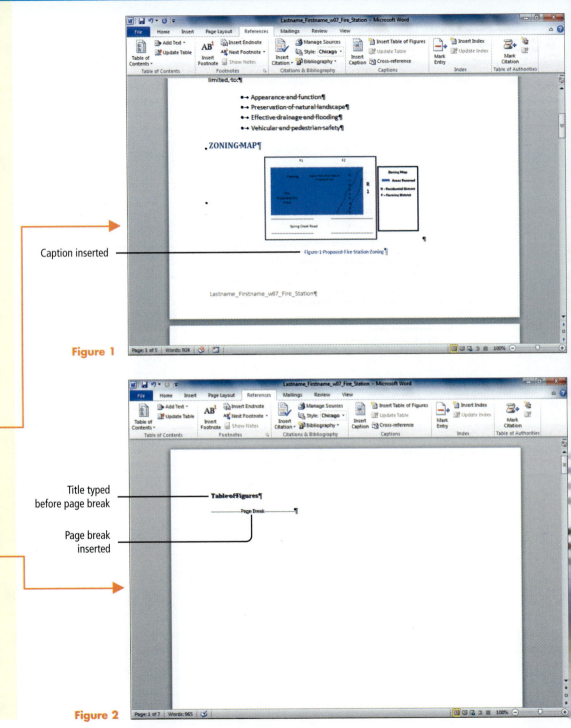

Caption inserted

Figure 1

Title typed before page break

Page break inserted

Figure 2

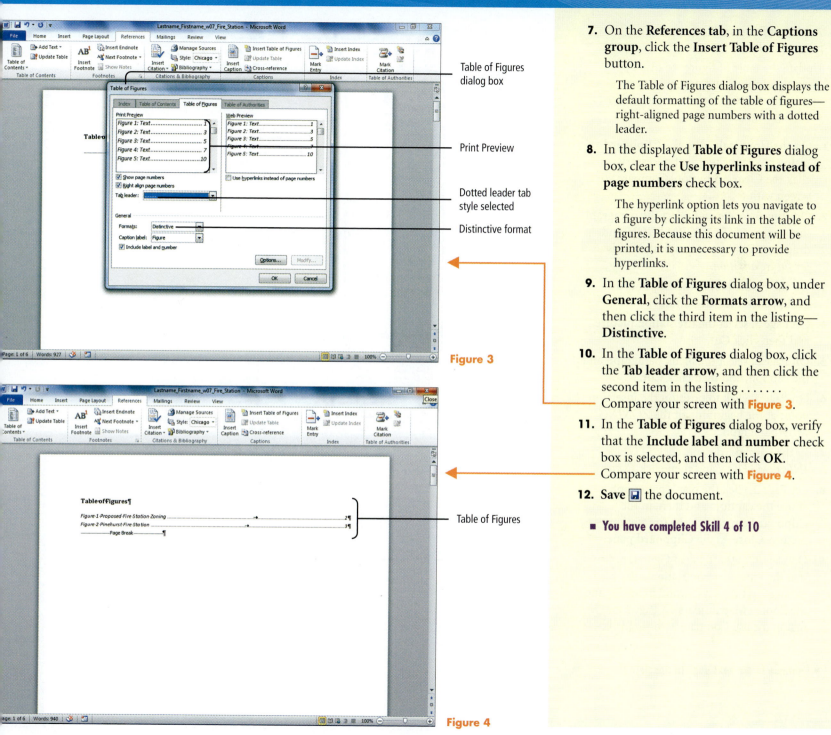

Table of Figures dialog box

Print Preview

Dotted leader tab style selected

Distinctive format

Figure 3

Table of Figures

Figure 4

7. On the **References tab**, in the **Captions group**, click the **Insert Table of Figures** button.

> The Table of Figures dialog box displays the default formatting of the table of figures—right-aligned page numbers with a dotted leader.

8. In the displayed **Table of Figures** dialog box, clear the **Use hyperlinks instead of page numbers** check box.

> The hyperlink option lets you navigate to a figure by clicking its link in the table of figures. Because this document will be printed, it is unnecessary to provide hyperlinks.

9. In the **Table of Figures** dialog box, under **General**, click the **Formats arrow**, and then click the third item in the listing—**Distinctive**.

10. In the **Table of Figures** dialog box, click the **Tab leader arrow**, and then click the second item in the listing . . . . Compare your screen with **Figure 3**.

11. In the **Table of Figures** dialog box, verify that the **Include label and number** check box is selected, and then click **OK**. Compare your screen with **Figure 4**.

12. Save 🖫 the document.

> ■ **You have completed Skill 4 of 10**

▶ A table of figures will not update automatically.

▶ Update the table of figures to display accurate captions and page numbers anytime you insert, delete, or move figures or change figure captions.

1. On the **Home tab**, click the **Clipboard** dialog box launcher ⬜. If necessary, click the **Clear All** button. Compare your screen with **Figure 1**.

2. On Page 3, locate and select the paragraph that begins *SITE INFORMATION*, and drag through the paragraph that ends *for future addition*.

3. On the **Home tab**, in the **Clipboard group**, click the **Cut** button.

4. On Page 3, select the fire station picture, and then click **Cut**.

5. On Page 3, select the blank paragraph and the caption, and then click **Cut**.

6. On Page 2, click to position the insertion point at the beginning of the *ZONING MAP* paragraph.

7. In the **Clipboard** pane, click *SITE INFORMATION* and then click *Figure 2*.

8. On Page 3, click the blank paragraph above the caption, and then, in the **Clipboard** pane, click the fire station picture. **Close** ⬜ the **Clipboard** pane.

9. On Page 1, in the Table of Figures, notice that the Pinehurst Fire Station entry refers to Page 3 yet displays second in the list and the Zoning Map displays on Page 2 and is first in the list. Compare with **Figure 2**.

■ **Continue to the next page to complete the skill** ➤

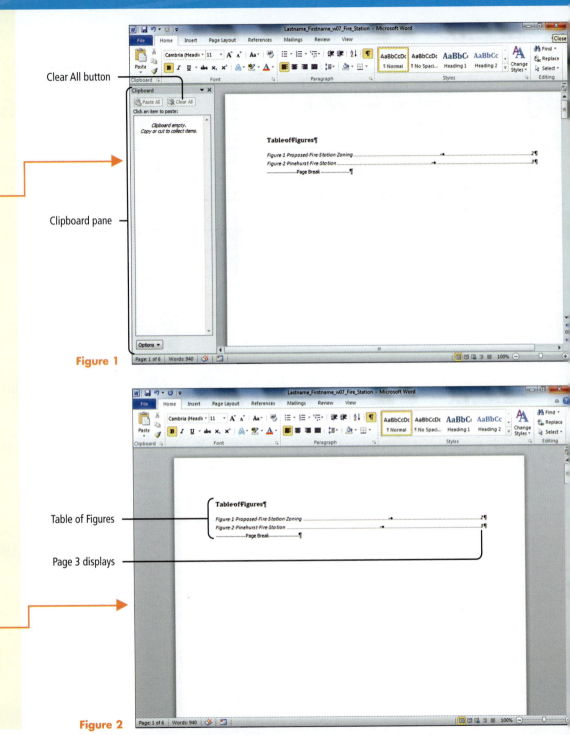

Clear All button

Clipboard pane

Figure 1

Table of Figures

Page 3 displays

Figure 2

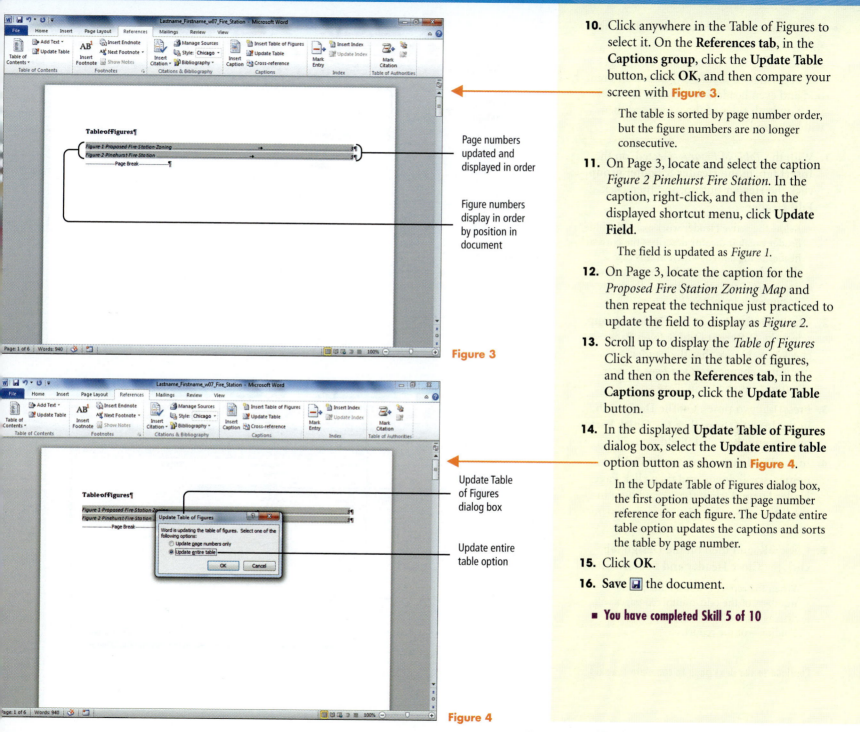

Figure 3

Figure 4

10. Click anywhere in the Table of Figures to select it. On the **References tab**, in the **Captions group**, click the **Update Table** button, click **OK**, and then compare your screen with **Figure 3**.

    The table is sorted by page number order, but the figure numbers are no longer consecutive.

11. On Page 3, locate and select the caption *Figure 2 Pinehurst Fire Station*. In the caption, right-click, and then in the displayed shortcut menu, click **Update Field**.

    The field is updated as *Figure 1*.

12. On Page 3, locate the caption for the *Proposed Fire Station Zoning Map* and then repeat the technique just practiced to update the field to display as *Figure 2*.

13. Scroll up to display the *Table of Figures* Click anywhere in the table of figures, and then on the **References tab**, in the **Captions group**, click the **Update Table** button.

14. In the displayed **Update Table of Figures** dialog box, select the **Update entire table** option button as shown in **Figure 4**.

    In the Update Table of Figures dialog box, the first option updates the page number reference for each figure. The Update entire table option updates the captions and sorts the table by page number.

15. Click **OK**.

16. Save 🖫 the document.

    ■ **You have completed Skill 5 of 10**

▶ Word contains several built-in page number styles.

▶ Headers or footers on odd and even pages can be formatted separately. Create different odd and even headers for reports that will print on both sides of the paper and then will be bound.

1. With the *Table of Figures* selected, on the **Insert tab**, in the **Header & Footer group**, click the **Header** button, and then click **Edit Header**.

   Below the active Header workspace, the blue header break indicator describes the current header being edited, which in this case is the header for section 1. Because you have not inserted any section breaks, the entire document is in section 1.

2. On the **Design tab**, in the **Options group**, select the **Different Odd & Even Pages** check box. Notice that the header indicator changes to *Odd Page Header -Section 1-* as shown in **Figure 1**.

3. Press Tab two times. On the **Design tab**, in the **Insert group**, click the **Quick Parts** button, and then click **Field**.

4. In the **Field** dialog box, under **Field names**, scroll down, and then click **Page**. Under **Format**, click the second item in the list— - 1 -, - 2 -, - 3 -, … —as shown in **Figure 2**.

5. Click **OK**, and then on the **Design tab**, click the **Close Header and Footer** button.

   When the report is bound, the page numbers of the odd-numbered pages will display on the outer side—opposite the binding—of the report.

■ **Continue to the next page to complete the skill**

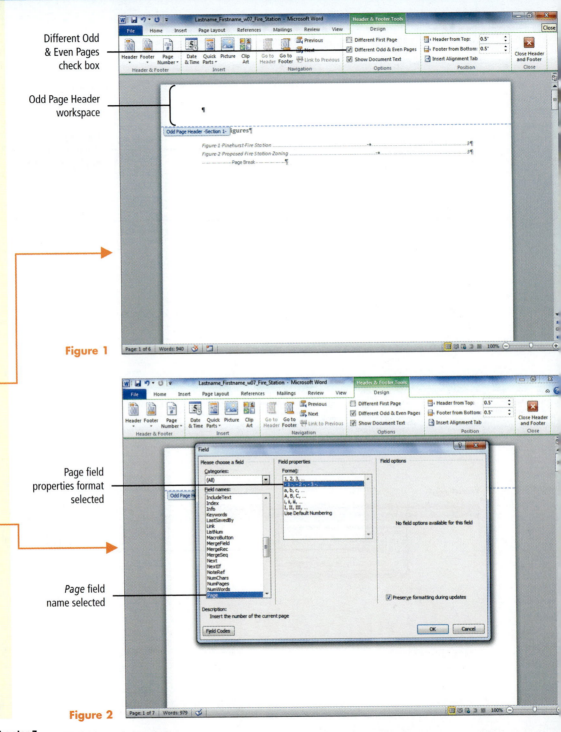

Different Odd & Even Pages check box

Odd Page Header workspace

Figure 1

Page field properties format selected

Page field name selected

Figure 2

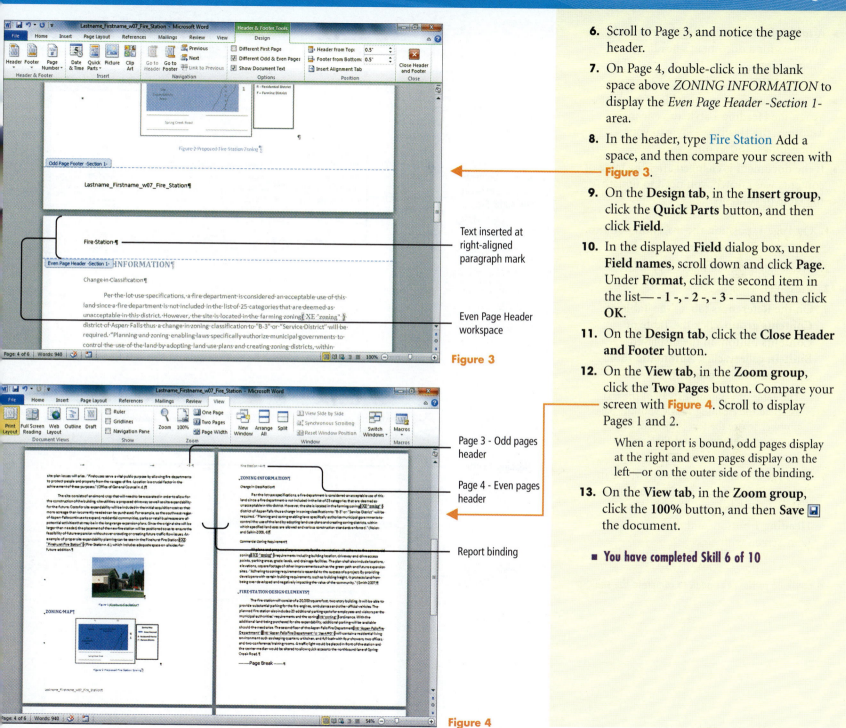

Text inserted at right-aligned paragraph mark

Even Page Header workspace

Figure 3

Page 3 - Odd pages header

Page 4 - Even pages header

Report binding

Figure 4

6. Scroll to Page 3, and notice the page header.

7. On Page 4, double-click in the blank space above *ZONING INFORMATION* to display the *Even Page Header -Section 1-* area.

8. In the header, type Fire Station Add a space, and then compare your screen with **Figure 3**.

9. On the **Design tab**, in the **Insert group**, click the **Quick Parts** button, and then click **Field**.

10. In the displayed **Field** dialog box, under **Field names**, scroll down and click **Page**. Under **Format**, click the second item in the list— - 1 -, - 2 -, - 3 - —and then click **OK**.

11. On the **Design tab**, click the **Close Header and Footer** button.

12. On the **View tab**, in the **Zoom group**, click the **Two Pages** button. Compare your screen with **Figure 4**. Scroll to display Pages 1 and 2.

When a report is bound, odd pages display at the right and even pages display on the left—or on the outer side of the binding.

13. On the **View tab**, in the **Zoom group**, click the **100%** button, and then **Save** the document.

■ **You have completed Skill 6 of 10**

► A *table of contents* displays entries and page numbers for a document's headings and *subheadings*—entries that are part of a broader entry.

► To include an item in the table of contents, assign the Heading 1 style to your main headings, the Heading 2 style to your subheadings, and so on.

► If the document is changed after the table of contents was created, you need to update the table of contents.

1. On Page 1, position the insertion point to the left of *Table of Figures*.

2. Press Ctrl + Enter to insert a page break.

3. Press Ctrl + Home.

4. On the **References tab**, in the **Table of Contents group**, click the **Table of Contents** button. In the displayed **Built-In** gallery, click **Automatic Table 2**. Compare your screen with **Figure 1**.

   The Table of Contents lists all of the text assigned the Heading 1 style with the page number where the text is located. In this report, four headings and *Bibliography* have been assigned the Heading 1 style.

5. On Page 2, locate and click anywhere in the title *Table of Figures*. On the **Home tab**, in the **Styles group**, click the **Heading 1** button, and then compare your screen with **Figure 2**.

■ **Continue to the next page to complete the skill**

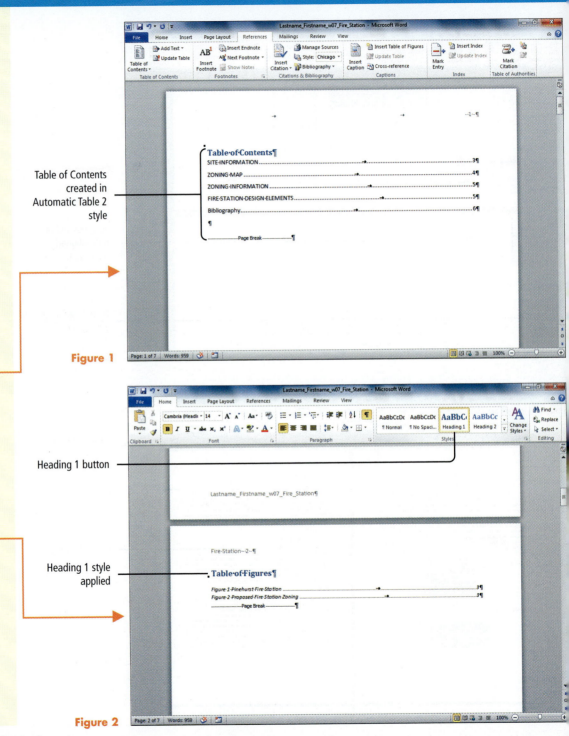

Table of Contents created in Automatic Table 2 style

Figure 1

Heading 1 button

Heading 1 style applied

Figure 2

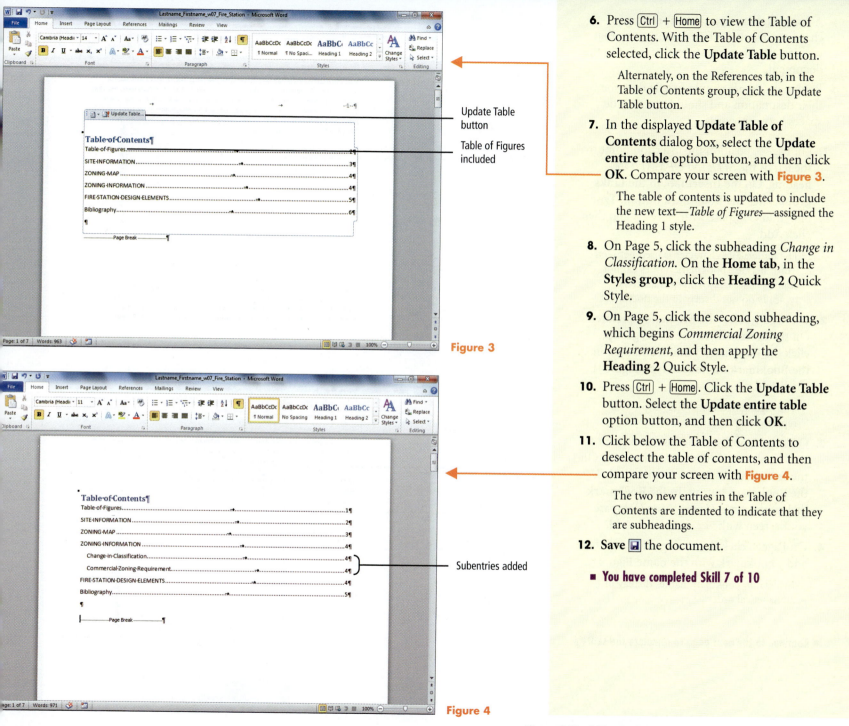

Figure 3

Figure 4

6. Press Ctrl + Home to view the Table of Contents. With the Table of Contents selected, click the **Update Table** button.

    Alternately, on the References tab, in the Table of Contents group, click the Update Table button.

7. In the displayed **Update Table of Contents** dialog box, select the **Update entire table** option button, and then click **OK**. Compare your screen with **Figure 3**.

    The table of contents is updated to include the new text—*Table of Figures*—assigned the Heading 1 style.

8. On Page 5, click the subheading *Change in Classification*. On the **Home tab**, in the **Styles group**, click the **Heading 2** Quick Style.

9. On Page 5, click the second subheading, which begins *Commercial Zoning Requirement,* and then apply the **Heading 2** Quick Style.

10. Press Ctrl + Home. Click the **Update Table** button. Select the **Update entire table** option button, and then click **OK**.

11. Click below the Table of Contents to deselect the table of contents, and then compare your screen with **Figure 4**.

    The two new entries in the Table of Contents are indented to indicate that they are subheadings.

12. Save the document.

■ **You have completed Skill 7 of 10**

▶ A **bookmark** is a special nonprinting character inserted into a document so that you can quickly navigate to that point in the document.

▶ Bookmark names should briefly describe their destination and should not include spaces between words.

1. On Page 3, position the insertion point to the left of the *SITE INFORMATION* heading. On the **Insert tab**, in the **Links group**, click the **Bookmark** button. Type Site_Info Compare with **Figure 1** and then click **Add**.

   The underscore character is used between words because bookmark names cannot contain spaces. Bookmark characters typically do not display in the document

2. On Page 4, select the fire station picture. On the **Insert tab**, in the **Links group**, click the **Bookmark** button, and then in the **Bookmark name** box, type Figure_1 Click **Add**.

   The highlighted text—Site_Info—was replaced with *Figure_1*.

3. On Page 4, position the insertion point to the left of the *ZONING MAP* heading. On the **Insert tab**, in the **Links group**, click the **Bookmark** button. In the **Bookmark** dialog box, type Zoning_Map Compare your screen with **Figure 2**. Click **Add**.

4. On Page 4, click the zoning map, and then add a bookmark with the name Figure_2

   By default, bookmark names display in alphabetical order.

■ **Continue to the next page to complete the skill**

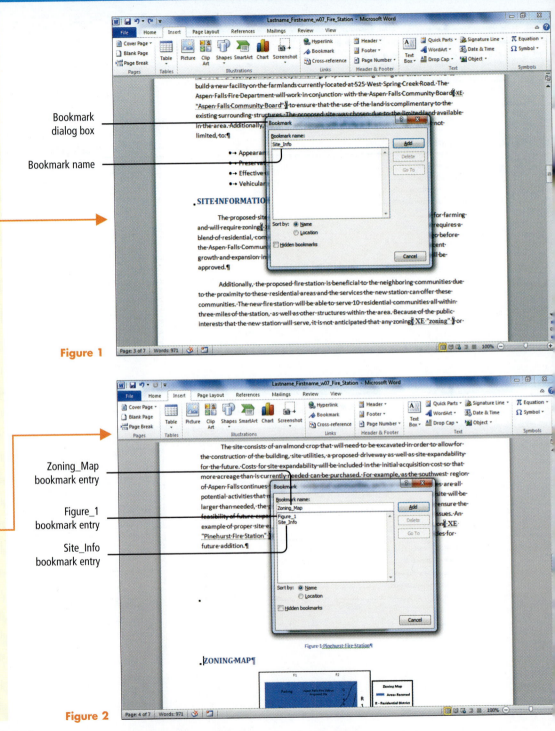

Bookmark dialog box

Bookmark name

Figure 1

Zoning_Map bookmark entry

Figure_1 bookmark entry

Site_Info bookmark entry

Figure 2

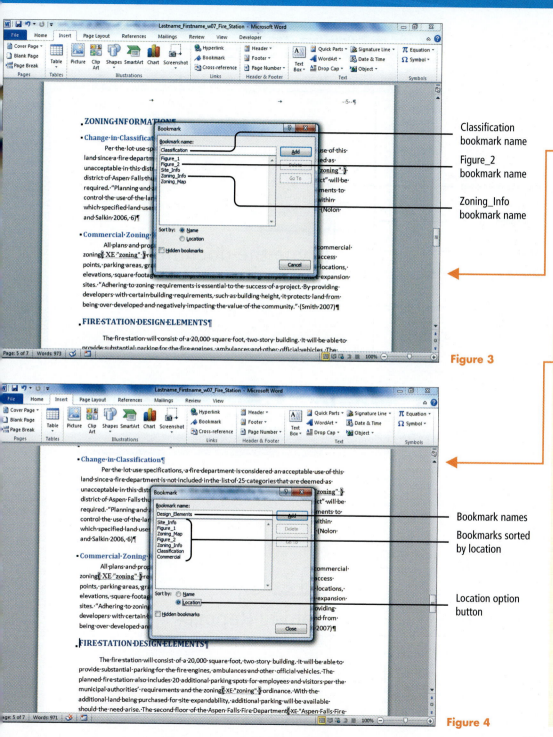

Figure 3

Figure 4

5. On Page 5, repeat the technique just practiced to add a bookmark before the heading *ZONING INFORMATION*. For the **Bookmark name**, type Zoning_Info

6. On Page 5, before the heading that begins *Change in Classification*, in the bookmark name box type Classification Compare your screen with **Figure 3** and then click **Add**.

7. On Page 5, before the heading *Commercial Zoning Requirement*, add a bookmark with the name Commercial

8. On Page 5, position the insertion point before the heading *FIRE STATION DESIGN ELEMENTS*, in the bookmark name box type Design_Elements

9. In the displayed **Bookmark** dialog box, to the right of **Sort by**, click the **Location** option button, and then compare your screen with **Figure 4**.

The bookmarks now display in the order in which they occur in the document.

10. Create a full-screen snip, and **Save** it in your **Word Chapter 7** folder as Lastname_Firstname_w07_Fire_Snip Close the Snipping Tool window.

11. In the **Bookmark** dialog box, click **Add**.

12. Save the document.

■ **You have completed Skill 8 of 10**

Classification bookmark name

Figure_2 bookmark name

Zoning_Info bookmark name

Bookmark names

Bookmarks sorted by location

Location option button

► A *cover page*, also called a title page, is usually the first page of a document. It displays document information such as the title and subtitle, the date, the document author's name, and the company name.

► Word provides several built-in cover pages with fields into which you insert your own document information.

1. Press ⌃Ctrl + ⌂Home.

2. On the **Insert tab**, in the **Pages group**, click the **Cover Page** button. Scroll down and then click the **Sideline** thumbnail. Compare your screen with **Figure 1**.

   A page break is automatically inserted along with the cover/title page. The cover page displays fields in which you type your own information.

3. On Page 1, on the **File tab**, click the **Properties** button, and then click **Advanced Properties**.

4. On the **Summary tab**, if necessary, record the existing text on a sheet of paper. Under **Author**, type Maria Martinez, City Manager

5. Under **Company**, type City of Aspen Falls and then click **OK**. Click the **Home tab**.

6. Locate the **Title** field with the text *[Type the document title]* click the field to select it, and then type Zoning Report

7. Locate the **Subtitle** field with the text *[Type the document subtitle]* click the field to select it, and then type Aspen Falls Fire Department Compare your screen with **Figure 2**.

■ **Continue to the next page to complete the skill** ▶

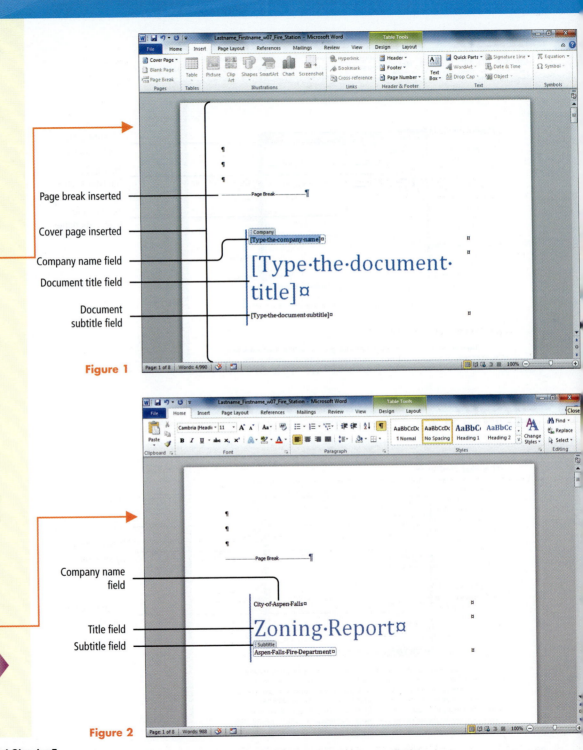

Page break inserted

Cover page inserted

Company name field

Document title field

Document subtitle field

Figure 1

Company name field

Title field

Subtitle field

Figure 2

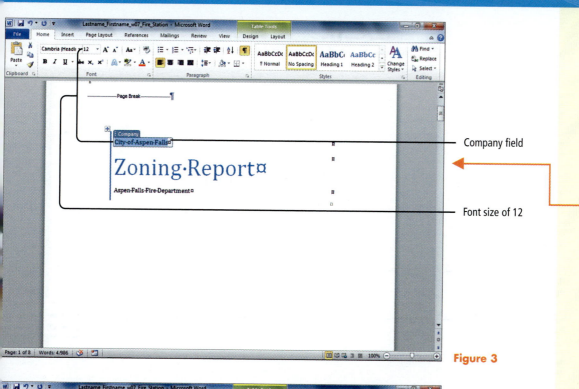

Company field

Font size of 12

Figure 3

Font size of 12

Cambria font

Author and Date fields

Figure 4

8. Click the **Date** field with the text *[Pick the date]* to select it. Click the displayed **Date field arrow**. Use the displayed **Date Picker arrow** to select *today's date.*

   The date displayed may vary.

9. On Page 1, click the text that begins *City of*, and then click the word *Company* to select the **Company** field. On the **Home tab**, in the **Font group**, click the **Font Size** button, and select **12**. Compare your screen with **Figure 3**.

10. On Page 1, click *Maria* to select the **Author** field, and then click the word **Author** to select the **Author** field. On the **Home tab**, in the **Font group**, click the **Font arrow**, and then click **Cambria (Headings)**.

11. In the **Font group**, click the **Font Size arrow**, and then click **12**.

12. Repeat the technique just practiced to change the **Date** field **Font** to **Cambria (Headings)** and the **Font Size** to **12**. Compare your screen with **Figure 4**.

■ **You have completed Skill 9 of 10**

► You can use the *Select Browse Object toolbar* to navigate long documents quickly.

► Each of the 12 buttons on the Select Browse Object toolbar refers to different types of objects—for example, bookmarks, figures, tables, fields, or sections.

1. Press [Ctrl] + [Home] to move to the beginning of the document.

2. On the vertical scroll bar located at the right side of your Word window, click the **Select Browse Object** button [○], as shown in **Figure 1**.

3. In the displayed Select Browse Object toolbar, click the **Browse by Graphic** button [🖼]. Notice that the document scrolls to the first figure—*Figure 1*

4. Select the graphic. On the **Format tab**, in the **Picture Styles group**, click the **Picture Border** button, and then click the fourth color in the first row—**Dark Blue**, **Text 2**. In the **Picture Styles group**, click the **Picture Border** button, click **Weight**, and then select **2 1/4pt**.

5. At the bottom of the vertical scroll bar, click the **Next Graphic** button [⯯] to move to the next graphic in the document—*Figure 2*.

6. Select the map. On the **Format tab**, in the **Picture Styles group**, click the ninth style in the gallery—**Simple Frame, Black**. Compare your screen with **Figure 2**.

■ **Continue to the next page to complete the skill**

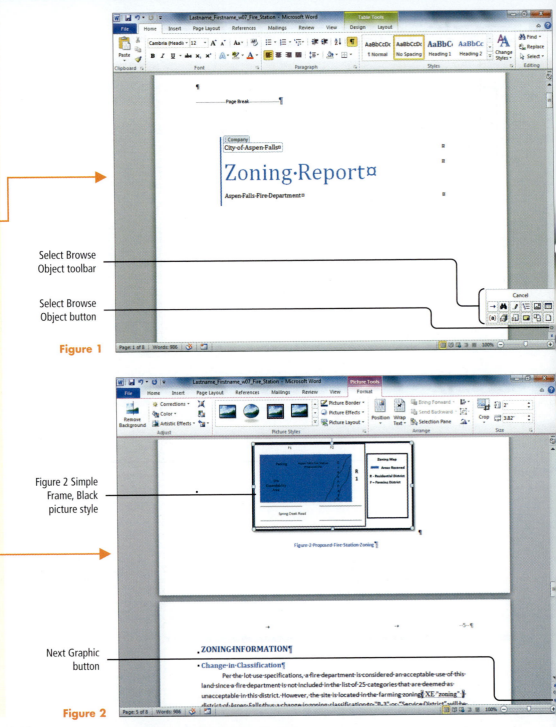

Select Browse Object toolbar

Select Browse Object button

Figure 1

Figure 2 Simple Frame, Black picture style

Next Graphic button

Figure 2

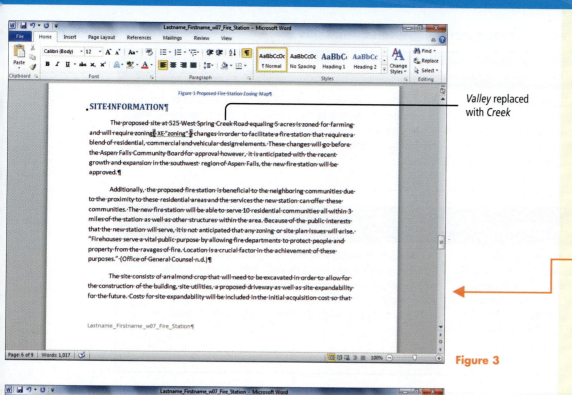

Valley replaced with Creek

Figure 3

Table of Figures heading

Font size changed

Figure 4

7. Click the **Select Browse Object** button, and then click the **Go To** button.

8. In the displayed **Find and Replace** dialog box, verify that the **Go To tab** displays. Under **Go to what**, scroll up to select **Bookmark**.

9. Click the **Enter bookmark name box arrow**, click **Site_Info**, click the **Go To** button, and then **Close** the dialog box.

10. In the paragraph that begins *The proposed site* replace the word *Valley* with Creek and then compare your screen with **Figure 3**.

11. Click the **Select Browse Object** button, and then click the **Browse by Heading** button.

12. Click the **Previous Heading** button two times to move to the *Table of Figures* heading. Select the figure entries, and then change the **Font Size** to 12 points. Compare your screen with **Figure 4**.

13. On the **File tab**, click **Properties**, and then click **Advanced Properties**.

14. In the displayed **Properties** dialog box, on the **Summary tab**, under **Author** and **Company**, reset the text to what you wrote down in Skill 9, Step 4.

15. If necessary, deselect the **Save Thumbnails for All Word Documents** check box, and then click **OK**.

16. **Save** the document. Print or submit the files as directed by your instructor. **Exit** Word.

Done! You have completed Skill 10 of 10 and your document is complete!

More Skills

The following More Skills are located at **www.pearsonhighered.com/skills**

More Skills Navigate Footnotes and Convert Footnotes to Endnotes

Each footnote can display at the bottom of the page on which it is inserted, or the footnotes can be placed as a single group at the end of the document as endnotes. The only difference between footnotes and endnotes is the location where they display in the document. For example, endnotes are edited and formatted in the same manner as footnotes.

In More Skills 11, you will convert footnotes to endnotes and then modify the format of the endnotes. To begin, open your web browser, navigate to www.pearsonhighered.com/skills, locate the name of your textbook, and then follow the instructions on the website.

More Skills Add Citations in the APA Style

Recall that Source Manager stores references that you commonly use so that you can quickly add them as citations and create a bibliography. Several types of references are supported, including books, periodicals, journals, and web pages. You can also choose the style—American Psychological Association (APA), Chicago Manual of Style, or Modern Language Association (MLA), for example—that you need your citations and bibliography to follow.

In More Skills 12, you will add sources using Source Manager and then add citations and a bibliography in APA style. To begin, open your web browser, navigate to www.pearsonhighered.com/skills, locate the name of your textbook, and then follow the instructions on the website.

More Skills Manage Versions

You can have Word do background saving every so many minutes, based on the number of minutes you select in the Word Options dialog box under the Save tab. In the event your machine shuts down while you are in the middle of working on your document, you may be able to recover the text from the last time Word AutoSaved your document. Versions enable you to select how far back you would like to go to recover your AutoSaved data.

In More Skills 13, you will make changes to your document and review AutoSaved versions. To begin, open your web browser, navigate to www.pearsonhighered.com/skills, locate the name of your textbook, and then follow the instructions on the website.

More Skills Create Table of Authorities

A Table of Authorities lists legal cases, statutes and laws, and other authorities that are referenced in a document's citations. Before building a Table of Authorities, you need to mark the citations that will be used to create the table's entries.

In More Skills 14, you will insert legal citations, mark the citations, and then create the Table of Authorities. To begin, open your web browser, navigate to www.pearsonhighered.com/skills, locate the name of your textbook, and then follow the instructions on the website.

Key Terms

Online Help Skills

1. **Start** ⊙ Word. In the upper right corner of the Word window, click the **Help** button ⊙. In the **Help** window, click the **Maximize** 🔲 button.

2. Click in the search box, type recover and then click the **Search** button 🔍. In the search results, click **Recover earlier versions of a file in Office 2010**.

3. Read the article's introduction, and then below **Learn more about** click **When you close without saving**. Compare your screen with **Figure 1**.

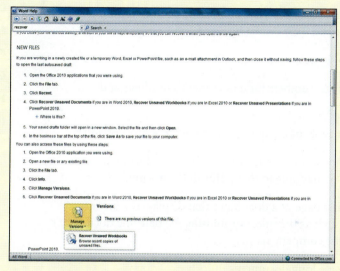

Figure 1

4. Read the section to see if you can answer the following: On what tab will you click to view recovered versions? On what button can you view Recovered Unsaved Documents?

Matching

Match each term in the second column with its correct definition in the first column by writing the letter of the term on the blank line in front of the correct definition.

____ **1.** A list of words and phrases found in a document along with their corresponding page numbers.

____ **2.** Words, phrases, or cross-references that will go in the index.

____ **3.** An index entry associated with a different word or phrase that is similar in context.

____ **4.** References to figures, equations, and tables in the document.

____ **5.** Entries and page numbers for a document's headings and subheadings.

____ **6.** An entry in a Table of Contents that is part of a broader entry.

____ **7.** A special nonprinting character inserted into a document so that you can quickly navigate to that point in the document.

____ **8.** Usually the first page of a document that displays document information such as the title and subtitle, the date, the document's author, and the company name.

____ **9.** Used to navigate long documents quickly.

A Bookmark

B Cover page

C Cross-reference

D Index

E Index entry field

F Select Browse Object toolbar

G Subheading

H Table of Contents

I Table of Figures

Multiple Choice

Choose the correct answer.

1. The location on a built-in cover page where the author, date, title, and subtitle entries are entered.
   A. Database
   B. Field
   C. Report heading

2. The Word feature used to display cross-references at the end of a document.
   A. Footnote
   B. Index
   C. Table of Contents

3. The button in the Mark Index Entry dialog box used to identify all occurrences of a word in the document.
   A. Identify
   B. Mark
   C. Mark All

4. The word in the Mark Index Entry dialog box that displays before a cross-reference.
   A. Cross-reference
   B. Mark
   C. See

5. The button used to change a label for a selected figure or table.
   A. Insert Caption
   B. Picture
   C. Text Box

6. The check box selected to help format the document so that the cover page does not display a page number.
   A. Different First Page
   B. Different Odd & Even Pages
   C. Pages

7. The option in the Update Table of Contents dialog box used to change all items that have been modified in the Table of Contents.
   A. Update All
   B. Update entire table
   C. Update page numbers only

8. The item that cannot be included in bookmark entries of two or more words.
   A. Capital Letter
   B. Space
   C. Underline

9. The button not available when using the Select Browse Object toolbar.
   A. Find
   B. Go To
   C. Replace

10. The type of source commonly used when the reference is located online.
    A. Book
    B. Journal Article
    C. Web site

Topics for Discussion

1. Imagine you are the office manager for a small architectural/engineering firm who has been asked to prepare a report for the city planner to explain the proposed plans for a new civic center. What types of items might you add to your report to enhance it? What images would you include?

2. Imagine you are preparing a report for a nonprofit organization. What types of items might you include on a cover page? In an index?

Skill Check

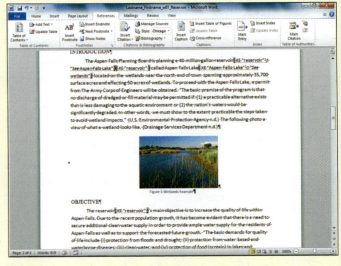

Figure 1

To complete this project, you will need the following file:

- w07_Reservoir

You will save your files as:

- Lastname_Firstname_w07_Reservoir
- Lastname_Firstname_w07_Reservoir_Snip

1. **Start** Word, and open the student data file **w07_Reservoir**. Save the file in your **Word Chapter 7** folder with the name Lastname_Firstname_w07_Reservoir Add the file name to the footer. Display the formatting marks.

2. On Page 2, in the paragraph that begins *The Aspen* select *reservoir*. On the **References tab**, in the **Index group**, click the **Mark Entry** button. In the **Mark Index Entry** dialog box, click **Mark All**.

3. In the **Mark Index Entry** dialog box, click the **Cross-reference** option button. Position the insertion point to the right of *See* and then type Aspen Falls Lake Click **Mark**, and then click **Close**. Compare your screen with **Figure 1**.

4. Press Ctrl + End. On the **References tab**, in the **Index group**, click the **Insert Index** button. In the **Index** dialog box, select the **Right align page numbers** check box. Click the **Formats arrow**, click **Fancy**, and then click **OK**.

5. On Page 1, position the insertion point before the page break. On the **References tab**, in the **Captions group**, click the **Insert Table of Figures** button.

6. In the **Table of Figures** dialog box, click the **Formats arrow**, and then select **Distinctive**. Click the **Tab leader arrow**, and select **dot leader—.......** Clear the **Use hyperlinks instead of page numbers** check box, and then click **OK**. Compare your screen with **Figure 2**.

7. Press Ctrl + Home. Press Ctrl + Enter. Press Ctrl + Home. On the **References tab**, in the **Table of Contents group**, click the **Table of Contents** button, and then click **Automatic Table 2**.

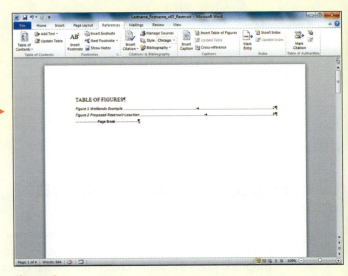

Figure 2

■ **Continue to the next page to complete this Skill Check**

8. On Page 2, locate and select the heading *TABLE OF FIGURES*. On the **Insert tab**, in the **Links group**, click the **Bookmark** button. In the **Bookmark** dialog box, type TOF and then click **Add**.

9. On Page 3, select *INTRODUCTION*. In the **Links group**, click the **Bookmark** button, and then type Intro With the **Bookmark** dialog box open, create a full-screen snip. **Save** it in your **Word Chapter 7** folder as Lastname_Firstname_w07_Reservoir_Snip and then close the Snipping Tool window.

10. In the **Bookmark** dialog box, click **Add**.

11. On the **Insert tab**, in the **Header & Footer group**, click the **Header** button, and then click **Edit Header**. On the **Design tab**, in the **Options group**, select the **Different Odd & Even Pages** check box.

12. In the **Odd Page Header**, tab two times, type Planning Report Scroll down and click in the **Even Page Header**, and then in the **Header & Footer group**, click the **Page Number** button, point to **Top of Page**, and then click **Plain Number 1**. Click **Close Header and Footer**. On Page 3, scroll up to view the header. Compare your screen with **Figure 3**.

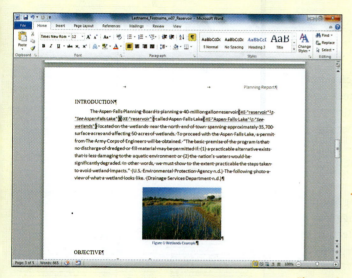

Figure 3

13. On Page 3, select the *INTRODUCTION* heading *According to the* through the caption. Be sure to include the paragraph symbol at the end of the caption. On the **Home tab**, in the **Clipboard group**, click **Cut**. Position the insertion point to the left of *DESIGN* and then in the **Clipboard group**, click **Paste**.

14. Press Ctrl + End. Click anywhere in the index. Right-click to display the shortcut menu, and then click **Update Field**.

15. Press Ctrl + Home. Click **Update Table**. Select the **Update entire table** option button, and then click **OK**.

16. Click the **Select Browse Object** button, and then click **Go To**. In the **Find and Replace** dialog box, click **Bookmark**, select *TOF* from the list, and then click **Go To**. **Close** the dialog box.

17. Click the reference to *Figure 1* to select the Table of Figures object. Right-click to display the shortcut menu, and then click **Update Field**. Select **Update entire table**, and then click **OK**.

18. Press Ctrl + Home. On the **Insert tab**, in the **Pages group**, click the **Cover Page** button, and then click **Sideline**.

19. In the **Company** field, type Aspen Falls Change the **Title** field to Reservoir and the **Subtitle** field to Planning Report Change the **Author** field to Your Name and the **Date** field to 5/31/2012 Compare your screen with **Figure 4**.

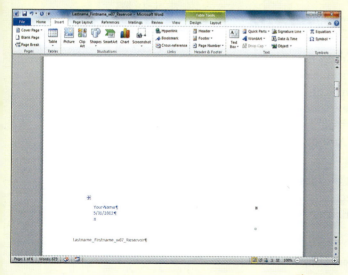

Figure 4

20. **Save** the document. Print or submit the files as directed by your instructor. If necessary, in the displayed message, click **No**. **Exit** Word.

Done! **You have completed the Skill Check**

Assess Your Skills 1

To complete this project, you will need the following file:

- w07_Convention_Center

You will save your file as:

- Lastname_Firstname_w07_Convention_Center

1. **Start** Word, and open the student data file **w07_Convention_Center**. Save the file in your **Word Chapter 7** folder with the name Lastname_Firstname_w07_Convention_Center Add the file name to the footer.

2. On Page 1, in the paragraph that begins *The planning board* select *low impact design* and then mark all occurrences of the phrase as an index entry. For the first occurrence of *LID* create a cross-reference to the *low impact design* index entry. Mark all occurrences of the word *parking* as an index entry.

3. At the end of the document, insert a page break. On the new page, type INDEX and press Enter. Insert an index that has page numbers right-aligned and that displays the **Modern** format. Apply the **Heading 1** style to *INDEX*.

4. At the top of Page 1, insert a page break. In the new Page 1, insert a Table of Contents using the **Automatic Table 2** style.

5. At the top of Page 2, insert a page break. Before the page break on Page 2, type TABLE OF FIGURES and press Enter. Insert a Table of Figures using the **Centered** format, and clear the **Use hyperlinks instead of page numbers** check box. On Page 2, apply the **Heading 1** style to *TABLE OF FIGURES*.

6. On Page 1, open the header, and then select the **Different Odd & Even Pages** check box. For the **Odd Page Header**, tab two times, and then type Convention Center For the **Even Page Header**, insert the **Bold Numbers 1** page number built-in at the top of the page.

7. On Page 4, select the paragraph that begins *CONSIDERATIONS* through the *Figure 2* caption, and click **Cut**. **Paste** the selection on Page 3, before the paragraph that begins *PROJECT DESCRIPTION*.

8. On Page 4, remove the page break, and then press Enter six times.

9. Update the captions, Table of Contents, the Table of Figures, and the Index.

10. At the beginning of the document, insert the **Transcend** cover page. In the **Date** field, pick **5/31/2012**. In the **Company** field, type City of Aspen Falls In the **Title** field, type Parking Lot Expansion In the **Subtitle** field, type Convention Center and then in the **Author** field, type your first and last name.

11. **Save** the document. Print or submit the files as directed by your instructor. If necessary, in the displayed message, click **No**. **Exit** Word.

Done! You have completed Assess Your Skills 1

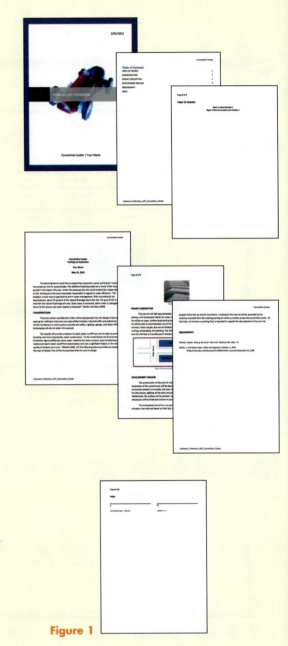

Figure 1

Assess Your Skills 2

To complete this project, you will need the following file:

- w07_Office

You will save your files as:

- Lastname_Firstname_w07_Office
- Lastname_Firstname_w07_Office_Snip

1. **Start** Word, and open the student data file **w07_Office**. Save the file in your **Word Chapter 7** folder with the name Lastname_Firstname_w07_Office Add the file name to the footer. Display the formatting marks.

2. At the top of Page 1, insert a page break. On Page 1, before the page break, insert a Table of Contents with the **Automatic Table 2** style.

3. On Page 1, open the header, and then select the **Different Odd & Even Pages** check box. For the **Odd Page Headers**, tab two times, and then type Community Office For the **Even Page Headers**, insert the **Plain Number 1** page number built-in at the top of the page.

4. Scroll to the top of Page 2. Insert a page break. On Page 2, click before the page break notation, type TABLE OF FIGURES and then press Enter.

5. Insert a Table of Figures using the **Simple** format, and clear the **Use hyperlinks instead of page numbers** check box.

6. On Page 1, select the *Table of Contents* heading, and insert a bookmark named TOC On Page 2, select the *TABLE OF FIGURES* heading, and then create a bookmark named *TOF*.

7. Display the **Bookmark** dialog box. Create a full screen snip named Lastname_Firstname_w07_Office_Snip

8. On Page 3, select the heading *MERGER OBJECTIVES* through the paragraph below the *FUNDING* heading, and **Cut**.

9. On Page 4, in the blank paragraph directly above BIBLIOGRAPHY, click **Paste**.

10. Use the **Select Browse Object** button to **Go To** the *TOF* **Bookmark**.

11. Apply the **Heading 1** style to the *TABLE OF FIGURES* paragraph. Update the Table of Figures.

12. Use the **Select Browse Object** button to **Go To** the *TOC* **Bookmark**. Update the Table of Contents.

13. At the top of Page 1, insert the **Sideline** cover page. In the **Company** field, type City of Aspen Falls In the **Title** field, type Community Office In the **Subtitle** field, type Merger In the **Author** field, type Your Name In the **Date**, pick 7/16/2012

14. **Save** the document. Print or submit the files as directed by your instructor. **Exit** Word.

Done! You have completed Assess Your Skills 2

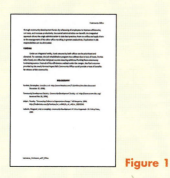

Figure 1

Assess Your Skills Visually

To complete this project, you will need the following file:

- w07_Winery_Grant

You will save your file as:

- Lastname_Firstname_w07_Winery_Grant

Open the student data file **w07_Winery_Grant**. Save the file in your **Word Chapter 7** folder with the name Lastname_Firstname_w07_Winery_ Grant On Page 1, add the file name to the footer. At the beginning of the document, use the **Stacks** format to create the **Cover Page** shown in **Figure 1**. In the document, mark the index entries and cross-reference entries as needed to create the **Modern** index page that will display on the last page of the report, as shown in **Figure 2**. Update the Table of Contents and the Table of Figures. Print or submit the file as directed by your instructor. **Exit** Word.

Done! You have completed Assess Your Skills Visually

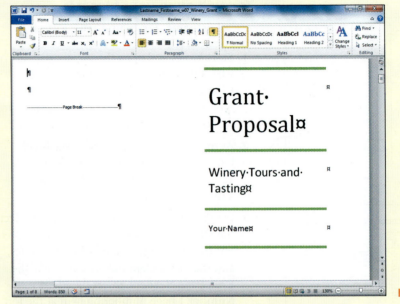

Figure 1

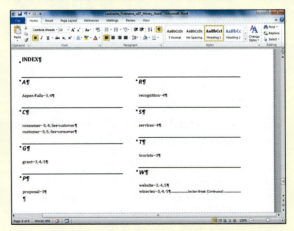

Figure 2

Skills in Context

To complete this project, you will need the following file:

- w07_Playground_Equipment

You will save your file as:

- Lastname_Firstname_w07_Playground_Equipment

The City of Aspen Falls is getting ready to purchase new playground equipment for special needs children. Using the skills you practiced in this chapter, create a report using the file **w07_Playground_Equipment**. Read the report. Insert a cover page with a style appropriate to the content. On the cover page, add appropriate information, including the current date and your own name as author. Based on the report contents, determine 15 to 20 of the most important key words or phrases, and then create an index that includes each. Include at least two cross-references. In the header, insert odd and even page numbers.

Save the file in your **Word Chapter 7** folder with the name Lastname_Firstname_w07_Playground_ Equipment Add the file name to the footer. Print or submit the file as directed by your instructor. **Exit** Word.

Done! You have completed Skills in Context

Skills and You

To complete this project, you will need the following file:

- New, blank Word document

You will save your file as:

- Lastname_Firstname_w07_Interest_Report

Using the skills you have practiced in this chapter, prepare a 3-4 page report about a topic of interest to you. Be sure the report includes at least two pictures, two tables, and two figures with captions, and then prepare a Table of Figures. Insert odd and even page numbers. Include a cover page, an index with at least two entries marked and at least one cross reference, a Table of Contents, and at least two bookmarks.

Save your report as Lastname_Firstname_w07_Interest_Report Print or submit the file as directed by your instructor. **Exit** Word.

Done! You have completed Skills and You

CHAPTER 8

Collaborate and Share with Others

▶ Review tools help you collaborate with others while building documents. Team members can add comments and track their changes so that their input can be used to create the final version of a document.

▶ Review tools also help you prepare your documents. For example, you can count the number of words or estimate the grade level needed to read your document.

Your starting screen will look like this:

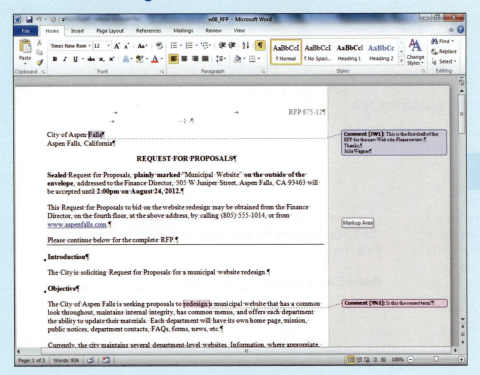

SKILLS

Skills 1-10 Training

At the end of this chapter, you will be able to:

Skill 1 Track Changes and Insert Comments

Skill 2 Check Document Statistics and Compatibility

Skill 3 Modify and Delete Comments

Skill 4 Change Tracking Options

Skill 5 Restrict Editing Options

Skill 6 Review Documents

Skill 7 Print Markups

Skill 8 Combine Documents

Skill 9 Accept or Reject Tracked Changes

Skill 10 Mark Documents as Final

MORE SKILLS

More Skills 11 Print Envelopes Using Mail Merge

More Skills 12 Apply Saved Themes

More Skills 13 Create Blog Posts

More Skills 14 Change Grammar and Style Options

Outcome

Using the skills listed to the left will enable you to create documents like these:

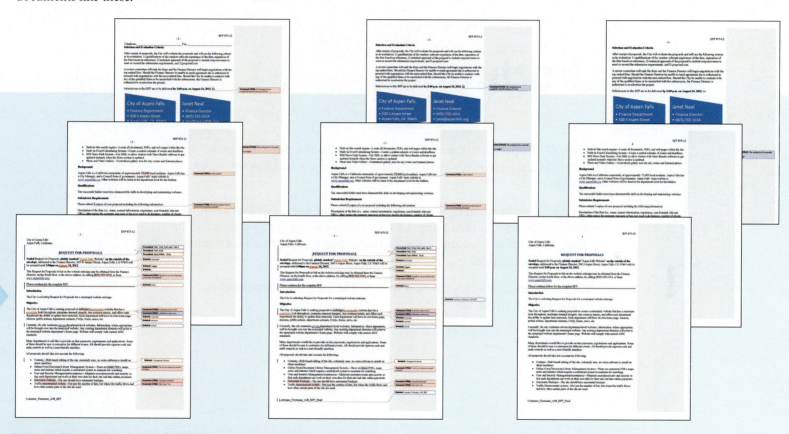

You will save your files as:

Lastname_Firstname_w08_RFP
Lastname_Firstname_w08_RFP_Draft
Lastname_Firstname_w08_RFP_Final

In this chapter, you will work with documents for the Aspen Falls City Hall, which provides essential services for the citizens and visitors of Aspen Falls, California.

Introduction

- ▸ When you collaborate to create a document, you may be asked to be a reviewer. As a reviewer, you can track each change you make in the Word document.

- ▸ When Word tracks changes, the original author can see the changes that a reviewer proposes and then accept or reject each change. The changes can be printed, and the final document can be marked as final so that no additional changes can be included.

- ▸ When reviewers have made changes in multiple files, the documents can be combined into a single file.

**Time to complete all
10 skills – 50 to 90 minutes**

Find your student data files here:

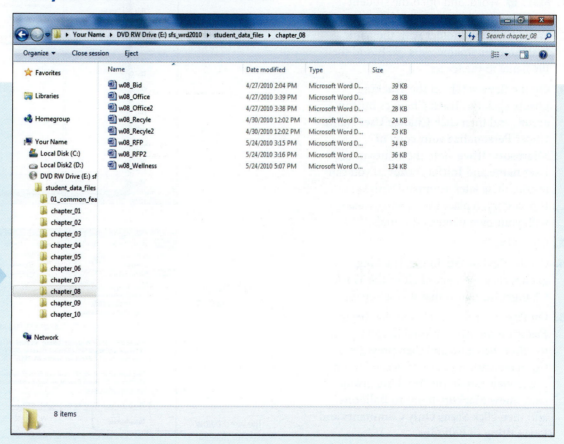

Student data files needed for this chapter:

- w08_RFP
- w08_RFP2

▶ Review tools can be used to mark each change you make in a document so that others can see your revisions.

▶ A *comment* is a message inserted by those reviewing a document. A comment is inserted at a specific location within the document.

1. **Start** ⊕ Word, and open the student data file **w08_RFP**. Save the file in your **Word Chapter 8** folder with the name Lastname_Firstname_w08_RFP Add the file name to the footer.

2. On the **Review tab**, in the **Tracking group**, click the **Track Changes button arrow**, and then click **Change User Name**. Under **Personalize your copy of Microsoft Office**, note the values in the **User name** and **Initials** boxes so you can restore these later. Compare with **Figure 1**. If necessary, replace the existing values with your own name and initials.

3. Click **OK**.

4. On the **Review tab**, in the **Tracking group**, click the upper half of the **Track Changes** button so that it is selected.

5. On Page 1, in the paragraph that begins *Please continue below*, double-click *below* to select the word, and then press Delete. Compare with **Figure 2**. If necessary, on the **Review tab**, in the **Tracking group**, click **Show Markup**, point to **Balloons**, and then click **Show Only Comments and Formatting in Balloons**.

> The deleted word displays in a new color and has a line through it indicating that the word has been marked for deletion.

■ **Continue to the next page to complete the skill**

Your own name should display

Your own initials should display

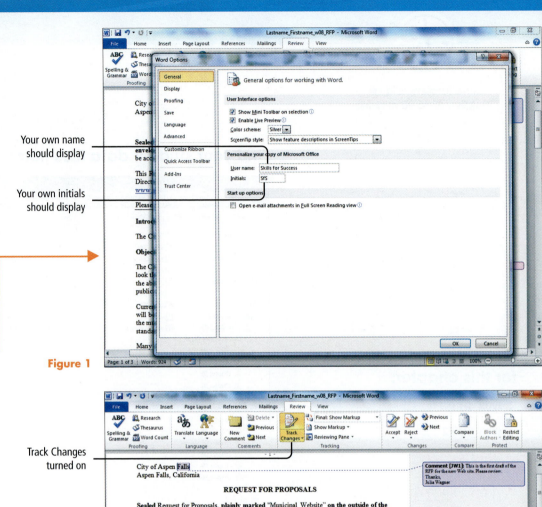

Figure 1

Track Changes turned on

The word *below* marked for deletion

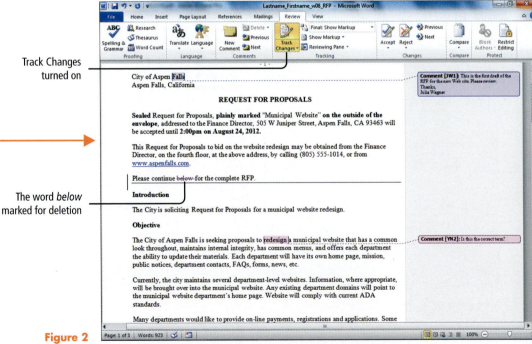

Figure 2

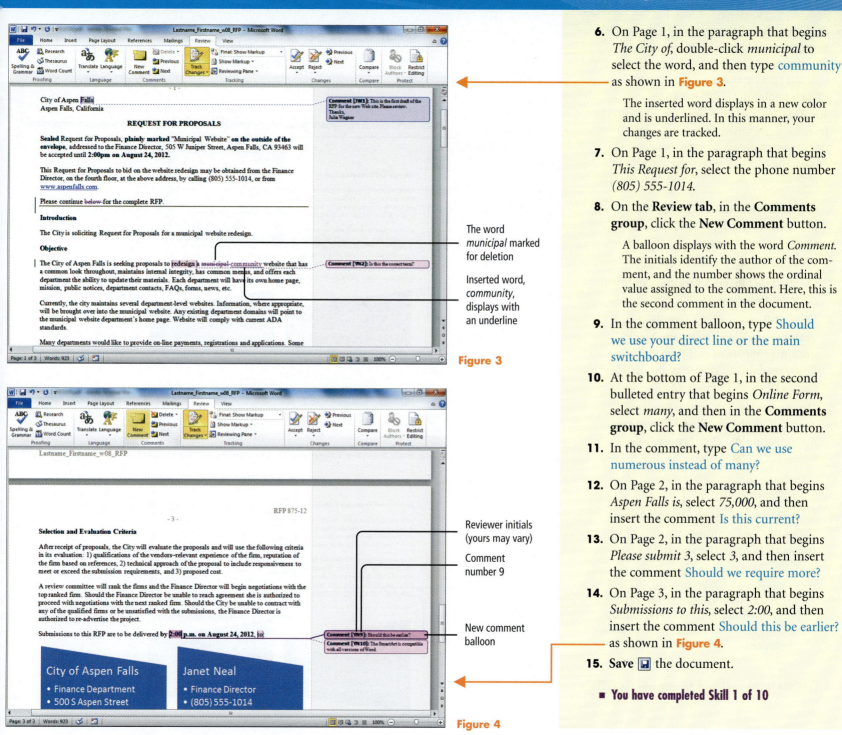

Figure 3

Figure 4

The word *municipal* marked for deletion

Inserted word, *community*, displays with an underline

Reviewer initials (yours may vary)

Comment number 9

New comment balloon

6. On Page 1, in the paragraph that begins *The City of*, double-click *municipal* to select the word, and then type community as shown in **Figure 3**.

   The inserted word displays in a new color and is underlined. In this manner, your changes are tracked.

7. On Page 1, in the paragraph that begins *This Request for*, select the phone number *(805) 555-1014*.

8. On the **Review tab**, in the **Comments group**, click the **New Comment** button.

   A balloon displays with the word *Comment*. The initials identify the author of the comment, and the number shows the ordinal value assigned to the comment. Here, this is the second comment in the document.

9. In the comment balloon, type Should we use your direct line or the main switchboard?

10. At the bottom of Page 1, in the second bulleted entry that begins *Online Form*, select *many*, and then in the **Comments group**, click the **New Comment** button.

11. In the comment, type Can we use numerous instead of many?

12. On Page 2, in the paragraph that begins *Aspen Falls is*, select *75,000*, and then insert the comment Is this current?

13. On Page 2, in the paragraph that begins *Please submit 3*, select *3*, and then insert the comment Should we require more?

14. On Page 3, in the paragraph that begins *Submissions to this*, select *2:00*, and then insert the comment Should this be earlier? as shown in **Figure 4**.

15. **Save** 🔲 the document.

   ■ **You have completed Skill 1 of 10**

▶ ***Document statistics*** are data that summarize document features such as the number of pages, words, characters without spaces, characters including spaces, paragraphs, and lines.

▶ ***Readability statistics*** measure the reading level for a document based on certain document statistics such as the length of words, the number of syllables in words, and the length of sentences and paragraphs.

1. On the **Review tab**, in the **Proofing group**, click the **Word Count** button. Compare your screen with **Figure 1**.

2. **Close** the **Word Count** dialog box.

3. On the **File tab**, click **Options**, and then click the **Proofing tab**.

4. Under **When correcting spelling and grammar in Word**, select the **Mark grammar errors as you type** and the **Show readability statistics** check boxes. Click **OK**.

5. On the **Review tab**, in the **Proofing group**, click the **Spelling & Grammar** button, and then click **Ignore Rule** 9 times.

   In this document, ignoring these rules is acceptable.

6. Read the displayed message, and then click **OK**. Take a moment to review the **Readability Statistics** shown in **Figure 2**.

   The ***Flesch Reading Ease*** is a 100-point scale that measures readability. A score of 100 indicates an easy-to-understand document. The ***Flesch-Kincaid Grade Level*** estimates the U.S. grade level needed to understand a document.

■ **Continue to the next page to complete the skill**

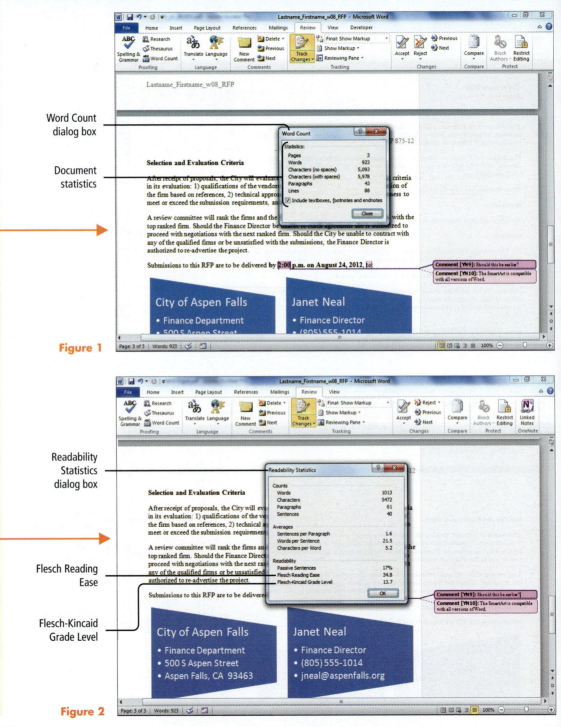

Word Count dialog box

Document statistics

Figure 1

Readability Statistics dialog box

Flesch Reading Ease

Flesch-Kincaid Grade Level

Figure 2

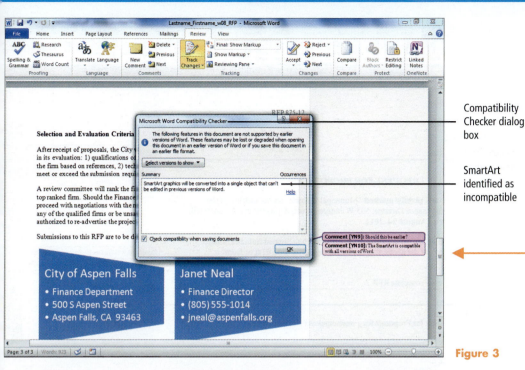

Compatibility Checker dialog box

SmartArt identified as incompatible

Figure 3

Word 2010 Features Incompatible with Word 2007 and Earlier

Alternative text on tables	New shapes and text boxes
Blocking authors	New WordArt effects
New content controls	OpenType features
New numbering formats	Text effects

Word 2010 Features Incompatible with Word 97-2003

Charts and diagrams	Margin tabs
Content controls	SmartArt graphics
Equations	Themes
Bibliographies and citations	Tracked moves
Relative positioning text boxes	Major/minor fonts
Open XML embedded objects	Building blocks

Figure 4

7. Record the **Flesch-Kincaid Grade Level** value on a piece of paper to refer to in the next skill, and then click **OK**.

8. On the **File tab**, click **Options**, and then click the **Proofing tab**.

9. Under **When correcting spelling and grammar in Word**, clear the **Mark grammar errors as you type** and the **Show readability statistics** check boxes, and then click **OK**.

10. On the **File tab**, click the **Check for Issues** button, and then click **Check Compatibility**. Compare your screen with **Figure 3**.

   The *Compatibility Checker* locates features in a Word 2010 document that are not supported in earlier versions of Word. Individuals using earlier versions of Word may not be able to see these features correctly.

   Here, the SmartArt would be converted to a picture if the document were opened in an earlier version of Word. Features supported in Word 2010 that are not supported in earlier versions are summarized in the table shown in **Figure 4**.

11. In the displayed dialog box, click **OK**, and then **Save** 🔲 the document.

   ■ **You have completed Skill 2 of 10**

► Comments already inserted into a document can be edited or deleted in their comment balloons or in the Reviewing Pane.

► When a comment is deleted, the remaining comments are automatically renumbered.

1. Press Ctrl + Home.

2. On the **View tab**, in the **Zoom group**, click the **Zoom** button.

   Zoom is the magnification level of the document as displayed on the screen. Increasing the zoom percentage increases the size of the text and comments as displayed on the screen, but it does not increase the actual font size.

3. In the **Zoom** dialog box, in the **Percent** box, select the current setting, for example, *100*, type 130 and then click **OK**.

4. Scroll to the right to view the first comment, and then compare your screen with **Figure 1**.

   Comments are often easier to work with when the zoom percentage is higher than 100%.

5. On the **Review tab**, in the **Comments group**, click the **Next** button one time to move to the comment that begins *This is the first draft*. Read the comment, and then in the **Comments group**, click the **Delete** button. In the **Comments group**, click the **Next** button one time, and then compare your screen with **Figure 2**.

6. On the **Review tab**, in the **Comments group**, click the **Next** button one time. With the second comment active, select the word *term*, and then type word

■ **Continue to the next page to complete the skill**

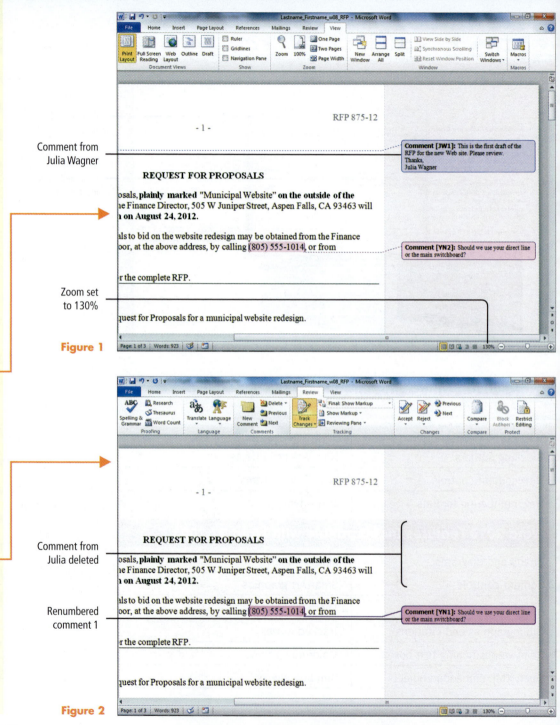

Comment from Julia Wagner

Zoom set to 130%

Figure 1

Comment from Julia deleted

Renumbered comment 1

Figure 2

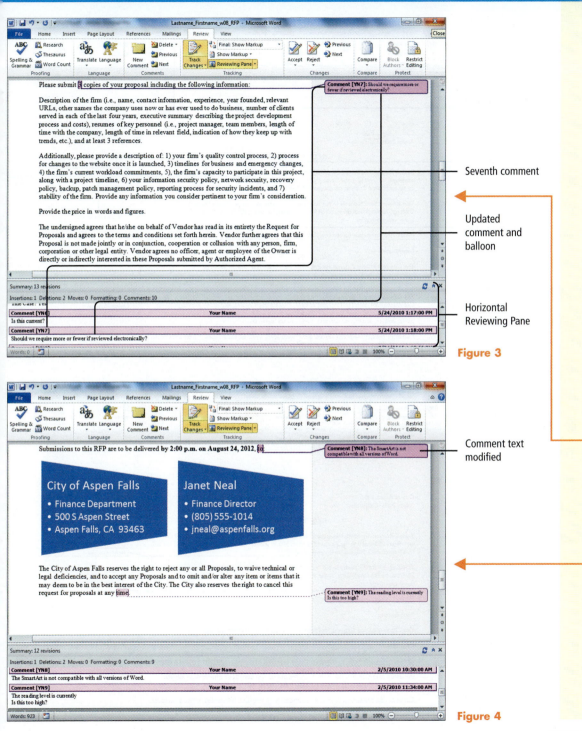

Seventh comment

Updated comment and balloon

Horizontal Reviewing Pane

Figure 3

Comment text modified

Figure 4

7. In the bottom right corner of the status bar, click the **Zoom Out** button three times to set the zoom to **100%**.

8. On the **Review tab**, in the **Tracking group**, click the **Reviewing Pane button arrow**, and then click **Reviewing Pane Horizontal**.

   The *Reviewing Pane* displays at the left—vertically, or at the bottom—horizontally, of the screen and lists all comments and tracked changes.

9. In the **Reviewing Pane**, scroll to locate the fourth comment, [YN4] or your initials. In the comment, select the text *Should this be*. Press Delete two times.

   When a comment is edited in the Reviewing Pane, the comment balloon also changes.

10. In the **Comments group**, click the **Next** button. In the **Reviewing Pane**, click the end of the fifth comment. Add a space, and then type Yes

11. Locate the seventh comment, [YN7] or your initials, and click before the ?. Add a space. Type or fewer if reviewed electronically as shown in **Figure 3**.

12. Click the entire eighth comment that begins *Should this*, and in the **Comments group**, click the **Delete** button.

13. In the renumbered eighth comment, click before the *c* in *compatible*, type not and then add a space. Compare your screen with **Figure 4**.

14. Locate the ninth comment, click the end of the first line, and then type the **Flesh-Kincaid Grade Level** value recorded in the previous skill. Add a period.

15. **Close** ✕ the **Reviewing Pane**, and then **Save** 🖫 the document.

■ **You have completed Skill 3 of 10**

► When tracking changes, you can alter how revisions display.

► Proposed revisions can be placed in balloons or displayed in the document in final form with the changes made.

1. On Page 1, in the paragraph that begins *Sealed Request for Proposals*, select *Municipal*, and then type Aspen Falls

   By default, tracked changes display as *Final: Show Markup*—a document view that displays the revised text in the document and the original text in balloons.

2. On the **Review tab**, in the **Tracking group**, click the **Display for Review button arrow** ▾, and then click **Original: Show Markup**.

3. In the **Tracking group**, click the **Show Markup** button, point to **Balloons**, and then click **Show Revisions in Balloons**. Compare your screen with **Figure 1**.

   Original: Show Markup is a document view that displays the original text in the document and the proposed changes in balloons. Here, the deleted word *Municipal* is crossed out and the inserted words—*Aspen Falls*—display in the balloon.

4. On Page 1, in the paragraph that begins *Sealed Request for*, select the space after the word *August*, and then press `Ctrl` + `Shift` + `Space` to create a nonbreaking space, as shown in **Figure 2**.

   Recall that a nonbreaking space is used to keep words or phrases from separating if they display toward the end of a line.

■ **Continue to the next page to complete the skill**

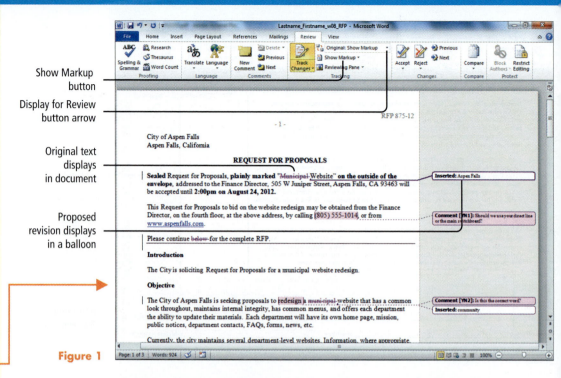

Show Markup button

Display for Review button arrow

Original text displays in document

Proposed revision displays in a balloon

Figure 1

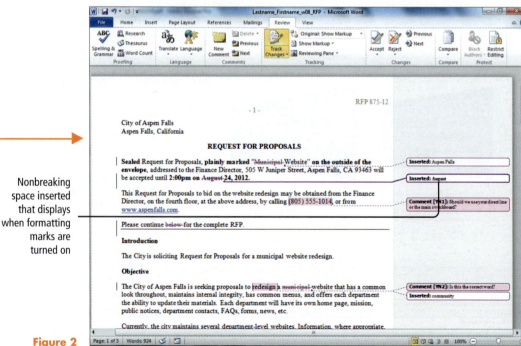

Nonbreaking space inserted that displays when formatting marks are turned on

Figure 2

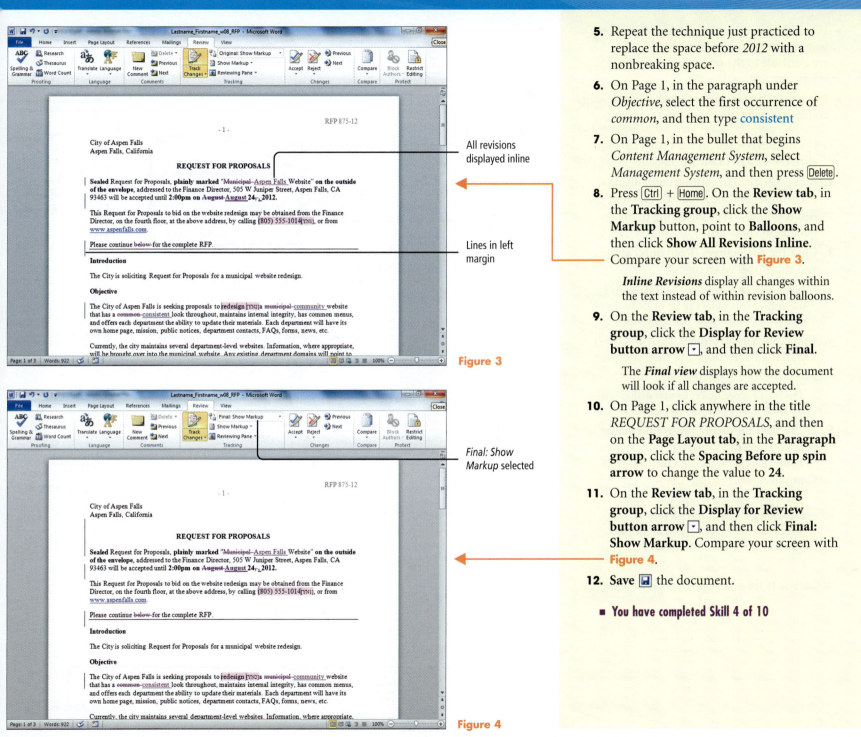

All revisions displayed inline

Lines in left margin

Figure 3

Final: Show Markup selected

Figure 4

5. Repeat the technique just practiced to replace the space before *2012* with a nonbreaking space.

6. On Page 1, in the paragraph under *Objective*, select the first occurrence of *common*, and then type consistent

7. On Page 1, in the bullet that begins *Content Management System*, select *Management System*, and then press ⌈Delete⌉.

8. Press ⌈Ctrl⌉ + ⌈Home⌉. On the **Review tab**, in the **Tracking group**, click the **Show Markup** button, point to **Balloons**, and then click **Show All Revisions Inline**. Compare your screen with **Figure 3**.

   Inline Revisions display all changes within the text instead of within revision balloons.

9. On the **Review tab**, in the **Tracking group**, click the **Display for Review button arrow** ⌈▾⌉, and then click **Final**.

   The *Final view* displays how the document will look if all changes are accepted.

10. On Page 1, click anywhere in the title *REQUEST FOR PROPOSALS*, and then on the **Page Layout tab**, in the **Paragraph group**, click the **Spacing Before up spin arrow** to change the value to **24**.

11. On the **Review tab**, in the **Tracking group**, click the **Display for Review button arrow** ⌈▾⌉, and then click **Final: Show Markup**. Compare your screen with **Figure 4**.

12. Save ⌈▾⌉ the document.

   ■ **You have completed Skill 4 of 10**

► When sharing a Word document for review, you may need to restrict what options are available to the reviewer during the reviewing process.

► Editing options include tracked changes, comments, filling in forms, and no changes.

1. On the **Review tab**, in the **Protect group**, click the **Restrict Editing** button.

2. In the **Restrict Formatting and Editing** pane, under **Editing Restrictions**, select the **Allow only this type of editing in the document** check box.

3. Click the **No changes (Read only) arrow**, and click **Tracked changes**.

   When editing restrictions are enforced, the only changes that can be made to the document are the ones that are tracked.

4. Under **Start enforcement**, click **Yes, Start Enforcing Protection**, and then compare your screen with **Figure 1**.

   The Start Enforcing Protection dialog box is used to enter an optional password.

5. In the **Start Enforcing Protection** dialog box, type Success! Press [Tab], type Success! to confirm, and then click **OK**. Compare your screen with **Figure 2**.

   When protection is enforced, the Restrict Formatting and Editing task pane options do not display. At the bottom of the pane, the Stop Protection button displays.

■ **Continue to the next page to complete the skill**

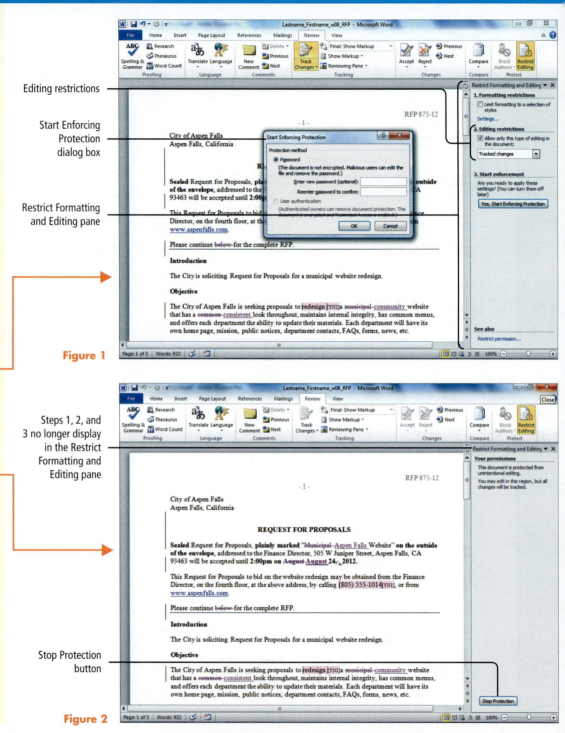

Editing restrictions

Start Enforcing Protection dialog box

Restrict Formatting and Editing pane

Figure 1

Steps 1, 2, and 3 no longer display in the Restrict Formatting and Editing pane

Stop Protection button

Figure 2

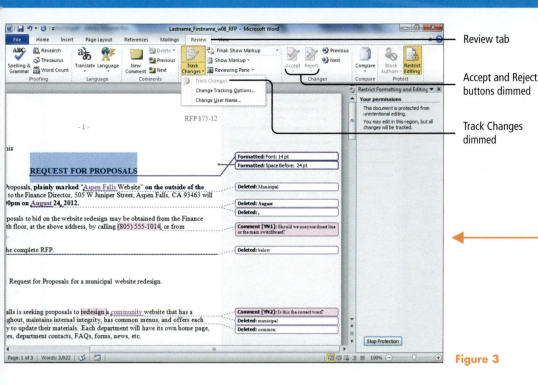

Review tab

Accept and Reject buttons dimmed

Track Changes dimmed

Figure 3

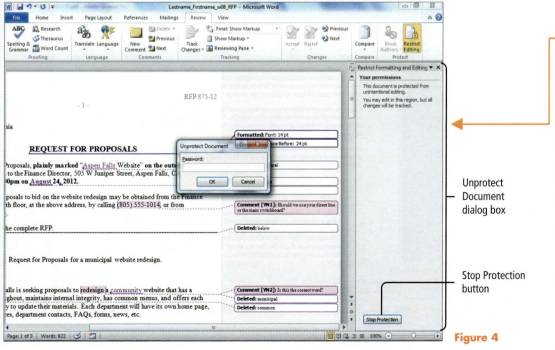

Unprotect Document dialog box

Stop Protection button

Figure 4

6. On the **Review tab**, in the **Tracking group**, click the **Show Markup** button, point to **Balloons**, and then click **Show Revisions in Balloons**.

7. Select the title that begins *REQUEST FOR*, and then on the **Home tab**, in the **Font group**, change the **Font Size** to **14**. Scroll to the right, and notice that the balloon displays the tracked change.

8. On the **Review tab**, in the **Tracking group**, click the **Track Changes button arrow**, and then compare your screen with **Figure 3**.

   The Track Changes command is dimmed, and in the Changes group, the Accept and Reject buttons are also dimmed. With the current editing restrictions, all changes will be tracked.

9. Click the document. In the **Restrict Formatting and Editing** pane, click the **Stop Protection** button.

10. Notice that the **Unprotect Document** dialog box asks for a password, as shown in **Figure 4**.

    Only individuals with the password will be able to stop enforcing the protection. In this manner, only those who are authorized can make untracked changes.

11. Click **Cancel** to leave protection in place.

12. **Close** ☒ the **Restrict Formatting and Editing** pane.

13. **Save** 🖫 the document.

   ■ **You have completed Skill 5 of 10**

▶ In a collaborative project, documents are often revised by multiple reviewers.

▶ Different colors are assigned to each reviewer's balloons and inline revisions to help distinguish each team member's proposed changes and comments.

1. On the **Review tab**, in the **Tracking group**, click the **Show Markup** button, point to **Balloons**, and then click **Show All Revisions Inline**.

2. On the **Review tab**, in the **Tracking group**, click the **Track Changes button arrow**, and then click **Change User Name**.

3. In the **Word Options** dialog box, on the **General tab**, under **Personalize your copy of Microsoft Office**, in the **User name** box, type Jack Ruiz and then change the initials to JR Compare your screen with **Figure 1**.

    Word relies on the user name value to track which reviewer is working with the document. Here, Jack Ruiz is now reviewing the document.

4. Click **OK** to close the dialog box.

5. On the **Review tab**, in the **Tracking group**, click the **Reviewing Pane** button.

6. In the **Reviewing Pane**, click the end of the comment, [YN2], that begins *Is this the.*

7. On the **Review tab**, in the **Comments group**, click the **New Comment** button. Type I think this is okay as is. Compare your screen with **Figure 2**.

    The revision made by Jack Ruiz displays in a different color.

■ **Continue to the next page to complete the skill** ▶

Initials and User name changed

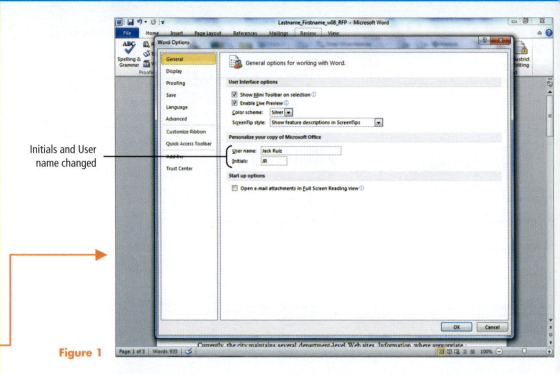

Figure 1

Revision made by Jack Ruiz

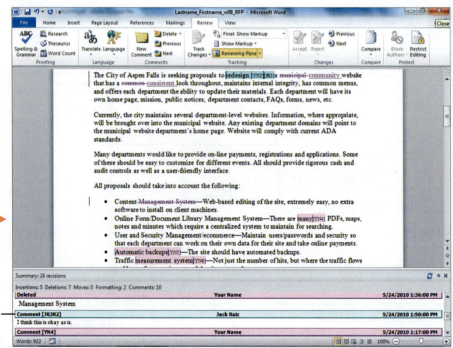

Figure 2

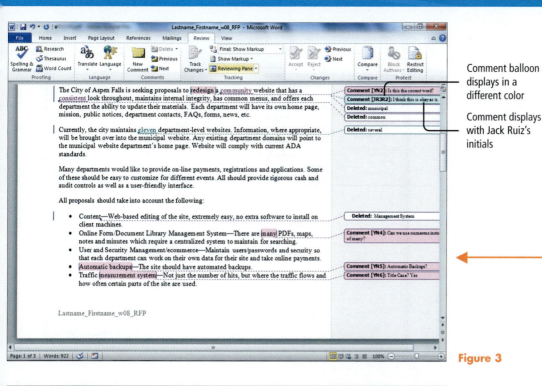

Figure 3

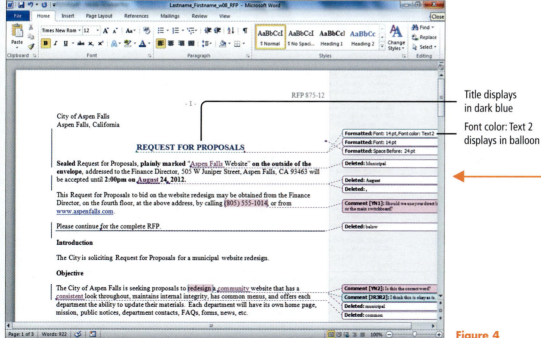

Figure 4

Comment balloon displays in a different color

Comment displays with Jack Ruiz's initials

Title displays in dark blue

Font color: Text 2 displays in balloon

8. In the middle of Page 1, in the paragraph that begins *Currently, the city maintains*, select *several*, and then type eleven

9. On the **Review tab**, in the **Tracking group**, click the **Show Markup** button, point to **Balloons**, and then click **Show Revisions in Balloons**.

   Comments by each reviewer are assigned a unique color and identified by the initials, here *JR*.

10. In the **Tracking group**, click the **Reviewing Pane** button to turn it off. Compare your screen with **Figure 3**.

11. On Page 1, select the title *REQUEST FOR PROPOSALS*. On the **Home tab**, in the **Font group**, click the **Font Color button arrow**, and then click the fourth color in the first row—**Dark Blue, Text 2**. Click anywhere in the document to deselect the highlighting. Notice that the proposed formatting changes to the title display. Compare your screen with **Figure 4**.

   Because the tracked changes feature assigns a color for each reviewer, the colors assigned to some text may not display the color you choose. Here, the assigned color is indicated in the balloon.

12. On the **Review tab**, in the **Tracking group**, click the **Display for Review button arrow**, and then click **Final**.

13. **Save** the document.

   ■ **You have completed Skill 6 of 10**

► A *split window* is a window separated into two parts to allow scrolling through each window independently to view different areas of the document at the same time.

► When printing, you can choose to include the *markups*—the balloons and inline revisions in a reviewed document.

1. On the **File tab**, click **Save As**. Save the file in your **Word Chapter 8 folder** with the name Lastname_Firstname_w08_RFP_Draft Open the footer. Delete the existing footer, and then add the new file name to the footer.

   The original file will retain all the tracked changes and comments you and Jack made.

2. On the **Review tab**, in the **Tracking group**, click the **Track Changes button arrow**, and then click **Change User Name**.

3. In the **Word Options** dialog box, on the **General tab**, under **Personalize your copy of Microsoft Office**, in the **User name** box, delete the text. Type Julia Wagner Change the **Initials** to JW as shown in **Figure 1**. Click **OK**.

   Julia Wagner, the original author of the document, is now the current reviewer.

4. On the **Review tab**, in the **Protect group**, click the **Restrict Editing** button.

5. In the **Restrict Formatting and Editing** pane, click **Stop Protection**. Compare your screen with **Figure 2**.

6. In the **Unprotect Document** dialog box, type Success! and then click **OK**.

7. Close ☒ the **Restrict Formatting and Editing** pane.

■ **Continue to the next page to complete the skill**

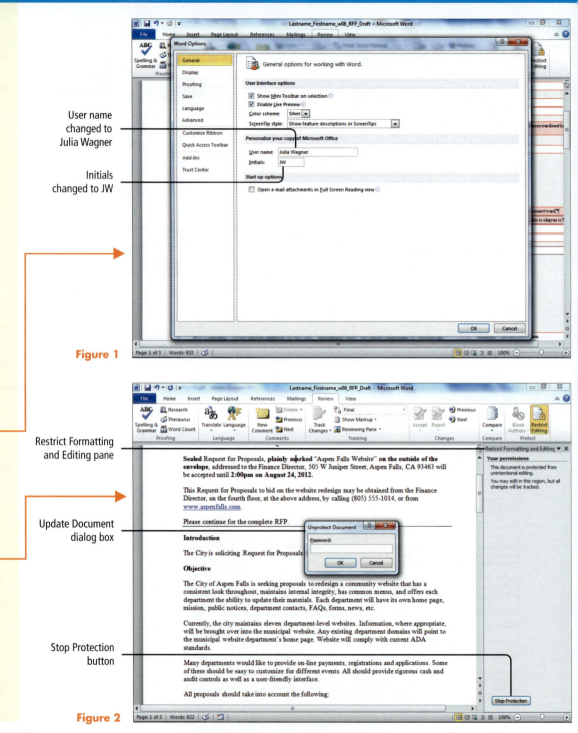

User name changed to Julia Wagner

Initials changed to JW

Figure 1

Restrict Formatting and Editing pane

Update Document dialog box

Stop Protection button

Figure 2

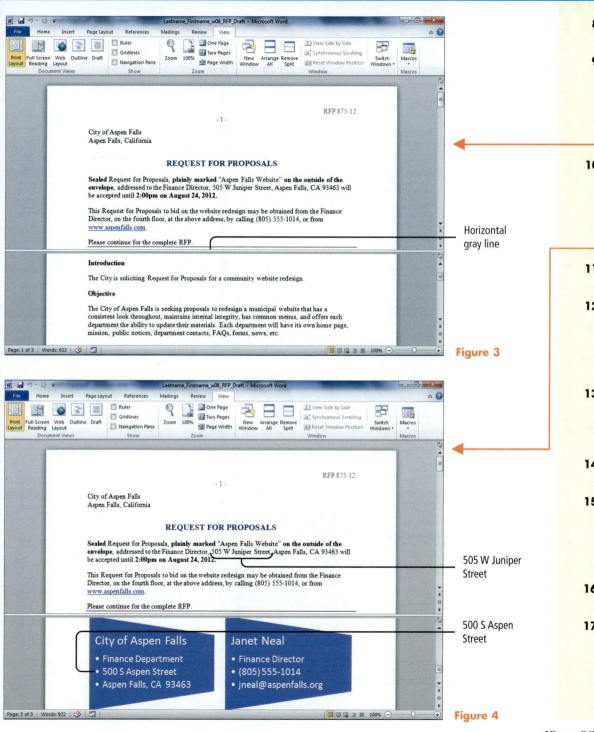

Horizontal gray line

Figure 3

505 W Juniper Street

500 S Aspen Street

Figure 4

8. Press `Ctrl` + `Home` to move to the beginning of the document.

9. On the **View tab**, in the **Window group**, click the **Split** button. Position the ⬍ pointer and horizontal gray line above the paragraph that begins *Introduction*, and click one time. Compare your screen with **Figure 3**.

10. In the lower window, scroll to Page 3, and then display the address in the SmartArt shape. Notice that the address in the upper window does not match the address in the lower window, as shown in **Figure 4**.

11. In the upper window, select *505 W Juniper*, and then type 500 S Aspen

12. On the **View tab**, in the **Window group**, click the **Remove Split** button.

    Alternately, double-click the Resize bar located above the horizontal ruler in the lower window.

13. On the **Review tab**, in the **Tracking group**, click the **Display for Review button arrow** , and then click **Final: Show Markup**.

14. On the **View tab**, in the **Zoom group**, click **Two Pages**.

15. On the **File tab**, click **Print**. Under **Settings**, click **Print All Pages**, and then verify that **Print Markup** is checked. If you are printing your work for this chapter, click **Print**.

16. On the **View tab**, in the **Zoom group**, click the **100%** button.

17. Save the document.

■ **You have completed Skill 7 of 10**

- When copies of a document are tracked in separate files, the changes may need to be compared so that they can be combined into a single file.

- To compare two documents at the same time, you can use *Side by Side* view—a view that displays two different documents in vertical windows so that they can be compared.

1. If necessary, open **Lastname_Firstname_w08_RFP_Draft**.

2. On the **Review tab**, in the **Tracking group**, click the **Display for Review button arrow** ⏷, and then click **Original: Show Markup**.

3. On the **File tab**, click **Open**. Open the student data file **w08_RFP2**.

4. In the taskbar, click the Word icon ⬛, and then click **Lastname_Firstname_w08_RFP_Draft** to make it the active window.

5. On the **View tab**, in the **Window group**, click the **View Side by Side** button, and then compare your screen with **Figure 1**.

    The two documents display in their own window so that both can be viewed at the same time. If more than two documents are open, the names of all open windows would display in a dialog box. You would click one of the RFP files.

6. In **Lastname_Firstname_w08_RFP_Draft**, scroll to the right to display the balloons. Compare your screen with **Figure 2**.

    In Side by Side view, *synchronous scrolling* scrolls both windows when you scroll either the vertical or horizontal scroll bar in either window.

■ **Continue to the next page to complete the skill**

Two documents viewed side by side

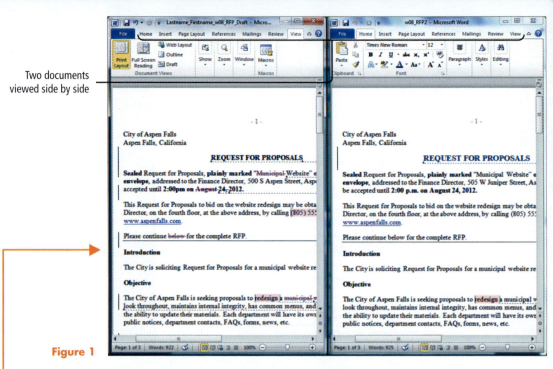

Figure 1

Windows display with synchronous horizontal scrolling

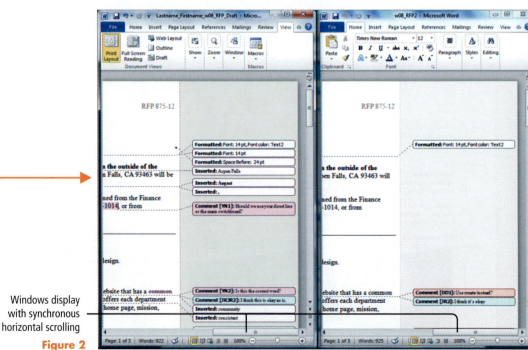

Figure 2

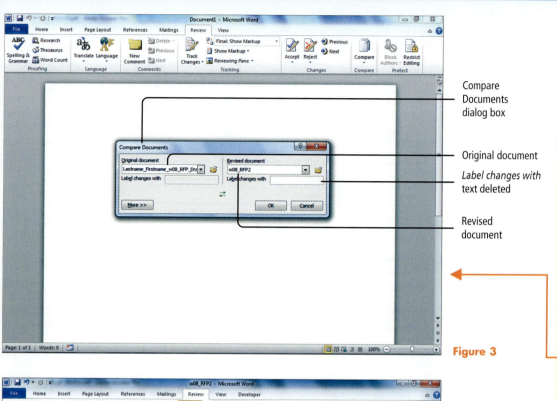

Compare
Documents
dialog box

Original document

Label changes with
text deleted

Revised
document

Figure 3

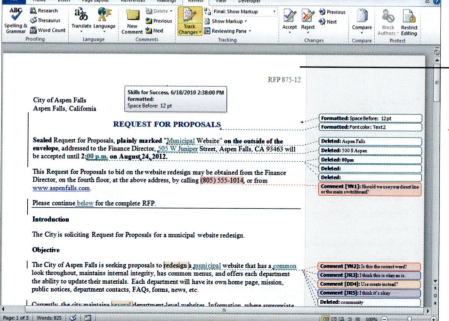

Compared
Document

Figure 4

7. Click **Save** 🖫. **Close** ❌ both documents. If necessary, start Word to display a new, blank document.

8. On the **Review tab**, in the **Compare group**, click the **Compare** button, and then click **Compare**.

9. In the **Compare Documents** dialog box, to the right of the **Original document** box, click **Open** 🖼. In the **Open** dialog box, navigate to where you are saving your files, click **Lastname_Firstname_w08_ RFP_Draft**, and then click **Open**.

10. In the **Compare Documents** dialog box, to the right of the **Revised document** box, click **Open** 🖼. Navigate to the student data files, click **w08_RFP2**, and then click **Open**.

11. Under **Revised document**, delete the text in the **Label changes with** box, as shown in **Figure 3**.

When comparing documents, the *revised document* is the document that has changes that you want to merge with the original document.

12. Click **OK**. Read the displayed message, and then click **Yes**. Compare your screen with **Figure 4**.

When documents are compared, the tracked changes are moved into a single, new compared document.

13. View the displayed changes to the compared document, and then click **Save** 🖫. Save the document in your **Word Chapter 8** folder as Lastname_Firstname_ w08_RFP_Final

■ **You have completed Skill 8 of 10**

► After a document has completed the review process, the original author can accept or reject each change.

► Content can be revised based on the comments, and the comments can then be deleted.

1. If necessary, verify that the insertion point is in the Compared Document, **Lastname_Firstname_w08_RFP_Final** window. On the **Review tab**, in the **Tracking group**, click the **Show Markup** button, point to **Balloons**, and then click **Show Revisions in Balloons**.

2. In the **Tracking group**, click the **Track Changes** button to turn it off.

3. If necessary, press [Ctrl] + [Home]. In the **Changes group**, click the **Next** button.

   The title that includes formatting changes is selected.

4. On the **Review tab**, in the **Changes group**, click the **Reject** button, and then compare your screen with **Figure 1**.

   The formatting change is rejected—made final—and the spacing before is not changed to 12 point.

5. In the balloon, read the proposed change, and then in the **Changes group**, click the **Reject** button two times to reject the changes, keep *Aspen Falls Website*, and move to the next balloon.

6. Read the proposed address change, and then in the **Changes group**, click the **Reject** button three times. Compare your screen with **Figure 2**.

   When evaluating text that has been replaced, two changes have been made. Different text has been inserted and text has been deleted.

■ **Continue to the next page to complete the skill**

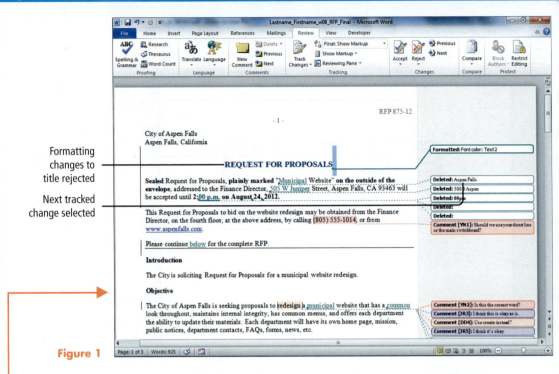

Formatting changes to title rejected

Next tracked change selected

Figure 1

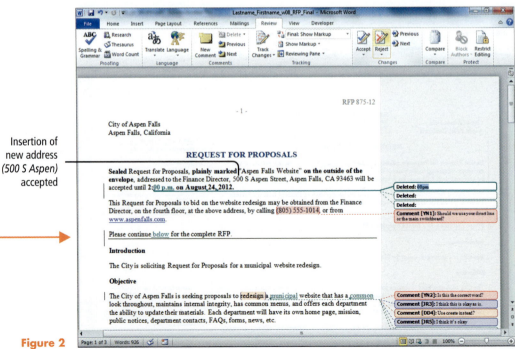

Insertion of new address *(500 S Aspen)* accepted

Figure 2

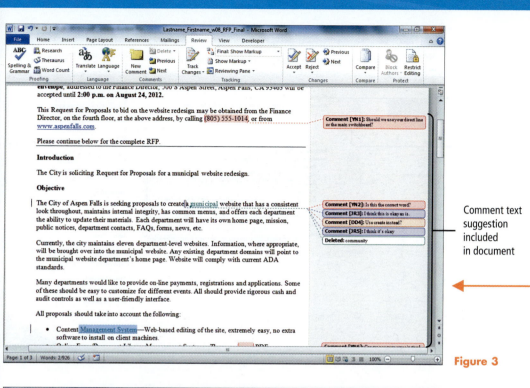

Comment text
suggestion
included
in document

Figure 3

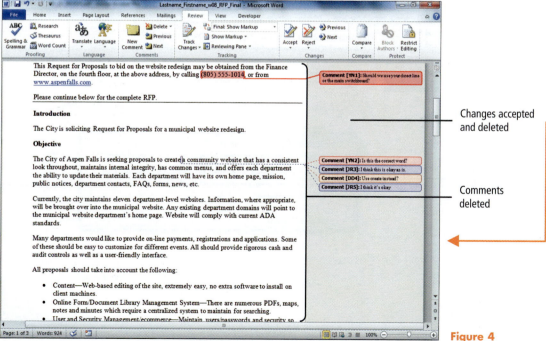

Changes accepted
and deleted

Comments
deleted

Figure 4

7. **Accept** the next two changes. **Reject** the next four changes. In the **Changes group**, click **Next**. **Accept** the insertion of *below*.

8. In the paragraph that begins *The City of*, observe the comment [DD4]. Select *redesign*, and then type create In the same paragraph, select *common*. In the **Changes group**, click **Reject** three times. Compare your screen with **Figure 3**.

9. In the paragraph that begins *Content Management*, select *Management System* and the space before, if necessary, and then click **Reject**.

10. In the paragraph that begins *Online Form*, select *many*, and then type numerous

11. In the paragraph that begins *Automatic backups*, select the *b* and then type B

12. In the next paragraph, repeat the technique to replace the M on *measurement* and the S on *system*.

13. Open the footer, and locate the suggested deletions. On the **Review tab**, in the **Changes group**, click the **Accept** button. Click **Yes**.

14. In the **Changes group**, click the **Reject** button arrow, and then click **Reject All Changes in Document**. Compare your screen with **Figure 4**.

15. Delete all comments with the exception of the comment related to the reading level.

16. On the **File tab**, click **Options**, and then on the **General tab**, replace the values in the **User name** and **Initial** boxes with the information you recorded on paper in Skill 1, Step 2. Click **OK**.

17. Add the file name to the footer. **Save** 💾 the document.

■ **You have completed Skill 9 of 10**

► When a document is *marked as final*, it is locked—no one can type, edit, or use the proofing tools to make additional changes.

► Documents can be marked as final to prevent those reading the document from making changes to it.

1. In **Lastname_Firstname_w08_RFP_Final**, on the **Review tab**, in the **Tracking group**, ensure that the **Track Changes** button is not selected.

2. On the **File tab**, under **Permissions**, click the **Protect Document** button, and then click **Mark as Final**.

3. Read the displayed dialog box, as shown in **Figure 1**, and then click **OK** to mark the document as final and save.

4. Read the displayed dialog box shown in **Figure 2**, and then click **OK**.

The displayed message indicates the document has been marked as final, all edits have been made, and the final version of the document has been created.

When no one can type, edit, or use the proofing tools within the document, it is considered to be marked as final.

■ **Continue to the next page to complete the skill**

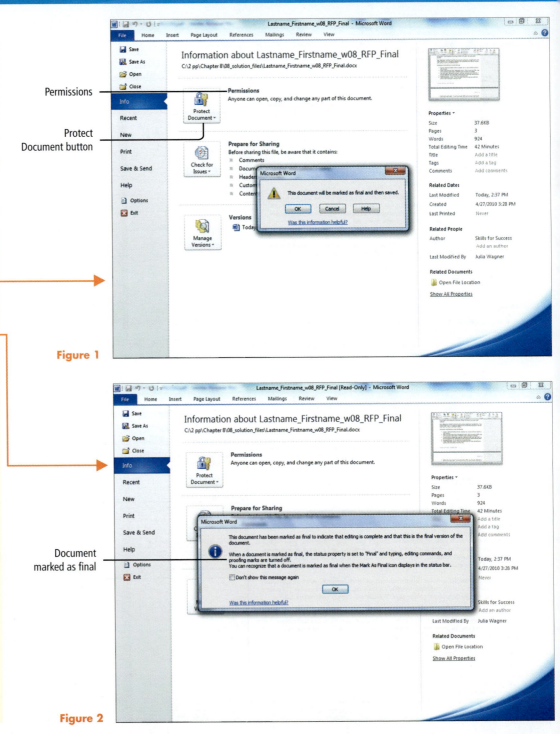

Figure 1

Figure 2

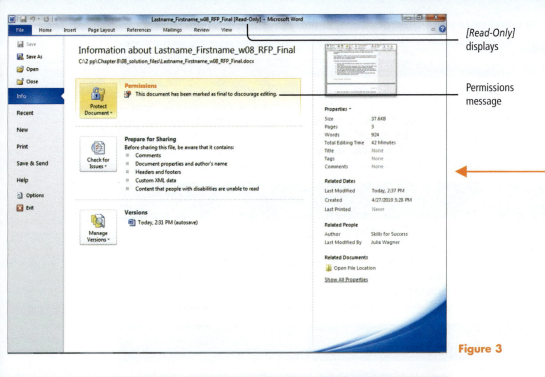

[Read-Only] displays

Permissions message

Figure 3

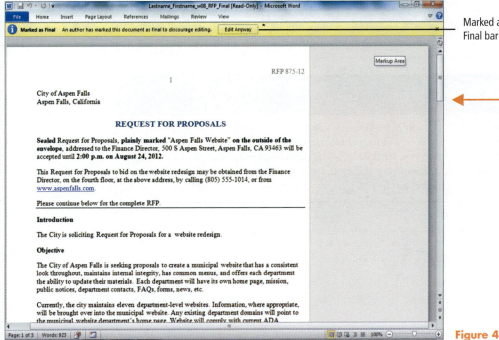

Marked as Final bar

Figure 4

5. Observe that *[Read-Only]* displays in the title bar after the file name to indicate that you can only read the document and not make any changes to it.

6. On the **File tab**, observe the message under **Permissions**. Compare your screen with **Figure 3**.

7. On the **Home tab**, observe that the only buttons available are **Show/Hide ¶**, **Find**, and **Select**.

    These three buttons are available because they can be used without making any changes to the current document.

8. Scroll through the document, and try to type something.

    You cannot type in the document because it is marked as final.

9. Observe the other tabs.

    Some buttons on the Ribbon are no longer available because changes cannot be made.

10. In the displayed **Lastname_Firstname_ w08_RFP_Final**, compare your screen with **Figure 4**.

    Marked as Final displays in the bar at the top.

11. Print or submit the files as directed by your instructor. **Exit** Word.

Done! You have completed Skill 10 of 10 and your document is complete!

More Skills

The following More Skills are located at **www.pearsonhighered.com/skills**

More Skills Print Envelopes Using Mail Merge

You can use mail merge to print envelopes for each recipient in your data source. To print an envelope, you will need to specify that you are using an envelope for your main document.

In More Skills 11, you will use the Mailings tab to create an envelope that merges addresses from a data source. To begin, open your web browser, navigate to www.pearsonhighered.com/skills, locate the name of your textbook, and then follow the instructions on the website.

More Skills Apply Saved Themes

Themes can be saved and then applied to other documents. When you download a previously-saved theme, the theme set file you download includes theme colors, theme fonts, and theme effects. You can then apply the theme set to your documents.

In More Skills 12, you will browse for a previously-saved theme and then apply the theme to a newsletter. To begin, open your web browser, navigate to www.pearsonhighered.com/skills, locate the name of your textbook, and then follow the instructions on the website.

More Skills Create Blog Posts

Word provides a template that can be used to prepare and publish a blog. The blog can be posted to the web for others to read.

In More Skills 13, you create a new blog post that could be published to the web. To begin, open your web browser, navigate to www.pearsonhighered.com/skills, locate the name of your textbook, and then follow the instructions on the website.

More Skills Change Grammar and Style Options

You can set the Grammar and Style Options to change the types of grammatical errors Word checks. For example, the Grammar checker can flag whenever there are two spaces after a punctuation mark. In this manner, you can customize Word to match the grammatical style of your organization.

In More Skills 14, you will change the grammar and style options and then check a document. To begin, open your web browser, navigate to www.pearsonhighered.com/skills, locate the name of your textbook, and then follow the instructions on the website.

Key Terms

Online Help Skills

1. **Start** 🌀 Word. In the upper right corner of the Word window, click the **Help** button 🔘. In the **Help** window, click the **Maximize** 🔲 button.

2. Click in the search box, type use mail merge and then click the **Search** button 🔍. In the search results, click **Use mail merge to create and print letters and other documents**.

3. Read the article's introduction, and then below **What do you want to do?** click **Add different headers and footers or page numbers in different parts of the document**. Compare your screen with **Figure 1**.

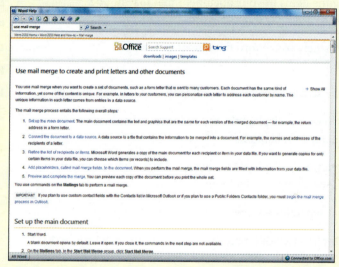

Figure 1

4. Read the section to see if you can answer the following: When might you connect to another data source? Why might you add a placeholder to a merged document?

Matching

Match each term in the second column with its correct definition in the first column by writing the letter of the term on the blank line in front of the correct definition.

___ **1.** A message that is inserted by those reviewing a document.

___ **2.** Data that summarizes document features such as the number of pages, words, characters without spaces, characters including spaces, paragraphs, and lines.

___ **3.** Feature listing the items in your document that may not be compatible with earlier versions of Word.

___ **4.** Feature used to view your Word document in various magnifications.

___ **5.** Displays on the screen and lists all comments and tracked changes.

___ **6.** A document view that displays the revised text in the document and the original text in balloons.

___ **7.** A document view that displays the original text in the document and the proposed changes in balloons.

___ **8.** A window that separates a single document into two parts.

___ **9.** A view that displays two different documents in two synchronized windows.

___ **10.** A way to move windows when you scroll either the vertical or horizontal scroll bar in either window.

A Comment

B Compatibility Checker

C Document statistics

D Final: Show Markup

E Original: Show Markup

F Reviewing pane

G Side by Side view

H Split window

I Synchronous scrolling

J Zoom

Multiple Choice

Choose the correct answer.

1. The value used when assigning colors to tracked changes and comments.
   - A. Changes
   - B. Tracking Options
   - C. User name

2. In addition to the ordinal number, the other item included in the comment balloon.
   - A. Document name
   - B. Initials
   - C. User name

3. The location where the reading level needed to understand text as determined by the length of words, the number of syllables in words, and the length of sentences and paragraphs can be found.
   - A. Compatibility Checker
   - B. Readability Statistics
   - C. Word Count

4. The number of points possible on the Flesch Reading Ease that measures how simple a Word document is to comprehend.
   - A. 50
   - B. 75
   - C. 100

5. The Word feature used to increase the size of the text and comments as displayed on the screen without increasing the actual font size.
   - A. 100%
   - B. Two Pages
   - C. Zoom

6. The pane where comments can be viewed when not in a balloon.
   - A. Clipboard
   - B. Restrict Formatting and Editing
   - C. Reviewing

7. A document view that displays how the document will look if all changes are accepted without the insertions or deletions displayed on the screen.
   - A. Final
   - B. Final: Show Markup
   - C. Original

8. A window separated into two parts so that you can scroll through each window independently to view different areas of the document at the same time.
   - A. Side by Side
   - B. Split Window
   - C. Synchronous Scrolling

9. The button used to move both windows at the same time when the vertical scroll bar or horizontal scroll bar is selected.
   - A. Side by Side
   - B. Split Window
   - C. Synchronous Scrolling

10. When comparing documents, the document that you want to merge with the original document.
    - A. Compared document
    - B. Original document
    - C. Revised document

Topics for Discussion

1. Imagine you are the office manager for a small medical office. You need to update the existing patient information form to comply with Health Information Privacy, or HIPAA. The existing form includes only a home telephone number and address as methods of contacting the patient. The form does not contain a statement about the types of information that can be disclosed. Feel free to use the Internet to search for HIPAA information. What types of changes might you make to this form? What features of Word would you include in the document?

2. Imagine you are reviewing a report for a team project. What Word features might you use to offer comments?

Skill Check

To complete this project, you will need the following files:

- w08_Office
- w08_Office2

You will save your file as:

- Lastname_Firstname_w08_Office
- Lastname_Firstname_w08_Office_Final

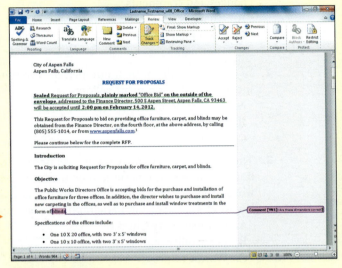

Figure 1

1. **Start** Word, and open the student data file **w08_Office**. Save the file in your **Word Chapter 8** folder with the name Lastname_Firstname_w08_Office Add the file name to the footer.

2. On the **Review tab**, in the **Tracking group**, click the **Track Changes button arrow**, and then click **Change User Name**. Under **Personalize your copy of Microsoft Office**, note the values in the **User name** and **Initials** boxes so you can restore these values later. If necessary, replace the existing values with your own name and initials, and then click **OK**.

3. On the **File tab**, click **Options**. In the **Word Options** dialog box, click the **Proofing tab**. Select the **Mark grammar errors as you type** and the **Show readability statistics** check boxes, and then click **OK**.

4. On the **File tab**, click **Check for Issues**. Click **Check Compatibility**, and then click **OK**.

5. Press [Ctrl] + [Home]. On the **Review tab**, in the **Comments group**, click the **Next** button, read the comment, and then in the **Comments group**, click **Delete**.

6. In the **Tracking group**, click **Track Changes**.

7. Locate the paragraph that begins *The Public Works*, and then click the end of the paragraph. In the **Comments group**, click **New Comment**, and then type Are these dimensions correct? Compare your screen with **Figure 1**.

8. Locate the paragraph that begins *Office furniture*, and then in the last sentence, select *including* through *requirements*, and then press [Delete].

9. Select the last paragraph. On the **Home tab**, in the **Font group**, click the **Font Size button arrow**, and then select **10**. Compare your screen with **Figure 2**.

10. Press [Ctrl] + [Home] to move to the beginning of the document.

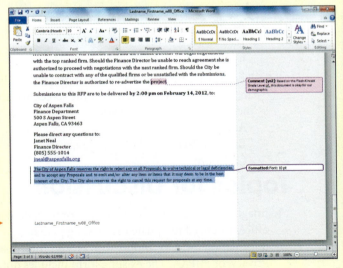

Figure 2

- **Continue to the next page to complete this Skill Check**

11. On the **Review tab**, in the **Proofing group**, click the **Spelling & Grammar** button. Click **Ignore Once** two times. Click **OK**. Record the **Flesch-Kincaid Grade Level** on a piece of paper, and then click **OK**. Edit the last comment in the document to include this number.

12. In the **Tracking group**, click the **Display for Review button arrow**, and then click **Final**.

13. In the **Protect group**, click the **Restrict Editing** button. Under **Editing restrictions**, select the **Allow only this type of editing in the document** check box. Click the **No changes (Read only) arrow**, and then click **Tracked changes**.

14. Under **Start enforcement**, click **Yes, Start Enforcing Protection**. Type Success! for both passwords, and then click **OK**. Compare your screen with **Figure 3**.

15. Locate the paragraph that begins *Office furniture*, and in the phone number, replace *27* with *14*

16. In the **Restrict Formatting and Editing** pane, click **Stop Protection**. Type Success! Click **OK**. **Close** the **Restrict Formatting and Editing** pane.

17. **Save** and **Close** the document. Open a new, blank document.

18. On the **Review tab**, in the **Compare group**, click the **Compare** button, and then click **Compare**. Under **Original document**, click the button arrow, and then click **Lastname_Firstname_w08_Office**. Under **Revised document**, click the **Open** button and open **w08_Office2**.

19. Delete the text in all **Label changes with** boxes, and then click **OK**. Click **Yes**. **Save** the document as Lastname_Firstname_w08_Office_Final Add the file name to the footer.

20. Press Ctrl + Home. On the **Review tab**, in the **Changes group**, click the **Accept** button ten times. Click the **Reject** button ten times. Accept all changes through the end of the document. Click **Yes**. Compare your screen with **Figure 4**.

21. On the **File tab**, click **Print**. Click the **Print All Pages** button, and verify that **Print Markup** is selected. If you are printing your work for this chapter, click **Print**.

22. On the **File tab**, click **Info**. Under **Permissions**, click the **Protect Document** button, and then click **Mark as Final**. Click **OK** two times.

23. On the **File tab**, click **Options**. In the **Word Options** dialog box, on the **General tab**, return the **User name** and **Initials** boxes to their original values. On the **Proofing tab**, clear the **Mark grammar errors as you type** and the **Show readability statistics** check boxes. Click **OK**.

24. Print or submit the files as directed by your instructor. **Exit** Word.

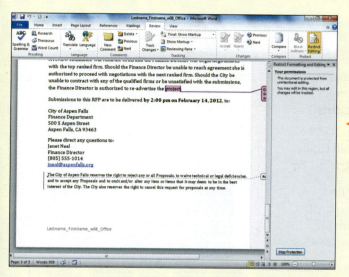

Figure 3

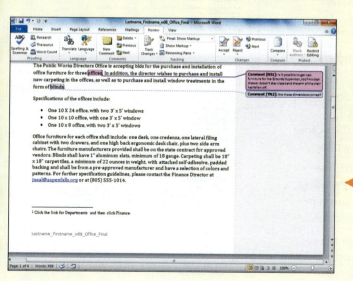

Figure 4

Done! You have completed the Skill Check

Assess Your Skills 1

To complete this project, you will need the following file:

- w08_Bid

You will save your file as:

- Lastname_Firstname_w08_Bid

1. **Start** Word. Open **w08_Bid**, and then save it in your **Word Chapter 8** folder as Lastname_Firstname_w08_Bid Add the file name to the footer.

2. If necessary, change the **User name** and **Initials** to your own. Note the values in the **User name** and **Initials** boxes so that you can restore these values later.

3. Turn on the **Track Changes** feature.

4. In the first paragraph below *Project Bid*, select *month*, and then insert the comment Or as often as needed

5. In the same paragraph, select the first occurrence of *11 pools*, and then insert the comment Or 13 if the new pools are completed in time

6. On the **Show Markup** button, use the **Balloons** menu to select **Show Only Comments and Formatting in Balloons** from the submenu.

7. Delete the first comment to Mr. Berhe.

8. In the paragraph that begins *The scope of*, click before *May*, and type end of and add a space. Click before *September*, and type beginning of and add a space.

9. Run the **Compatibility Checker**, and read the displayed dialog box. Modify the last comment to include what was mentioned in the **Compatibility Checker** dialog box as not displaying.

10. Use **Word Options** to change the **Proofing** settings to include **Mark grammar errors as you type** and to **Show readability statistics**.

11. Check **Spelling & Grammar**. Ignore everything. Record the **Flesch-Kincaid Grade Level** in the second to last comment.

12. **Print** the document showing markups.

13. Use the **Accept button arrow** to **Accept All Changes in Document**, and then turn off **Track Changes**.

14. **Save** the document.

15. **Restrict Editing** to **allow only Tracked changes editing in the document. Start Enforcing Protection**, and use Success! as the password.

16. Use permissions, and mark the document as final.

17. On the **Home tab**, at the top of the document, select the **Edit Anyway** button, **Stop Protection**, type the password, and then **Close** the **Restrict Formatting and Editing** pane.

18. If necessary, in **Word Options**, restore the **User name** and **Initials**, and under **Proofing**, clear the **Mark grammar errors as you type** and **Show readability statistics** check boxes.

19. **Save** the document. Print or submit the file as directed by your instructor. Compare your completed document with **Figure 1**. **Exit** Word.

Done! You have completed Assess Your Skills 1

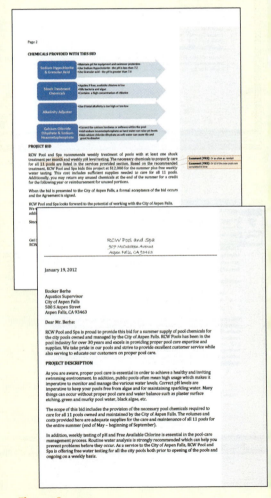

Figure 1

Assess Your Skills 2

To complete this project, you will need the following files:

- w08_Recycle
- w08_Recycle2

You will save your files as:

- Firstname_Lastname_w08_Recycle
- Firstname_Lastname_w08_Recycle_Final

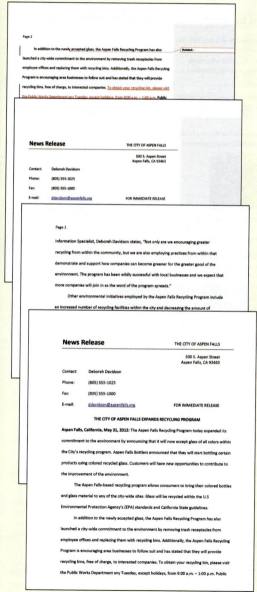

Figure 1

1. **Start** Word. Open **w08_Recycle**, and then save it in your **Word Chapter 8** folder as Lastname_Firstname_w08_Recycle Add the file name to the footer.

2. If necessary, change the **User name** and **Initials** to your own. Turn on **Track Changes**.

3. Locate the paragraph that begins *Aspen Falls, California*. In the word *city's*, capitalize the *C*. Select *Bottlers*, and then type glass supplier Replace *start* with begin

4. Delete the comment.

5. Locate the paragraph that begins *In addition to*, and then replace the *hyphen* in *newly-accepted* with a space.

6. On Page 2, delete the paragraph that begins *Other environmental initiatives*.

7. Scroll up until the paragraph that begins *The Aspen Falls-based recycling program* displays as the first paragraph, and split the screen below the paragraph.

8. In the bottom window, scroll to display the paragraph that begins *About the Aspen Falls*. Select the heading and the next paragraph. Select **Cut**.

9. In the upper window, position the insertion point at the beginning of the *The Aspen Falls-based* paragraph. Click **Paste**. Remove the split view.

10. Click the beginning of the inserted *The Aspen Falls Recycling Program is the* paragraph, and then press Tab. Select *nine*,

and then insert the comment Please double-check the number

11. **Show Revisions in Balloons**. Press Ctrl + Home. Accept the first seven changes.

12. Locate and open **w08_Recycle2**. View the two documents in **Side by Side** view. Make **w08_Recycle2** the active window. At the bottom of Page 1, select the inserted sentence, and **Copy**. **Close** the active window. In **Lastname_Firstname_08_Recycle**, locate the paragraph that begins *In addition to the*, and then **Paste** the sentence before the text *Public Information*. If necessary, add a space. **Save** the document.

13. **Close** the file. In a new Word document, **Compare** the original document, **Lastname_Firstname_w08_Recycle**, with **w08_Recycle2**. Delete the text in the **Label changes with** box. **Save** the new document as **Lastname_Firstname_w08_Recycle_Final**. Add the file name to the footer.

14. Press Ctrl + Home. **Accept** the first five changes. **Reject** the next two. **Accept** the next seven changes. **Reject** the next two. **Accept** the last seven changes. Turn off **Track Changes**.

15. If necessary, restore the **User name** and **Initials**.

16. **Save** the document. Print or submit the files as directed by your instructor. **Exit** Word.

Done! You have completed Assess Your Skills 2

Assess Your Skills Visually

To complete this project, you will need the following file:

- w08_Wellness

You will save your file as:

- Lastname_Firstname_w08_Wellness

Start Word, and open the student data file **w08_Wellness**. Save the file in your **Word Chapter 8** folder with the name Lastname_Firstname_w08_Wellness Add the file name to the footer. In **Word Options**, change the **User name** to Leah Kim and the **Initials** to LK

Turn on **Track Changes**, and then insert the comments and changes to the flyer as shown in **Figure 1** and **Figure 2**. Turn off Track Changes. Print or submit the files electronically as directed by your instructor. Restore the User name and Initials. **Save** the document. Print or submit the file as directed by your instructor. **Exit** Word.

Done! You have completed Assess Your Skills Visually

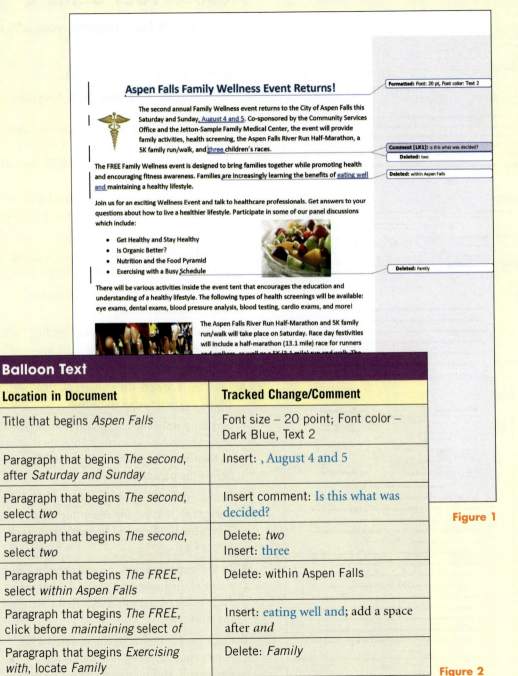

Figure 1

Balloon Text	
Location in Document	**Tracked Change/Comment**
Title that begins *Aspen Falls*	Font size – 20 point; Font color – Dark Blue, Text 2
Paragraph that begins *The second*, after *Saturday and Sunday*	Insert: , August 4 and 5
Paragraph that begins *The second*, select *two*	Insert comment: Is this what was decided?
Paragraph that begins *The second*, select *two*	Delete: *two* Insert: three
Paragraph that begins *The FREE*, select *within Aspen Falls*	Delete: within Aspen Falls
Paragraph that begins *The FREE*, click before *maintaining* select *of*	Insert: eating well and; add a space after *and*
Paragraph that begins *Exercising with*, locate *Family*	Delete: Family

Figure 2

Skills in Context

To complete this project, you will need the following file:

- New, blank Word document

You will save your files as:

- Lastname_Firstname_w08_City_Flyer
- Lastname_Firstname_w08_City_2
- Lastname_Firstname_w08_City_Final

Start Word, and open a new Word document. Save the file in your **Word Chapter 8** folder with the name Lastname_Firstname_w08_City_Flyer Add the file name to the footer. Prepare a one-page flyer that includes highlights of your city. Insert at least three comments. After you have prepared the document and inserted the comments, save the file as Lastname_Firstname_w08_City_2 Add the file name to the footer. Turn on Track Changes, and

insert text into five locations anywhere in the document. Delete text in at least two locations in the document. Save the file. Close all files. Use the Compare feature to compare the two documents. You decide what changes to accept and reject. Name the document Lastname_Firstname_w08_City_Final Add the file name to the footer. Print or submit the file as directed by your instructor. **Exit** Word.

Done! You have completed Skills in Context

Skills and You

To complete this project, you will need the following file:

- Word document you have prepared for this or another class

You will save your file as:

- Lastname_Firstname_w08_My_Changes

Start Word, and open a Word document you have prepared for this class or another class. Record the user name and initials, and change the user name to your name, if necessary. Turn on Track Changes, and edit the document for spelling and grammar. Run the Compatibility Checker, and record the results in a comment at the end of the document. Check the Readability Statistics, and record the Flesch-Kincaid Grade Level in a comment at the end of the document. Record the word count in a separate comment.

Save the file in your **Word Chapter 8** folder with the name Lastname_Firstname_w08_My_Changes Add the file name to the footer. If asked to print your document, include the markups, or submit the file electronically as directed. Change the user name and initials back to what you recorded earlier. **Exit** Word.

Done! You have completed Skills and You

CHAPTER 9

Work with Styles

▶ Formatting documents using styles results in professional-looking documents and helps maintain consistent formatting.

▶ Documents can be saved as web pages so that they can be viewed on the Internet using a web browser.

Your starting screen will look like this:

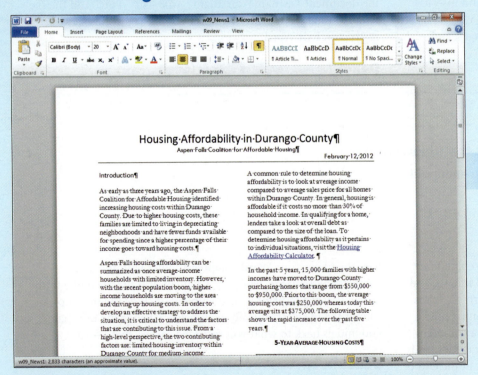

SKILLS

Skills 1-10 Training

At the end of this chapter, you will be able to:

Skill 1 Create and Apply Character Styles

Skill 2 Create and Apply List Styles

Skill 3 Change Style Pane Options

Skill 4 Create and Apply Table Styles

Skill 5 Apply Link Styles

Skill 6 Set Styles to Update Automatically

Skill 7 Work with Paragraph Spacing Styles

Skill 8 Add Hyperlinks to Pictures

Skill 9 Change Hyperlink Styles and Save Documents as HTML Files

Skill 10 Use the Organizer to Copy Styles

MORE SKILLS

More Skills 11 Insert Hyphenation

More Skills 12 Create Styles Based on Existing Styles

More Skills 13 Assign Styles Using the Outline View

More Skills 14 Create New Theme Colors

Outcome

Using the skills listed to the left will enable you to create documents like these:

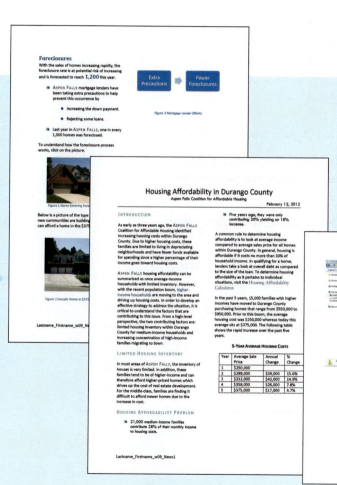

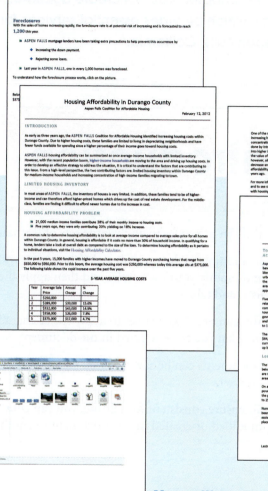

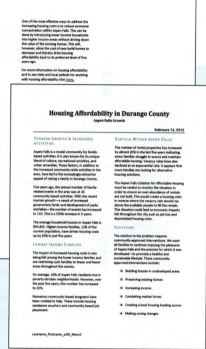

You will save your files as:

Lastname_Firstname_w09_News1

Lastname_Firstname_w09_News1_HTML

Lastname_Firstname_w09_News1_HTML (folder)

Lastname_Firstname_w09_News2

In this chapter, you will create documents for the Aspen Falls City Hall, which provides essential services for the citizens and visitors of Aspen Falls, California.

Introduction

- ▶ You can use styles to apply large sets of formatting choices with a single click.

- ▶ In addition to the prebuilt styles that come with Word 2010, you can create and modify your own styles and then apply them to characters, paragraphs, lists, and tables.

- ▶ You can use linked styles to apply either character or paragraph styles, based on what you have selected in the document.

- ▶ Documents can be saved as web pages so that they can be viewed in a web browser.

- ▶ To ensure consistent formatting, you can copy the styles that you have modified or created in one document to another document.

Time to complete all
10 skills – 50 to 90 minutes

Find your student data files here:

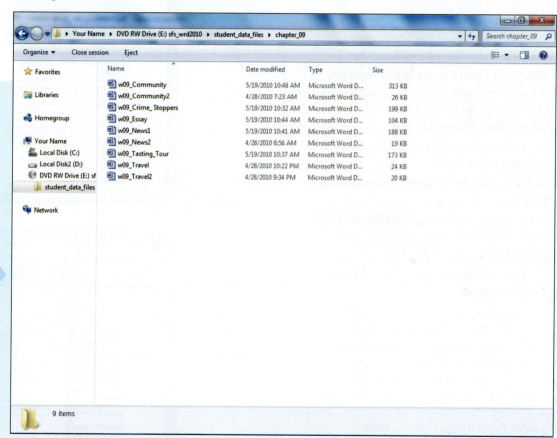

Student data files needed for this chapter:

- w09_News1
- w09_News2

▶ Recall that Word 2010 has several built-in styles that display in the Quick Style gallery and Styles pane.

1. **Start** 🌐 Word, and open the student data file **w09_News1**. Save the file in your **Word Chapter 9** folder with the name Lastname_Firstname_w09_News1 Add the file name to the footer. Display the formatting marks.

2. On the **Home tab**, in the **Styles group**, click the **Styles Dialog Box Launcher** 🔲.

3. If necessary, point to the **Styles** pane title bar, and then with the 🔲 pointer, double-click to dock the pane to the right edge of the window, as shown in **Figure 1**.

4. In the first paragraph that begins *As early as*, select *Aspen Falls*.

5. At the bottom of the **Styles** pane, click the **New Style** button 🔲.

6. In the **Create New Style from Formatting** dialog box, in the **Name** box, replace the existing value with Aspen Falls

7. Click the **Style type arrow** 🔽, and then click **Character**.

> A *character style* is a style type that formats selected letters, numbers, and symbols.

> In the Styles pane, the ¶ symbol labels each *paragraph style*—a style type that formats an entire paragraph. The letter **a** 🄰 symbol labels each character style—here, the *Aspen Falls* character style.

8. Under **Formatting**, click the **Font arrow**—the first box—and then click **Calibri (Body)**. Compare your screen with **Figure 2**.

■ **Continue to the next page to complete the skill**

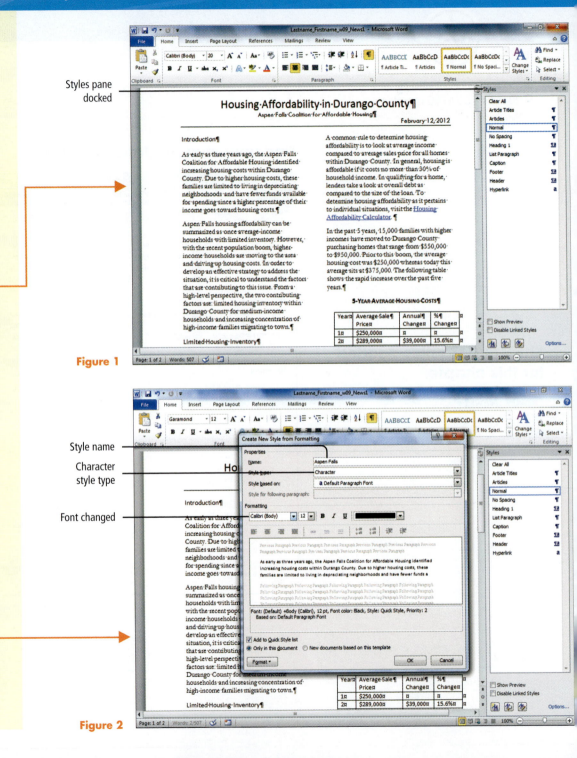

Styles pane docked

Figure 1

Style name
Character style type
Font changed

Figure 2

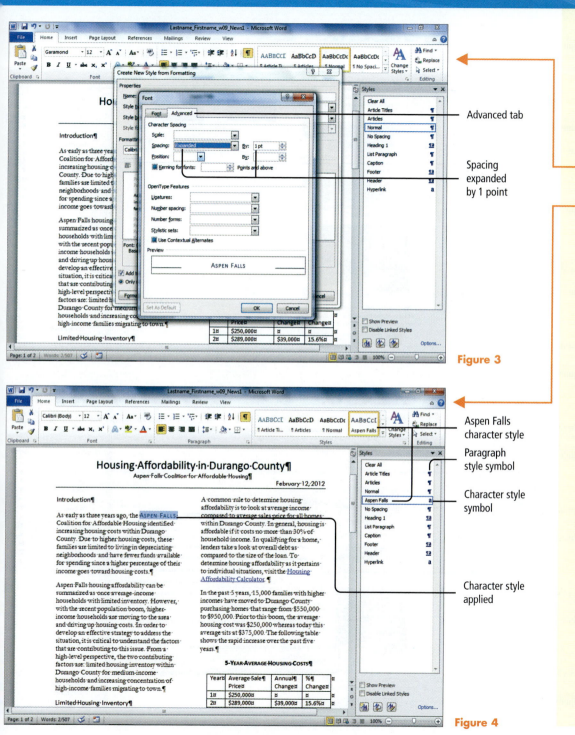

Advanced tab

Spacing expanded by 1 point

Figure 3

Aspen Falls character style

Paragraph style symbol

Character style symbol

Character style applied

Figure 4

9. Click the **Format** button, and then in the displayed list, click **Font**.

10. In the **Font** dialog box, click the **Font color arrow**, and then select the fifth color in the sixth row—**Blue, Accent 1, Darker 50%**. Select the **Small caps** check box. On the **Advanced tab**, click the **Spacing arrow**, and then click **Expanded**. Compare your screen with **Figure 3**.

11. Click **OK** two times, and then compare your screen with **Figure 4**.

    The formatting is applied to the selected text, and the character style name— *Aspen Falls*—displays in the Quick Styles gallery and Styles pane.

12. In the second paragraph, select the text *Aspen Falls*, and then in the **Styles** pane, click **Aspen Falls** to apply the character style.

    Recall that to apply a paragraph style, you may position the insertion point anywhere in the paragraph. To apply a character style, you must first select the text.

13. Repeat the technique just practiced to locate the three remaining occurrences of *Aspen Falls*, and then apply the **Aspen Falls** character style to each. Do not apply the style to the newsletter subtitle.

14. Save the document.

■ **You have completed Skill 1 of 10**

► A *list style* is a style type that formats bullets, numbers, and indent settings.

► List styles store the bullet style or number settings and the indent settings applied to the list items.

1. On Page 2, triple-click the paragraph that begins *Aspen Falls mortgage*, press and hold Ctrl, and then triple-click the paragraph that begins *Last year in*.

2. In the **Styles** pane, notice that the **List Paragraph** style has been applied, as shown in **Figure 1**.

   List Paragraph is the default paragraph style applied to bulleted lists.

3. At the bottom of the **Styles** pane, click the **New Style** button.

4. In the **Create New Style from Formatting** dialog box, in the **Name** box, replace the existing value with Aspen List

5. Click the **Style type arrow**, and then click **List**. Compare your screen with **Figure 2**.

   When a List style type is selected, the dialog box displays options for formatting lists. A preview pane displays the formatting for list level.

6. In the box with the text *Bullet:* •, click the arrow, scroll to the bottom of the list, and then click **New Picture**.

7. In the **Picture Bullet** dialog box, scroll to the bottom of the gallery, and then click the second bullet in the fourth to last row.

■ **Continue to the next page to complete the skill**

Styles pane

List Paragraph style

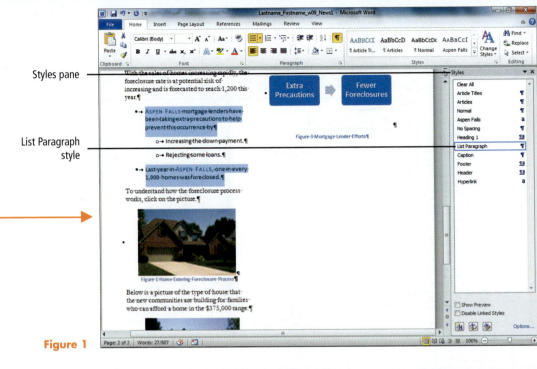

Figure 1

List style type

List formatting options

Preview pane

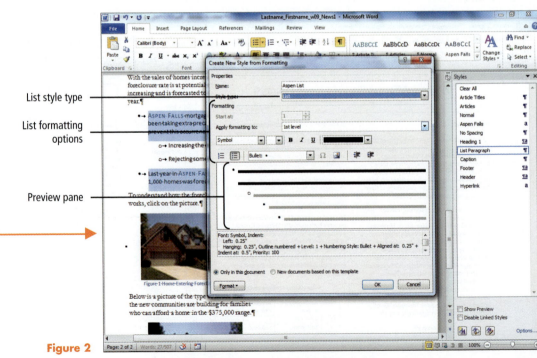

Figure 2

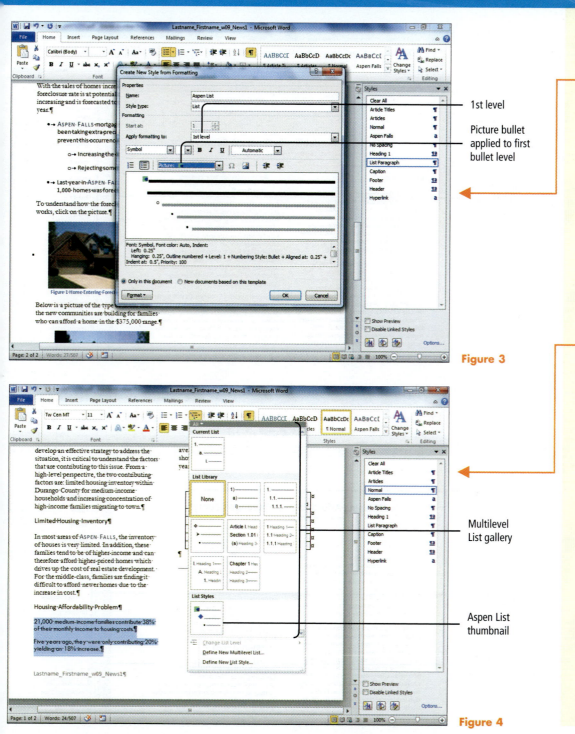

Figure 3

Figure 4

8. Click **OK** to close the **Picture Bullet** dialog box, and then in the preview, notice that the picture bullet is applied to the first level, as shown in **Figure 3**.

> By default, list styles do not display in the Quick Styles gallery or the Styles pane.

9. Click the **Apply formatting to arrow**, and then click **2nd level**.

10. In the box with the **Bullet**, click the arrow, scroll to the bottom of the list, and then click **New Picture**. Select the first bullet in the second to last row, and then click **OK** two times.

11. Scroll to Page 1, and at the bottom of the left column, select the two paragraphs that begin *21,000 medium-income*. On the **Home tab**, in the **Paragraph group**, click the **Multilevel List** button. Compare your screen with **Figure 4**.

> The list styles you create can be found at the bottom of the Multilevel List gallery.

12. In the **Multilevel List** gallery, under **List Styles**, click the **Aspen List** thumbnail to apply the list style to the selected paragraphs.

13. On Page 2, select the two bulleted paragraphs that begin *Increasing the down*. On the **Home tab**, in the **Paragraph group**, click the **Multilevel List** button. Under **List Styles**, click the **Aspen List** thumbnail.

> The type of bullet applied is determined by the indent level assigned to the bullet.

14. Press Ctrl + Home.

15. Save the document.

■ **You have completed Skill 2 of 10**

▶ The Style Pane Options dialog box is used to change how styles display in the Styles pane.

▶ The *Normal template* is a Word template that stores the default styles that are applied when a new document is created.

1. At the bottom of the **Styles** pane, click **Options**.

2. In the **Style Pane Options** dialog box, click the **Select styles to show arrow**, and then click **All styles**. Click **OK**, and then compare your screen with **Figure 1**.

  With the All styles option selected, the Styles pane displays all of the styles stored in the Normal template.

3. In the **Styles** pane, click **Options**. In the **Style Pane Options** dialog box, click the **Select styles to show arrow**, and then click **In current document**.

4. Click the **Select how list is sorted arrow**, and then click **By type**.

5. Select the **Bullet and numbering formatting** check box, and then click **OK**.

6. In the **Styles** pane, select the **Show Preview** check box, and then compare your screen with **Figure 2**.

  The document's character styles are listed first, followed by the paragraph styles.

■ **Continue to the next page to complete the skill** ➤

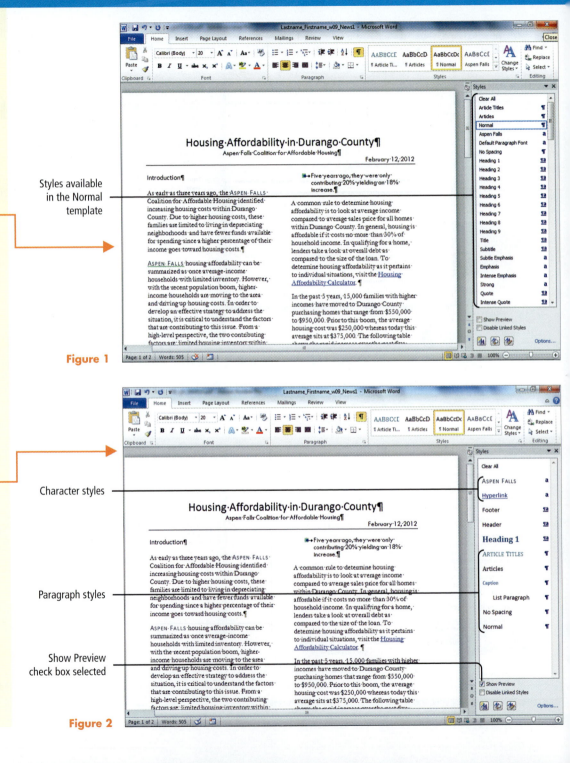

Styles available in the Normal template

Figure 1

Character styles

Paragraph styles

Show Preview check box selected

Figure 2

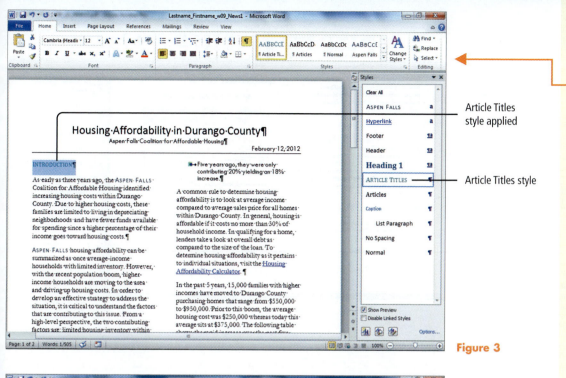

Article Titles style applied

Article Titles style

Figure 3

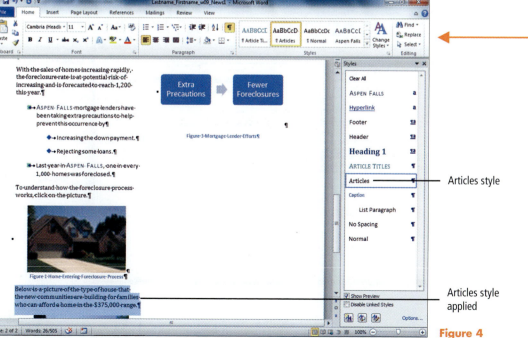

Articles style

Articles style applied

Figure 4

7. At the top of Page 1, click the first article title, *Introduction*, and then in the **Styles** pane, click **Article Titles** to apply the paragraph style. Compare your screen with **Figure 3**.

    The Article Titles style is a character style created for this skill and previously saved with the file. It is not one of the default styles in Word.

8. Repeat the technique just practiced to apply the **Article Titles** style to the article titles *Limited Housing Inventory* and *Housing Affordability Problem*.

9. In the first article, select the paragraphs that begin *As early as* and *ASPEN FALLS housing*, and then in the **Styles** pane, click **Articles**.

    The Articles style is a paragraph style previously created and saved for this skill.

    When a paragraph style is applied, any character styles in the paragraph retain their formatting. Previously-formatted character styles remain unchanged.

10. Repeat the technique just practiced to apply the **Articles** style to paragraphs that begin as follows: *In most areas of Aspen Falls, A common rule to determine, In the past 5 years, With the sales of homes, To understand,* and *Below is a picture.* Compare your screen with **Figure 4**.

11. In the **Styles** pane, click **Options**. In the **Style Pane Options** dialog box, click the **Select how list is sorted arrow**, click **Alphabetical**, and then click **OK**.

12. **Save** the document.

    ■ **You have completed Skill 3 of 10**

► A *table style* is a style type that formats rows, columns, and cells.

► Table style options include separate formatting settings for row and column headers, alternate rows or columns, and summary rows or columns.

1. At the bottom of Page 1, click any cell in the first row of the table. On the **Layout tab**, in the **Table group**, click the **Select** button, and then click **Select Row**. Alternately, point to the row with the 🔁 pointer and click.

2. In the **Styles** pane, notice that the **Normal** style has been applied to the selected row, as shown in **Figure 1**.

3. In the **Styles** pane, click the **New Style** button 🔳, and then in the **Create New Style from Formatting** dialog box, replace the **Name** box value with Table Heading Format

4. Click the **Style type arrow**, click **Table**, and then compare your screen with **Figure 2**.

When the Table style type is selected, the Create New Style from Formatting dialog box displays style options for formatting tables.

■ **Continue to the next page to complete the skill**

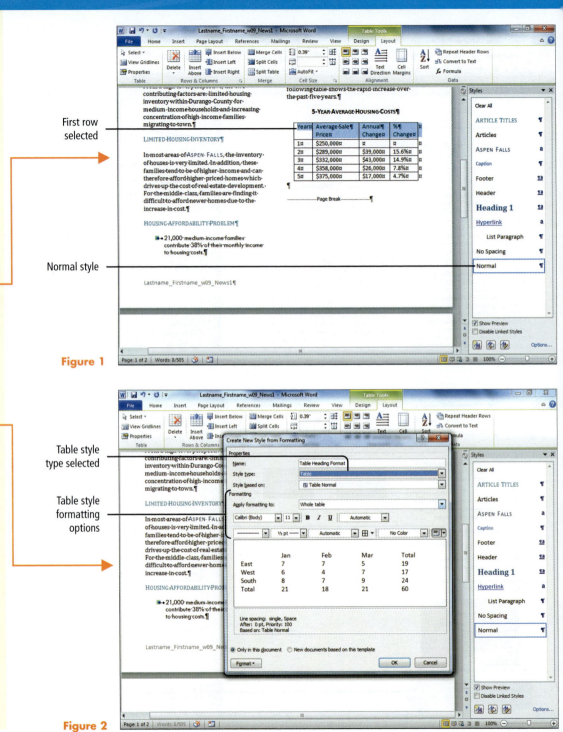

First row selected

Normal style

Figure 1

Table style type selected

Table style formatting options

Figure 2

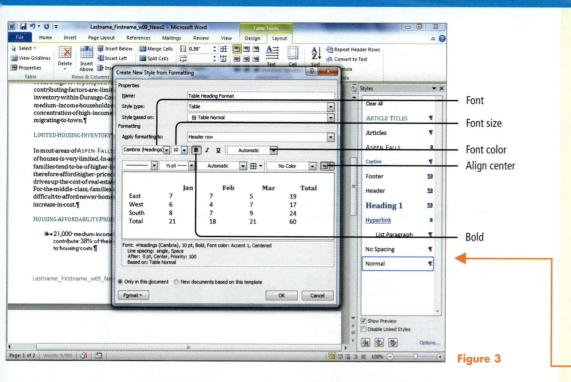

Font
Font size
Font color
Align center
Bold

Figure 3

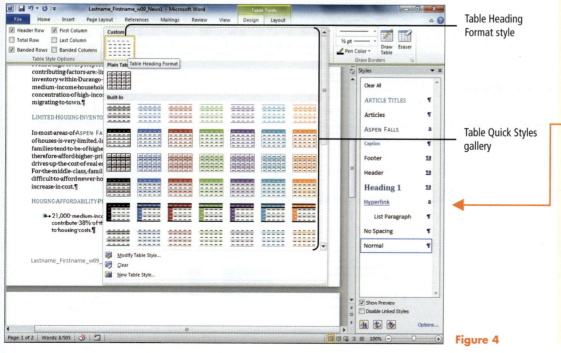

Table Heading Format style

Table Quick Styles gallery

Figure 4

5. Under **Formatting**, click the **Apply formatting to arrow**, and then click **Header row**.

6. Under **Formatting**, click the **Font arrow**—the first empty box, and then click **Cambria (Headings)**.

7. Under **Formatting**, click the **Font Size arrow**—the second box—, and then click **10**.

8. Under **Formatting**, click the **Bold** B button.

9. Under **Formatting**, next to Underline icon, click the **Font Color arrow**, and then click the fifth color in the sixth row—**Blue, Accent 1, Darker 50%**.

10. Click the **Align button arrow**—the last button to the right above the Preview— and then click the second style in the second row—**Align Center**. Compare your screen with **Figure 3**.

11. Verify that the **Only in this document** option button is selected, and then click **OK**.

12. On the **Design tab**, in the **Table Styles group**, click the **More** button, and then in the displayed gallery, under **Custom**, point to the **Table Heading Format** thumbnail, as shown in **Figure 4**. Click **Custom**.

    Table styles you create display in the Table Quick Styles gallery.

13. **Save** the document.

■ **You have completed Skill 4 of 10**

▶ A *linked style* is a style type that can be applied as a character style in one place and as a paragraph style in another. The Heading 1 style is an example of a linked style.

▶ When a linked style is applied to a word or a phrase, only the text level formatting is applied. When a linked style is applied to an entire paragraph, both the text level and paragraph formatting are applied.

1. At the top of Page 2, click the blank paragraph and then type Foreclosures

   Foreclosures displays with the Normal style, as displayed on the Home tab.

2. In the **Styles** pane, click **Heading 1**, as shown in **Figure 1**.

   The Heading 1 style has both a paragraph and a character symbol next to it, indicating that it is a linked style that can be formatted with either style format, depending on what is selected in the document.

3. In the **Styles** pane, click the **Style Inspector** button. Point to the **Style Inspector** title bar, and then with the pointer, double-click to dock the pane to the right edge of the window. Compare your screen with **Figure 2**.

   The *Style Inspector* pane displays the paragraph and text level formatting for the current style.

■ **Continue to the next page to complete the skill**

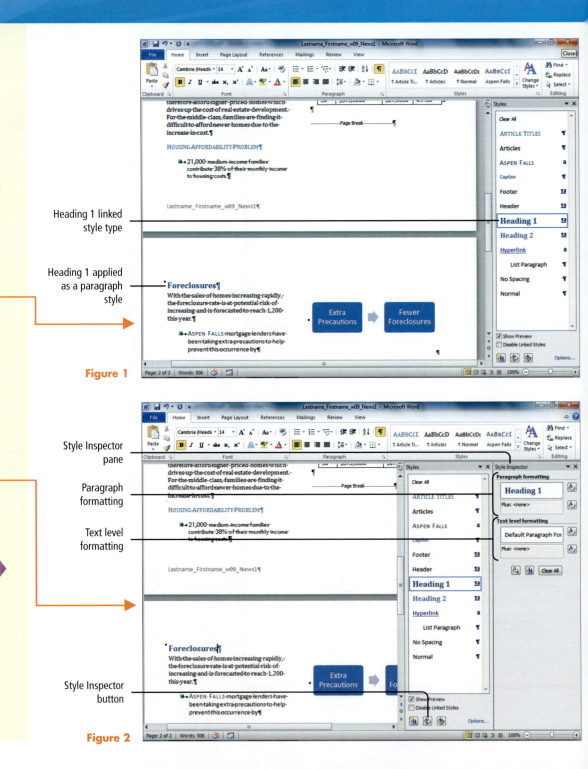

Heading 1 linked style type

Heading 1 applied as a paragraph style

Figure 1

Style Inspector pane

Paragraph formatting

Text level formatting

Style Inspector button

Figure 2

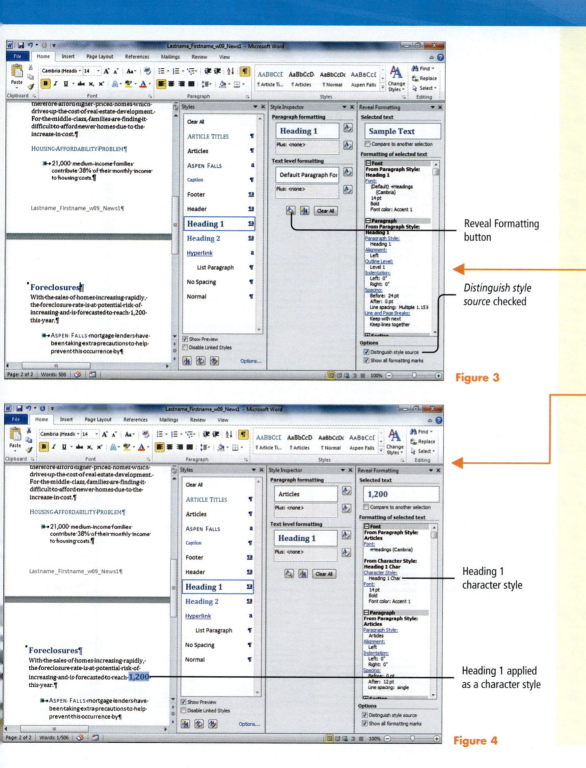

Reveal Formatting
button

*Distinguish style
source* checked

Figure 3

Heading 1
character style

Heading 1 applied
as a character style

Figure 4

4. In the **Style Inspector** pane, click the **Reveal Formatting** button. The Reveal Formatting pane should dock to the right of your screen. If necessary, point to the **Reveal Formatting** pane title bar, and then with the pointer, double-click to dock the pane to the right of the window.

> The *Reveal Formatting* pane displays the selected text and the font, paragraph, and section formatting currently in use.

5. In the **Reveal Formatting** pane, below **Options**, select the **Distinguish style source** check box. Compare your screen with **Figure 3**.

6. In the paragraph that begins *With the sales*, select *1,200*.

> In the Style Inspector pane and the Reveal Formatting pane, observe that the Articles paragraph style is in use.

7. In the **Styles** pane, click **Heading 1**, and then compare your screen with **Figure 4**.

> Heading 1 is applied as a character style.

8. **Close** the **Reveal Formatting** pane and the **Style Inspector** pane.

9. **Save** the document.

- **You have completed Skill 5 of 10**

▶ When a style is set to update automatically, you can modify the style by formatting the text directly instead of using the Modify style dialog box to apply the formatting.

▶ When a style is updated automatically, all occurrences of text assigned that style are changed when formatting changes are made to a single occurrence.

1. Press [Ctrl] + [Home] to move to the top of the document.

2. Click anywhere in the first Article Titles style, *INTRODUCTION*.

   Recall that the Article Titles style has been applied to all of the newsletter titles.

3. In the **Styles** pane, point to **Article Titles**, click the displayed arrow, and then click **Modify**.

4. In the **Modify Style** dialog box, select the **Automatically update** check box as shown in **Figure 1**, and then click **OK**.

5. Select the text *INTRODUCTION*, and then on the **Home** tab, click the **Font Dialog Box Launcher** [⌐].

6. In the **Font** dialog box, on the **Advanced tab**, click the **Spacing arrow**, and then click **Expanded**.

7. Click the **Spacing By** up spin arrow **5** times to display **1.5 pt**. Compare your screen with **Figure 2**, and then click **OK**.

   The Article Titles style is updated automatically, and all of the article titles are formatted with expanded character spacing.

■ **Continue to the next page to complete the skill** ▶

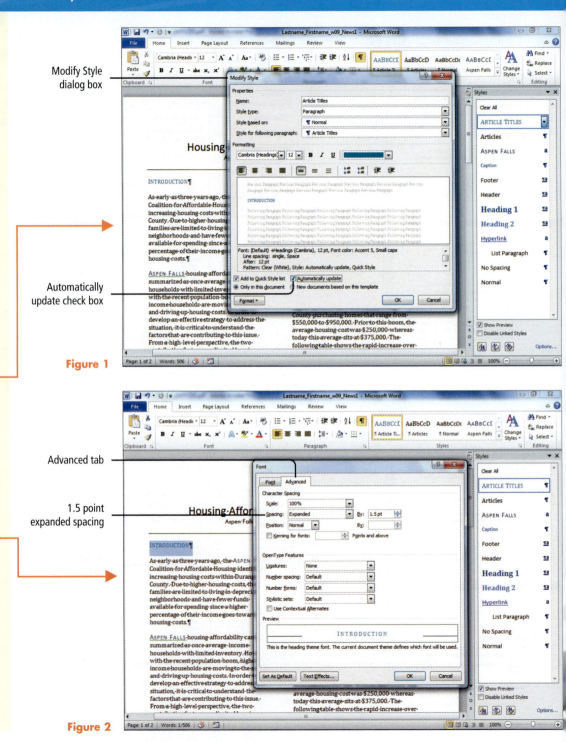

Modify Style dialog box

Automatically update check box

Figure 1

Advanced tab

1.5 point expanded spacing

Figure 2

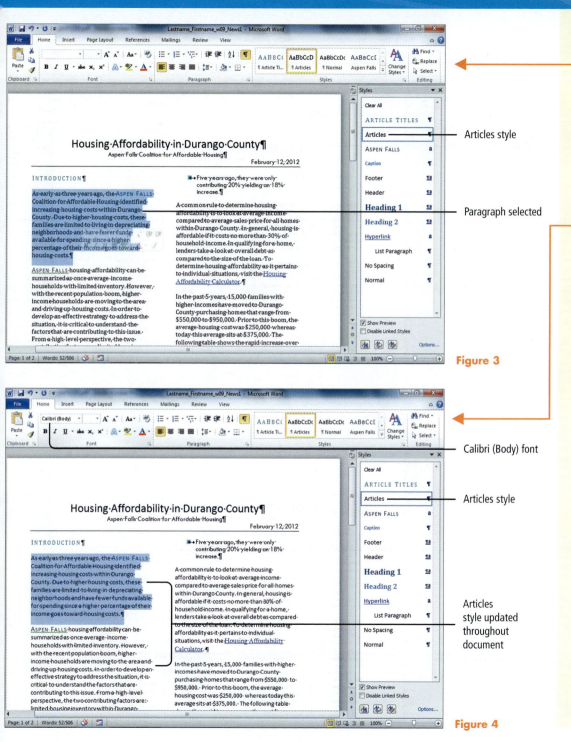

Figure 3

Figure 4

8. Select the paragraph that begins *As early as three years*, as shown in **Figure 3**.

9. In the **Styles** pane, display and click the **Articles arrow**, and then click **Modify**.

10. In the **Modify Style** dialog box, select the **Automatically update** check box, and then click **OK**.

11. On the **Home tab**, in the **Font group**, click the **Font arrow**, and then click **Calibri (Body)**. Compare your screen with **Figure 4**.

    The style is updated automatically, and all paragraphs assigned the Articles style are updated, including the document title.

12. In the displayed **Styles** pane, clear the **Show Preview** check box.

13. Click **Options**. In the **Style Pane Options** dialog box, click **Select how list is sorted**, click **As Recommended**, clear the **Bullet and numbering formatting** check box, and then click **OK**.

14. **Close** ⊠ the **Styles** pane, and then **Save** 🔲 the document.

■ **You have completed Skill 6 of 10**

► Word has six built-in Paragraph Spacing styles that you can use to assign paragraph spacing. You can also create your own custom paragraph spacing style.

► The default Paragraph Spacing style is the Open Built-In style.

1. Press Ctrl + Home to move to the top of the document.

2. On the **Home tab**, in the **Styles group**, click the **Change Styles** button.

3. Point to **Style Set**, and point to **Modern**, as shown in **Figure 1**. Click to select **Modern**.

4. In the **Styles** group, click the **Change Styles** button, and then point to **Paragraph Spacing**.

5. Under **Built-In**, point to **Double**, as shown in **Figure 2**, and then click to select it.

6. On Page 2, click anywhere in the *Foreclosures* paragraph.

7. On the **Home tab**, click the **Paragraph Dialog Box Launcher**.

8. In the **Paragraph** dialog box, on the **Indents and Spacing tab**, verify that the line spacing displays **Double**, and then click **OK**.

9. Click **Undo** three times.

■ **Continue to the next page to complete the skill** ►

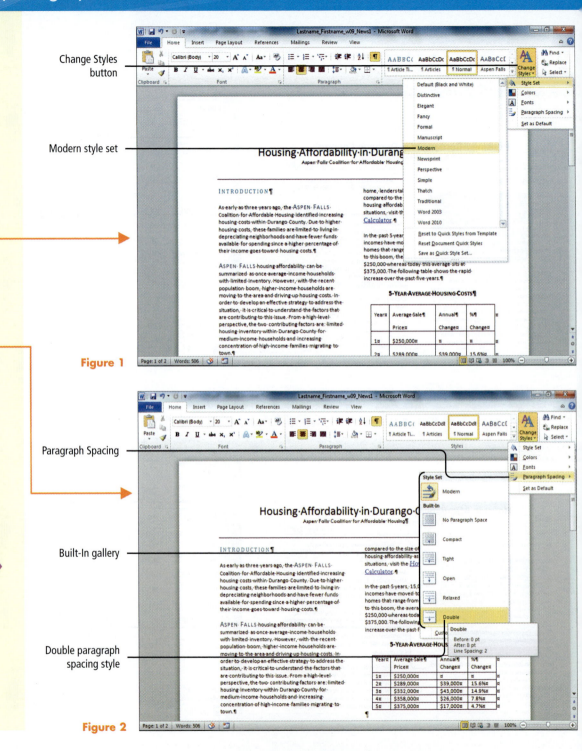

Change Styles button

Modern style set

Figure 1

Paragraph Spacing

Built-In gallery

Double paragraph spacing style

Figure 2

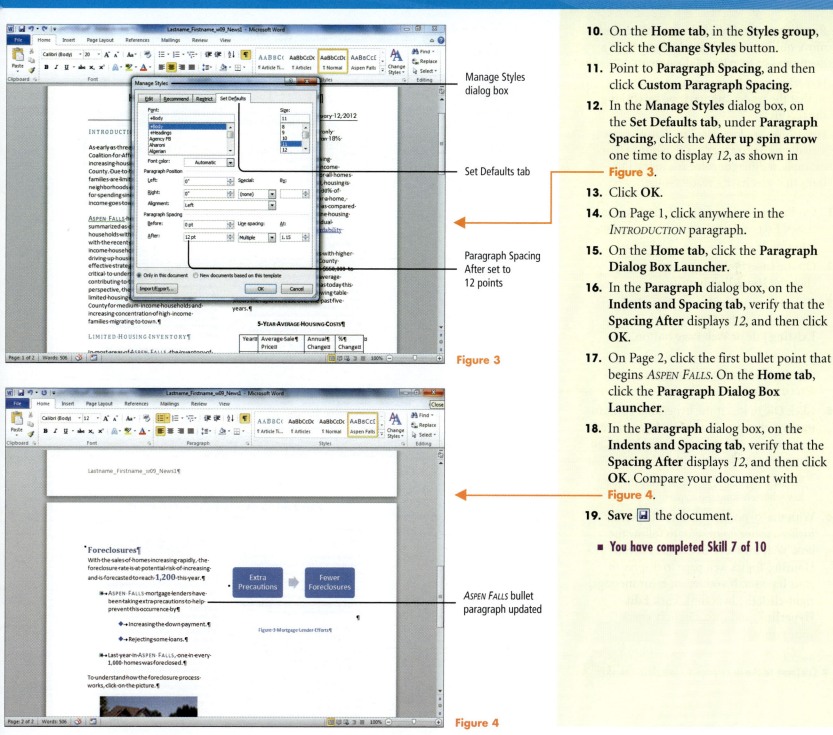

Manage Styles dialog box

Set Defaults tab

Paragraph Spacing After set to 12 points

Figure 3

Lastname_Firstname_w09_News1¶

ASPEN FALLS bullet paragraph updated

Figure 4

10. On the **Home tab**, in the **Styles group**, click the **Change Styles** button.

11. Point to **Paragraph Spacing**, and then click **Custom Paragraph Spacing**.

12. In the **Manage Styles** dialog box, on the **Set Defaults tab**, under **Paragraph Spacing**, click the **After up spin arrow** one time to display *12*, as shown in **Figure 3**.

13. Click **OK**.

14. On Page 1, click anywhere in the *INTRODUCTION* paragraph.

15. On the **Home tab**, click the **Paragraph Dialog Box Launcher**.

16. In the **Paragraph** dialog box, on the **Indents and Spacing tab**, verify that the **Spacing After** displays *12*, and then click **OK**.

17. On Page 2, click the first bullet point that begins *ASPEN FALLS*. On the **Home tab**, click the **Paragraph Dialog Box Launcher**.

18. In the **Paragraph** dialog box, on the **Indents and Spacing tab**, verify that the **Spacing After** displays *12*, and then click **OK**. Compare your document with **Figure 4**.

19. Save 💾 the document.

■ **You have completed Skill 7 of 10**

▶ Recall that hyperlinks help the online reader move quickly to predefined areas within a document or to external documents.

▶ Hyperlinks can be inserted into pictures so that the reader can navigate by clicking the picture.

▶ Hyperlinks are formatted so that you can visually recognize them as hyperlinks. For example, a different color is assigned to links that you have already visited.

1. On Page 1, in the paragraph that begins *ASPEN FALLS*, select the text *higher-income households*.

2. On the **Insert tab**, in the **Links group**, click the **Hyperlink** button.

3. If necessary, in the **Insert Hyperlink** dialog box, under **Link to**, click the **Existing File or Web Page** button.

4. In the **Address** box, type http://www. census.gov/hhes/www Compare your screen with **Figure 1**.

5. Click **OK** to insert the hyperlink. Point to the hyperlink just inserted—*higher-income households*—and then press and hold Ctrl. Compare your screen with **Figure 2**.

    To use a hyperlink in Word, press the Ctrl key while clicking the hyperlink.

6. With the pointer, click the hyperlink *higher-income households* to follow the link. Wait for the U.S. Census Bureau Housing Topics web page to display in your browser. If you see an error message, right-click the hyperlink, click **Edit Hyperlink**, and then carefully check your typing.

■ **Continue to the next page to complete the skill** ➡

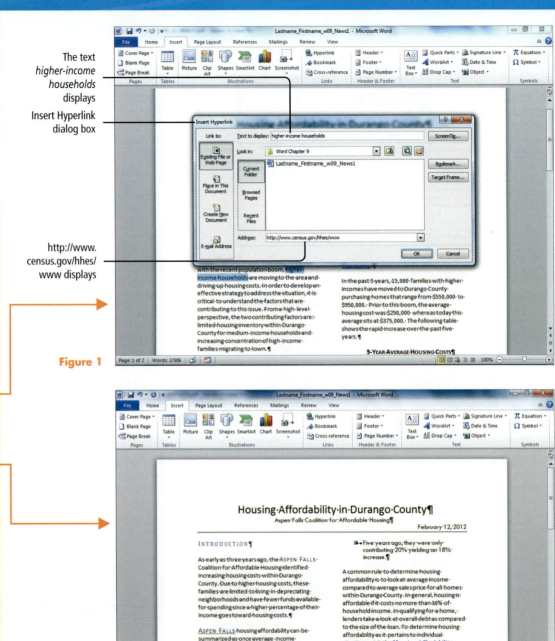

The text *higher-income households* displays

Insert Hyperlink dialog box

http://www. census.gov/hhes/ www displays

Figure 1

Hyperlink pointer

Figure 2

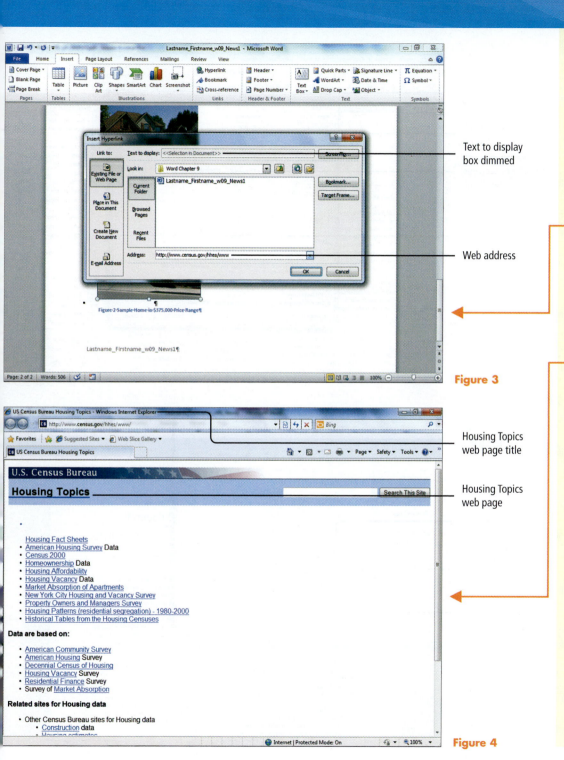

Text to display box dimmed

Web address

Figure 3

Housing Topics web page title

Housing Topics web page

Figure 4

7. **Close** the browser window. On Page 2, right-click the second picture, which has the caption that begins *Figure 2*, and then in the displayed shortcut menu, click **Hyperlink**.

8. If necessary, in the **Insert Hyperlink** dialog box, under **Link to**, click the **Existing File or Web Page** button.

9. In the **Address** box, type http://www. census.gov/hhes/www Compare your screen with **Figure 3**, and then click **OK**.

As you begin to type the URL in the Address box, the URLs previously typed begin to display to help you save time.

10. Click anywhere in the document so that the picture is no longer selected. While pressing Ctrl, click the *Figure 2* picture to open the page in your web browser. Compare your screen with **Figure 4**. If you see an error message, right-click the picture, click **Edit Hyperlink**, and then carefully check your typing.

11. **Close** the browser window. Press Ctrl + Home.

The hyperlink *higher-income households* displays in magenta to indicate that it has been followed. The *Housing Affordability Calculator* hyperlink displays in blue to indicate that you have not yet clicked the link.

12. On the **Home tab**, in the **Styles group**, click the **Styles Dialog Box Launcher**, and then click **Options**.

13. Click the **Select styles to show arrow**, click **All styles**, and then click **OK**.

14. **Save** the document.

■ **You have completed Skill 8 of 10**

► You can convert Word documents to **HTML files**—text documents with special markup codes that enable web pages to display the document in a web browser.

1. In the **Styles** pane, scroll down, and then point to **Hyperlink**. Click the arrow, and then click **Modify**.

2. In the **Modify Style** dialog box, click the **Underline** button $\underline{\text{U}}$ ▾ to deselect it, and then click **OK**.

   The Hyperlink style stores the formatting for links that have not yet been followed. The formatting for the visited links is stored in the FollowedHyperlink style. Here, the *higher-income households* link is still underlined because the Hyperlink style, not the FollowedHyperlink style, was changed.

3. In the **Styles** pane, point to **FollowedHyperlink**, click the arrow, and then click **Modify**. Click the **Underline** button $\underline{\text{U}}$ ▾ to deselect it, as shown in **Figure 1**.

4. Click **OK**.

5. In the **Styles** pane, click **Options**. Click the **Select styles to show arrow**, click **In current document**, and then click **OK**.

6. **Close** ☒ the **Styles** pane, and then **Save** 🖫 the document.

7. On the **File tab**, click **Save As**. In the **Save As** dialog box, click the **Save as type arrow**. In the list of file types, click **Web Page**. If necessary, navigate to your Word Chapter 9 folder. In the **File name** box, type Lastname_Firstname_w09_News1_HTML as shown in **Figure 2**.

■ **Continue to the next page to complete the skill** ▶

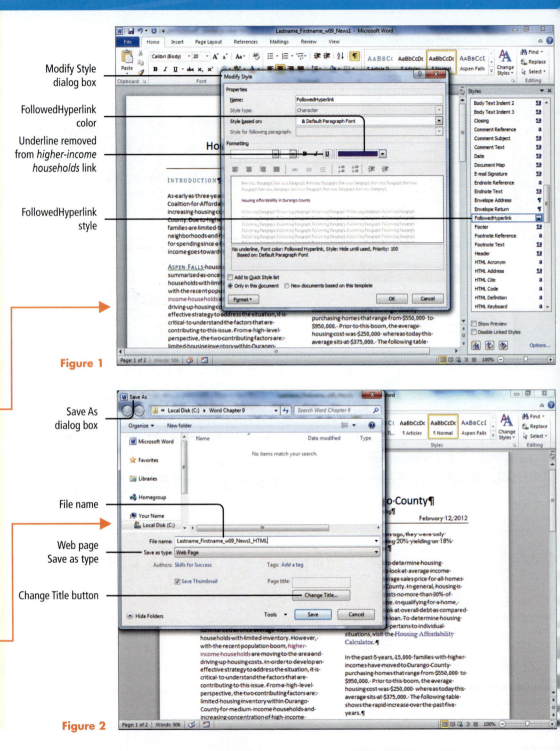

Modify Style dialog box

FollowedHyperlink color

Underline removed from *higher-income households* link

FollowedHyperlink style

Figure 1

Save As dialog box

File name

Web page Save as type

Change Title button

Figure 2

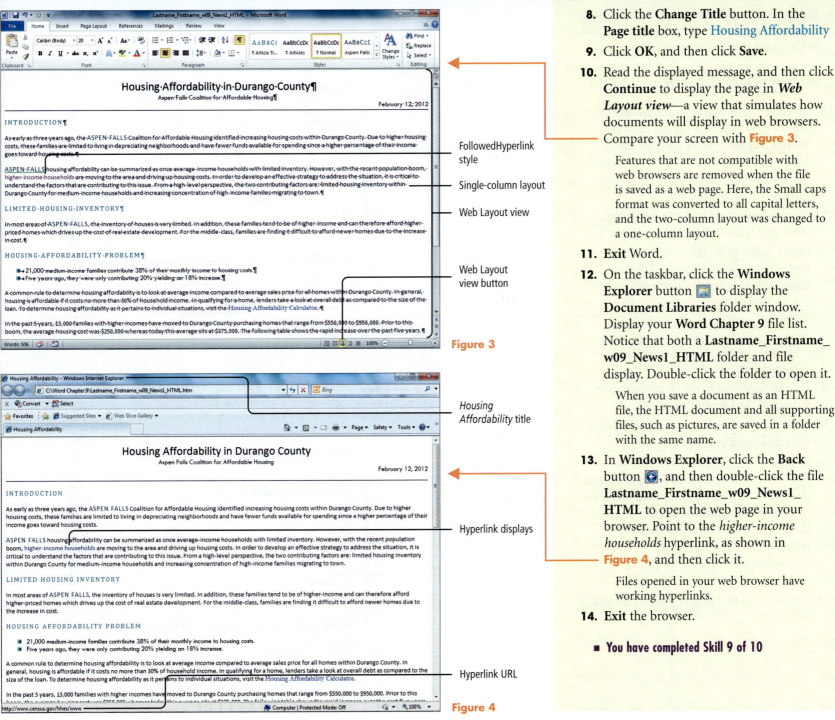

Figure 3

Figure 4

FollowedHyperlink style

Single-column layout

Web Layout view

Web Layout view button

Housing Affordability title

Hyperlink displays

Hyperlink URL

8. Click the **Change Title** button. In the **Page title** box, type Housing Affordability

9. Click **OK**, and then click **Save**.

10. Read the displayed message, and then click **Continue** to display the page in *Web Layout view*—a view that simulates how documents will display in web browsers. Compare your screen with **Figure 3**.

    Features that are not compatible with web browsers are removed when the file is saved as a web page. Here, the Small caps format was converted to all capital letters, and the two-column layout was changed to a one-column layout.

11. **Exit** Word.

12. On the taskbar, click the **Windows Explorer** button 🗔 to display the **Document Libraries** folder window. Display your **Word Chapter 9** file list. Notice that both a **Lastname_Firstname_ w09_News1_HTML** folder and file display. Double-click the folder to open it.

    When you save a document as an HTML file, the HTML document and all supporting files, such as pictures, are saved in a folder with the same name.

13. In **Windows Explorer**, click the **Back** button ⬅, and then double-click the file **Lastname_Firstname_w09_News1_ HTML** to open the web page in your browser. Point to the *higher-income households* hyperlink, as shown in **Figure 4**, and then click it.

    Files opened in your web browser have working hyperlinks.

14. **Exit** the browser.

■ **You have completed Skill 9 of 10**

► The Organizer is a dialog box that displays styles available in the current document and in the Normal template.

► You can use the Organizer to copy styles from one document to another.

1. **Start** 🌐 Word, and open the student data file **w09_News2**. Save the file in your **Word Chapter 9** folder with the name **Lastname_Firstname_w09_News2** Add the file name to the footer, and if necessary, display the formatting marks.

2. On the **Home tab**, in the **Styles group**, click the **Styles Dialog Box Launcher** 🔲.

3. In the **Styles** pane, click the **Manage Styles** button 🔳, and then click the **Import/Export** button. Compare your screen with **Figure 1**. ———►

   The Organizer displays the styles in the open document on one side of the dialog box and the styles in the Normal template— *normal.dotm*—on the other side.

4. On the right side of the **Organizer** dialog box, click the **Close File** button.

5. On the right side of the **Organizer** dialog box, click the **Open File** button.

6. In the bottom right corner of the **Open** dialog box, click **All Word Templates**, and then from the list, click **All Files**. Navigate to your **Word Chapter 9** folder, and then double-click **Lastname_Firstname_w09_News1** to display the styles in the original newsletter, as shown in **Figure 2**. ———►

■ **Continue to the next page to complete the skill** ►

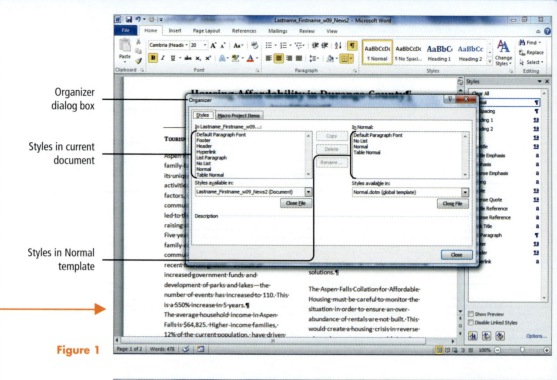

Organizer dialog box

Styles in current document

Styles in Normal template

Figure 1

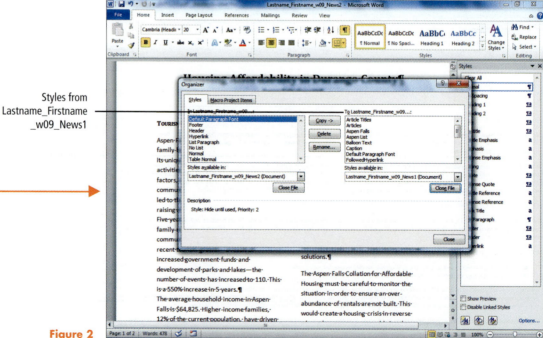

Styles from Lastname_Firstname _w09_News1

Figure 2

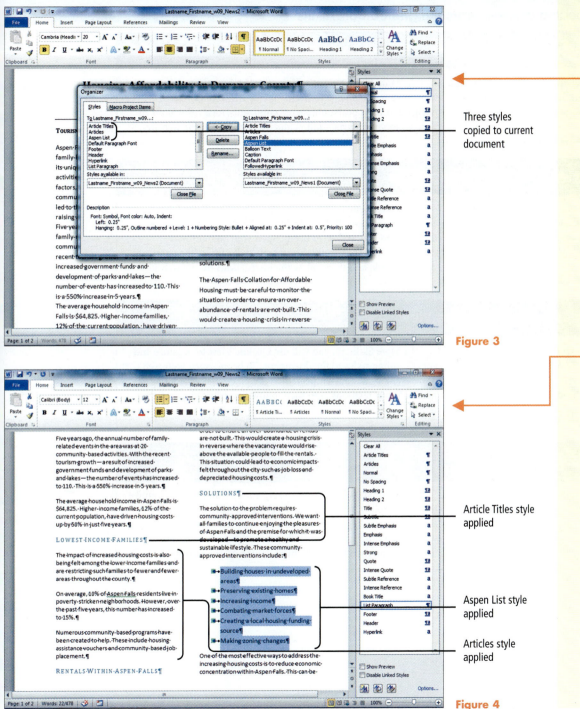

Figure 3

Figure 4

Three styles copied to current document

Article Titles style applied

Aspen List style applied

Articles style applied

7. Under **To Lastname_Firstname_w09_ News1**, click **Article Titles**, and then click the **Copy** button. Repeat this technique to copy the **Articles** and **Aspen List** styles as shown in **Figure 3**.

    In this manner, you can copy styles into the current, open document, where they can be saved with the document for future use.

8. **Close** the **Organizer** dialog box. Using the techniques practiced in this chapter, apply the **Article Titles** style to the four article titles in the newsletter.

9. For each body paragraph in the newsletter, apply the **Articles** style.

10. On Page 1, select the six bulleted items. On the **Home tab**, in the **Paragraph group**, click the **Multilevel List** button, and then at the bottom of the gallery, click the last thumbnail— **Aspen List**. Compare your screen with **Figure 4**.

11. **Close** the **Styles** pane.

12. On Page 1, at the bottom of column 1, click the beginning of the paragraph that begins *RENTALS WITHIN*. On the **Page Layout tab**, in the **Page Setup group**, click the **Breaks** button, and then click **Columns**.

13. **Save** the document. Print or submit the files as directed by your instructor. **Exit** Word.

Done! You have completed Skill 10 of 10 and your document is complete!

More Skills

The following More Skills are located at **www.pearsonhighered.com/skills**

More Skills Insert Hyphenation

Many publications divide words between two lines by placing a hyphen between the syllables in a word. You can use Word 2010 to hyphenate words in a document.

In More Skills 11, you will use the Hyphenation tool to hyphenate a document. To begin, open your web browser, navigate to www.pearsonhighered.com/skills, locate the name of your textbook, and then follow the instructions on the website.

More Skills Create Styles Based on Existing Styles

New styles can be based on an existing style. When changes are made to the base style, both the base style and the new style are updated. Several styles can be based on a single style so that you can change many styles at once.

In More Skills 12, you will create a new style based on an existing style. You will then modify the base style to change both the new and base styles. To begin, open your web browser, navigate to www.pearsonhighered.com/skills, locate the name of your textbook, and then follow the instructions on the website.

More Skills Assign Styles Using the Outline View

When documents are organized in Outline view, styles are automatically assigned to each level in the outline. For example, Level 1 text is assigned the Heading 1 style. When you return to Print Layout view, all of the document headings will be assigned an appropriate style.

In More Skills 13, you will use Outline View to organize and apply heading styles to the document. To begin, open your web browser, navigate to www.pearsonhighered.com/skills, locate the name of your textbook, and then follow the instructions on the website.

More Skills Create New Theme Colors

You can modify prebuilt themes, and you can also create new theme colors, fonts, and effects. You can then apply the new theme to your documents.

In More Skills 14, you will apply a theme and then customize the theme colors, fonts, and effects. You will then create a new theme color. To begin, open your web browser, navigate to www.pearsonhighered.com/skills, locate the name of your textbook, and then follow the instructions on the website.

Key Terms

Online Help Skills

1. **Start** 🕭 Word. In the upper right corner of the Word window, click the **Help** button 🔲. In the **Help** window, click the **Maximize** 🔲 button.

2. Click in the search box, type headers and footers and then click the **Search** button 🔍. In the search results, click **Add or remove headers, footers, and page numbers**.

3. Read the article's introduction, and then below **What do you want to do?** click **Add different headers and footers or page numbers in different parts of the document**. Compare your screen with **Figure 1**.

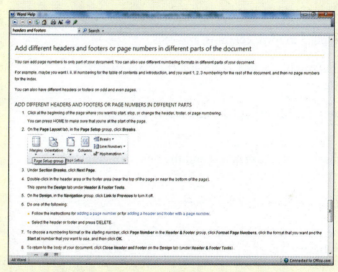

Figure 1

4. Read the section to see if you can answer the following: What are two reasons for using a different number format in the same document? What Tab is used to make changes to headers and footers?

Matching

Match each term in the second column with its correct definition in the first column by writing the letter of the term on the blank line in front of the correct definition.

____ **1.** The style type applied to selected letters, numbers, and symbols.

____ **2.** The style type used to format spacing, indents, and alignment.

____ **3.** A style type applied to bullets, numbers, and indent settings.

____ **4.** A Word template that stores the default styles that are applied when a new document is created.

____ **5.** A style type applied to rows, columns, and cells.

____ **6.** A style type that can be applied as either a character style or a paragraph style.

____ **7.** A pane that describes the paragraph and text level formatting for the selection.

____ **8.** A pane that displays the selected text and the font, paragraph, and section formatting currently in use.

____ **9.** A hyperlink that has been previously visited.

____ **10.** A text document with special mark up codes that enable it to display in a web browser.

A Character

B FollowedHyperlink

C HTML file

D Linked style

E List style

F Normal

G Paragraph

H Reveal Formatting

I Style Inspector

J Table style

Multiple Choice

Choose the correct answer.

1. The button clicked to access a stored list style thumbnail.
   A. Bullets
   B. More Styles
   C. Multilevel List

2. The button clicked to display table styles in the Table Quick Styles gallery.
   A. Manage Styles
   B. Styles More
   C. More

3. The dialog box used to update the style's formatting settings.
   A. Manage Styles
   B. Modify Style
   C. Update Style

4. A feature that updates a style as soon as the formatting is changed in the Ribbon.
   A. Add to Quick Style list
   B. Automatically update
   C. List formatting to permitted styles

5. The style type used to change the link color for a website not yet visited.
   A. FollowedHyperlink
   B. HTML
   C. Hyperlink

6. The style type used to change the link color for a website that has been previously visited.
   A. FollowedHyperlink
   B. HTML
   C. Hyperlink

7. The file format commonly used to publish pages on the Internet.
   A. FollowedHyperlink
   B. HTML
   C. Hyperlink

8. The dialog box used to copy styles from other documents.
   A. Modify Styles
   B. Organizer
   C. Style Pane Options

9. Template in which the styles inserted into a new document are stored
   A. Master
   B. Normal
   C. Styles

10. The file that must be closed in the Organizer before another document can be opened.
   A. Master.dotm
   B. Normal.dotm
   C. Style.dotm

Topics for Discussion

1. Assume that you are designing a website to raise money to purchase a new fire truck for your city's fire station. What types of hyperlinks, styles, and themes might you add to your website to enhance it? Why?

2. Assume that you are preparing a newsletter for a nonprofit organization. What types of styles and themes might you include to achieve a professional-looking newsletter that reflects the personality of the organization?

Skill Check

To complete this project, you will need the following files:

- w09_Community
- w09_Community2

You will save your files as:

- Lastname_Firstname_w09_Community
- Lastname_Firstname_w09_Community_Web
- Lastname_Firstname_w09_Community_Web (folder)

1. **Start** Word, and then open the student file **w09_Community**. Save the file in your **Word Chapter 9** folder with the name Lastname_Firstname_w09_ Community Add the file name to the footer.

2. On the **Home tab**, in the **Styles group**, click the **Styles Dialog Box Launcher**, and then select the **Show Preview** check box.

3. In the **Styles** pane, point to **Hyperlink**, and then click the **Hyperlink arrow**. Click **Modify**. Click the **Underline** button to deselect it. Change the **Font Color** to the fifth color in the sixth row—**Blue, Accent 1, Darker 50%**. Click **OK**. Press Ctrl + End to view the hyperlink. Compare your screen with **Figure 1**.

4. On Page 1, under the *Features* section, select all of the paragraphs. In the **Styles** pane, click the **New Style** button. In the **Name** box, type CommunityList and then change the **Style type** to **List**.

5. In the box with the **Number/Bullet**, click the arrow, scroll down, and then click **New Picture**. In the **Picture Bullet** dialog box, click the second thumbnail in the fourth row—**blue box**. Click **OK** two times, and then compare your screen with **Figure 2**.

6. Deselect the text. In the **Styles** pane, click the **Manage Styles** button, and then click **Import/Export**. On the right side of the **Organizer** dialog box, click the **Close File** button.

7. Click **Open File**, click **All Word Templates**, and then select **All Files**. Navigate to your student data files, and then open **w09_Community2**.

8. At the right, click **Article Titles**, and then hold Ctrl while clicking **Articles** and **Table Heading**. Click **Copy**, and then **Close** the Organizer.

9. For the five article titles, such as *Introduction*, apply the **Article Titles** style. For each body paragraph—but not the bulleted list—apply the **Articles** style.

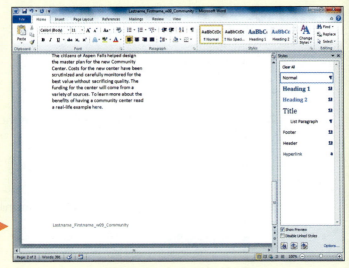

Figure 1

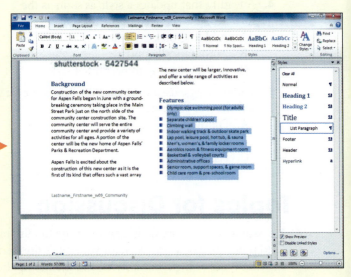

Figure 2

■ Continue to the next page to complete this Skill Check ▶

10. Select the table's first row. On the **Design tab**, in the **Table Styles group**, click the **More** button, and then under **Custom** click the **Table Heading** style.

11. Select the remaining rows of the table. In the **Styles** pane, click the **New Style** button. In the **Name** box, type CommunityRows Click the **Style type arrow**, and click **Table**. Click the **Apply formatting to arrow**, and then click **Even banded rows**. Click the **Fill Color arrow**, click the fifth color in the third row—**Blue, Accent 1, Lighter 60%**, and then click **OK**.

12. On Page 2, select the *COST* heading. In the **Styles** pane, display and click the **Article Titles arrow**, and then click **Modify**. Select the **Automatically update** check box, and then click **OK**. On the **Home tab**, click the **Paragraph Dialog Box Launcher**. Change the **Spacing Before** to 12 points, and then click **OK**. Compare your screen with **Figure 3**. Deselect the heading.

13. Click the **New Style** button. Create a character style named Community Apply **Small caps**, **Bold**, and the font color **Blue, Accent 1**. Click **OK** two times, and then apply **Community** to each occurrence of *community center*, except in the title.

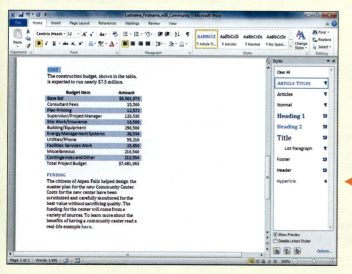

Figure 3

14. In the paragraph that begins *Construction of*, select *Aspen Falls*. In the **Styles** pane, click **Heading 1** to apply a linked style.

15. In the **Styles** pane, clear the **Show Preview** check box. **Close** the **Styles** pane.

16. Select the second picture. On the **Insert tab**, in the **Links group**, click the **Hyperlink** button. Under **Address**, type http://archive.gao.gov/t2pbat7/143871.pdf and then click **OK**.

17. At the top of Page 1, click the date. On the **Home tab**, in the **Styles group**, click the **Change Styles** button, point to **Paragraph Spacing**, and then click **Double**.

18. Click before the *Cost* heading, and then press Ctrl and Enter.

19. **Save** the document. On the **File tab**, click **Save As**. If necessary, navigate to your **Word Chapter 9** folder. Name the new file Lastname_Firstname_w09_Community_Web Click the **Save as type arrow**, and then click **Web Page**. Click **Save**, and then click **Continue**. Compare your screen with **Figure 4**.

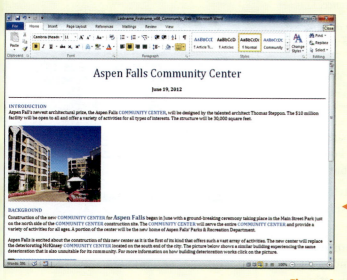

Figure 4

20. On the taskbar, click the **Windows Explorer** button to display the **Document Libraries** folder window. Display your **Word Chapter 9** file list. Double-click the **Lastname_Firstname_w09_Community_Web_files** folder.

21. In **Windows Explorer**, click the **Back** button, and then double-click the file **Lastname_Firstname_w09_Community_Web**.

22. Print or submit the files and folders as directed by your instructor. **Exit** your browser and Word.

Done! You have completed the Skill Check

Assess Your Skills 1

To complete this project, you will need the following files:

- w09_Travel
- w09_Travel2

You will save your files as:

- Lastname_Firstname_w09_Travel
- Lastname_Firstname_w09_Travel_Snip

1. **Start** Word, and open the student data file **w09_Travel**. Save the file in your **Word Chapter 9** folder with the name Lastname_Firstname_w09_Travel Add the file name to the footer.

2. In the paragraph that begins *6:00 a.m.*, select the word *Flight*. Create a new character style type named Flight For the new style, apply **Bold**, change the **Font Color** to **Blue, Accent 1**, and then apply **Small caps**.

3. Apply the **Flight** style to the other two occurrences of the word *Flight*.

4. Select the last five paragraphs, beginning with *In-room movies*. Create a new **List** style type named Travel List For the first-level bullet, in the box with the **Numbers/Bullet**, assign the second picture in the second row.

5. Use the **Organizer** to import the *Travel Table Heading* and *Travel Title* styles from the file **w09_Travel2**.

6. In the **Styles** pane, display the styles available **In current document** sorted **By type** and with the **Bullet and numbering formatting** displayed. Create a full-screen snip of the **Style Pane Options** dialog box, **Save** it in your **Word Chapter 9** folder as Lastname_Firstname_w09_Travel_Snip and then close the Snipping Tool window.

7. In the first row of the table that begins *Item*, apply the **Travel Table Heading** style.

8. Select all rows in the table beginning with *Air*. Create a new **Table** style named Travel Rows Apply the formatting to **Even banded rows**. Change the **Fill Color** to **Blue, Accent 1**. If necessary, apply the **Travel Rows** style.

9. Apply the **Travel Title** style to the newsletter title that begins *International Conference*.

10. In the paragraph that begins *Please adhere*, select *guidelines*, and then apply the **Heading 1** style as a linked style.

11. Set the **Travel Title** style to update automatically.

12. Select the title that begins *International*. Use the Ribbon to make the following changes: apply **Center** alignment, change the **Font Size** to **14**, and use a **Dark Blue, Text 2 Font Color**.

13. Deselect the text. Use the **Change Styles** button to apply the **Relaxed Paragraph Spacing**.

14. In the **Styles** pane, show the **Recommended** styles available sorted **As Recommended**, and clear the **Bullet and numbering formatting** check box. **Close** the **Styles** pane.

15. **Save** the document, and then compare your screen with **Figure 1**. Print or submit the files as directed by your instructor. **Exit** Word.

Done! You have completed Assess Your Skills 1

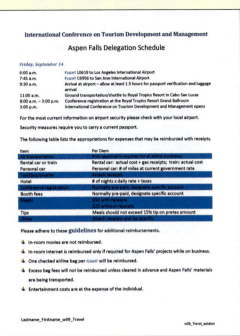

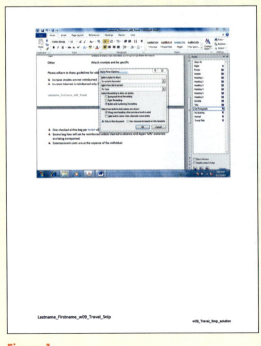

Figure 1

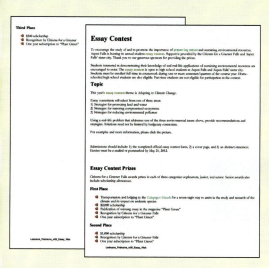

Figure 1

Assess Your Skills 2

To complete this project, you will need the following file:

- w09_Essay

You will save your files as:

- Lastname_Firstname_w09_Essay
- Lastname_Firstname_w09_Essay_Web

1. **Start** Word, and then open the student file **w09_Essay**. Save the file in your **Word Chapter 9** folder with the name Lastname_Firstname_w09_Essay Add the file name to the footer.

2. Modify the **Heading 2** style to update automatically.

3. Select the *Topic* paragraph, and then use the Ribbon to change the **Spacing Before** to 6 points and the **Spacing After** to 12 points.

4. In the paragraph that begins *To encourage*, select *essay contest*. Create a new Character style named Essay that includes **Bold** and a **Font Color** of **Olive Green, Accent 3, Darker 25%**. Apply the **Essay** style to all occurrences of *essay contest*, except in headings.

5. In the paragraph below the *Essay Contest* title, select the text *preserving nature*, and then insert a hyperlink that opens the web page at www.nps.gov Follow the link, and then close your browser.

6. Select the picture, and then create a hyperlink to www.nrcs.usda.gov/

7. In the **Styles** pane, display **All styles** sorted **By type**.

8. Modify the **Hyperlink** style by removing the **Underline** and changing the font color to **Green**. Modify the **FollowedHyperlink** color by applying **Bold**, removing the **Underline**, and changing the font color to **Tan, Background 2, Darker 50%**.

9. On Page 2, under *First Place*, select the five bulleted list paragraphs. Create a new **List** style type named Essay List For the first-level bullet, assign the first picture in the first row of the **Picture Bullet** dialog box. Use the Ribbon to apply the **Essay List** style to the bullets below *Second Place* and *Third Place*.

10. In the **Styles** pane, display the **Recommended** styles in the current document sorted **As Recommended**. **Close** the **Styles** pane.

11. **Save** the document.

12. **Save** the file as a **Web Page** named Lastname_Firstname_w09_Essay_Web and assign the title Aspen Falls Essay Contest

13. **Exit** Word. Print or submit the files as directed by your instructor.

Done! You have completed Assess Your Skills 2

Assess Your Skills Visually

To complete this project, you will need the following file:

- w09_Tasting_Tour

You will save your file as:

- Lastname_Firstname_w09_Tasting_Tour

Start Word, and open the student data file **w09_Tasting_Tour**. Save the file in your **Word Chapter 9** folder with the name Lastname_Firstname_w09_Tasting_Tour Add the file name to the footer.

Apply the following styles as shown in **Figure 1**. The flyer title, *Winery Tasting and Tour,* is the **Title** style. *Tour Duration, Group Size, Destinations, Season, Price per Person, Best Time to Go,* and *Activities* have been assigned the **Heading 1** style. The **Heading 1** has been modified to use the **Verdana** font, a **14** point font size, and the font color **Olive Green, Accent 3, Darker 50%**. The body paragraphs have been assigned a new paragraph style named Tour Body Text The Tour Body Text style uses the **Verdana** font and the **11** point font size. From the **Change Styles** button, apply **Tight Paragraph Spacing**. If necessary, move the picture(s). Print or submit the file as directed by your instructor.

Done! You have completed Assess Your Skills Visually

Winery Tasting and Tour

Tour Duration: 4 hours

Group Size: 6-15 people

Destinations: Aspen Falls Wine Region

Season: May-October

Price per Person: $100

Have you considered a wine tour but are unsure of the best place to visit? The Aspen Falls Wine region offers a beautiful and peaceful atmosphere that is sure to offer a memorable experience.

The Aspen Falls Wineries in Durango County are known for their breath-taking views, fine dining, spa resorts, and peaceful and relaxing settings far from the stresses of everyday living.

Walk among the vines as you take in the fresh air while sipping on an award-winning wine.

Enjoy delicious dining offered by our famous chefs who have been awarded the 5-star medal of accommodation. Escape to our romantic bed and breakfasts at the end of the day, or relax with a massage from one of our specially-trained masseuses.

Best Time to Go

The best time to plan your trip is in May or during the fall harvest in September and October. The views are spectacular and the crowds are smaller. You can still enjoy all the services offered during peak-season.

Activities

If you desire a planned trip, Aspen Falls' wineries offer an array of activities. Experience one of our winery tours in the comforts of a limousine. Take a winemaking class taught by some of the best wine makers in the region. And, finally, relax while enjoying the full-service spas around the area.

Lastname_Firstname_w09_Tasting_Tour

Figure 1

Skills in Context

To complete this project, you will need the following file:

- w09_Crime_Stoppers

You will save your file as:

- Lastname_Firstname_w09_Crime_Stoppers

Open the student file **w09_Crime_ Stoppers**. Review the newsletter, and then create styles with formatting appropriate to the content. Create at least one character, list, linked, and table style. Apply the styles to format the newsletter effectively. Format the hyperlink to display with no underline for both the normal and followed links.

Save the file in your **Word Chapter 9** folder with the name Lastname_Firstname_w09_Crime_Stoppers Add the file name to the footer. Print or submit the file as directed by your instructor.

Done! You have completed Skills in Context

Skills and You

To complete this project, you will need the following file:

- Blank document

You will save your files as:

- Lastname_Firstname_w09_Aware

Create a new blank document. Prepare a one-page or two-page flyer for an organization you are involved in or wish you had time to be involved in. Include a table, at least one list, and two hyperlinks, and then create and apply appropriate styles for each of the items. Create a character and a linked style. Format the flyer to reflect the content by creating a Custom Paragraph Spacing style.

Save the file in your **Word Chapter 9** folder with the name Lastname_Firstname_ w09_Aware Add the file name to the footer. Print or submit as directed by your instructor.

Done! You have completed Skills and You

CHAPTER 10

Create Forms and Macros

- ► You can create forms in Word that users can complete.
- ► Macros let you perform a series of common tasks with a single click.
- ► You can customize the Ribbon and change the buttons on the Quick Access Toolbar.

Your starting screen will look like this:

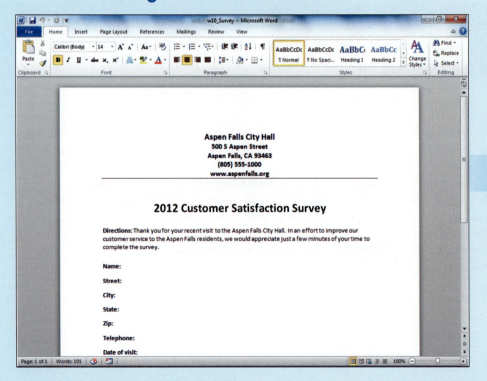

SKILLS

Skills 1–10 Training

At the end of this chapter, you will be able to:

Skill 1 Display the Developer Tab and Insert Text Controls
Skill 2 Insert Date Picker Controls
Skill 3 Insert Drop-Down Lists and Check Boxes
Skill 4 Insert Legacy Tools
Skill 5 Protect and Distribute Forms
Skill 6 Test Online Forms and Remove Protection
Skill 7 Record Macros and Set Macro Security
Skill 8 Run and Step into Macros
Skill 9 Customize the Ribbon
Skill 10 Change Buttons on the Quick Access Toolbar

MORE SKILLS

More Skills 11 Create Multilevel Lists
More Skills 12 Edit Macros in Visual Basic for Applications
More Skills 13 Add XML and Save Forms as XML Documents
More Skills 14 Insert Signature Lines

Outcome

Using the skills listed to the left will enable you to create documents like these:

Aspen Falls City Hall
500 S Aspen Street
Aspen Falls, CA 93463
(805) 555-1000
www.aspenfalls.org

2012 Customer Satisfaction Survey

Directions: Thank you for your recent visit to the Aspen Falls City Hall. In an effort to improve our customer service to the Aspen Falls residents, we would appreciate just a few minutes of your time to complete the survey.

Name: Click here to enter text.

Street: Click here to enter text.

City: Click here to enter text.

State: CA

Zip: Click here to enter text.

Telephone: Click here to enter text.

Date of visit: 3/19/2012

Department visited: Choose an item.

Nature of visit:

Please request the Planning Commission member(s) you wish to call you:

☐Richie Bona   ☐Jung Ortolano

☐Hisako Lavoy   ☐Jerrold Calhaun

☐Octavio Coogan   ☐Gwyneth Rondeau

☐Barton Bierschbach   ☐Tammi Markewich

Comments:

Lastname_Firstname_w10_Survey

Aspen Falls City Hall
500 S Aspen Street
Aspen Falls, CA 93463
(805) 555-1000
www.aspenfalls.org

2012 Customer Satisfaction Survey

Directions: Thank you for your recent visit to the Aspen Falls City Hall. In an effort to improve our customer service to the Aspen Falls residents, we would appreciate just a few minutes of your time to complete the survey.

Name: Your First and Last Name

Street: Your Street Address

City: Your City

State: CA

Zip: Your Postal Code

Telephone: Your Telephone Number

Date of visit: May 2, 2012

Department visited: Engineering

Nature of visit: Drop off specifications for Donald.

Please request the Planning Commission member(s) you wish to call you:

☒Richie Bona   ☐Jung Ortolano

☐Hisako Lavoy   ☐Jerrold Calhaun

☐Octavio Coogan   ☐Gwyneth Rondeau

☐Barton Bierschbach   ☒Tammi Markewich

Comments: Call Me At (805) 555-2668

Lastname_Firstname_w10_Survey_Locked

Aspen Falls City Hall
500 S Aspen Street
Aspen Falls, CA 93463
(805) 555-1000
www.aspenfalls.org

2012 Customer Satisfaction Survey

Directions: Thank you for your recent visit to the Aspen Falls City Hall. In an effort to improve our customer service to the Aspen Falls residents, we would appreciate just a few minutes of your time to complete the survey.

Name: Click here to enter text.

Street: Click here to enter text.

City: Click here to enter text.

State: CA

Zip: Click here to enter text.

Telephone: Click here to enter text.

Date of visit: 3/19/2012

Department visited: Choose an item.

Nature of visit:

Please request the Planning Commission member(s) you wish to call you:

☐Richie Bona   ☐Jung Ortolano

☐Hisako Lavoy   ☐Jerrold Calhaun

☐Octavio Coogan   ☐Gwyneth Rondeau

☐Barton Bierschbach   ☐Tammi Markewich

Comments:

3/26/2010 4:59:32 PM Lastname_Firstname_w10_Survey_Macro

You will save your files as:

Lastname_Firstname_w10_Survey
Lastname_Firstname_w10_Survey_Locked
Lastname_Firstname_w10_Survey_Macro

In this chapter, you will create documents for the Aspen Falls City Hall, which provides essential services for the citizens and visitors of Aspen Falls, California.

Introduction

▶ You create online forms so that others can enter information by typing text, inserting dates, selecting items from a list, or selecting check boxes.

▶ Form documents can be locked so that only the form fields can be filled in— no other changes can be made.

▶ You can create macros that perform a series of common tasks with a single click or a keyboard shortcut.

▶ You can customize the Ribbon and change buttons on the Quick Access Toolbar for the tasks you use the most.

Time to complete all
10 skills – 50 to 90 minutes

Find your student data files here:

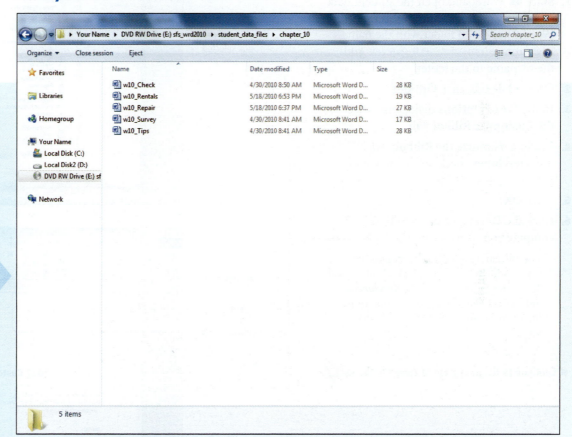

Student data file needed for this chapter:

- w10_Survey

► The Developer tab has tools for working with forms, macros, and XML. The Developer tab does not display until it is selected in the Word Options dialog box.

► To design a form, you insert *controls*—interactive objects such as text boxes, buttons, or list boxes.

1. **Start** ⊕ Word, and open the student data file **w10_Survey**. Save the file in your **Word Chapter 10** folder with the name Lastname_Firstname_w10_Survey Add the filename to the footer.

2. On the **File tab**, click **Options**.

3. In the **Word Options** dialog box, select the **Customize Ribbon tab**.

4. Under **Customize the Ribbon**, select the **Developer** check box as shown in **Figure 1**.

5. Click **OK**.

6. Click the **Developer tab**, and then compare your screen with **Figure 2**.

   The Developer tab displays six groups—Code, Add-Ins, Controls, XML, Protect, and Templates—that are used by *developers*—individuals who design documents with interactive content such as forms and macros.

■ **Continue to the next page to complete the skill**

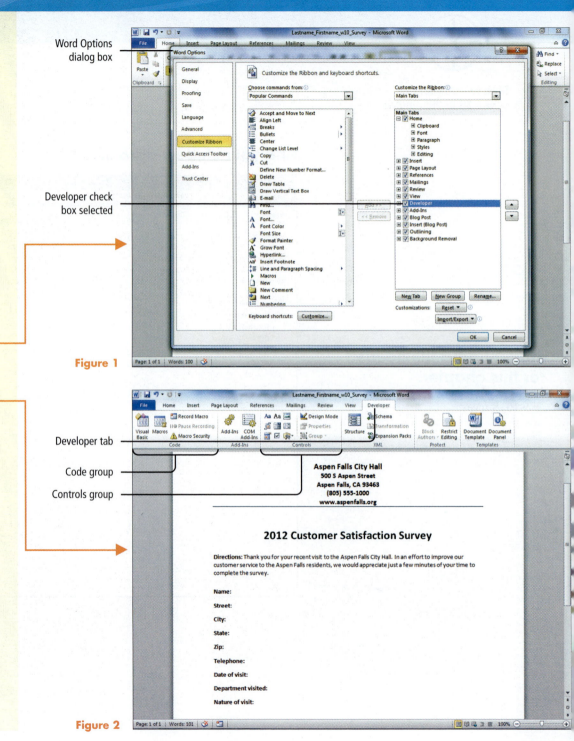

Word Options dialog box

Developer check box selected

Figure 1

Developer tab

Code group

Controls group

Figure 2

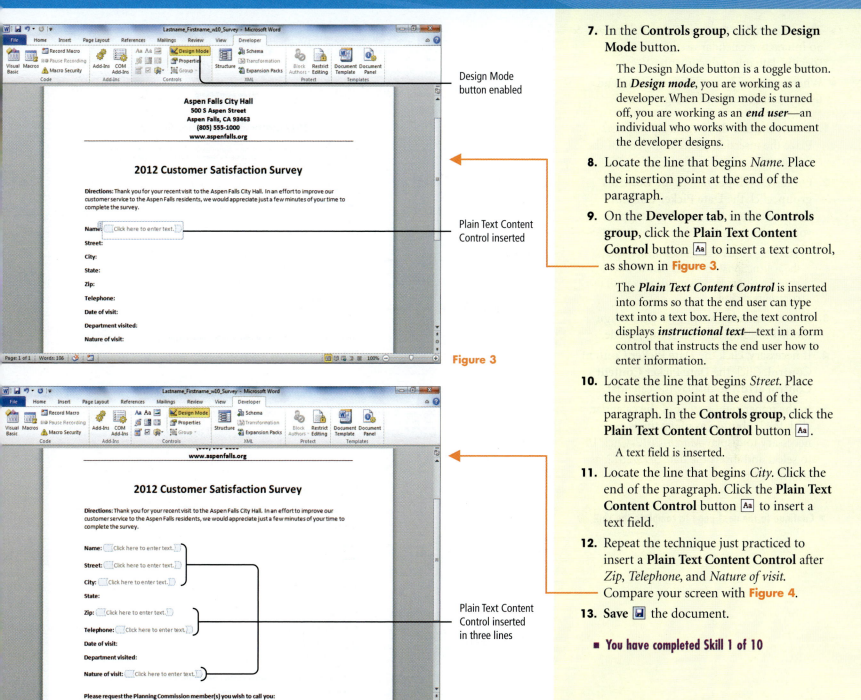

Design Mode button enabled

Plain Text Content Control inserted

Figure 3

Plain Text Content Control inserted in three lines

Figure 4

7. In the **Controls group**, click the **Design Mode** button.

   The Design Mode button is a toggle button. In **Design mode**, you are working as a developer. When Design mode is turned off, you are working as an **end user**—an individual who works with the document the developer designs.

8. Locate the line that begins *Name*. Place the insertion point at the end of the paragraph.

9. On the **Developer tab**, in the **Controls group**, click the **Plain Text Content Control** button Aa to insert a text control, as shown in **Figure 3**.

   The **Plain Text Content Control** is inserted into forms so that the end user can type text into a text box. Here, the text control displays **instructional text**—text in a form control that instructs the end user how to enter information.

10. Locate the line that begins *Street*. Place the insertion point at the end of the paragraph. In the **Controls group**, click the **Plain Text Content Control** button Aa.

    A text field is inserted.

11. Locate the line that begins *City*. Click the end of the paragraph. Click the **Plain Text Content Control** button Aa to insert a text field.

12. Repeat the technique just practiced to insert a **Plain Text Content Control** after *Zip*, *Telephone*, and *Nature of visit*. Compare your screen with **Figure 4**.

13. **Save** 🖫 the document.

   ■ **You have completed Skill 1 of 10**

► The *Date Picker Content Control* displays an interactive calendar used to insert a specific date into a document.

► When you need to use the form as an end user, you must turn off Design mode.

1. Locate the line that begins *Date of visit*. Place the insertion point at the end of the paragraph.

2. On the **Developer tab**, in the **Controls group**, click the **Date Picker Content Control** button 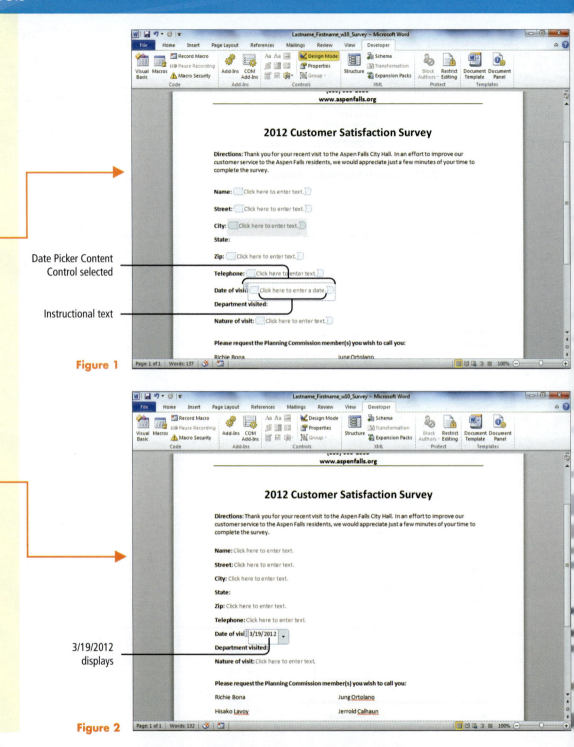, and then compare your screen with **Figure 1**.

   The Date Picker Content Control displays the instructional text *Click here to enter a date*. The calendar will not display until the control is clicked.

3. In the **Controls group**, click the **Design Mode** button to turn off Design mode.

4. If necessary, click the **Date Picker Content Control**. Click the **Date Picker Content Control arrow** to display the calendar.

5. In the upper right corner of the calendar, click the ▶ button as many times as necessary to display *March, 2012*. Click **19** to select and insert the date *3/19/2012*, as shown in **Figure 2**.

▪ **Continue to the next page to complete the skill**

Date Picker Content Control selected

Instructional text

Figure 1

3/19/2012 displays

Figure 2

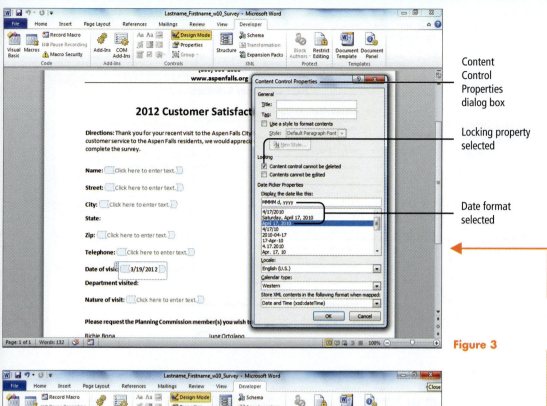

Figure 3

Figure 4

6. Click the **Design Mode** button to turn on Design mode.

7. With the **Date Picker Content Control** still selected, on the **Developer tab**, in the **Controls group**, click the **Properties** button.

8. In the **Content Control Properties** dialog box, under **Locking**, select the **Content control cannot be deleted** check box.

   The Locking properties are used to prevent the end user from deleting form controls.

9. Under **Display the date like this**, notice that the current date displays in different formats. Click the following date format: **March 19, 2012**, or similar date, to display **MMMM d, yyyy**. Compare your screen with **Figure 3**.

10. Click **OK** to close the dialog box, and then notice that the *Date of visit* displays in the selected format, as shown in **Figure 4**.

11. Save 🖫 the document.

   ■ **You have completed Skill 2 of 10**

Content Control Properties dialog box

Locking property selected

Date format selected

Formatted date

▶ When clicked, a *Drop-Down List Content Control* displays a list of choices.

▶ A *Check Box Content Control* is a form field with a box that can be selected or cleared. In a group of check boxes, multiple choices may be selected.

1. Locate the paragraph that begins *Department visited*. Place the insertion point at the end of the paragraph.

2. On the **Developer tab**, in the **Controls group**, click the **Drop-Down List Content Control** button .

3. With the insertion point in the **Drop-Down List Content Control**, in the **Controls group**, click the **Properties** button.

4. In the **Content Control Properties** dialog box, under **Locking**, select the **Content control cannot be deleted** check box, and then compare your screen with **Figure 1**.

5. In the **Display Name** box, click **Choose an item**, and then click **Remove**.

6. Click **Add**, and then in the **Add Choice** dialog box, type City Management as shown in **Figure 2**.

You use the Add Choice dialog box to add items to drop-down lists. Here, *City Management* will be the first item in the Value list box.

■ **Continue to the next page to complete the skill**

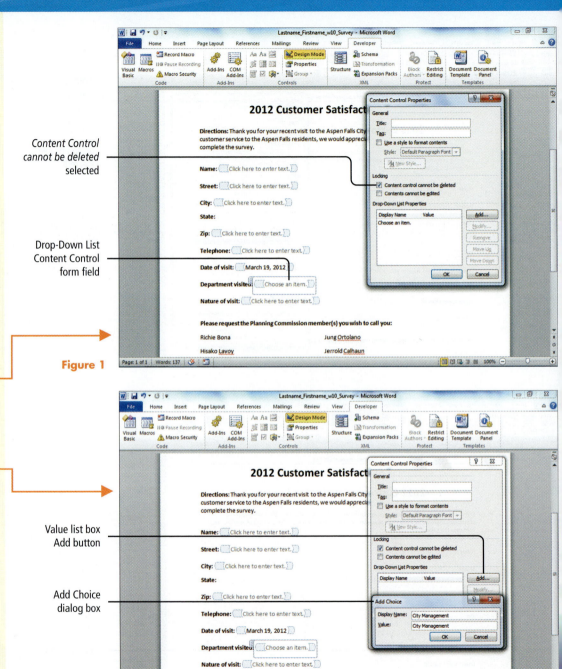

Content Control cannot be deleted selected

Drop-Down List Content Control form field

Figure 1

Value list box
Add button

Add Choice dialog box

Figure 2

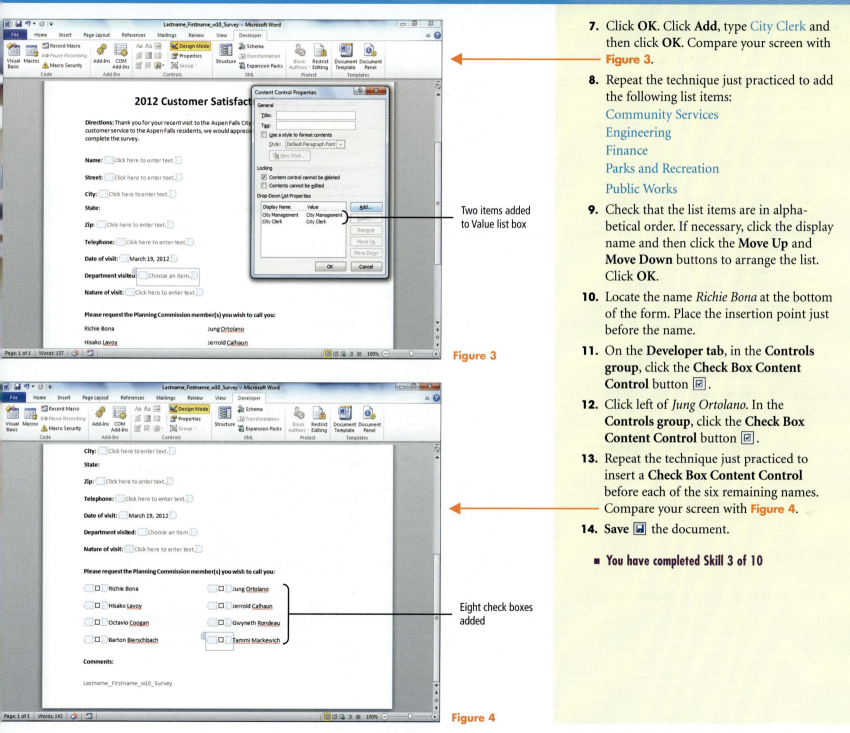

Figure 3

Figure 4

Two items added
to Value list box

Eight check boxes
added

7. Click **OK**. Click **Add**, type City Clerk and then click **OK**. Compare your screen with **Figure 3**.

8. Repeat the technique just practiced to add the following list items:

   Community Services

   Engineering

   Finance

   Parks and Recreation

   Public Works

9. Check that the list items are in alphabetical order. If necessary, click the display name and then click the **Move Up** and **Move Down** buttons to arrange the list. Click **OK**.

10. Locate the name *Richie Bona* at the bottom of the form. Place the insertion point just before the name.

11. On the **Developer tab**, in the **Controls group**, click the **Check Box Content Control** button ☑ .

12. Click left of *Jung Ortolano*. In the **Controls group**, click the **Check Box Content Control** button ☑ .

13. Repeat the technique just practiced to insert a **Check Box Content Control** before each of the six remaining names. Compare your screen with **Figure 4**.

14. **Save** 🔲 the document.

■ **You have completed Skill 3 of 10**

► *Legacy Tools* are a set of controls that work with earlier versions of Word.

► Legacy Tools include the following form fields: text, check box, and drop-down box.

1. Locate the paragraph that begins *State*. Place the insertion point at the end of the paragraph.

2. On the **Developer tab**, in the **Controls group**, click the **Legacy Tools** button.

3. In the displayed **Legacy Tools** gallery, under **Legacy Forms**, point to **Text Form Field**, as shown in **Figure 1**. Click **Text Form Field**.

   In the Legacy Tools gallery, the form controls display below Legacy Forms.

   A ***text form field*** is a legacy tool that creates a placeholder for entering text in an online form.

4. Select the *State* **Text Form Field**, and then click the **Properties** button.

5. In the **Text Form Field Options** dialog box, click the **Default text** box and then type CA

6. Click the **Maximum length up spin arrow** two times to change the maximum length to *2*.

7. Click the **Text Format arrow**, and then click **Uppercase**. Compare your screen with **Figure 2**.

8. Click **OK**.

■ **Continue to the next page to complete the skill**

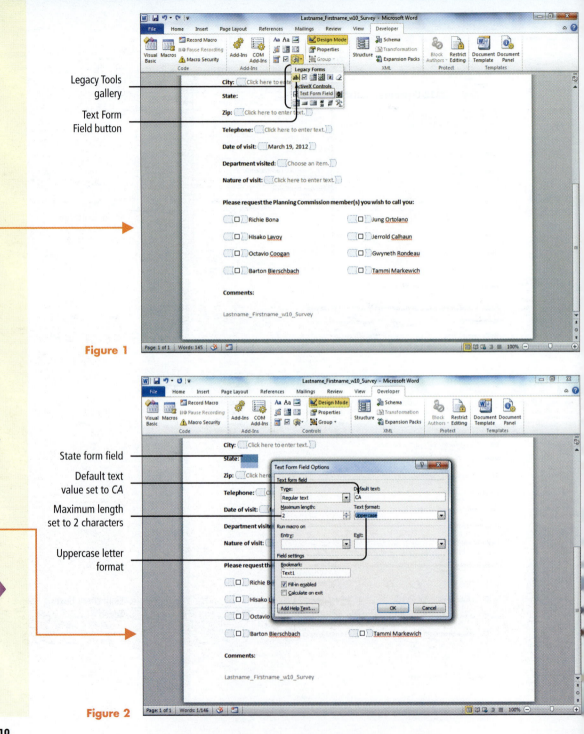

Legacy Tools gallery

Text Form Field button

Figure 1

State form field

Default text value set to CA

Maximum length set to 2 characters

Uppercase letter format

Figure 2

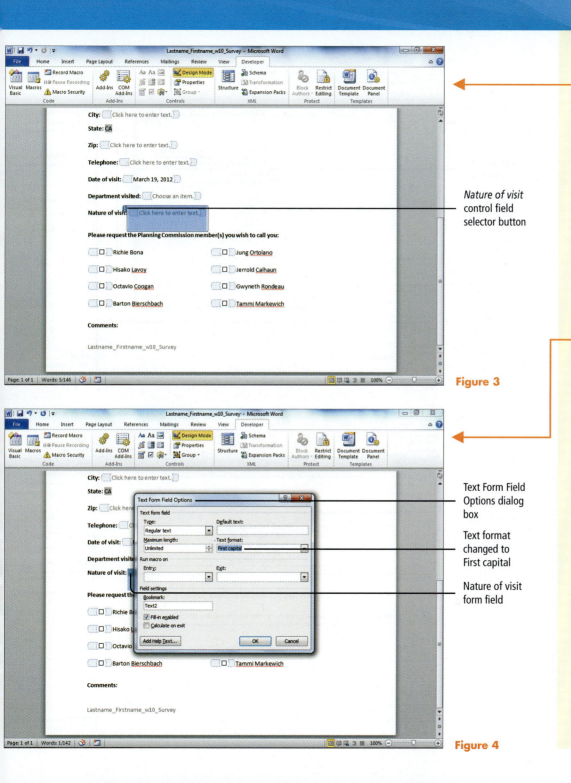

Figure 3

Figure 4

Nature of visit control field selector button

Text Form Field Options dialog box

Text format changed to First capital

Nature of visit form field

9. Click the *Nature of visit* control field, click the control field selector button as shown in **Figure 3**, and then press Delete.

The control is deleted.

10. On the **Developer tab**, in the **Controls group**, click the **Legacy Tools** button.

11. In the displayed **Legacy Tools** gallery, under **Legacy Forms**, click **Text Form Field** ab.

12. If necessary, select the *Nature of visit* **Text Form Field**, and then in the **Controls group**, click the **Properties** button.

13. In the **Text Form Field Options** dialog box, click the **Text Format arrow**, and then click **First capital**. Compare your screen with **Figure 4**, and then click **OK**.

14. Repeat the technique just practiced to insert a **Legacy Forms Text Form Field** after *Comments* with the **Title case** property.

15. **Save** the document.

■ **You have completed Skill 4 of 10**

▶ Before making an online form available for use, you should protect it.

▶ When a form is protected, the form fields can be filled in, but the form's design cannot be changed.

1. Press **Ctrl** + **Home**.

2. On the **Developer tab**, in the **Controls group**, click the **Design Mode** button to turn off Design mode.

   To enable document protection, the Design Mode must be turned off.

3. On the **Developer tab**, in the **Protect group**, click the **Restrict Editing** button.

4. In the **Restrict Formatting and Editing** pane, under **Formatting restrictions**, select the **Limit formatting to a selection of styles** check box, and then click **Settings**.

5. In the **Formatting Restrictions** dialog box, click the **None** button. Compare your screen with **Figure 1**.

   The Formatting Restrictions dialog box is used to specify which styles can be formatted. When no styles are selected, formatting changes cannot be made.

6. Click **OK**, read the displayed message, and then click **No**.

7. In the **Restrict Formatting and Editing** pane, under **Editing Restrictions**, select the **Allow only this type of editing in the document** check box.

8. Click the **Editing restrictions arrow**, and then click **Filling in forms**. Compare your screen with **Figure 2**.

■ **Continue to the next page to complete the skill**

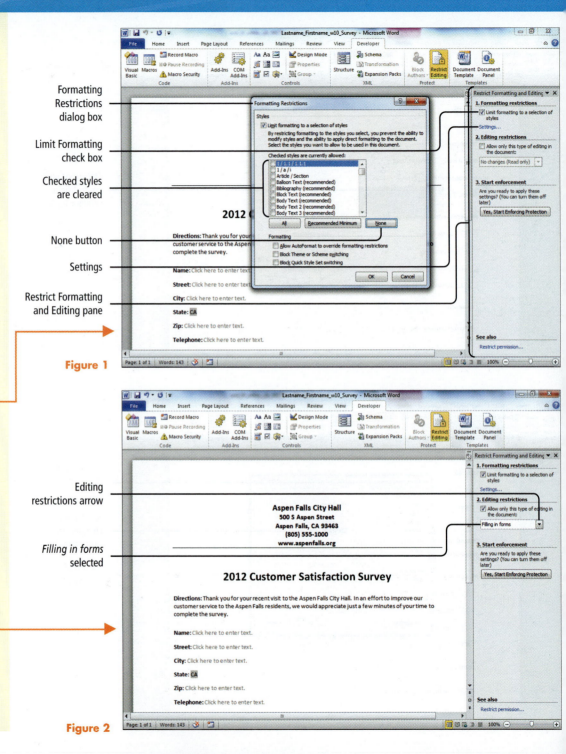

Formatting Restrictions dialog box

Limit Formatting check box

Checked styles are cleared

None button

Settings

Restrict Formatting and Editing pane

Figure 1

Editing restrictions arrow

Filling in forms selected

Figure 2

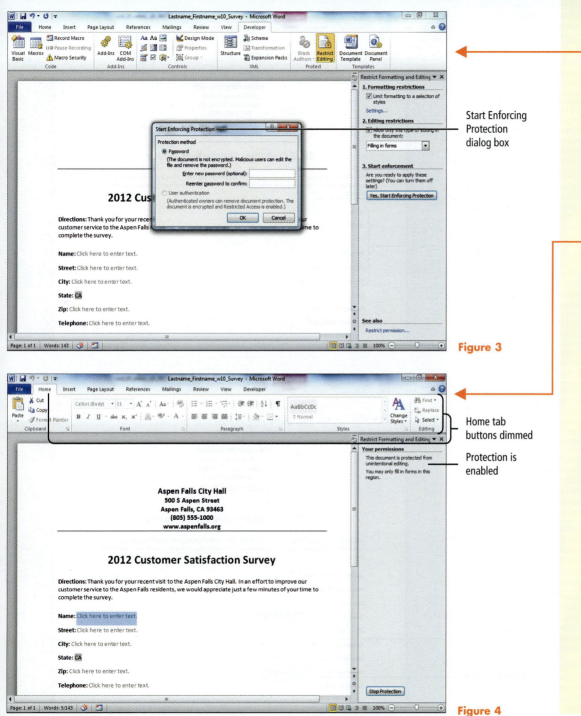

Figure 3

Figure 4

9. Click the **Yes, Start Enforcing Protection** button, and compare your screen with **Figure 3**.

> When a password is assigned, only those who know the password will be able to make changes to the document. Assigning a password is optional. When the password field is left blank, the end user will be able to remove the protection.

10. In the **Start Enforcing Protection** box, type Success! and then press Tab. Type Success! again, and then click **OK**.

11. Click the **Home tab**, and then compare your screen with **Figure 4**.

> Most of the buttons on the Home tab are dimmed, and the Restrict Formatting and Editing pane explains that the document is protected from unintentional editing.

12. **Close** ☒ the **Restrict Formatting and Editing** pane.

13. Click the form title, *2012 Customer Satisfaction Survey*, and then verify that the insertion point cannot be placed in the paragraph.

14. **Save** 🔲 the document.

15. On the **File tab**, click **Save As**. Navigate to your **Word Chapter 10** folder, and then save the file as Lastname_Firstname_w10_Survey_Locked

> The form is ready to distribute electronically—as an e-mail attachment for example.

■ **You have completed Skill 5 of 10**

► Once a form is created, the designer should test the form by filling in the fields as the end user will.

► To make changes to the design of the form, protection must first be disabled.

1. In **Lastname_Firstname_w10_Survey_ Locked**, if necessary, click the **Name** form field, and then type your first and last name

2. Press Tab, and then in the **Street** form field, type your own street address

3. Press Tab, and then in the **City** form field, type your city

4. Repeat this technique to insert your state—if different from the default *CA*— ZIP Code, and telephone number. Compare your screen with **Figure 1**.

   In this manner, the end user will be able to quickly fill out the fields on the form. The size of the Text controls will resize to fit the information entered.

5. For the date of your visit, use the Date Picker to replace the date with *May 2, 2012*.

6. Click the **Department visited** Drop-Down List field, and then click the displayed **arrow**. Compare your screen with **Figure 2**.

   The list box displays the items that you add to the control's properties.

7. From the displayed list, click *Engineering*.

■ **Continue to the next page to complete the skill**

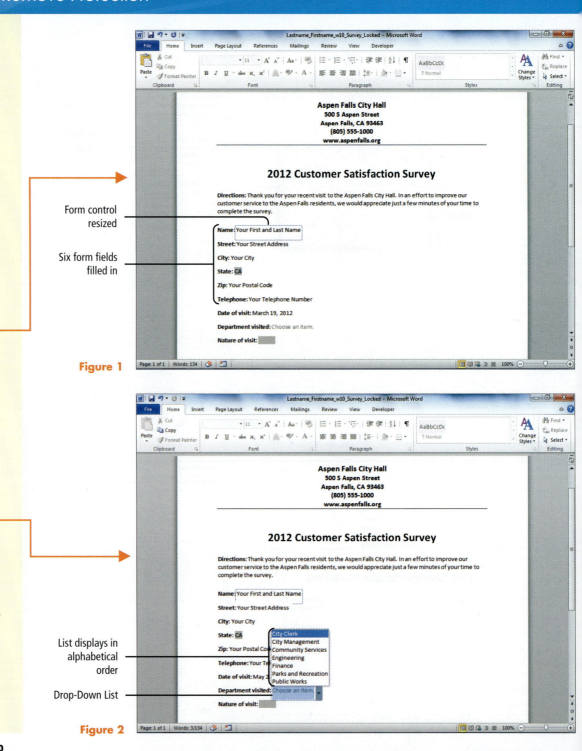

Form control resized

Six form fields filled in

Figure 1

List displays in alphabetical order

Drop-Down List

Figure 2

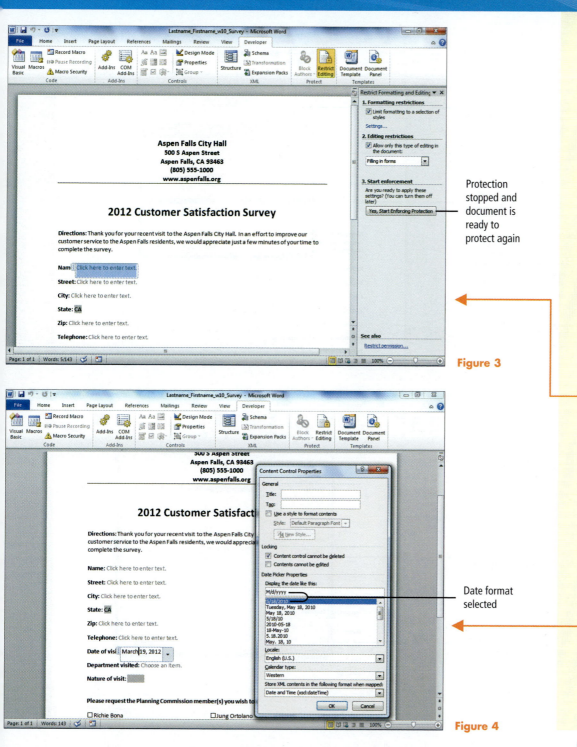

Protection stopped and document is ready to protect again

Figure 3

Date format selected

Figure 4

8. Click the **Nature of visit** text field, and then type drop off specifications for Donald. Press [Tab].

> The *d* on *drop* updates to *D* because Title capital is selected.

9. Select the check boxes for *Richie Bona* and *Tammi Markewich*.

> A selected check box is the equivalent of yes. A cleared check box is the equivalent of no.

10. In the **Comments** field, type call me at (805) 555-2668 and then press [Tab].

11. **Save** 🖫, and then **Close** ✖ the document. Open **Lastname_Firstname_ w10_Survey**.

12. On the **Developer tab**, in the **Protect group**, click the **Restrict Editing** button.

13. In the **Restrict Formatting and Editing** pane, click the **Stop Protection** button.

14. In the **Unprotect Document** box, type Success! and then click **OK**. Compare your screen with **Figure 3**.

> When the correct password is entered, protection is stopped.

15. **Close** ✖ the **Restrict Formatting and Editing** pane, and then **Save** 🖫 the document.

16. Locate the paragraph that reads *Date of visit*, and then click the **Date Picker** form field. On the **Developer tab**, in the **Controls group**, click **Properties**.

17. In the **Content Control Properties** dialog box, select date format **M/d/yyyy**—the first format in the list. Compare your screen with **Figure 4**, and then click **OK**.

18. Press [Ctrl] + [Home].

19. **Save** 🖫 the document.

- **You have completed Skill 6 of 10**

- A *macro* is a stored set of instructions that automate common tasks.

- Create a macro by using the macro recorder to record all of the steps you perform. The recorded steps are then performed whenever the macro is run.

1. On the **Developer tab**, in the **Code group**, click the **Record Macro** button. In the **Macro name** box, type AddDateTime

2. Click the **Store macro in arrow**. Click **Lastname_Firstname_w10_Survey (document)**, as shown in **Figure 1**.

   The macro is available only in the current document. Storing a macro to the Normal template makes the macro available for all files created from the Normal template.

3. Under **Assign macro to**, click the **Keyboard** button.

4. In the **Customize Keyboard** dialog box, press and hold Ctrl, and then press F.

5. Click the **Assign** button. Compare your screen with **Figure 2**.

   Assign keyboard shortcuts before the macro is created. Here, Ctrl + F will run the macro.

6. Click **Close**.

   The pointer displays to indicate that the macro recorder is recording each step.

7. On the **Insert tab**, in the **Header & Footer group**, click the **Footer** button, and then click **Edit Footer**.

8. On the **Design tab**, in the **Insert group**, click the **Date & Time** button.

9. In the **Date and Time** dialog box, click the format **9/19/2012 12:36:16PM**—or today's date/time. If necessary, select the **Update automatically** check box. Click **OK**.

■ **Continue to the next page to complete the skill**

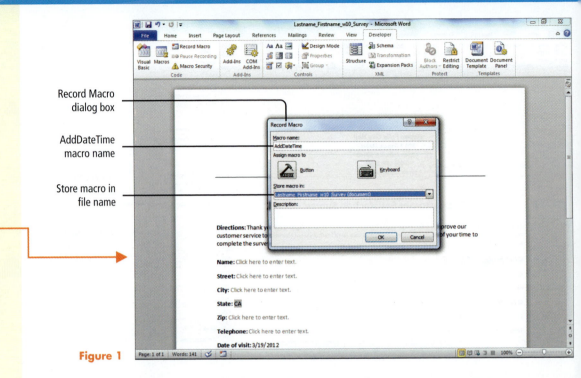

Record Macro dialog box

AddDateTime macro name

Store macro in file name

Figure 1

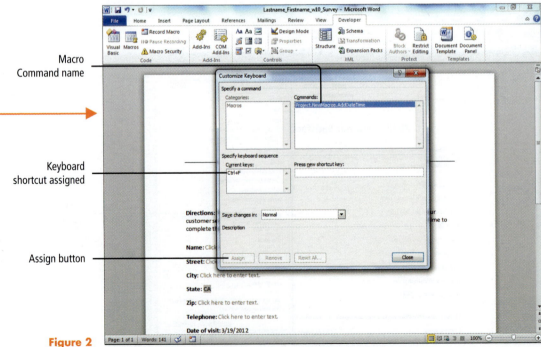

Macro Command name

Keyboard shortcut assigned

Assign button

Figure 2

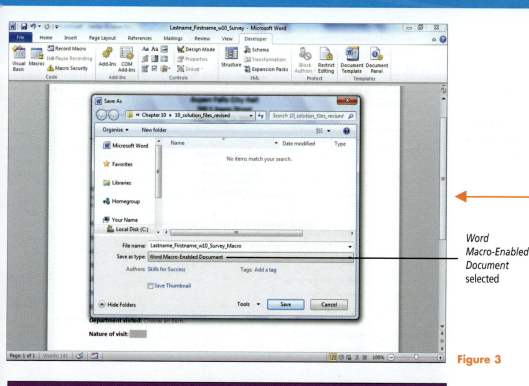

Figure 3

*Word
Macro-Enabled
Document
selected*

Macro Security Options

Macro Option	Description
Disable all macros without notification	Disables all macros and security alerts.
Disable all macros with notification	Disables all macros, and displays security alerts if macros are present in document.
Disable all macros except digitally signed macros	Enables macros that have a digital signature from a publisher that you have added to your trusted publishers list. Disables unsigned macros, and displays security alerts.
Enable all macros	Enables all macros without a security alert.

Figure 4

10. Press the Spacebar one time to insert a space between the date and the filename.

11. In the **Close group**, click **Close Header and Footer**.

12. On the **Developer tab**, in the **Code group**, click the **Stop Recording** button.

   The macro recorder has recorded each step.

   If you make a mistake while recording a macro, on the Developer tab, in the Code group, click the Macros button. In the displayed Macros dialog box, select the macro, and then click Delete. You can then name and record a new macro.

13. On the **File tab**, click **Save As**. In the **Save As** dialog box, type Lastname_Firstname_w10_Survey_Macro Click **Save as type**, and then click **Word Macro-Enabled Document**, as shown in **Figure 3**.

   Documents that contain macros must be saved in a file format that has the *.docm* file extension.

14. Click **Save**. On the **Developer tab**, in the **Code group**, click the **Macro Security** button.

15. In the **Trust Center** dialog box, if necessary, select the **Disable all macros with notification** option button, and then click **OK**. Macro security settings are summarized in **Figure 4**.

   With the current security setting, Word will ask your permission before enabling a macro. Macros are sometimes used to spread viruses. Only enable macros that are from trusted sources.

16. **Save** 🖫 the document, and then **Close** ❎ the file.

   ■ **You have completed Skill 7 of 10**

▶ When you run a macro, the macro performs the steps you completed while recording the macro.

▶ When macros do not work as intended, you can have the macro perform one step at a time to discover where the error occurs.

1. Open **Lastname_Firstname_w10_ Survey_Macro**, and then compare your screen with **Figure 1**.

   Recall that macros were disabled in the previous skill. The Microsoft Office Security Options box informs you when a document contains macros and provides an option to enable the macros.

2. In the **Security Warning**, click the **Enable Content** button. If the button does not display, on the **Developer tab**, in the **Code group**, click the **Macro Security** button. In the **Trust Center** dialog box, click the **Trusted Documents tab**, and then click **Clear**. In the message box, click **Yes**, and then click **OK**.

   In this manner, macros are enabled and the document becomes a trusted document.

3. Press Ctrl + End. Point to the footer, and then double-click the mouse. In the footer, select the date/time field. Press Delete.

4. Press Ctrl + F to run the **AddDateTime** macro.

   The AddDateTime macro ran as intended.

5. Observe the footer. Repeat the steps above to delete the date/time field. On the **Developer tab**, in the **Code group**, click the **Macros** button. Compare your screen with **Figure 2**.

■ **Continue to the next page to complete the skill** ➡

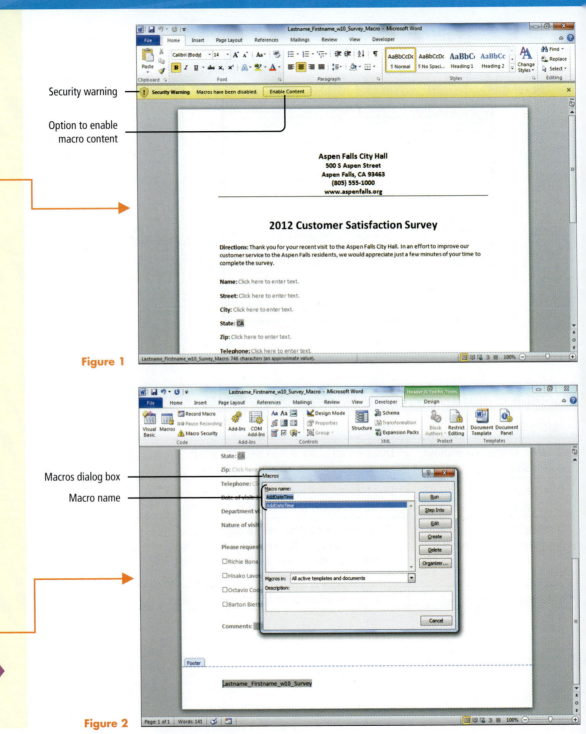

Security warning

Option to enable macro content

Figure 1

Macros dialog box

Macro name

Figure 2

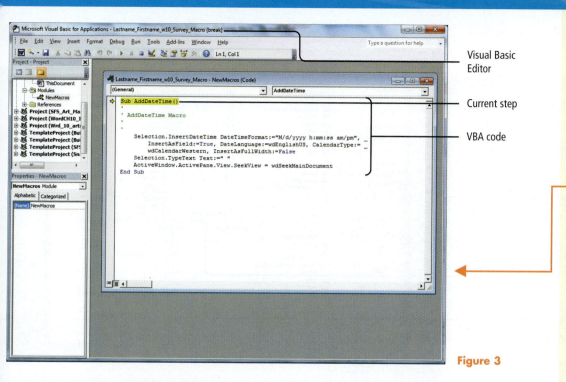

Visual Basic Editor

Current step

VBA code

Figure 3

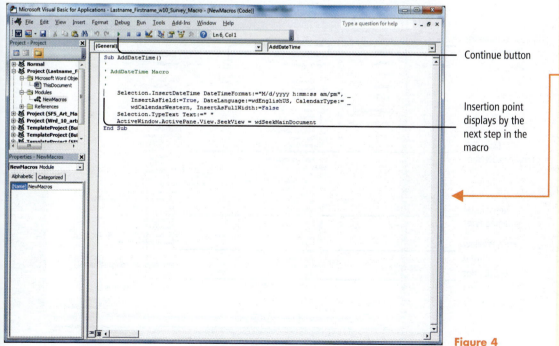

Continue button

Insertion point displays by the next step in the macro

Figure 4

6. In the **Macros** dialog box, with the **AddDateTime** macro selected, click the **Run** button.

   In this manner, you can run macros from the Macros dialog box.

7. In the **Code group**, click the **Macros** button. With the **AddDateTime** macro selected in the **Macros** dialog box, click **Step Into**, and then compare your screen with **Figure 3**.

   When you record a macro, the macro recorder writes instructions in *Visual Basic for Applications (VBA)*—a programming language that can be used to write and modify macros.

   Here, the Visual Basic Editor displays the VBA code in the AddDateTime macro. The yellow arrow and highlight indicates the current step the macro will perform.

8. From the menu bar, click **Debug**, and then click **Step Into**.

   To *debug* is to check for errors. Here, the next step is highlighted.

9. On the Standard toolbar, click the **Continue** button ▶. Compare your screen with **Figure 4**.

   The remaining steps in the macro are performed.

   The macro completed, so none of the VBA code is highlighted.

10. From the **File** menu, click **Close and Return to Microsoft Word**.

11. Notice that the date/time displays where the insertion point is located. Keep only one occurrence of the date/time in the footer. Delete any other occurrences.

    During the Debug phase, the macro is run.

12. Save 🖫 the document.

■ **You have completed Skill 8 of 10**

- ▶ In Word 2010, you can customize the Ribbon.
- ▶ The Ribbon can display new tabs and new groups, that can both be renamed.

1. On the **File tab**, click **Options**.

2. In the **Word Options** dialog box, select the **Customize Ribbon tab**.

3. Under **Customize the Ribbon**, clear the **Developer** check box.

4. In the **Word Options** dialog box, click the **New Tab** button. Compare your screen with **Figure 1**.

5. Under **Main Tabs**, click **New Tab** **(Custom)**, and then click **Rename**.

6. In the **Rename** dialog box, type Student and then click **OK**.

7. Under **Main Tabs**, click **New Group** **(Custom)**, and then click **Rename**.

8. In the **Rename** dialog box, type Print and then click **OK**.

9. In the list at the left, under the **Choose commands from** list, scroll down, click **Print Preview and Print**, and then click **Add**.

10. Scroll down and then repeat the technique just practiced to add **Quick Print** to the **Print Group**. Compare your screen with **Figure 2**.

11. Under **Main Tabs**, click **Student** **(Custom)**, and then click **New Group**.

12. In the list at the left, under **Choose commands from**, click the **Choose commands from arrow**, and then click **All Commands**.

■ **Continue to the next page to complete the skill**

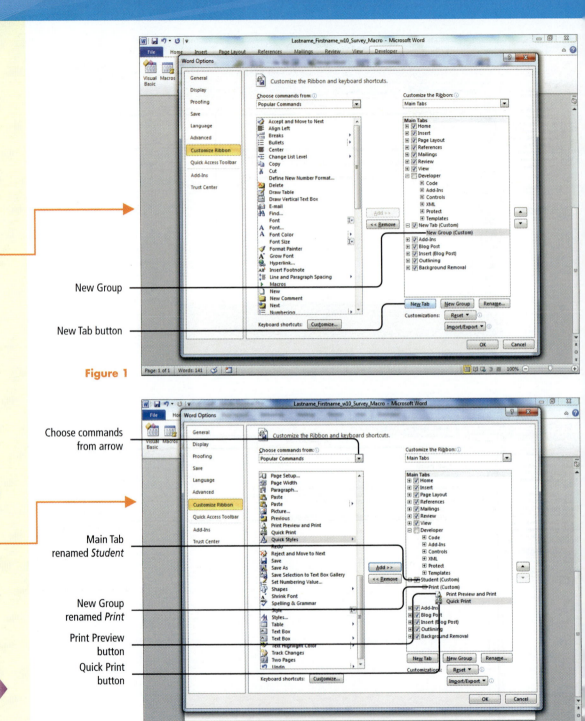

New Group

New Tab button

Figure 1

Choose commands from arrow

Main Tab renamed *Student*

New Group renamed *Print*

Print Preview button

Quick Print button

Figure 2

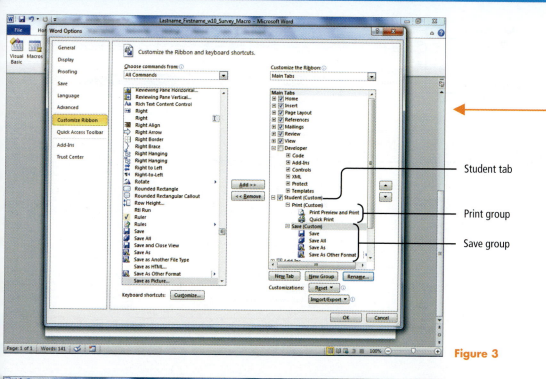

Student tab

Print group

Save group

Figure 3

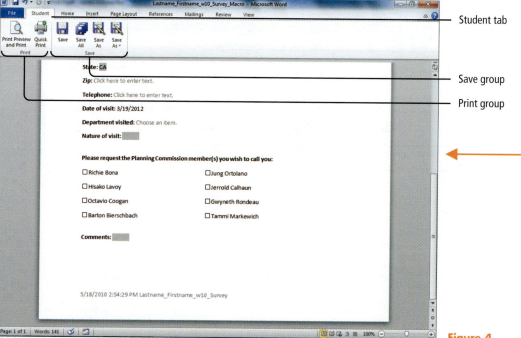

Student tab

Save group

Print group

Figure 4

13. Scroll down to locate and click **Save**, and then click **Add**.

14. Repeat the technique just learned to add the **Save All**, **Save As**, and **Save As Other Format** commands.

15. Under **Main Tabs**, click **New Group** (**Custom**), and then click **Rename**.

16. In the **Rename** dialog box, type Save and then click **OK**. Compare your screen with **Figure 3**.

17. Click **OK**. In the Ribbon at the top of the screen, click the **Student tab**.

    The Student tab is available in any Word document.

18. On the **Student tab**, in the **Save group**, click the **Save** button.

19. On the **File tab**, click **Options**.

20. In the **Word Options** dialog box, select the **Customize Ribbon tab**.

21. Under **Customize the Ribbon**, in the **Main Tabs** list, click **Student (Custom)**, and then click the **Move Up** button ▲ eight times to display the tab name at the top of the list.

22. Click **OK**. Compare your screen with **Figure 4**.

    The Student tab now displays as the second tab in the ribbon.

23. On the **File tab**, click **Options**.

24. In the **Word Options** dialog box, select the **Customize Ribbon tab**.

25. Under **Customizations**, click **Reset**, and then click **Reset all customizations**. In the message box, click **Yes**.

26. Click **OK**, and then click **Save** 🖫 the document.

■ **You have completed Skill 9 of 10**

► You can add your own buttons to the Quick Access Toolbar, QAT, to perform common tasks. For example, you can add Ribbon commands, commands not found on the Ribbon, and buttons to run macros.

1. Click the **Quick Access Toolbar arrow** ⬇, and then from the displayed list, click **More Commands**.

2. In the dialog box, click the **Customize Quick Access Toolbar arrow**, and then click **For Lastname_Firstname_w10_Survey_Macro**. Compare with **Figure 1**.

    The changes to the Quick Access Toolbar will apply only to the current document.

3. In the list of **Popular Commands**, click **<Separator>**, and then click **Add**.

    A *separator* is a vertical line that groups buttons or commands. Here, the separator will divide the default Quick Access Toolbar buttons and the custom buttons you add.

4. In the list of **Popular Commands**, click **New Comment**, and then click **Add**.

5. Click the **Choose commands arrow**, click **File Tab**. In the list, scroll down, click **Save As**. Click **Add**.

6. Click the **Choose commands arrow**, and then click **Developer Tab**. In the list, click **Date Picker Content Control**. Click **Add**. Compare with **Figure 2**. Repeat the steps just practiced to add the **Plain Text Content Control**.

7. Click the **Choose commands arrow**, and then click **Macros**.

■ **Continue to the next page to complete the skill** ▶

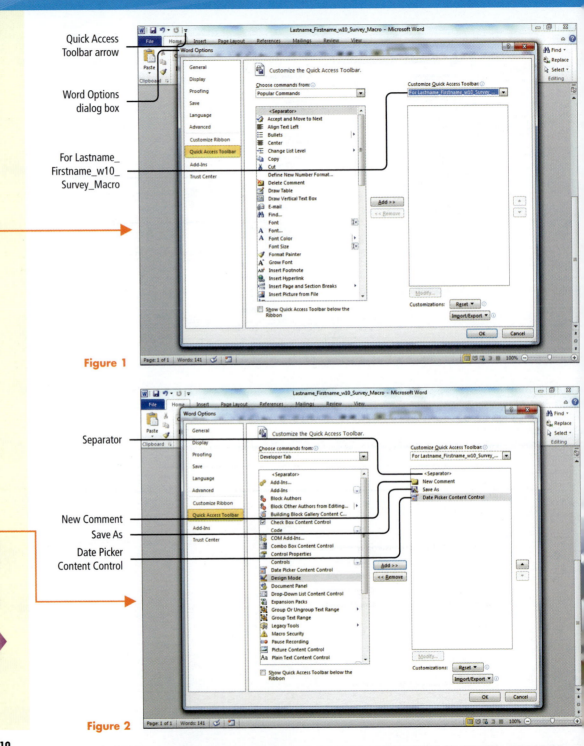

Quick Access Toolbar arrow

Word Options dialog box

For Lastname_Firstname_w10_Survey_Macro

Figure 1

Separator

New Comment
Save As
Date Picker Content Control

Figure 2

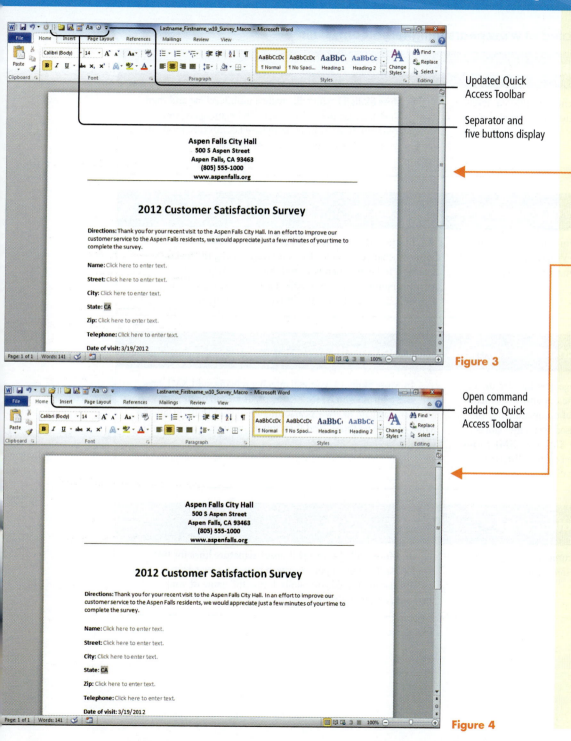

Updated Quick Access Toolbar

Separator and five buttons display

Figure 3

Open command added to Quick Access Toolbar

Figure 4

8. In the **Macros** list, click **Project. NewMacros.AddDateTime**, and then click **Add**.

9. In the list at the right, click **Project. NewMacros.AddDateTime**. Click **Modify**.

10. In the dialog box, click the ninth button in the fourth row—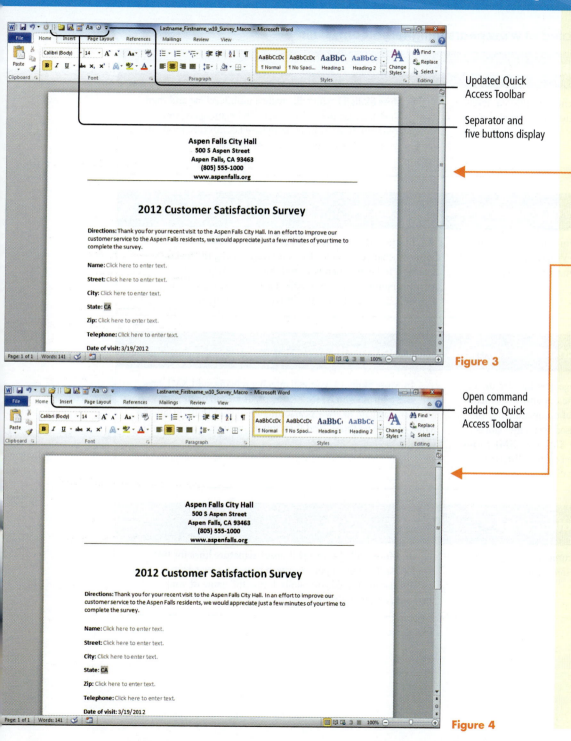. Click **OK** two times. Compare your screen with **Figure 3**.

   The commands display on the QAT. The macro button displays the custom clock.

11. Click the **Quick Access Toolbar arrow** ⊡. Click **Open**, and then compare with **Figure 4**.

   The button displays before the separator. When you add a button to the QAT using this technique, the button is added to all documents.

12. Point to the footer, and then double-click. In the footer, delete the previous date/time occurrence.

13. On the QAT, click the **Project. NewMacros.AddDateTime** button ⊙.

   In this manner, you can run macros with Quick Access Toolbar buttons.

14. Click the **Customize Quick Access Toolbar arrow** ⊡. Click **More Commands**. At the right, click the **Customize Quick Access Toolbar arrow**. Click **For Lastname_ Firstname_w10_Survey_Macro**.

15. In the dialog box, click **Reset**. Click **Reset Only Quick Access Toolbar**, and then click **Yes**. Click **OK**.

16. **Save** 🖫 the document. Print or submit the files as directed by your instructor. **Exit** Word.

Done! You have completed Skill 10 of 10 and your document is complete!

More Skills

The following More Skills are located at **www.pearsonhighered.com/skills**

More Skills Create Multilevel Lists

The items in a multilevel list are indented at different levels, and each level is assigned a unique character or number type. Multilevel lists can also be formatted.

In More Skills 11, you will create a multilevel list and then increase and decrease the indent levels. To begin, open your web browser, navigate to www.pearsonhighered.com/skills, locate the name of your textbook, and then follow the instructions on the website.

More Skills Edit Macros in Visual Basic for Applications

You can create and edit macros by working directly with the Visual Basic for Applications code. In the Visual Basic Editor, you can edit a macro that was created by the macro recorder.

In More Skills 12, you will use the Visual Basic Editor to change a macro that was created using the macro recorder. To begin, open your web browser, navigate to www.pearsonhighered.com/skills, locate the name of your textbook, and then follow the instructions on the website.

More Skills Add XML and Save Forms as XML Documents

In XML, eXtensible Markup Language, text files are used to store information. An XML tag defines the document's structure and meaning. An XML element consists of an opening tag, the content, and a closing tag. In an XML-based form, the data is entered between the opening and closing XML tags. XML forms can be saved as XML text files to be shared among different computers, operating systems, and applications.

In More Skills 13, you will attach a schema, add XML tags, and save a form as an XML document. To begin, open your web browser, navigate to www.pearsonhighered.com/skills, locate the name of your textbook, and then follow the instructions on the website.

More Skills Insert Signature Lines

You can add your signature to a document automatically. Signatures can be verified for document integrity.

In More Skills 14, you will insert signature lines for two employees. To begin, open your web browser, navigate to www.pearsonhighered.com/skills, locate the name of your textbook, and then follow the instructions on the website.

Key Terms

Online Help Skills

1. **Start** 🪟 Word. In the upper right corner of the Word window, click the **Help** button 🔵. In the **Help** window, click the **Maximize** 🔲 button.

2. Click in the search box, type enable macros and then click the **Search** button 🔍. In the search results, click **Enable or disable macros in Office files**.

3. Read the article's introduction, and then below **In this article** click **Change macro settings in the Trust Center**. Compare your screen with **Figure 1**.

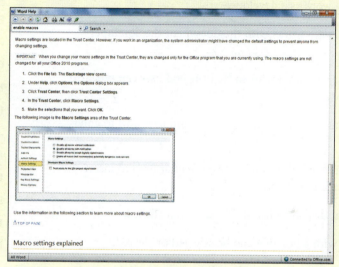

Figure 1

4. Read the section to see if you can answer the following: Why would the system administrator change the default settings for macros? What is affected when macro settings are changed in the Trust Center?

Matching

Match each term in the second column with its correct definition in the first column by writing the letter of the term on the blank line in front of the correct definition.

____ **1.** An interactive object such as a text box, a button, or a list box.

____ **2.** A person who designs documents with interactive content such as forms and macros.

____ **3.** Allows you to work as a developer.

____ **4.** An individual who works with the document the developer designs.

____ **5.** A control inserted into forms so that the end user can type text into a text box.

____ **6.** Text in a form control that instructs the end user how to enter information.

____ **7.** A control that displays an interactive calendar used to insert a specific date into a document.

____ **8.** A control that displays a list of choices when clicked.

____ **9.** A form field with a box that can be selected or cleared.

____ **10.** A set of controls that work with earlier versions of Word.

____ **11.** A legacy tool that creates a placeholder for entering text in an online form.

____ **12.** A stored set of instructions that automate common tasks.

____ **13.** A programming language that can be used to write and modify macros.

____ **14.** A mode that checks for errors.

____ **15.** A vertical line that groups buttons or commands.

A Check Box Content Control

B Control

C Date Picker Content Control

D Debug

E Design mode

F Developer

G Drop-Down List Content Control

H End user

I Instructional text

J Legacy Tools

K Macro

L Plain Text Content Control

M Separator

N Text Form Field

O Visual Basic for Applications

Multiple Choice

Choose the correct answer.

1. Used to make only the form fields available on a form.
   - A. Debug
   - B. Disable
   - C. Lock

2. Another name for the document designer.
   - A. Developer
   - B. End user
   - C. VBA

3. The type of control used to select multiple items.
   - A. Check Box
   - B. Drop-Down List
   - C. Text Form Field

4. The type of control used to select one item from a single box containing several choices.
   - A. Check Box
   - B. Drop-Down List
   - C. Text Form Field

5. Format selected from the Content Control Properties dialog box to have the date display as *September 19, 2012*.
   - A. d-MM-yy
   - B. MMMM yy
   - C. MMMM d, yyyy

6. By default, where macros are stored.
   - A. Buttons
   - B. Desired files
   - C. Normal template

7. Button used to cancel the Restrict Editing feature.
   - A. Cancel
   - B. Disable
   - C. Stop Protection

8. Feature that tests a macro.
   - A. Edit
   - B. Run
   - C. Step Into

9. Button that allows macros to be available in the current document.
   - A. Allow
   - B. Enable Content
   - C. Macro

10. Toolbar that contains Save, Undo, and Redo by default.
    - A. Mini
    - B. Quick Access Toolbar
    - C. Ribbon

Topics for Discussion

1. Imagine you are interested in promoting an Art in the Park weekend event. What types of forms might you need? What types of information would you need to collect, and which form controls would work best for collecting that information?

2. Imagine you are preparing a donor form for a non-profit organization. What buttons might you display in the Quick Access Toolbar?

Skill Check

To complete this project, you will need the following file:

- w10_Check

You will save your files as:

- Lastname_Firstname_w10_Check
- Lastname_Firstname_w10_Check_Macro

1. **Start** Word. Open **w10_Check**. Save it in the **Word Chapter 10** folder as Lastname_Firstname_w10_Check Add the file name to the footer.

2. On the **File tab**, click **Options**. Click the **Customize Ribbon tab**, and then select the **Developer** check box.

3. Click the **New Tab** button. Click **New Tab (Custom)**. Click **Rename**, and then type Student Click **OK**. Click **New Group (Custom)**, click **Rename**, type Macros and then click **OK**.

4. Click the **Choose commands arrow**, click **All Commands**, select **Macros**, and then click **Add**. Select **Macro Security**. Click **Add**. Compare with **Figure 1**. Click **OK**. On the **Developer tab**, in the **Controls group**, click **Design Mode**.

5. Position the insertion point to the right of the space after *Date*. In the **Controls group**, click the **Date Picker Content Control** button. Click the space after *Officer*. In the **Controls group**, click the **Plain Text Content Control** button. Click the space after *Type*. In the **Controls group**, click the **Drop-Down List Content Control** button. In the **Controls group**, click the **Properties** button. Click **Choose an item**, and then click **Remove**.

6. Click **Add**, type Car and then click **OK**. Repeat the technique just practiced to add SUV and Truck and Van Click **OK**. Click the space after *Description*. In the **Controls group**, click the **Legacy Tools** button. Click **Text Form Field**. Click left of *Oil*. In the **Controls group**, click the **Check Box Content Control** button. Compare your screen with **Figure 2**.

7. Click **Design Mode** to turn it off. **Save** the file.

- Continue to the next page to complete this Skill Check

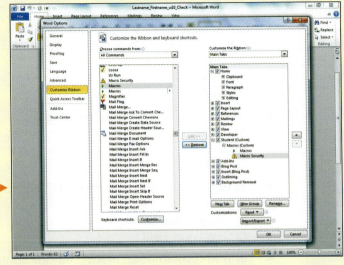

Figure 1

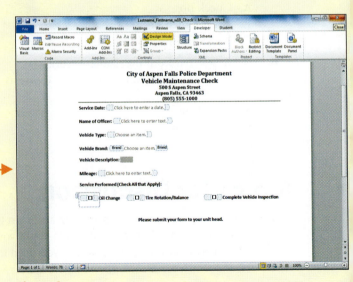

Figure 2

Data for Vehicles Form

Field	Text to Type
Service Date	9/7/2012
Officer	Larry Danner
Vehicle Type	SUV
Vehicle Brand	GMC
Vehicle Description	Yukon
Mileage	10,531
Service Performed	Oil Change

Figure 3

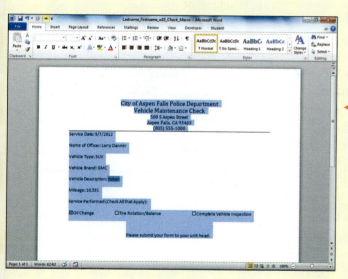

Figure 4

8. In the **Protect group**, click the **Restrict Editing** button. In the **Restrict Formatting and Editing** pane, select the **Allow only this type of editing in the document** check box. Click the **Editing Restrictions arrow**, and then click **Filling in forms**.

9. Click **Yes, Start Enforcing Protection**. In the **Start Enforcing Protection** box, type Success! in both password boxes. Click **OK**. Fill in the form using the information in **Figure 3**. **Save** the file.

10. In the **Restrict Formatting and Editing** pane, click **Stop Protection**, and type Success! Click **OK**. **Close** the **Restrict Formatting and Editing** pane.

11. On the **Developer tab**, in the **Code group**, click the **Record Macro** button, and then type UnBold to select the entire document and remove bold. Click the **Store macro in arrow**, and select **Lastname_ Firstname_w10_Check**.

12. Under **Assign macro to**, click **Button**. In the dialog box, click the **Quick Access Toolbar arrow**, and then click **For Lastname_Firstname_w10_ Check**. Click **Project.NewMacros.UnBold**, and then click **Add**. At the right, click **Project. NewMacros.Unbold**, and then click **Modify**. In the dialog box, click the first button in the third row—**triangle**. Click **OK** two times.

13. On the **Home tab**, in the **Editing group**, click the **Select** button, and then click **Select All**. Click **Bold** to turn it off in this step. On the **Developer tab**, in the **Code group**, click the **Stop Recording** button.

14. **Save** the file in the **Word Chapter 10** folder as Lastname_Firstname_w10_Check_ Macro as a **Word Macro-Enabled Document**. Update the file name in the footer.

15. On the **Student tab**, in the **Macros group**, click the **Macros** button, and then click **Step Into**. On the **Debug** menu, click **Step Into**, and then click **Continue**. On the **File** menu, click **Close and Return to Microsoft Word**.

16. On the **Student tab**, in the **Macros group**, click the **Macro Security** button. Select the **Disable all macros with notification** option. Click **OK**. **Save** and **Close** the file.

17. Open **Lastname_Firstname_w10_Check_Macro**, and then click **Enable Content**.

18. In the Quick Access Toolbar, click the **Project.NewMacros.UnBold** button. Compare with **Figure 4**.

19. Click the **Customize Quick Access Toolbar arrow**, click **More Commands**, click the **Quick Access Toolbar arrow**, and then select **For Lastname_ Firstname_ w10_Check_Macro**. Click **Reset**, and then click **Reset only Quick Access Toolbar**. Click **Yes**, and then click **OK**.

20. **Save** the document. Print or submit the files as directed by your instructor. **Exit** Word.

Done! You have completed the Skills Check

Assess Your Skills 1

To complete this project, you will need the following file:

- w10_Repair

You will save your files as:

- Lastname_Firstname_w10_Repair
- Lastname_Firstname_w10_Repair_Macro

1. **Start** Word. Open **w10_Repair**. Save the file in your **Word Chapter 10** folder as Lastname_Firstname_w10_Repair Add the file name to the footer.

2. Display the **Developer tab**. Turn on **Design Mode**. After *Date of Request*, insert a **Date Picker Content Control**.

3. Insert a **Drop-Down List Content Control** after *City Neighborhood* that contains Neighborhood 1, Neighborhood 2 and Neighborhood 3.

4. Insert a **Plain Text Content Control** after *Name of Applicant*.

5. From the **Legacy Tools**, insert a **Text Form Field** after *Zip*. Insert a **Check Box Content Control** before *Sidewalk*.

6. Turn off **Design Mode**. Protect the document so forms can be filled in only by using the password Success!

7. Fill in the form using the information in **Figure 1**.

8. **Stop Protection**. Enter the password. Close the **Restrict Formatting and Editing** pane. **Save** the file.

9. Press Ctrl + Home. **Save** the file as a **Word Macro-Enabled Document** with the name Lastname_Firstname_w10_Repair_Macro Double-click the footer, and then right-click the footer to **Update Field**.

10. Record a macro with the name NoBold that is stored in the current document. Assign the macro to a button on the Quick Access Toolbar in the current file. Modify the button to display with the first button in the sixth row—the green box.

11. The macro should select the entire document and remove bold.

12. **Stop Recording** the macro, and deselect the text. If necessary, change the **Macro Security** to **Disable all macros with notification**. **Save** and **Close** the file.

13. Open **Lastname_Firstname_w10_Repair_ Macro** and **Enable Content**. Select the entire document and **Bold**. From the Quick Access Toolbar, run the **NoBold** macro. Compare your screen with **Figure 2**.

14. Remove the **Developer tab** from the Ribbon. Remove the NoBold button from the Quick Access Toolbar.

15. **Save** and **Close** the document.

16. Print or submit the files as directed by your instructor. **Exit** Word.

Done! You have completed Assess Your Skills 1

Data for Repair Form	
Field	**Text to Type**
Date of Request	12/15/2012
City Neighborhood	Neighborhood 3
Name of Applicant	Tonya D. Batright
Address	907 Kensington Drive
Zip	93463
Daytime Phone	(805) 555-0412
Repair or Maintenance	Sidewalk

Figure 1

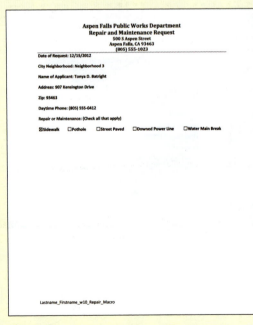

Figure 2

Tips Form Data

Character	Description
Name	Ima Criminal
Alias	Dandy Lyon
Age	55
Address	Unknown
City	Aspen Falls
State	CA
Zip	93463
Telephone	(805) 555-4622
Markings	Scars
Last Seen	Neighborhood 2
Date	June 19, 2012
Password	Hardyboyz56

Figure 1

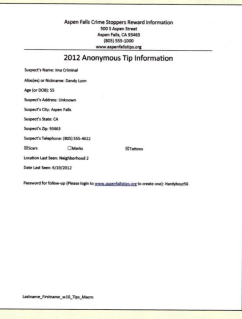

Figure 2

Assess Your Skills 2

To complete this project, you will need the following file:

- w10_Tips

You will save your files as:

- Lastname_Firsname_w10_Tips
- Lastname_Firsname_w10_Tips_Macro

1. **Start** Word. Open **w10_Tips**. **Save** the file as Lastname_Firstname w10_Tips Add the file name to the footer.

2. Display the **Developer tab**. Add a **New Tab** named Student **Rename** the **New Group (Custom)** as Macros Add the **Macros** and **Macro Security** buttons from the **All Commands group**.

3. Turn on the **Design Mode**. After *Suspect's Name*, insert a **Plain Text Content Control**.

4. After *Suspect's State*, from the **Legacy Tools**, insert a **Text Form Field**.

5. Add a **Check Box Content Control** in front of *Scars*, *Marks*, and *Tattoos*.

6. After *Location Last Seen*, insert a **Drop-Down List Content Control** that includes Neighborhood 1, Neighborhood 2, and Neighborhood 3

7. After *Date Last Seen*, insert a **Date Picker Content Control**. Turn off **Design Mode**. **Save** the file.

8. Protect the document so that forms can be filled in only by using the password Success!

9. Fill in the form using the information in **Figure 1**. Stop protection. Close the **Restrict Formatting and Editing** pane. **Save** the file.

10. Record a macro with the name CrimeTip that is stored in the current document and is assigned to a macro button stored in

Lastname_Firstname_w10_Tips. Assign the macro to a button on the Quick Access Toolbar in the current file. Modify the button to display with the first button in the third row—the triangle. The macro should remove bold from all text.

11. **Stop Recording** the macro. Use the **Student tab** to change the **Macro Security** to **Disable all macros with notification**.

12. Use the **Student tab** to **View Macros**, **Step Into**, and close Visual Basic. Stop the debugger. **Bold** all text. Use the **Student tab** to **View Macros**, and then **Run** the macro.

13. **Save** the file in your **Word Chapter 10** folder as a **Word Macro-Enabled Document** named Lastname_Firstname_w10_Tips_Macro Double-click the footer, and then right-click the footer to **Update Field**. **Save**. **Close** the document.

14. Open **Lastname_Firstname_w10_Tips_Macro** and **Enable Content**. **Bold** all text. From the Quick Access Toolbar, run the **CrimeTip** macro.

15. For the current document, select **Reset only Quick Access Toolbar** and **Reset all customizations**, and then click Save. Compare with **Figure 2**. Print or submit the files as directed by your instructor. **Exit** Word.

Done! You have completed Assess Your Skills 2

Assess Your Skills Visually

To complete this project, you will need the following file:

- w10_Rentals

You will save your file as:

- Lastname_Firstname_w10_Rentals

Start Word. Locate and open **w10_Rentals**. **Save** the file in your **Word Chapter 10** folder as Lastname_Firstname_w10_Rentals Add the file name to the footer.

Add controls to create the form shown in **Figure 1**.

Insert a **Plain Text Content Control** after *Name of Applicant, Name of Organization, Address, City, State, Zip, Daytime Phone, Fax Number, Email, No. of Occupants,* and *No. of Rental Hours Requested.* Insert a **Check Box Content Control** before *Wedding* and *Reception.* Insert the **Date Picker Content Control** next to *Date of Event.* Insert a **Drop-Down List Content Control** for *Location Requested.* Include these items in the drop-down list:

Cobblestone Pavilion

Maple Shelter

President Pavilion

Sandy Beach

Vista Shelter

Done! You have completed Assess Your Skills Visually

Aspen Falls Parks and Recreation Department
Facility Reservation Application and Permit
500 S Aspen Street
Aspen Falls, CA 93463
(805) 555-1000

Name of Applicant: Click here to enter text.

Name of Organization: Click here to enter text.

Address: Click here to enter text.

City: Click here to enter text.   **State:** Click here to enter text.   **Zip:** Click here to enter text.

Daytime Phone: Click here to enter text.   **Fax Number:** Click here to enter text.

Email: Click here to enter text.

Type of Event: (Check all that apply.)

☐Wedding ☐Reception ☐Reunion ☐Work Function ☐School Function ☐Sporting Function

Date of Event: Click here to enter a date.

Location Requested: Choose an item.

No. of Occupants: Click here to enter text.

No. of Rental Hours Requested: Click here to enter text.

FACILITY USE FEES: All *areas* are $40.00 per hour. All events must end by 10:00 p.m. The City of Aspen Falls is not responsible for any accidents or injuries.

Rental Fee will be computed at a rate of $40.00 per hour per shelter. Each shelter will be assessed a $150.00 refundable deposit. Renters are responsible for cleanup of the shelter area after use. Failure to clean up the area as found will result in forfeiture of $150.00 deposit. Deposit must be submitted with application in order to secure the requested location. Deposit is forfeited if the event is cancelled with seven (7) business days of scheduled event. Please allow 1 to 2 weeks to process deposit/refund after your event/function or cancellation. All rentals are subject to availability.

Authorized Signature of Applicant/Organization:

Make checks payable to: Aspen Falls Parks and Recreation Department.
Retain receipt and approved permit to present to authorized staff during your event.

Lastname_Firstname_w10_Rentals

Figure 1

Skills in Context

To complete this project, you will need the following file:

- New blank Word document

You will save your file as:

- Lastname_Firstname_w10_Sports

Open a new Word document. Prepare a one-page Word survey form to be sent to the parents of children participating in the summer sports programs in Aspen Falls. Include fields appropriate for application date, name, contact information, and emergency phone number. Include check boxes for the following sports: Baseball, Soccer, Swimming, and Tennis. Additionally, include a drop-down list for the following age groups: 3 to 5, 6 to 7, 8 to 9, 10 to 11, 12 to 13, 14 to 15, and 16 to 17. Test the form by filling it in for a fictitious child.

Save the file as Lastname_Firstname_w10_Sports Add the file name to the footer. Submit as directed by your instructor.

Done! You have completed Skills in Context

Skills and You

To complete this project, you will need the following file:

- New blank Word document

You will save your files as:

- Lastname_Firstname_w10_Volunteer_Survey

Open a new Word document.   Prepare a one-page Word survey form that a volunteer organization of your choosing could use for its current membership or for members of the community. Design a form that includes a date picker, at least five text fields, and a drop-down list. Test the form by filling it in with sample information.

Save the file as Lastname_Firstname_w10_Volunteer_Survey Add the file name to the footer. Submit as directed by your instructor.

Done! You have completed Skills and You

Glossary

Anchor A symbol to the left of a paragraph mark that indicates which paragraph the picture is associated with.

APA style The publication style used by the American Psychological Association.

Aspect ratio A Picture Tools layout option that keeps the height and width of an object proportionate.

AutoCorrect Corrects common spelling errors as you type; for example, if you type teh, Word will automatically correct it to the.

AutoRecover The feature in Word that automatically saves the document being worked on. The default for AutoRecover is every 10 minutes.

AutoSave entry The day of the week, the current date, and the time of the version.

Bibliography A list of sources referenced in a document and listed on a separate page at the end of the document.

Blog A message board posted to the web that is used to share information that can be read by others, also known as a weblog.

Bookmark Special nonprinting character inserted into a document to allow quick navigation to that point in the document.

Building block Any object or group of objects in a Word document that can be saved for later retrieval.

Bulleted list A list of items with each item introduced by a symbol such as a small circle or check mark.

Cell The box formed by the intersection of a row and column.

Cell reference A number on the left side and a letter on the top of a spreadsheet that addresses a cell.

Character graphic A small graphic character that can be formatted as text.

Character style A style type that formats selected letters, numbers, and symbols.

Chart A graphic representation of the data in a worksheet or table.

Check Box Content Control A form field with a box that can be selected or cleared. In a group of check boxes, multiple choices can be selected.

Citation A note in the document that refers the reader to a source in the bibliography.

Clip art A set of images, drawings, photographs, videos, and sound included with Microsoft Office or accessed from Microsoft Office Online.

Clipboard A temporary storage area that holds text or an object that has been cut or copied.

Column break An applied column end that forces the text following the break to the top of the next column but does not automatically create a new page.

Comment A message that is inserted by those reviewing a document.

Compatibility Checker A check done to locate features in a Word 2010 document that are not supported in earlier versions of Word.

Content control In a template, text or a field that is formatted as a placeholder and is designated by a border when you click the placeholder text.

Continuous section break A break that is inserted into a document and is used to format each section differently.

Control An interactive object such as a text box, a button, or a list box.

Copy A command that places a copy of the selected text or object in the Clipboard.

Cover page Usually the first page of a document that displays document information such as the title and subtitle, the date, the document's author, and the company name.

Crop Reduces the size of a picture by removing unwanted vertical or horizontal edges.

Cross-reference An index entry associated with a different word or phrase that is similar in context to the initial entry.

Cut A command that removes the selected text or object and stores it in the Clipboard.

Data point A value that originates in a datasheet cell.

Data series Data points that are related to one another.

Data source The part of the Word mail merge feature that contains the information, such as names and addresses, that changes with each letter or label.

Date Picker Content Control A control that displays an interactive calendar used to insert a specific date into a document.

Debug A mode that checks a macro for errors.

Design mode A mode in which an individual can work as a developer.

Developer An individual who designs documents with interactive content such as forms and macros.

Dialog box A box where you can select multiple settings.

Document properties Information about a document that can help you identify or organize your files, such as the name of the document author, the file name, and keywords.

Document statistics Data that summarizes document features such as the number of pages, words, characters without spaces, characters including spaces, paragraphs, and lines.

Dot leader A series of evenly spaced dots that precede a tab stop.

Double-spacing The equivalent of a blank line of text displayed between each line of text in a paragraph.

Drag To move the mouse while holding down the left mouse button and then to release it at the appropriate time.

Drop cap The first letter (or letters) of a paragraph, enlarged and either embedded in the text or placed in the left margin.

Drop-Down List Content Control A control that displays a list of choices when clicked.

Edit To insert text, delete text, or replace text in an Office document, spreadsheet, or presentation.

Em dash Word processing name for a long dash in a sentence, which marks a break in thought, similar to a comma but stronger.

End User An individual who works with the document the developer designs.

Endnote A reference placed at the end of a section or a document.

eXtensible Markup Language (XML) A language that uses text files to store information.

Field (Word) A category of data—such as a file name, a page number, or the current date—that can be inserted into a document.

Final view A view that displays how the document will look if all changes are accepted.

Final: Show Markup A document view that displays the revised text in the document and the original text in balloons.

First line indent The location of the beginning of the first line of a paragraph to the left edge of the remainder of the paragraph.

Flesch Reading Ease A 100-point scale that measures readability. A score of 100 indicates an easy-to-understand document.

Flesch-Kincaid Grade Level An estimate of the U.S. grade level needed to understand a document.

Floating object An object or graphic that can be moved independently of the surrounding text.

Font A set of characters with the same design and shape.

Font style Bold, italic, or underline emphasis added to text.

Footer (Word) Reserved area for text, graphics, and fields that displays at the bottom of each page in a document.

Footnote A reference placed at the bottom of the page.

Format To change the appearance of the text, such as changing the text color to red.

Format Painter A command that copies formatting from one selection of text to another.

Formatting mark A character that displays on the screen, but does not print, indicating where the Enter key, the Spacebar, and the Tab key were pressed; also called non-printing characters.

Gallery A visual display of choices from which you can choose.

Glyph A picture or symbol used to represent data.

Grid line A line between the cells in a table or spreadsheet.

Hanging indent The first line of a paragraph extends to the left of the rest of the paragraph.

Header Reserved area for text, graphics, and fields that displays at the top of each page in a document.

Horizontal alignment The orientation of the left or right edges of the paragraph—for example, flush with the left or right margins.

Horizontal line A line that separates document text so that it is easier to read.

HTML file A text document with special markup codes that enable web pages to display the document in a web browser.

Hyperlink Text or other object that displays another document, location, or window when it is clicked.

Hyphen A character that divides a word between the end of one line and the beginning of the next.

Indent The position of paragraph lines in relation to the page margins.

Index A list of words and phrases found in a document along with their corresponding page numbers.

Index entry field A word, phrase, or cross-reference that will go in the index.

Inline Revision A notation that displays all changes within the text instead of within revision balloons.

Insertion point A vertical line that indicates where text will be inserted when you start typing.

Inside address The placeholder located in the middle of an envelope document that contains the address information of the person receiving the envelope.

Instructional text Text in a form control that instructs the end user how to enter information.

Justified Paragraph text is aligned flush with both the left margin and the right margin.

Keep Source Formatting A paste option that copies text using the formatting from the original location.

Keep Text Only A paste option that copies text with all formatting removed.

Keyboard shortcut A combination of keys on the keyboard, usually using the Ctrl key, the Shift key, or the Alt key, that provides a quick way to activate a command.

KeyTip An icon that displays in the Ribbon to indicate the key that you can press to access Ribbon commands.

Landscape orientation A page orientation in which the printed page is wider than it is tall.

Leader A series of characters that form a solid, dashed, or dotted line that fills the space preceding a tab stop.

Leader character A character such as a dash or a dot that is repeated to fill the space preceding a tab stop.

Legacy Tools A set of controls that work with earlier versions of Word.

Ligature A graphic character that displays when two or more symbols are combined.

Line spacing The vertical distance between lines of text in a paragraph.

Linked object An object that is updated whenever the original source file is updated.

Linked style A style type that can be applied as a character style in one place and as a paragraph style in another.

Linked text box A Word feature that is used so that text automatically flows between one or more text boxes.

List style A style type that formats bullets, numbers, and indent settings.

Live Preview A feature that displays the result of a formatting change if you select it.

Macro A stored set of instructions that automate common tasks.

Mail merge A Word feature that creates customized letters or labels by combining a main document with a data source.

Main document The part of the Word mail merge feature that contains the text that remains constant.

Manage Versions The feature that allows the recovery of AutoSaved data.

Manual line break Moves the remainder of the paragraph following the insertion point to a new line while keeping the text in the same paragraph.

Manual page break Forces a page to end, and places subsequent text at the top of the next page.

Margin The space between the text and the top, bottom, left, and right edges of the paper when you print the document.

Marked as final When no one can type, edit, or use the proofing tools within the document.

Markup The balloons and inline revisions in a reviewed document.

Merge Formatting A paste option that copies text and applies the formatting in use in the new location.

Metadata Information and personal data that is stored with a document.

Mini toolbar A toolbar with common formatting buttons that displays after you highlight text.

Mixed content Both normal text and XML data in an XML document.

Multilevel list Items in this type of list are indented at different levels, and each level is assigned a unique character or number type.

Nonprinting character A character that displays on the screen, but does not print, indicating where the Enter key, the Spacebar, and the Tab key were pressed; also called formatting marks.

Normal template A Word template that stores the default styles that are applied when a new document is created.

Nudge The action of moving an object in small increments by using the directional arrow keys.

Numbered list A list of items with each item introduced by a consecutive number or letter to indicate definite steps, a sequence of actions, or chronological order.

Object Item such as graphics, charts, or spreadsheets created by Word or other programs—or text from a Word file.

Office Clipboard A temporary storage area maintained by Office that can hold up to 24 items.

OpenType feature A feature that contains fonts that work on multiple platforms, including Macintosh and Windows.

OpenType font A font made up of two or more symbols or characters combined; similar to typesetting.

Original: Show Markup A document view that displays the original text in the document and the proposed changes in balloons.

Outline A Word feature that displays headings and body text, formatted so that headings and all associated subheadings and body text move along with the heading.

Page Layout view A view where you prepare your document or spreadsheet for printing.

Paragraph spacing The vertical distance above and below each paragraph.

Paragraph style A style type that formats an entire paragraph.

Paste To insert a copy of the text or an object stored in the Clipboard.

Paste Options Provide formatting choices when pasting text into the current document.

Placeholder text Reserved space in shapes into which personalized text is entered.

Plain Text Content Control A control inserted into forms so that the end user can type text into a text box.

Point Measurement of the size of a font; each point is 1/72 of an inch.

Portrait orientation A page orientation in which the printed page is taller than it is wide.

Protected View A view applied to documents downloaded from the Internet that allows you to decide if the content is safe before working with the document.

Quick parts Saved text and objects that can be retrieved from the Quick Parts gallery.

Quick Style A style that can be accessed from a Ribbon gallery of thumbnails.

Quick Table A built-in table that can be used to insert a formatted table into your document.

RAM The computer's temporary memory.

Range Two or more cells that are adjacent or nonadjacent.

Read-only mode A mode where you cannot save your changes.

Readability statistics A check that measures the reading level for a document based on certain document statistics such as the length of words, the number of syllables in a word, and the length of sentences and paragraphs.

Return address The placeholder located in the top left corner of an envelope document that contains the address information of the person sending the envelope.

Reveal Formatting A pane that displays the selected text and the font, paragraph, and section formatting currently in use.

Reviewing Pane A pane that displays either at the left—vertically—or at the bottom—horizontally—of the screen and lists all comments and tracked changes.

Revised document The document that has changes that you want to merge with the original document.

Right-click Click the paragraph with the right mouse button.

Root element The XML element in which all other XML elements must be placed.

Schema An XML file that specifies what elements can and cannot go in an XML file.

Schema Library The location on a computer where XML schemas are stored.

Screen shot A picture of your computer screen, a window, or a selected region saved as a file that can be printed or shared electronically.

ScreenTip Informational text that displays when you point to commands or thumbnails in the Ribbon.

Section A portion of a document that can be formatted differently from the rest of the document.

Section break Marks the end of one section and the beginning of another section.

Select Browse Object toolbar Toolbar consisting of 12 buttons used to find different types of objects—for example, bookmarks, figures, tables, fields, or sections. Using the buttons allows quicker navigation of long documents.

Selection and Visibility pane A view that displays a list of shapes, including pictures and text boxes, located on the current page.

Separator A vertical line that groups buttons or commands.

Separator character In a list, a character such as a comma or a tab that separates elements of the paragraph.

Shape A drawing object such as a rectangle, arrow, and callout that is inserted into a document.

Shortcut menu A list of commands related to the type of object that you right-click.

Side by Side view A view that displays two different documents in vertical windows so that they can be compared.

Single-spacing No extra space is added between lines of text in a paragraph.

Sizing handle A small square or circle at the corner or side of a selected object that is dragged to increase or decrease the size of the object.

SmartArt graphic A designer-quality visual representation of information used to communicate messages or ideas effectively by choosing from among many different layouts.

Snip A screen capture created with the Snipping Tool.

Sources Master List All sources that have been cited in previous documents or in the current document.

Split bar A border that separates two different parts of a document that has been split into two sections.

Split window A window separated into two parts to allow scrolling through each window independently to view different areas of the document at the same time.

Style A predefined set of formats that can be applied to text, a paragraph, a table cell, or a list.

Style Inspector A pane that displays the paragraph and text level formatting for the current style.

Subheading An entry in a Table of Contents that is part of a broader entry.

Synchronous scrolling A way to move both windows when scrolling either the vertical or horizontal scroll bar in either window.

Tab stop A specific location on a line of text, marked on the Word ruler, to which you can move the insertion point by pressing GF; used to align and indent text.

Table Text or numbers displayed in a row and column format to make the information easier to read and understand.

Table of Authorities A case, statute, and other authority marked in the document.

Table of Authorities entry field A word, phrase, or cross-reference that will go in the table of authorities.

Table of Contents Entries and page numbers for a document's headings and subheadings.

Table of Figures References to figures, equations, and tables in the document.

Table style A style type that formats rows, columns, and cells.

Template A preformatted document structure that defines the basic document settings, such as font, margins, and available styles.

Text box (Word) A movable, resizable container for text or graphics.

Text effect A set of decorative formats, such as outlines, shadows, text glow, and colors that make text stand out in a document.

Text Form Field A legacy tool that creates a placeholder for entering text in an online form.

Text wrapping The manner in which text displays around an object.

Theme A coordinated set of font choices, color schemes, and graphic effects.

Thesaurus A research tool that lists words that have the same or similar meaning to the word you are looking up.

Toggle button A button used to turn a feature both on and off.

Triple-click Click three times fairly quickly without moving the mouse.

Value axis The side of the chart that displays numeric values.

Visual Basic for Applications (VBA) A programming language that can be used to write and modify macros.

Watermark A semitransparent image often used for letters and business cards.

Web Layout view A view that simulates how documents will display in web browsers.

Windows Live A free online storage that can be used to save and open your files from any computer connected to the Internet.

Windows Live ID A unique name and password—a Hotmail or Windows Live e-mail user name and password, for example.

Windows Live network A group of people whom you have invited to share files or to chat using Instant Messenger.

Word wrap Automatically moves text from the right edge of a paragraph to the beginning of the next line as necessary to fit within the margins.

WordArt A set of graphic text styles that can be used to make text look like a graphic.

XML Another name for eXtensible Markup Language.

XML element An opening tag, the content, and a closing tag—for example, <firstname>content</firstname>

XML tag A definition or mark for the document's structure and meaning.

XML text file A text file marked up in way that allows different computers, operating systems, and applications to share data.

Zoom The magnification level of the document as displayed on the screen. Increasing the zoom percentage increases the size of the text and comments as displayed on the screen but does not increase the actual font size.

Index

Numbers and Symbols

= (equal sign), 187
© (copyright), 170
¶ (paragraph mark), 7, 176, 206, 306
® (registered symbol), 54, CW Word ch 1, More Skills 12

A

Add Choice dialog box, 344
address bar, in Internet Explorer, 89
Address Block dialog box, 153
Add Shape button, 149
Adjust group, 107
Advanced tab, on Font dialog box, 24
After down spin arrow, 111, CW Word ch 3,
    More Skills 11
After up spin arrow, 72–73, 78–79
alignment
    in documents, 70–71
    of paragraphs, 91
    tab, 108
    table, 113, CW Word ch 3, More Skills 13
All Programs command, 6
anchor symbol, 105
APA (American Psychological Association) style for
    citations, 258, CW Word ch 7, More Skills 12
Arial Black font, 42–43
Arrange group, 23, 45, 105
arranging windows, 54
Artistic Effect button, 107
aspect ratio, 220
assessment
    collaboration, 293–301
    creating, 55–57
    formatting and layout settings, 192–199
    formatting and organizing, 89–91
    forms and macros, 361–369
    graphics, tabs, and tables, 123–125
    Office functions, common features, 27–29
    references, 259–267
    special formats, 157–159
    styles, 327–335

AutoCorrect entries, 88, CW Word ch 2, More Skills 11
AutoFit feature, CW Word ch 3, More Skills 13
AutoFormat, 88, CW Word ch 2, More Skills 12
Automatic numbered lists check box, CW Word ch 2,
    More Skills 12
automatic updates, 81
AutoRecover, CW Word ch 7, More Skills 13
AutoShapes, 223
Available formats button, for date and time, 81
Avery US Letter labels, 153
Axis Title, 217

B

backgrounds, removing, 180–181, 202
Backspace key, deleting with, 36
Backstage Print page, 52–53
Backstage view, CW Word ch 2, More Skills 14
balloons
    comments in, 273
    revisions in, 278, 281
Before down spin arrow, 154
Before up spin arrow, 25
Bevel effects, 107
bibliographies, 86–87. *See also* citations
blank document, in Word, 6
blog posts, 292, CW Word ch 8, More Skills 13
blue wavy lines, in proofing, 46
bold font style, 42–43, 68
bookmarks, 252–253
borders, in documents, 106–107, 120, 134, 144–145
breaks
    column, 138–139
    line, 73
    page, 40, 73
Browse Folders button, 10
Browse Object toolbar, 256–257
building blocks
    for page numbers, 224, CW Word ch 6, More Skills 11
    for Quick Parts, 182, 184–185
    for watermarks, 224, CW Word ch 6, More Skills 14
Built-in gallery, 206–207

built-in text boxes, 202, 206–207
bullets
    Bullets button, 21
    characters for, 170
    in documents, 66, 78–79
    libraries of, CW Word ch 2, More Skills 13
    styles for, 308

C

Calibri font, 42
Cambria font, 42
camera, digital, 100
cell references, 12
cells
    Merge Cells button, 189
    ranges of, 215
    table, 118–119, 188
    in table formulas, 186
    table style for, 312
character graphics, 170
character styles, 304, 306–307
charts, 214–217
Chart Title, 216–217
check boxes, 344–345
Chicago center alignment button, 38, 70, 140
style, for citations, 84
citations, 66. *See also* bibliographies
    in APA style, 258, CW Word ch 7, More Skills 12
    in *Chicago* style, 84–85
    in table of authorities, CW Word ch 7, More Skills 14
clip art, 44, 134, 146–147, 158
Clipboard
    for collecting, CW Word ch 1, More Skills 13
    Cut button, 76
    Format Painter in, 74–75
    overview, 18–19
    text and objects collected on, 54
clustered column charts, 214
collaboration
    assessment, 293–301
    blog posts, 292, CW Word ch 8, More Skills 13

The internet icon represents Index entries found within More Skills
on the Companion Website: www.pearsonhighered.com/skills

SINGLE PC LICENSE AGREEMENT AND LIMITED WARRANTY

READ THIS LICENSE CAREFULLY BEFORE OPENING THIS PACKAGE. BY OPENING THIS PACKAGE, YOU ARE AGREEING TO THE TERMS AND CONDITIONS OF THIS LICENSE. IF YOU DO NOT AGREE, DO NOT OPEN THE PACKAGE. PROMPTLY RETURN THE UNOPENED PACKAGE AND ALL ACCOMPANYING ITEMS TO THE PLACE YOU OBTAINED THEM. *THESE TERMS APPLY TO ALL LICENSED SOFTWARE ON THE DISK EXCEPT THAT THE TERMS FOR USE OF ANY SHAREWARE OR FREEWARE ON THE DISKETTES ARE AS SET FORTH IN THE ELECTRONIC LICENSE LOCATED ON THE DISK:*

1. GRANT OF LICENSE and OWNERSHIP: The enclosed computer programs ("Software") are licensed, not sold, to you by Prentice-Hall, Inc. ("We" or the "Company") and in consideration of your purchase or adoption of the accompanying Company textbooks and/or other materials, and your agreement to these terms. We reserve any rights not granted to you. You own only the disk(s) but we and/or our licensors own the Software itself. This license allows you to use and display your copy of the Software on a single computer (i.e., with a single CPU) at a single location for academic use only, so long as you comply with the terms of this Agreement. You may make one copy for back up, or transfer your copy to another CPU, provided that the Software is usable on only one computer.

2. RESTRICTIONS: You may not transfer or distribute the Software or documentation to anyone else. Except for backup, you may not copy the documentation or the Software. You may not network the Software or otherwise use it on more than one computer or computer terminal at the same time. You may not reverse engineer, disassemble, decompile, modify, adapt, translate, or create derivative works based on the Software or the Documentation. You may be held legally responsible for any copying or copyright infringement which is caused by your failure to abide by the terms of these restrictions.

3. TERMINATION: This license is effective until terminated. This license will terminate automatically without notice from the Company if you fail to comply with any provisions or limitations of this license. Upon termination, you shall destroy the Documentation and all copies of the Software. All provisions of this Agreement as to limitation and disclaimer of warranties, limitation of liability, remedies or damages, and our ownership rights shall survive termination.

4. DISCLAIMER OF WARRANTY: THE COMPANY AND ITS LICENSORS MAKE NO WARRANTIES ABOUT THE SOFTWARE, WHICH IS PROVIDED "AS-IS." IF THE DISK IS DEFECTIVE IN MATERIALS OR WORKMANSHIP, YOUR ONLY REMEDY IS TO RETURN IT TO THE COMPANY WITHIN 30 DAYS FOR REPLACEMENT UNLESS THE COMPANY DETERMINES IN GOOD FAITH THAT THE DISK HAS BEEN MISUSED OR IMPROPERLY INSTALLED, REPAIRED, ALTERED OR DAMAGED. THE COMPANY DISCLAIMS ALL WARRANTIES, EXPRESS OR IMPLIED, INCLUDING WITHOUT LIMITATION, THE IMPLIED WARRANTIES OF MERCHANTABILITY AND FITNESS FOR A PARTICULAR PURPOSE. THE COMPANY DOES NOT WARRANT, GUARANTEE OR MAKE ANY REPRESENTATION REGARDING THE ACCURACY, RELIABILITY, CURRENTNESS, USE, OR RESULTS OF USE, OF THE SOFTWARE.

5. LIMITATION OF REMEDIES AND DAMAGES: IN NO EVENT, SHALL THE COMPANY OR ITS EMPLOYEES, AGENTS, LICENSORS OR CONTRACTORS BE LIABLE FOR ANY INCIDENTAL, INDIRECT, SPECIAL OR CONSEQUENTIAL DAMAGES ARISING OUT OF OR IN CONNECTION WITH THIS LICENSE OR THE SOFTWARE, INCLUDING, WITHOUT LIMITATION, LOSS OF USE, LOSS OF DATA, LOSS OF INCOME OR PROFIT, OR OTHER LOSSES SUSTAINED AS A RESULT OF INJURY TO ANY PERSON, OR LOSS OF OR DAMAGE TO PROPERTY, OR CLAIMS OF THIRD PARTIES, EVEN IF THE COMPANY OR AN AUTHORIZED REPRESENTATIVE OF THE COMPANY HAS BEEN ADVISED OF THE POSSIBILITY OF SUCH DAMAGES. SOME JURISDICTIONS DO NOT ALLOW THE LIMITATION OF DAMAGES IN CERTAIN CIRCUMSTANCES, SO THE ABOVE LIMITATIONS MAY NOT ALWAYS APPLY.

6. GENERAL: THIS AGREEMENT SHALL BE CONSTRUED IN ACCORDANCE WITH THE LAWS OF THE UNITED STATES OF AMERICA AND THE STATE OF NEW YORK, APPLICABLE TO CONTRACTS MADE IN NEW YORK, AND SHALL BENEFIT THE COMPANY, ITS AFFILIATES AND ASSIGNEES. This Agreement is the complete and exclusive statement of the agreement between you and the Company and supersedes all proposals, prior agreements, oral or written, and any other communications between you and the company or any of its representatives relating to the subject matter. If you are a U.S. Government user, this Software is licensed with "restricted rights" as set forth in subparagraphs (a)-(d) of the Commercial Computer-Restricted Rights clause at FAR 52.227-19 or in subparagraphs (c)(1)(ii) of the Rights in Technical Data and Computer Software clause at DFARS 252.227-7013, and similar clauses, as applicable.

Should you have any questions concerning this agreement or if you wish to contact the Company for any reason, please contact in writing:

Multimedia Production
Higher Education Division
Prentice-Hall, Inc.
1 Lake Street
Upper Saddle River NJ 07458